D0461700

THE
ANTIQUES
CARE & REPAIR
HANDBOOK

LIBRARY OF PAOLO HARDUZZI

THE
ANTIQUES
CARE & REPAIR
HANDBOOK

ALBERT JACKSON & DAVID DAY

Alfred A. Knopf
New York 1984

CONTENTS

The Antiques Care & Repair Handbook was conceived, edited and designed by Dorling Kindersley Limited, 9 Henrietta Street, London WC2E 8PS

Project Editor
Judith More

Art Editor
Nicholas Harris

Editor
Richard Dawes

Designer
Hugh Schermuly

Managing Editor
Alan Buckingham

Art Director
Stuart Jackman

All rights reserved under International and Pan-American Copyright Conventions.

THIS IS A BORZOI BOOK PUBLISHED BY ALFRED A. KNOPF, INC.

Published in the United States by Alfred A. Knopf, Inc., New York, and simultaneously in Canada by Random House of Canada Limited, Toronto. Distributed by Random House, Inc., New York.

Copyright © 1984 by Dorling Kindersley Limited London

Library of Congress Cataloging in Publication Data

Jackson, Albert 1943– Antiques care and repair handbook Includes Index.
1. Antiques—Conservation and restoration.
I. Day, David, 1944–. II. Title.
NK1127.5.J32   1984
745.1′028′8   83–48845
ISBN 0–394–53492–1
First American Edition

Filmsetting by Advanced Filmsetters, Glasgow Reproduction by Reprocolor Llovet S.A., Barcelona Printed and bound in Italy by L.E.G.O.

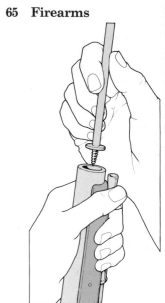

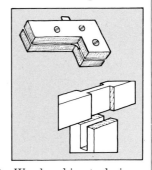

INTRODUCTION

Every collector of antiques aims to find examples in perfect condition, but the mere fact that pieces have been in existence for many years means that the majority of items offered to the average collector will benefit from some sort of restoration. Enormous pleasure can be gained from turning what appears to be an unattractive piece of junk into a beautiful antique. Indeed, many of the objects for sale in antique shops have been through a similar process. If you are able, like a dealer, to spot the potential of less-than-perfect items, then the techniques in this book will help you to restore them to their former glory.

This book is divided into chapters covering the major categories applicable to antiques. And even if the item you want to restore does not fit obviously into one of these categories, you should find an explanation of the techniques you need applied to similar or related items that *are* covered. You may have to consider what material your antique is made from in order to find the relevant information on how to restore it. For example, a broken limb on an antique china doll can be remodeled in the same way as that of a china figurine (see p. 33). And although antique tools do not have their own section, material in the metalware and furniture chapters should give you the information you need. Similarly, in a section like jewelry we have considered the obvious precious and semi-precious materials. However, many other materials have been used to manufacture jewelry, so you may find other chapters useful too. Use the Index to help you find the relevant information.

What is an antique?

There is a considerable difference of opinion among collectors as to what exactly constitutes an antique. An item was once regarded as antique if it had been made before 1830, but then the definition shifted to mean anything more than one hundred years old. Now, many experts consider the "cut-off point" to be 1930.

Unless you collect for investment only, these matters are mostly irrelevant. What matters is whether you like some-

thing enough to want to preserve it. There are a great
many old things that can be admired for their beauty,
standard of craftsmanship, sense of history, or simply for
their curiosity value. These are the items that we would
like to encourage you to collect and restore, whether they
are, strictly speaking, antiques or not.

Should amateurs be encouraged to restore antiques?

Although there are areas of this book that will appeal
to experienced amateur restorers, we have nevertheless
assumed that most readers will be beginners with no previous experience. Consequently, we have tried to explain
each operation simply, using as little technical jargon as
possible. For the same reason, we have suggested that you
use materials and tools which are easily available, in
preference to more specialized items, unless there is really
no alternative. We have even included basic woodworking, metalworking and sewing skills at the back of the
book for those readers with little practical experience.
Eventually, if you build up your experience carefully and
slowly, you should be able to carry out all the jobs in this
book. However, avoid employing a complicated technique
without practicing it first, and do not start
a difficult repair job before mastering
easier ones.

Even though there are a considerable number of jobs that a novice restorer can undertake without the slightest risk to the antique, inexperienced amateurs ought to think twice about attempting the renovation of a rare or valuable item. Consequently, throughout this book we have advised caution and have suggested that whenever you are dealing with costly or fragile items, or when you are faced with a task that seems beyond you, you should contact an expert.

If you decide to put an item in the hands of a professional restorer, always make it perfectly clear what you want done. If you are not sure yourself, ask the professional to explain exactly what he or she intends to do. This is in order to determine the degree of restoration. Some restorers like to return the object to its original condition, while others like to preserve only what exists, without any attempt to disguise the scars of its previous history. To avoid disappointment, you must agree beforehand on exactly what is to be done and how much it will cost.

Buying antiques

Wear and damage often stems either from the way an object is used or the way it is constructed. It is often possible, therefore, to predict the type of damage you will find when you examine certain antiques. In each chapter we have included "buying tips" and "damage checks" to help you when you are buying antiques.

There are several ways to locate and buy antiques, each of which has its particular advantages and pitfalls for the restorer. The most obvious source of antiques is a dealer. However, there are many kinds of dealers selling at a wide variety of price levels. A dealer in a fancy location will have high overheads, so you must expect to pay higher prices. Also, such a dealer is unlikely to have many items in need of restoration. Local dealers are a better source. Often they acquire damaged items in job lots, and are usually willing to sell you such pieces cheaply.

Antique markets are fun, but you may have to sort through a lot of rubbish before you come across something that is worth buying. Often, the only way to find anything interesting at a market is to go early, before the dealers and professional restorers skim off the best pieces.

Auction sales are potentially the most profitable way of acquiring antiques. Collectors can expect to find objects of interest fairly regularly, and the restorer is often in luck, especially at local auctions where there can be a

lot of damaged material. Prices are usually cheaper than
at an antique shop because auction sales are one of the
sources for dealers' stock.

When you are viewing the lots in advance, inspect any
you are interested in carefully to determine condition.
Take a flashlight so that you can see into dark corners.
A magnifying glass is useful for detecting small faults, as
well as to examine any makers' marks or proofs.

Displaying antiques

Once you have bought and restored your antiques, you
will want to display them attractively. In many chapters
we have given specific advice on this, but you will also
find the following general information useful.

A display case or cabinet is an obvious choice to house a collection of small antiques such as ceramics, especially if the items are delicate or should be kept dust-free. However, many collectors who accumulate general, unrelated objects will find that they look out of place in a showcase.

Open shelving is suitable for many antiques. You can mount glass sliding doors between shelves to form small display cases for particular sections of your collection, but make sure that the shelves are sturdy and cannot sag, or the doors will jam.

Grouping objects on coffee or side tables is also attractive. They can be mixed up randomly, chosen merely because you feel that they complement each other. On the other hand, you could adopt a thematic approach to your selection, or link the objects by color or material.

To display your collection well you should consider "accent" lighting. Spotlights or downlights set into the ceiling will create pools of light over groups of objects or individual pictures, while striplights hidden behind deep battens on the front of shelving will light items displayed on shelves. And special, brass-cased striplights for lighting pictures are available from some lighting specialists.

Safety measures

Throughout the book we have identified potentially harmful substances used to restore certain antiques. As long as you take adequate precautions, and follow the manufacturer's instructions, these chemicals are quite safe to use. You should always wear protective gloves and eye glasses when using corrosive or caustic materials. Workshops or work areas should always be adequately ventilated and well-lit to prevent accidents. Some chemicals are very flammable, and should never be used near an open flame. All dangerous chemicals should be clearly labeled, and kept in a locked cupboard out of the reach of small children.

POTTERY AND PORCELAIN

Identifying ceramics

Ceramics are made of clay fired in kilns and given a variety of treatments. Identifying these treatments is important because they affect both the value and the method of repair. Start by examining the body of the piece, then look at the glaze and decoration.

Pottery

This opaque earthenware is made from baked clay. It is porous and requires a glaze to protect it and make it waterproof.

Hard paste porcelain

First developed in China in the ninth century, the secret of making hard paste porcelain remained undiscovered in Europe until 1705. Hard paste is a mixture of kaolin (white china clay) and petuntse (china stone), fired at 900°C, then glazed and fired again at 1300°C. This fuses the glaze into the body of the china, making it extremely hard.

Soft paste porcelain

This type of porcelain was made before the technique for producing hard paste became widespread. Production ceased by the beginning of the nineteenth century. Soft paste was composed of white clay and a vitreous mixture of sand and flint. The glaze was fired at a lower temperature, and therefore lies on the surface of the body and looks thicker than the glaze on hard paste. Obviously, this type of porcelain is much softer than hard paste, and can be scratched easily with coarse abrasives. Air trapped in the clay mix may show up as lighter patches when you hold up a soft paste piece against the light.

Bone china

A hard paste porcelain with the addition of animal bone ash to make the china very white. It was developed in the late eighteenth century.

Biscuit

This unglazed white porcelain is also known as bisque. Matching colors for retouching unglazed wares is difficult.

Is it pottery or porcelain?

It is useful to be able to distinguish pottery from porcelain because the method of restoration will differ. A broken edge or a chip in pottery will reveal a coarse, granular body. Hold it in good daylight and you will see a distinct edge to the glaze against the earthenware. The body of porcelain is much finer, with an almost glassy appearance where the glaze is fused into it. You will find porcelain is very light and looks translucent when you hold it up to the light.

Parian

Fine, unglazed white porcelain that is smoother than biscuit is known as parian ware. Because of its appearance it was used to make busts and figurines.

Parian
wall bracket

Stoneware

A coarse, hard non-porous pottery made by adding flint or stone dust to clay. Salt-glazed stoneware, which has a slightly pitted appearance, is produced by adding salt to the kiln.

Wedgwood stoneware jug

Creamware

Stoneware fired at a lower temperature than normal is known as creamware. The cream colored lead glaze is not resistant to hot water.

Slipware

This term refers to pottery dipped in a creamy water and clay mixture. Slip itself is a decorative feature, and on some pieces this is taken still further by removing part of the slip to form patterns.

Black basaltware

A black colored stoneware containing ironstone, basalt was first produced at the Wedgwood factory in the eighteenth century.

Forms of applied decoration

The earliest pottery was decorated by cutting or pressing patterns into the soft clay. Later colored glazes were introduced. Since the Industrial Revolution, many mechanical forms of decoration have been applied to ceramics.

Pierced patterns are cut right through the body of the ceramic while the clay is still "leather-hard".

Crazing can be faked during the glazing process.

Molding involves pressing clay between molds. The process allows intricate three-dimensional decoration to be repeated both quickly and accurately.

Incised patterns and motifs are cut into dry clay in a similar way to engraving.

Painted and printed decoration

Much china is decorated with painted or printed designs. Hand painted patterns and motifs were worked directly onto the piece. The paint may be on or under the glaze, depending on whether it can withstand high temperatures or not. Overglaze work is very vulnerable to damage.

As early as the mid-eighteenth century a method was developed for printing patterns onto thin tissue paper and transferring them to ceramic. At first, only black line work was possible, but in the 1840's multi-colored transfer-printing techniques arrived. You can tell printing by its flat, almost photographic appearance. And sometimes you will see a mis-aligned join in a border pattern. You will also find china with printed black line work filled in by hand.

Real gold leaf was often used for gold pattern work and edging on quality pieces. Cheaper wares were gilded with liquid gold paint.

Painted decoration

Printed decoration

Special glazes

Silver luster cream jug

Luster Metallic finishes are produced by adding metallic salts to the glaze. It may be an all-over finish imitating metal work, as in the piece above, or applied in panels along with printed or painted patterns.

Crackle Any glaze can begin to craze, forming a network of extremely fine cracks across the surface. Some china, notably certain oriental ware, is deliberately crazed during manufacture. This type of finish is known as crackle or alligator glaze.

Collecting ceramics

When you are hunting for pieces to add to your collection, examine each one carefully for damage. A blemish, no matter how small, will reduce the value, and you should point it out to the vendor in case it is not reflected in the asking price.

A well-restored item will fetch more than a damaged one, but not as much as a perfect piece. So look out for signs of previous restoration when buying, and be prepared to limit your price when you come to sell any china you have restored yourself.

Damage checks

*A simple repair
**Some experience needed
***Skilled work—not for beginners

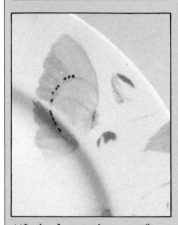

Is the **decoration worn? The centers of plates and saucers are often damaged where they have been stacked. You can retouch all damage, but the complexity of the pattern affects how easy this work will be.

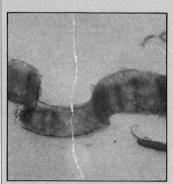

*Are there any **hairline cracks**? Hold the item up to the light to check. Another test is to place the piece in the palm of your hand and tap it gently with your fingernail. If it "rings" it is usually sound.
*Most **stains** can be bleached out, but if there is gilding present bleach may damage it.
Crazing of the glaze is quite common on old china. Do not expect a great deal of discount unless the crazing is stained. You will have to fake crazing on any restored area.
Is a **missing handle worth replacing? Making a new handle from scratch is time-consuming. If there is a matching item, you can mold a new handle.
*Salts** show up as a powdery white deposit on the surface of china. These will require treatment.
*Chipped edges** are often found, particularly on plates and saucers. If a plate hanger has been forced over the rim there may be four small, evenly spaced chips. Do not forget to look at the back for others.
Discolored paint or **glaze** from a previous, inferior restoration can mar the piece. If in doubt, view the piece against the light—such paint may show up as a darker patch. You can usually strip it off and repaint it.
*Badly joined pieces** can be dismantled and reglued.
Metal rivets were once used as a way of reinforcing a bad break. You can remove them, but this may be tricky.

Examining figures
It is rare to find a figure without some kind of damage— look for the points shown on the figure below.

**A missing limb or head will probably mean modeling a new one from scratch (see p. 29).

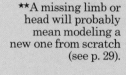

**Look at the extremities for missing fingers and toes.

**Check for broken or missing flowers (see pp. 29 and 34).

Using and displaying china

You can safely use most nineteenth and early twentieth century services as long as you handle them carefully and wash them by hand, never in the dishwasher. Store china in a dry cupboard, and try to avoid stacking it or overcrowding the shelves. If you have to stack plates, place a sheet of paper between each one to protect any decoration.

If an item has been restored, use it with discretion. A glued hairline crack should stand up to normal use, but painting applied to disguise a repair can easily be discolored or damaged. Such restorations are best kept for display or, at the most, used as a plant holder.

Glass-fronted cabinets provide ideal conditions for preserving china. However, many collectors feel that viewing their treasures through glass detracts from their appeal, and they prefer to display a collection on open shelves. If you wish to stand plates at the back of a shelf, there should be either a groove or raised lip to secure the rim. Otherwise, use a metal, plastic or wooden plate stand, making sure that it does not put undue strain on a repair or rub surface decoration.

Sprung metal hooks are useful if you want to hang plates on a wall. If the wire hooks are not sheathed with a softening, buy soft neoprene tubing from a model shop, or dip the hooks in silicon bath sealant, leaving it to harden off before you use the device. Protect the back of the plate by slipping thin cardboard between it and the springs.

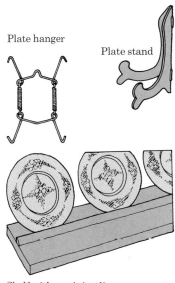

Plate hanger

Plate stand

Shelf with retaining lip

Dating china

Ceramic marks (see p. 232) are often the best way of dating and identifying pieces. If you have a lot of pottery and porcelain it may be worth your while buying a specialized dictionary of marks.

● Some potteries marked their china with the year mark. With the appropriate references you can therefore date such a piece very accurately.

● You can sometimes approximate the date of manufacture by the way the maker's mark has been applied, or by a change in its design. These changes were often instigated by a change of premises or the formation of a new partnership.

● Artist's marks were sometimes applied in addition to the factory mark. These can also help to date a piece.

● The marks that denote the country of origin of the piece give hints to dating, especially as they were sometimes applied as a result of legislation. In 1891, for instance, American import laws made such marks compulsory.

● In the absence of makers' marks, you can often date a piece by the style of decoration or by certain distinctive shapes. A book on the history of design should establish broad guidelines.

● Libraries and museums may have copies of famous makers' catalogs.

Dating by style The geometric shape and pattern of this "Bizarre" coffee set (by the English designer Clarice Cliff) are typical of the Art Deco style that was fashionable from about 1910 to the mid 1930s.

Tools and materials

You do not have to buy everything shown on these pages before making your first attempt at china repair. To mend a simple break you will need only a few of the items—glue, a sharp knife, modeling clay and razorblades. As you progress to more difficult repairs, start to build up your collection.

You can work satisfactorily in a spare room or even the kitchen. You will need good lighting, and color matching must be carried out in daylight or under daylight bulbs. The room must be well-ventilated (because some chemicals give off unhealthy fumes), and have access to hot and cold water. You should have a large worktable to spread out tools, materials and partly-assembled items—a cramped, cluttered bench will lead to costly, even dangerous spillages or breakages. Protect the tabletop with wipe-clean plastic or old newspaper. And keep dangerous materials in a lockable cupboard.

Materials

Hydrogen peroxide Bleaches stains from ceramics. Ask for the 100 volume type.

Ammonia Add a few drops to a bleaching solution.

Distilled water Professional restorers usually use this. However, you can use tap water unless the piece is very fine.

Mineral spirits Hydrochloric acid (mineral spirits) removes lime scale.

Rust remover Commercial removers eliminate rust stains.

Acetone Use this to clean and degrease broken edges. Buy a lanolin-free type.

Paint stripper Breaks down glues in unsatisfactory repairs.

Glues See p. 25.

Titanium dioxide Add to epoxy resin glue to reduce its tendency to yellow.

Kaolin Mix with epoxy glue to make a filler putty.

Fillers See p. 27.

Plaster of Paris Fills pottery and forms molds.

Molding material See p. 27.

Dental composition Use to make press molds (see p. 28).

Abrasive papers Use to rub down glue, filler and paintwork. For large areas of filler use 150 grit, then 220 grit. For finishing work and small repairs try plastic-backed silicon carbide.

Chrome polish For buffing filler and glaze buy polish from an auto accessory store.

Talcum powder Sprinkle onto molds to stop filler adhering to them. Mix it with epoxy glue to make a filler.

Silver sand This very fine sand from pet stores will support assemblies while glue sets.

Modeling clay Use this to support pieces, for taking impressions and to model a master of a missing component.

Denatured alcohol You will need a doctor's certificate to get clear denatured alcohol from a druggist. You can use normal denatured alcohol but do not soak ceramics in it as it may stain them.

Stainless steel and brass rod Use this to make reinforcing pins or dowels.

Cotton Swabs of cotton keep bleach and stain-removing chemicals in contact with the piece.

Adhesive tape Use this to strap glued pieces together.

Tools

Most forms of ceramic restoration can be carried out with a very basic set of tools, but a few specialized items will make your work easier.

Sharp knife Surgical scalpels are available from artist's suppliers. They have interchangeable blades—choose one to suit your particular needs.

Razorblades These are useful for scraping glue and filler flush with the surface of the ceramic, particularly as they can be bent to fit curved surfaces.

Pine modeling tools Wooden modeling tools from an artist's suppliers are ideal for shaping and smoothing epoxy paste.

Dental tools Shaped probes and spatulas will reach into awkward spaces when filling or modeling china. If your dentist cannot supply you with secondhand tools you can obtain them from specialist dental suppliers.

Needle files A small selection of fine needle files is essential for the initial shaping of fillers and modeling material. Your kit should include round, triangular and flat files.

Palette knife An artist's palette knife with a flexible steel blade will be useful for mixing resins and fillers.

Ceramic tile White tiles are ideal surfaces for mixing paints, but use old tin lids or disposable foil dishes for mixing adhesives.

Tweezers You will need a pair of tweezers to apply cotton swabs soaked in various solvents and bleach to your china.

Pliers These are useful for manipulating wire to make supports for modeling material.

Needle-nosed pliers These will enable you to reach into less accessible areas.

Junior hacksaw You will need this to cut the metal rod used to make reinforcing dowels.

Vise Have a small clamp-on bench vise to hold metal rod and other materials while they are cut and shaped.

Swizzle sticks These are useful for applying glue or filler.

Power drill A flexible drive attachment for a power drill will enable you to drill ceramics safely. The working end, containing the chuck, is connected by a flexible cable to the power drill (which must be clamped into a bench mounting). If you can afford them, miniature electric drills from model shops are much more accurate.

Drill bits Ceramics are so hard that only diamond-tipped drill bits (from dental suppliers) will penetrate them successfully. These are expensive, but you only need one or two finely-tapered bits for inserting reinforcing pins.

Brushes Keep worn-out toothbrushes and shaving brushes for cleaning ceramics.

Magnifying glass A magnifying glass is essential to inspect work closely at various stages.

Protective gloves You should wear rubber gloves when handling chemicals.

Safety glasses If you wear spectacles, they will provide sufficient protection for your eyes, but otherwise it is advisable to use protective glasses when drilling ceramics and using paint stripper.

Face mask You may need to wear a simple face mask to prevent you from inhaling fumes. If you have any history of bronchial disorders consult your doctor.

Painting equipment See p. 35.

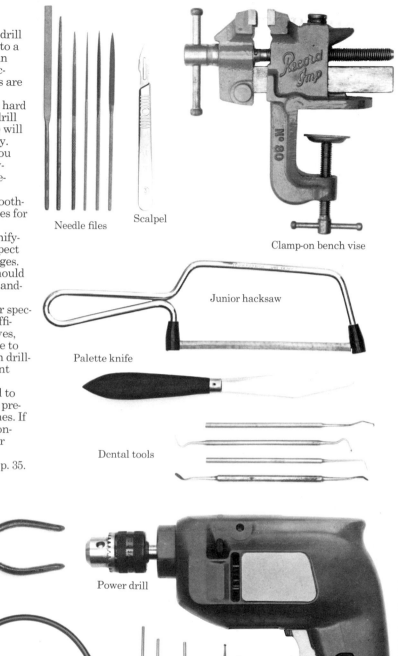

Needle files

Scalpel

Clamp-on bench vise

Junior hacksaw

Palette knife

Dental tools

Needle-nosed pliers

Power drill

Drill bits, brush and cutting wheel

Pine modeling tools

Flexible drive attachment

Cleaning ceramics

It is always worth dusting ceramics prior to washing them to prevent excess dirt entering any tiny cracks or crazing. Use a soft paintbrush or shaving brush. Never put antiques in a dishwasher. Instead lay the item on a sheet of foam or a folded cloth at the bottom of a plastic bowl filled with warm water and a little liquid detergent. If you intend to eat or drink from newly acquired items, sterilize them first in the mild bleach used for cleaning babies' bottles. Use a soft brush or non-abrasive cloth to coax out any dirt from raised ornament before rinsing the piece in clean water. Lay it on a cloth and leave it in a warm place to dry, or use a hairdryer. When dry, remove any greasy smears with acetone and treat stubborn dirty patches with chrome polish. Then gently burnish the piece with a soft cloth.

Removing stains

A ceramic often has ugly stains which washing will not remove. In such a case you should soak the piece in water, then use tweezers to apply bleach on cotton swabs. You must be particularly careful to treat stained edges of broken pieces before gluing, or an invisible joint will be impossible.

Pure household bleach will remove light staining. Otherwise use hydrogen peroxide (100 volume) from your druggist. Make a solution with one part bleach to three parts of water, plus a few drops of ammonia. Wear protective gloves and an apron. If you spill bleach on your skin, wash it off immediately with water.

Soak the piece in water before applying bleach. This will prevent stains being drawn into the body of the ceramic. Pottery is particularly absorbent, so resoak such pieces every time you apply bleach. Use tweezers to dip cotton swabs in the bleach solution and apply them to the stain. Leave them in position for several hours.

Cover the piece with a plastic sheet or seal it in a plastic container to keep swabs moist. Inspect the staining after a couple of hours, and repeat the bleaching process until the stain is completely removed. It may take several weeks to treat badly stained items—try increasing the concentration of bleach.

Caution: Gilding may be affected by strong bleach, so inspect a gilded piece frequently. When the stain has gone, rinse the item in water and leave to dry.

Pre-nineteenth-century glazes are unstable, so seek specialist advice if you have an early piece.

Removing lime scale

If a ceramic bowl has been used to house a potted plant, hard water may have left a deposit of calcium carbonate (lime scale). You can remove this with mineral spirits (hydrochloric acid), from a druggist.

Warning: You must always handle acid with care. Wear old clothing, protective gloves and safety glasses. *Never* add water to acid—it will boil over, causing a serious accident. Only add acid to water.

Pour water into the ceramic bowl to cover the stain. Slowly add acid until the lime scale starts to bubble, then leave this solution in the pot until it has dissolved the scale. If necessary, add more acid. When you have finished, pour the solution into a drain, then wash the piece.

Washing off salting

Salts present in the body of an object can accumulate on the surface, causing it to break up. To cure this, the salts must be washed out of the piece. If the surface is flaking, consolidate it first by brushing on a solution of polyvinyl alcohol powder and warm distilled water. This will fix the surface, yet still allow salts to be washed away. Then place the piece in a plastic container and add distilled water. Do not immerse the object entirely—some of its surface must be exposed. Change the water daily until all the salts have gone. To test this, hold a spoonful of the water over a flame so that the water evaporates. There should be no salts left.

Removing metallic stains

The copper and iron rivets once used to reinforce repairs (see p. 26) will often stain the surrounding ceramic. Ammonia applied with cotton swabs will remove copper stains, and you can use a commercial rust remover (phosphoric acid) on rust marks. When the stains have disappeared, wash the area thoroughly with distilled water.

Dismantling old repairs

When buying china, watch out for badly repaired pieces where the joints are poorly aligned and hardened glue is left on the surface. Even if the joint is satisfactory, old glues can often discolor with age. In all cases, the only remedy is to dismantle the item, clean off the remaining glue and restore the piece with a modern synthetic adhesive.

Dissolving glue in water

Brown animal-based glues can usually be broken down by immersing the piece in hot water. Polyvinyl acetate glues may also respond to this treatment. To avoid cracking the ceramic, lower it into a plastic bowl of warm water, then gradually add hot water to increase the temperature. As the glue softens, use a small, stiff paintbrush or toothbrush to remove it. Then try each joint to make sure that it closes perfectly. If it does not, inspect the edges closely for traces of glue. Either brush this away with water, or carefully pick off any specks with a pointed knife blade.

Dissolving glue with denatured alcohol

Shellac, which is also brown in color, may break down in hot water. If this has not worked, lay cotton swabs soaked in industrial denatured alcohol along each side of the joint. Apply fresh swabs until the spirit penetrates the joint. If this is unsuccessful, try paint stripper.

Dissolving glue with acetone

Acetone-soaked cotton swabs will soften cellulose-based and polyvinyl acetate glue. As acetone evaporates very fast, wrap the item in plastic as soon as you have applied the swabs.

Dissolving glue with paint stripper

Commercial strippers will soften modern epoxy and rubber-based glues, but they may also remove surface paintwork. This can be an advantage if it was from a previous, badly applied restoration, but you must avoid stripping original paint. Where possible, use stripper on the inside of the piece only. Wash it off as soon as the glue has softened, and take care not to smear any on the outside. Soak pottery in water before applying stripper.

Warning: Wear protective gloves, follow instructions and avoid contact with skin.

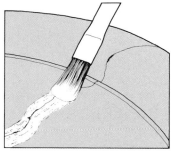

1 Paint stripper along both sides of the joint with a small brush. A type with a jelly-like consistency is best. Avoid very fluid strippers as these can run.

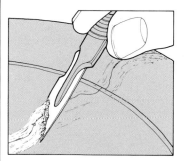

2 Once the glue has softened, lift off any excess left on the surface with a scalpel blade so that a second application of stripper can penetrate the joint.

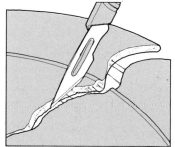

3 If the broken pieces will not separate of their own accord, try gently pulling them apart, cutting any strands of glue with a sharp scalpel blade.

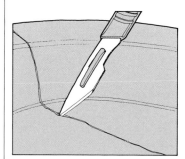

4 It may be possible to insert the point of a scalpel into a partially open joint or hole. The thickness of the blade may be enough to pry the joint open.

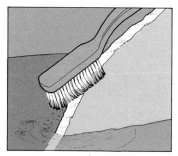

5 Wash pieces in water, using an old toothbrush to remove glue.
Warning: Brush away from yourself at all times to avoid flicking stripper into your eyes.

Bonding china

Gluing china is not a particularly difficult task, requiring patience more than skill, but it is an extremely important one. You should be prepared to persevere with each and every joint until it is perfect. If you do not you will have more problems, either because a subsequent piece will not fit, or because a slight misalignment will show through the paintwork.

Small hollow-ware objects such as cups or bowls are the best things to begin with. Although a plate might appear simpler, broken pieces with exaggerated curves will give you a more positive "feel" as you bring them together; this will indicate to you that they are mating exactly.

Bonding a simple break

It is a simple process to restore an item that has broken cleanly into two halves. Clean both pieces (see p. 22) and make sure that the joint closes satisfactorily. Then wipe the edges with a piece of silk soaked in acetone to remove any remaining grease and fingerprints. Before you start, warm the two tubes of epoxy resin glue on a radiator to encourage them to flow easily, mix up the glue and add a small amount of titanium dioxide (see p. 20). And pre-cut several 2–3 in (5–7.5 cm) lengths of adhesive tape or paper tape for strapping the pieces together. Or use a tape dispenser so that you can pull out the tape to the required length with one hand and steady the china with the other.

1 Stick several lengths of tape on both sides of one piece at right angles to the break line so that they overhang the edge by half their length. Fold them back so that they do not prevent you from mating the two halves.

2 Use a swizzle stick or knife blade to apply adhesive sparingly to the edge of the other half. Bring both pieces together, squeezing excess glue from the joint. A gentle, rocking action often encourages a perfect match.

3 Holding the joint together firmly, stretch each piece of tape across the break. There is no need for perfect alignment at this stage—just strap the halves together safely. Remove excess glue with denatured alcohol.

4 Lift the edges of the tape and stretch each piece tightly, making sure that tension is even on both sides. Run your fingernail or a knife blade across the joint to make sure that it is aligned correctly. Adjust any irregularities with a gentle sideways pressure. Use denatured alcohol to remove excess glue from areas which would be difficult to clean later. Scrape off glue under the tape when the joint has set.

Repairing multiple breaks

When an item is broken into more than two pieces, first determine the order in which to assemble broken components. Make sure that none of them is "locked out"—that is when one piece cannot be inserted without first dismantling others that surround it. Lay all the pieces out and try a dry run, taping larger bits together. Number each piece with a grease pencil, a wax crayon or numbered adhesive tape.

Having built up the article to your satisfaction, take the pieces apart carefully, making sure that you do not damage fragile edges as you remove the tape. Each piece must be completely clean before you glue together each joint. Follow the procedure for a simple break, but do not attempt to complete the assembly in one operation. Stick two, or at the most three, pieces together at any one time, and allow glue to set before further assembly. Clean excess adhesive from edges and corners as you go because even a speck of hardened glue will prevent a perfect join. Squeeze out excess glue as any increase in size will prevent the final bit from fitting.

Dealing with a warped piece

Often it will be impossible to coax two pieces of a broken item together, even when the edge is sound and perfectly clean. The reason for this is that when the ceramic broke, tensions were released within the item and one or more of the pieces has become distorted.

Slightly warped pieces can be "sprung" into place. Glue one half of the joint, then strap it together firmly with tape. Tape the unglued section of joint, but not too tightly. Leave the glue to set thoroughly—say for 2–3 days—then remove the tape and apply glue to the unbonded half with a knife blade. Warm the joint with a hairdryer. Pull the joint closed with tape, then apply tape all along the joint and leave the glue to set.

Mending a crack

Clean and bleach the crack (see p. 22), then warm the item on a radiator. Place a knife or razorblade in the crack to open it up a little. Take great care, because it is easy to turn the crack into a break. Scrape epoxy glue against the edge of the crack from both sides, remove the blade and strap the crack up tightly with adhesive tape.

Taping a cup handle

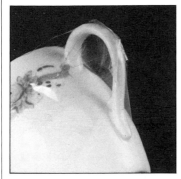

A broken cup handle must be taped back on carefully to ensure a first-rate joint. Apply glue to both surfaces. Then run one piece of tape straight across the handle. Next, apply diagonal tapes, stretching them first at one end, then the other for equal tension.

Supporting repaired china

A repair should be supported so that gravity helps to hold pieces together while the glue is setting. Modeling clay is the most useful material for this purpose—you can embed smaller items in it and use it to prop up larger pieces. Place plates and saucers in a plastic or wooden plate rack, using clay to hold them at the right angle. Do not use a metal rack—it might damage delicate decoration. You can also use modeling clay to prevent a cup rolling on the workbench when you are gluing on a handle.

Support very large items in a box filled with the very fine silver sand (see above) available from pet stores. If you let a large piece of china slip, you may find that sand adheres to it. To prevent this, loosely fill a plastic bag with sand and seal it.

Adhesives

There are a great many adhesives on the market that claim to bond almost anything permanently. Most of these will be suitable for mending ceramics. The glues described here are reliable, and are recommended for china restoration.

Epoxy resin glues

Epoxy adhesives are sold in two tubes, the glue itself and a hardener. When the two constituents are mixed, the glue begins to set. For most work, use standard epoxy adhesive which sets in about 6 hours. For small, hand-held sub-assemblies buy a quick-setting variety which hardens after only 5–10 minutes. A special, much thinner epoxy adhesive, available from specialist suppliers, makes it much easier to achieve a hairline joint. Always use this type of glue when casting components.

All epoxy glues have a tendency to yellow. To compensate, mix in a tiny amount of titanium dioxide to color the glue without reducing its adhesive quality. For colored ceramics, add a little pigment in place of the titanium dioxide.

Polyvinyl acetate glue

This is a white, water-based, single-tube adhesive that is ideal for gluing earthenware, terracotta and pottery. Dampen the edge of the joint with water before gluing to prevent adhesive being absorbed, thus weakening the bond.

Cyanoacrylate glues

These "superglues" are suitable for hard-paste china only. They are water-thinned, and so add nothing to the bulk of the work. This helps with multiple breaks, since a build-up of gap-filling glue may force the last pieces out of alignment. The fast setting time—10–15 seconds under finger pressure—is ideal for bonding tiny pieces which are impossible to tape together.

Warning: These glues bond skin. Acetone or some other solvent may dissolve them.

Reinforcing a joint

To reinforce a joint modern restorers use brass or stainless steel pins glued into holes made in both halves of the break. This type of repair will only be necessary where the joint is likely to take more than the average strain— for example a handle—or when the object is heavy, as in the case of a large bowl.

Inserting metal pins

Porcelain is so hard that it can only be drilled well with a diamond drill bit (see p. 21). Start the hole with a small bit, and work up to the required diameter. It is rarely necessary to use pins larger than $\frac{1}{8}$ in (3 mm) in diameter. Holes for pins this size should not be deeper than $\frac{3}{16}$ in (5 mm) and about one third the thickness of the ceramic.

tiny "bath" of cold water. With this method, only the drill is in water—your fingers and the motor are kept dry. Drill a hole slightly larger than the pin. Before gluing, assemble the joint and make any adjustment to the hole with a diamond bit.

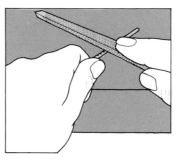

3 Roughen the rod with a file, then degrease it with acetone before cutting out the pins with a hacksaw.

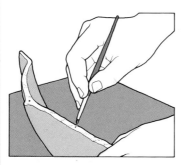

1 On one edge mark the position of the pins with small spots of paint. Bring the two halves together carefully so that the paint spots are transferred to the other edge.

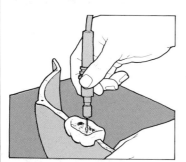

2 Diamond drill bits must be water-cooled while drilling. However, mixing electricity and water is dangerous. The safest way to cope with this is to construct a wall of modeling clay around the area of the hole so that the bit is running in a

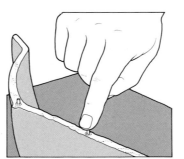

4 Scrape adhesive into the holes on both sides, bedding the pins in one half. Glue, assemble and clamp the joint in the normal way (see p. 25).

(see p. 21)
(see p. 25)

Removing rivets

Before the availability of superior glues, repairs on large items were often reinforced with rivets, staple-like fastenings which helped to clamp a joint together. As long as the joint is sound and the rivets do not disfigure the piece, there is little point in taking them out and risking further damage. However, if the joint lines are unsightly, remove the rivets and reinforce the joint with hidden metal pins.

Rivets are normally held in place with Plaster of Paris. Soften this by covering the rivet with a wet swab of cotton, or, if possible, immerse the whole piece in hot water. Pick out loose filler with a pointed tool then pull the rivet out straight with pliers.

If the rivet is stubborn, use a small hacksaw blade to saw it in half. Keep the blade parallel to the surface or the glaze could be badly marked. Grip one half of the rivet with pliers and twist it gently while pulling it directly from the hole. Repeat the procedure for the other half. Clean out old filler from holes with a carborundum drill bit.

Filling china

Very few repair jobs are straightforward—it is quite unusual to be able to just glue two pieces of china together and form a perfect joint. In most cases, the edges chipped when the item was broken, and often small pieces were lost. For an invisible repair you will need to fill these holes and then retouch the surface decoration (see pp. 35–8).

Types of filler

Epoxy putty To fill porcelain use epoxy putty from a hardware store. You buy this in two tubes, and mix the two components in equal proportions, setting the hardening process in motion. It sets very hard, but it can be filed and sanded to a smooth finish. The putty will not become too stiff to handle for from 45 to 60 minutes.

You can make your own putty by mixing epoxy resin glue with titanium dioxide to make it white and a powder such as kaolin or talc to give it body. First make the glue (see p. 25), but add a greater proportion of titanium dioxide. This mixture will be sticky, but if you add powder you can eventually knead it into a putty-like consistency.

Spackle To fill pottery use the spackle that comes in powdered form. This is the type that you mix with water to fill cracks in a plaster wall, and it is available from hardware stores. Plaster of Paris will work equally well. To prevent water being drawn from fillers into the body of the pottery, paint the broken edges with polyvinyl acetate adhesive before applying filler.

After filling porcelain, use a spackle primer over the epoxy putty as a final surface before finishing. This forms a good base for paintwork. As an alternative, you can use fine-surface spackle for small repairs to porcelain, as long as the piece is for display only. Once you have prepared spackle, clean your hands and tools with water or denatured alcohol before handling any china.

Filling a joint

Once the adhesive in a joint has set hard, remove the tape and scrape off any remaining glue with a sharp knife. Remove any smears of glue with a very fine abrasive paper.

Use a magnifying glass to look for small chips along the line of repair. Press filler into these with a palette knife or knife blade, working across the line from both directions. Then dampen the tool with denatured alcohol or water and draw it along the joint, pressing and smoothing the filler into low points.

When set, scrape the filler flush. Use a razor blade for flat surfaces and a round-tipped knife for internal curves. Then smooth the surface with the smallest piece of very fine abrasive paper that will cover your fingertip.

You may need to make further applications of filler. Continue until you can rub a finger across the repair without feeling a change in the texture of the surface. Finally, you should buff the whole piece lightly with chrome polish.

Filling holes

Back up holes which pass right through an object with adhesive tape to stop the filler falling out while it is still soft. Curved surfaces can be backed with modeling clay dusted with talc to prevent filler sticking to it.

Stretch two or three lengths of tape across the hole, and gently press filler into the recess. Start by concentrating on the edges, scraping filler against them. Gradually build up filler to the level of the ceramic or slightly above. Dip your finger in denatured alcohol or water and smooth the surface of the filler. When it has set, rub it down with abrasive paper and buff the surface with chrome polish.

Rebuilding chipped edges

The edges of bowls, plates and saucers are most vulnerable to damage, especially the characteristic shell chip. It can be difficult to make filler adhere in such a shallow depression. Apply adhesive (see p. 25) mixed with titanium dioxide to the damaged surface. Then press in filler, carefully smoothing it with a fingertip. Use a needle file for rough shaping before resorting to abrasive papers.

Fine edges may be completely broken away, leaving a gap which needs to be backed up to support the filler. Tape alone might bridge the gap, but it is usually safer to use thin plastic or cardboard, bent to follow the curve and taped tightly in place. Once again, dust the support with talc, and leave it in place until the glue has set.

Shell chips Examine the edges of pieces like plates and cups for these shallow marks, and fill them before they become stained.

Casting missing components

However carefully you collect up the broken pieces of a damaged item, sometimes you will assemble the components and find that something is missing. Perhaps it is part of a rim, or a cup handle. In these cases it is preferable to take a molding—from the remaining rim or from an identical piece—and cast a replacement, rather than try to model it from scratch.

Press molding

The simplest of all molding techniques requires a soft material which, when pressed against china, reproduces its shape exactly. White modeling clay is well suited to the job, and it is cheap and easy to obtain.

Mending a chipped dish
The dish shown above has a wavy edge and a slightly raised decoration on the inner rim. To cast the piece missing from the rim, first measure the area of damage and locate an identical spot along part of the edge which is intact. Use water to moisten the area against which the modeling clay will be pressed to prevent the clay sticking. In this example, the inner face was moistened in order to incorporate the decoration in the mold.

1 Roll out a $\frac{1}{2}$ in (12 mm) thick slab of modeling clay, large enough to cover the damaged portion with a 1 in (2.5 cm) margin all round.

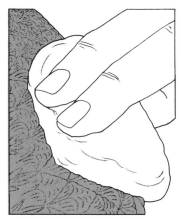

2 Press the clay firmly against the *undamaged* rim, making sure that it overlaps the outer edge enough to reproduce its wavy contour, but not so much that you cannot remove it without distorting the mold.

3 Gently pry the edge of the modeling clay with a knife until it is loose enough to pull straight from the dish. Put it in a refrigerator for a few hours to harden slightly. Meanwhile, mix some epoxy putty for the cast.

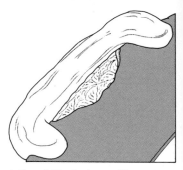

4 Carefully fit the mold over the damaged area. Press it in contact with the china around its outer edge, and fold it over the edge of the dish at each end to hold it firmly in place.

5 Lightly dust the clay with talcum powder. Use a palette knife to gently press putty against the mold. Work the putty carefully into the edges and decoration, gradually building it up flush with the outer surface of the dish. Dampen the knife with denatured alcohol, and smooth the putty so that it matches the contours of the china.

6 Leave the putty overnight to set hard. Then remove the mold and rub down the putty in the normal way, making good any slight imperfections on the inner surface.

Using dental composition

This composition sets hard, and therefore lasts longer than modeling clay. If you need to make a second or third casting, use composition for your press molding. Soften it by immersing it in hot water, then model it with your fingers into an even texture. You use this material in exactly the same way as modeling clay, except that you do not have to prepare the china by moistening it or dusting it with talcum powder. When you have taken an impression, allow the composition to become firm before removing it. Then leave it to harden naturally. You should hold the finished mold in place with adhesive tape when making a cast from it.

One-piece molds

Missing flower

Latex is an extremely versatile material for making molds. A finished latex mold is flexible enough to be peeled from an original which has "undercuts" —hollows or projections which would lock a more rigid material in place. As long as you remove the mold carefully you can use it more than once.

Latex emulsion is available from specialist suppliers, but it is more easily obtained in the form of the latex adhesive commonly used to glue fabrics.

Molding a flower
To make a mold of a missing flower (from the base of a figure, for example) find a suitable original, either on the same piece or on a similar one.

1 Clean the original with acetone. Buy Q-tips (or make one by wrapping a small ball of cotton around the end of a swizzle stick). Use a Q-tip to apply latex to the flower and some of the surrounding area. This first

layer is very important to achieve a faithful reproduction. Carefully prick out any air bubbles, and encourage the latex to flow into crevices or undercuts. Let the latex harden for several hours until it turns brown.

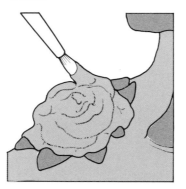

2 Apply five or six additional layers of latex over the first, leaving it to harden each time. If the item is small, the mold will now be strong enough to remove. But with larger moldings you should strengthen the mold by coating it with one more layer of latex mixed up to a thick paste with sawdust. Press this in place with a palette knife and leave it overnight to harden.

4 Lightly dust the surface of the mold with talc to make it easier to remove the casting, peel it off carefully, then fill it with epoxy putty. If the flower is very delicate, making it impossible to fill the mold with a paste, pour in some liquid epoxy glue mixed with a little titanium dioxide. This material is fluid enough to penetrate the finest detail. You must pour it in slowly to avoid trapping air in the mold, and prick out any bubbles that form. Arrange the mold so that the adhesive will stay in place while it hardens. When the casting has set, peel off the mold, attach the new part to your piece, then paint it (see p. 357) to match the rest.

Casting an arm

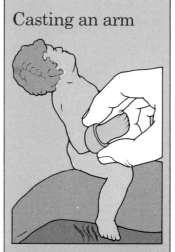

Latex is so flexible that it will even peel off easily from a hand with projecting fingers and thumb. Apply it exactly as you do for a flower (see left) but omit the final sawdust layer. Dust the outer surface of the mold with talc before peeling it off. This will stop it sticking to itself as you turn it inside out. Work the mold off the fingers slowly and carefully. Once you have successfully removed the mold, dust its inner surface with talc and turn it right way out.

To make a casting, pour enough liquid adhesive into the mold to fill the hand only, then squeeze the bottom end of the mold and tap it gently to encourage any trapped air to escape. Now fill the mold slowly to the top and leave the casting to harden. When set, remove the mold and attach the arm to the piece. You may need to use a dowel (see p. 27). Paint it to tone in with the piece.

Two-piece Plaster of Paris molds

With some items—for example, an open handle—you will find that it is impossible to withdraw a mold from the original in one piece. In such cases you must make the mold in two separate halves.

The choice of material for the mold will depend on the size or complexity of the object in question.

Plaster of Paris is most suitable for large, simple moldings such as a handle for a jug or vase like the one shown right. It is cheap, and rigid enough to be self-supporting.

1 Paint the area of the vase to be molded with a release agent —a light cooking oil—to prevent plaster sticking to it.

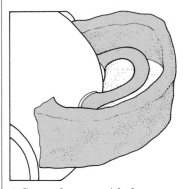

2 Set up the vase with the handle perfectly horizontal. Build an open-topped "box" of modeling clay around the handle, leaving at least $\frac{1}{2}$ in (12 mm) clearance all round and below it. The sides of this box should extend $\frac{1}{2}$ in (12 mm) above the level of the handle. Press the corners with your thumb to make sure that they are sealed. And check that the clay is pressed firmly against the vase so that no Plaster of Paris can leak out.

3 Pour enough water to fill the mold into a bowl, and mix in plaster to a creamy consistency. Slowly pour plaster into one side of the box—*not* into the center—to push air in one direction so that none is trapped. When the plaster half fills the mold, leave it to set. If the halfway mark is not obvious, draw it on the handle with a pencil.

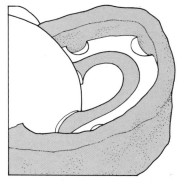

4 Before the plaster has set hard, cut notches around the edge. This forms a key to locate one half of the mold on the other.

5 Spread petroleum jelly on the surface of the plaster to act as a release agent between the two halves. Keep the handle free of it, or a bad casting will result.

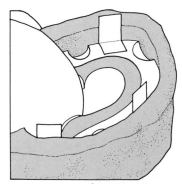

6 Cut three $1 \times \frac{3}{4}$ in (25×18 mm) rectangles from thick aluminum foil and fold them to form right-angles. Place them inside the mold—one at each end and one opposite the handle—with one

face resting on the plaster, the other pressed against the clay. These "tabs" will help you to separate the two halves.

7 Mix and pour the plaster as in step 3. Then leave it to set hard.

8 Remove the modeling clay box and locate the foil tabs. Starting at the end tabs, slide a knife blade down beside each one to open the mold. Do not start with the central tab, or you may break the handle as the mold tries to part.

Casting from a plaster mold

Always start by coating the inside of both halves of the mold with petroleum jelly. Then strap them together with elastic bands and pour in liquid epoxy adhesive (see p. 25). Leave the casting to set overnight. Then take the mold apart and remove the new handle. Finally, use a file and abrasive paper to smooth any roughness, and a carbon cutting disk on your drill to trim the handle to fit the piece.

Two-piece vinyl rubber molds

For delicate pieces, or items which have slight undercuts that would make it impossible to remove a rigid mold in one piece, use vinyl rubber to make a flexible two-part mold.

1 Cut the vinyl into small cubes and heat it gently in an old saucepan until it reaches the consistency of thick soup. It will then be ready for pouring over the area of china to be molded.

Warning: Follow the manufacturer's instructions carefully when warming vinyl rubber because overheated vinyl gives off toxic fumes. You must have a window open, and it is advisable to wear a face mask.

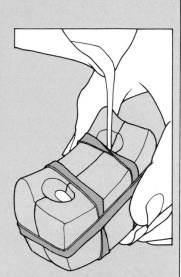

2 Prewarm the object on a radiator, then set it up as for plaster casting (see opposite), with a modeling clay box built around the area to be molded. You will not need a release agent or foil tabs to help you to separate the two halves.

3 Pour in rubber to halfway up the handle. Once cool, burn in "key-ways" with a hot needle. Pour in a second layer.

4 When set, remove the clay, cut around the joint and peel the two halves apart.

5 To make a casting, hold the two halves together with elastic bands, and pour liquid epoxy adhesive into one end in a steady stream to expel the air. Then set the piece up in a sand box (see p. 25) to harden.

Two-piece latex molds

You can use latex (see p. 29) to make a two-part mold for small items such as coffee-cup handles. Latex is very flexible, and will peel off undercuts easily.

Warning: Never use a repaired cup to serve hot liquids— the glue may weaken in time, and the joint will come apart, spilling the contents.

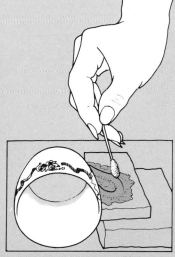

1 Roll out a slab of modeling clay and align it with the edge of your work bench. Embed half of the handle in the clay. Press "key-ways" into the clay around the handle with a knitting needle. Use some more clay to prop up both cup and clay support so that the handle is held horizontally.

2 Apply latex (see p. 29), including a stiff outer layer of sawdust mixture.

3 When the first half of the mold has set, leave it in place. Remove the clay, turn the cup over and dust the latex with talc. Make the second half of the mold in the same way.

4 Lightly dust both halves of the mold with talc and clamp them together with elastic bands. Pour liquid epoxy adhesive into one end, tilting the mold until glue begins to emerge from the other end. Gradually bring the mold back to horizontal, and continue pouring until it is full. Set the mold up in silver sand until the glue has set.

Modeling missing components

Many items have missing components that you cannot copy by molding—there is no "twin" part on the piece, and you cannot find an identical item to mold from. If you are unable to take a mold you will have to model the missing component yourself. You can either model a replacement directly onto the ceramic item, or make one up separately and then glue it in place once it has set hard. It is more difficult to obtain a perfect joint with the second method, but you will often find it easier to model a component.

Research

Before you begin to make a model, try to find out exactly what the missing part looks like. Visit libraries, museums and antique shops, and search through friends' collections, to find a piece in the same style, preferably by the same manufacturer. Museums can be particularly fruitful. Talk to museum staff if possible, as well as looking through the collections. There will often be something in store which matches the object. Some factories also have their own museums. Consulting dealers can also be useful. An experienced dealer will have seen so much material over the years that he or she may well have seen an identical piece of china at some time.

The object itself will often display traces of the missing part. For example, with a figure look for marks where a hand rested on a knee or fence post, or held an object. Bear in mind,

however, that correctly modeled limbs or features do not necessarily mean that scale has been properly observed or that the item has been modeled realistically. Many ceramic figures are rather stylized, and some, Victorian fairings for example, are quite crude. If one hand is complete you can copy the style, otherwise you will have to find a similar figure to copy.

The delicacy of floral or lace decoration varies enormously, depending on the standards of the manufacturer. If possible, find work by the same manufacturer, to see the style. When it is obvious that the figure should be holding an object—there may be a mark on the base or plinth that indicates this—it can be difficult to decide what it might be. The style of the clothing might provide a clue. Sporting clothes, for example, suggest that the object might be a gun, rod, or basket.

Modeling materials

Epoxy putty This is an ideal modeling material for most ceramics. Buy it ready-made or mix epoxy adhesive and kaolin (see p. 27). It is easy to work while soft, and as it begins to harden you can smooth it with a finger dipped in denatured alcohol or water. Once the putty has hardened, you can create a perfectly smooth finish by using abrasive papers and files.

Cellulose filler This filler is a better match for pottery than epoxy putty. Because of its brittle nature, you should reinforce it with metal pins whenever practicable. Mix it to a stiff consistency, and to increase its strength mix white adhesive with the first application. For a better finish, you can use a fine-surface filler for the final layer.

Replacing arms and hands

A determined restorer can model fingers, hands and even complete arms. This is perhaps the most daunting aspect of modeling, but with patience, good observation and a lot of practice you will achieve good results.

Once you have taken the measurements, you will need to make up a supporting structure for the arm. Use wire (see opposite) or sticks of hardened epoxy putty. Roll out putty into thin sticks, leave these to harden, then cut them up and glue them together. Model the arm separately on this core, then dowel it to the figure (see p. 26). With this method modeling is not affected by misplaced wire reinforcement.

Once you have made the support, build up an approximation of the arm in epoxy putty up to the wrist level, then leave it to harden. Next sculpt the rest, including the hand, up to the knuckles. Define each knuckle with a tiny ball of putty. After about 15 minutes the putty will be firm enough to smooth with a moistened tool or finger.

To make fingers, roll out thin "sausages" of epoxy and cut off the required length. If the fingers are large and far apart, you can push fine wire into the setting putty to reinforce them. If they are smaller and in a group of two or three, possibly touching the palm or thumb, or gripping some object, they will support each other. Use a knife to group fingers and trim knuckle line. Apply a speck of glue to the knuckle line and position the fingers together. Support them on modeling clay until the glue becomes tacky, when you can shape and pose them gently. Do not smooth the surface of the fingers at this stage. Add the thumb separately, placing it about halfway down in the center of the palm.

Let the fingers harden, then apply a final coat of putty. Place filler on the edge of a knife blade, put it in the gap between the fingers, and smooth it up over each finger from both sides. Fill any small holes on the arm before sanding the limb smooth.

1 Measure remaining limb with dividers—record shoulder to elbow, elbow to wrist, wrist to knuckles and length of fingers.

2 Glue the top of the wire into a hole drilled in the figure. Then bend wire to the correct shape and angle up to knuckle level.

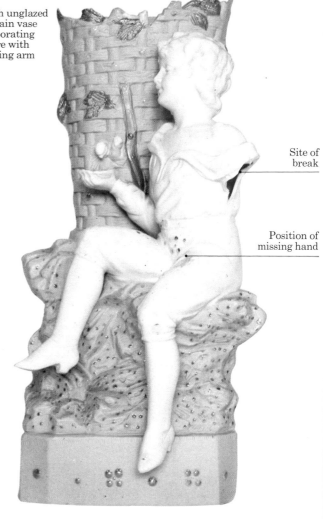

French unglazed porcelain vase incorporating a figure with a missing arm

Site of break

Position of missing hand

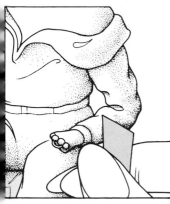

3 Build up the arm in epoxy putty up to wrist level. Once hard, sculpt the rest, including the hand up to the knuckles.

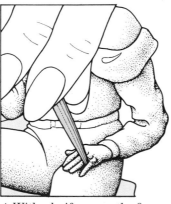

4 With a knife, group the fingers together carefully, making sure that they are all adequately supported.

5 To smooth the fingers sand carefully between them, using a small, tightly-creased piece of fine abrasive paper.

Repairing a teapot spout

The tip of a teapot spout is vulnerable, and many pots are spoiled because part of the spout has broken off. It is not practical to cast the missing piece, but you can model it directly onto the existing spout.

To make a support for the putty, plug the end of the spout with modeling clay, bending it until it follows the curve of the spout. Cut off any excess clay and dust the rest with talc. Spread a little neat epoxy adhesive on the broken edge, then build up the missing section with epoxy putty, smoothing it to flow into the existing shape. You may need to support the soft putty by wrapping adhesive tape around the spout. Once the putty has set, remove the clay, shape and roughen the repaired section, then paint it.

Modeling replacement parts

Delicate, three-dimensional moldings such as the handles of small cups or the flowers and leaves that decorate figures or bowls are often broken off and lost. They are easier to replace by modeling new parts than by casting. Leaves are cut out like petals, using a moist swizzle stick to imprint veins. Drape the leaf over a roll of clay to help it to set correctly.

Making a cup handle

Using your reference material (see p. 33), draw the outline of the proposed handle on card.

1 Cut around one edge of the cardboard so that you can match the drawing to the cup.

2 Shape a piece of reinforcing wire to run along the center line of the handle.

3 Drill holes in remaining handle stubs to take wire. If the cup is too delicate, or insufficient stubs remain, attach the new handle with glue alone.

4 Roughen ends of wire with a file, then scrape epoxy adhesive into each hole, and insert wire. Support the wire with a piece of modeling clay and build up adhesive around each end. Leave glue to set hard.

5 Dust fingers with talc and press putty along the wire. Finish is unimportant at this stage, but follow the shape of the handle to avoid unnecessary filing and abrading.

6 Let the putty harden, then apply the final layer, smoothing with a modeling tool and fingers moistened with de-natured alcohol or water. The new handle should match the stubs. When set, abrade, then buff with chrome polish.

Making flowers

Often if a whole flower is missing from a piece, you can copy its style from others still on the item. You can build up most flowers with epoxy putty, petal by petal.

1 Dust a glass or ceramic tile and a "rolling pin" made from wooden dowel with talc. Roll out a thin layer of epoxy putty.

2 Dampen a knife blade in water or denatured alcohol. Cut out the petals, then slide the blade underneath to lift them off the tile.

3 Moisten fingers to avoid leaving fingerprints in the putty, curl one petal and wrap another around it.

4 Attach two more petals at right angles to the first, repeating the process until you have attached the required number of petals.

5 Use the moistened tip of a paintbrush handle to coax the petals out to form the correct shape. Smooth any rough edges with a soft brush dipped in water.

6 Support the finished flower in a lump of modeling clay. When the putty has hardened, cut off the "stem" before you glue the flower in place.

Painting china

Even professional restorers find it difficult to disguise repairs successfully. And matching the original colors with paint and glazes requires a good deal of experience. Beginners should practice on cheap, domestic china before tackling antiques. Begin by working on patterned china, especially types with bold, free designs rather than intricate decoration. Decoration that incorporates fine, straight or regularly-spaced line work is very hard to copy. And the most arduous task of all is to retouch a white background.

Materials

Glaze Many professionals prefer a glaze they can cure by baking in an oven. Baking gives an experienced restorer the best results, but it has several drawbacks for the amateur. Heat can darken adhesives, accentuate minor cracks or crazing, and encourage fillers to shrink. And worst of all, if the piece has been repaired previously it could even disintegrate. Also ceramics must be baked in an oven reserved for this purpose, because even the slightest grease in a domestic oven could ruin paintwork. Therefore it is advisable to use a cold setting glaze.

Cold cure lacquer, available from hardware stores, is a good cold glaze for ceramics. You mix the lacquer with its own hardener, and it cures in 12 hours. For the final coat you must use the clear variety, but the lacquer is also produced in white and you can use this as a base for mixing colors.

Colored pigments You will need artists' powder pigments to match the groundwork of the china. A wide range of colors is available at an art supply store.

Acrylic paints These paints mixed with water, are perhaps the easiest medium for painting patterns on china. Once the paint is dry, you must seal your work with a coat of clear glaze.

Metallic powders If you want to simulate gilding mix colored gold and silver powders with glaze. You can buy these powders in art supply stores and some model shops.

Tools

Brushes Buy three or four good quality sable paint brushes ranging from size 00 down to a number 3. You will hardly ever need large brushes. When you buy brushes make sure that they come to a fine point. You should reserve at least one brush specifically for gilding. If you are using acrylic paint you should clean your brushes in water. However, when you are using glaze, you will need to use special thinner to clean them.

Palette You should use either a piece of clear glass or a white ceramic tile to mix your colors on.

Airbrush This is not an essential tool, but a practised restorer can use it to produce a very effective feathered edge to a repair. Airbrushes are expensive, however, especially if you buy a compressor to power it. But it is possible to start off with canned compressed air until you can afford the compressor. You must buy an airbrush that is capable of fine adjustment to enable you to paint very small areas without obliterating the surrounding paintwork.

Other tools and materials that you will need for retouching china are described in the main equipment section for this chapter (see pp. 20–1).

Choosing tools A beginner should start with paintbrushes, as these are easier to control. When you become more proficient, you may find that you get better results with an airbrush.

Color matching

The first step in all retouching work is to match the color accurately. Unfortunately, there is no magic formula that enables you to match the color of new paintwork to the original. Even a white background will need some coloring, as no ceramic is pure white. Professionals refer to white as having a "warm" or "cold" bias. Add a brown or reddish pigment to "warm" it slightly, and a blue or green to "cool" it.

If you intend to use acrylic paint as a base, to find the right mix lay a speck of white paint on a tile and add a little color. Repeat this procedure until you find a close match. Then try a speck of this on the piece. Use a rag moistened in thinner to clean the china between each test.

An alternative method is to mix white cold cure lacquer and pigments. Place some lacquer on a white tile; if it is fresh, its consistency will be perfect. If the lacquer is too thick, add some of the special thinners supplied with it. Lay a minute speck of pigment on the tile, and before adding any to the glaze crush it with a palette knife to remove lumps. Mix the pigment into the glaze with a palette knife. Once you are satisfied with the color and tone of the glaze, add hardener.

Coloring and glazing

Unless you already have experience of china restoring, it is best to start with inexpensive pieces before you tackle your best Meissen. The piece we used here is an Art Deco plate from a tag sale.

The basic procedure for painting china begins with mixing the right color of the paint and glaze mixture and then using it to retouch the ground color (as shown below). Next, any pattern colors are matched and retouched (right). Finally, a coat of clear glaze is applied to protect the work.

The purpose of painting restored china is to disguise any repairs as much as possible, by concealing the hard edge of the break. However, simple, applying a thick coat of color will do just the opposite—the line between the new color and the original glaze will be all too obvious.

In order to hide the repair you must "feather" the edge of the painted area, however small, until it merges imperceptibly with the surrounding color. Keep the area of new color as small as possible.

If you have to retouch a large area of groundwork or reproduce a shaded or speckled glaze you may find that you get a better effect if you use an airbrush. Once you have mastered the technique you will get very attractive results.

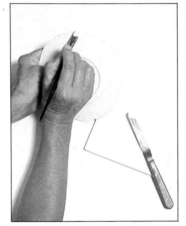

1 Start by applying a coat of tinted glaze onto clean china, working from the center outward. Load your brush with enough glaze so that it flows naturally, but does not flood the area. Avoid going back over any area twice because this may leave brush strokes. As you approach the edge of the section you are working on, squeeze excess color from the brush, leaving it with a flat (rather than pointed) tip.

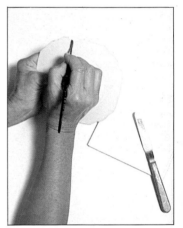

2 Next, working reasonably quickly so that the new paint does not dry, feather the edge with light strokes, dragging color out to the brink of the repair. Work in different directions to avoid a definite line.

3 While the paint is still wet, perform the same feathering operation again, this time with clear glaze. Use the glaze to pull the edge of the color out, thus thinning it further. If the edge of this clear glaze can be seen, wipe it away with a silk rag.

4 If you have painted over a surrounding pattern which was otherwise in good order, sharpen a wooden stick, moisten it with thinners and carefully remove the feathered paintwork up to the edge of the pattern.

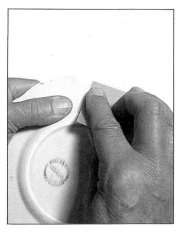

5 Once set, rub down the first layer of glaze with the finest plastic-backed silicon carbide paper. Use the lightest possible touch, concentrating on losing the edge and the brush strokes. Wipe away any dust with a damp cloth. Never use wet-and-dry paper.

Now apply another layer of tinted glaze, adjusting the color as necessary. There are no rules as to how many coats you should apply, but keep them to the minimum.

6 When you are satisfied with the base color, apply a coat of clear glaze over the whole repaired area feathering out the edge with a brush dampened in thinners. The final coat of glaze should be covered while it dries so that it does not attract specks of dust. Cover the piece with a shoebox or polyethylene sheet on a frame.

Retouching decorative patterns

Area of missing pattern

Once you have created a flat color which merges with the groundwork, but before you add clear glaze, you should retouch any area of pattern. Use acrylic paints thinned with water, and match colors as before. A fine-pointed sable brush is the most versatile tool for this work, but you may need pens or sharpened sticks to copy fine detail.

1 Mark the pattern on the piece with a soft pencil, using a series of dots rather than a line. Dividers will help you to space regular motifs, as shown above.

It is even possible to trace a section of pattern from another part of the piece and transfer it to the repaired section by rubbing the back of the tracing with a soft pencil before laying it in place. As you draw over the tracing, the marks will be reproduced on the groundwork.

2 Starting at the edge, block in your first color. If you accidentally paint over the next color, you can remove the excess paint with a stick moistened in thinner.

3 Fill in the other colors in the same way, following your predrawn lines. Once the pattern has dried, protect it with a coat of clear glaze (see left).

Restoring gilding

Many pieces of antique china have a gold edging or pattern and, in the case of the very best quality work, it is real gold leaf. But gold leaf is expensive and difficult to use, so if you want a top quality piece restored you should employ a professional. However, pieces not gilded with gold leaf can be successfully restored with metallic powders. Mix the powders together a little at a time until the proportions

look right, then add clear glaze, and finally hardener just before you paint the mixture onto the work with a fine brush. Use light, even strokes and try to apply gilding in one movement. The effect is likely to be more even if you avoid painting an area twice.

It is often easiest to paint the edge of items like cups or saucers by rotating the piece against the tip of the brush. Support your painting arm on a pile of books to hold it still at a convenient height.

When painting flat areas of gold it is difficult to lose brush strokes, and the gold particles have a tendency to separate out from the glaze. Try painting the pattern first with a clear glaze that has a touch of colored pigment added, this gives you a line to follow. Leave this glaze to turn "tacky." (A test strip on an old tile will indicate when it is ready.) Then sprinkle dry metallic powder from the tip of a soft brush over this glaze, and lightly stipple it down with the

same brush. Leave it for a few minutes, then tap excess powder onto folded card and return it to its container.

Dip a piece of tissue in clean water and squeeze it gently over the work to wash away any loose powder. Finally, pick off remaining powder from the edge of the gilded area with a swizzle stick dampened in water. Leave overnight to set, then protect it with a clear glaze.

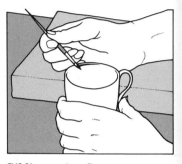

Gilding a rim Support one hand on a block and hold the brush still. Use the other hand to turn the cup.

Matching crazing

The glaze on antique china is often partly or wholly crazed. If a patch of newly restored paintwork is surrounded by crazing you should disguise the new work by faking the crazed effect on the retouched area.

The simplest method is to lightly draw the lines on to the dry paintwork with an extremely sharp, hard pencil. Sharpen it constantly to keep the thickness of the lines even. If you apply too much pencil, remove the excess by dabbing it lightly with a fingertip or soft eraser. If the crazing is stained you may have to use colored inks and a very fine pen.

Seal faked crazing with a coat of clear glaze. An airbrush is ideal for applying this, because a brush can sometimes disturb new pencil. However, you can get a satisfactory result with a paint brush if you apply the glaze very lightly and carefully.

Crazing Antique china often has areas of crazed glaze. You may need to match a retouched area by drawing on fake crazing.

GLASSWARE

Collecting glassware

Glass is made from silica derived from sand with the addition of lime and an alkali. In early glass this alkali was either wood ash (making potash glass) or burnt seaweed (making soda glass). However, in the seventeenth century the English glassmaker George Ravenscroft introduced lead oxide as the alkali, making the superior flint glass. Its strength and reflectivity made it ideal for the cut glass designs of the following centuries.

Damage checks

    *A simple repair
   **Some experience needed
 ***Skilled work—not for
    beginners

Badly chipped glass cannot be successfully restored, but tiny chips can be ground down or filled.
Cracks can be improved on as long as they are clean. Turn the piece while looking at it against the light so that any small cracks show up. Then hold the piece in your palm and tap it gently with your fingernail—if it rings it is sound.
***Stains** cannot always be removed easily.
*Is the **stopper** in a decanter original? It should be in proportion and have the same form of decoration as the rest of the piece.

Using and displaying glass

Never put antique glass in a dishwasher. Wash each piece separately by hand in clean, soapy water, then dry it very carefully as moisture will cloud it. With vessels like decanters a hairdryer is the best way to dry the inside. Store glass in dry conditions to avoid staining.

Concealed lighting in a display cabinet will show cut glass to advantage, and back lighting can show up engraving.

Dating glass

Dating glassware can be a difficult task, even for an expert. There are usually no maker's or registration marks to rely on, so you will have to date pieces by the quality of the glass and by their characteristic shapes (right). Unfortunately, quality glasses in "period" shapes continue to be made today, so you cannot rely on any of these features in isolation.

In addition, the "pontil mark" is often used as a means of dating glass. During manufacture, the base of a glass is attached to an iron rod known as a pontil. When the rod is removed from the finished glass it leaves a mark on the base. Early glasses have such a mark, but from the end of the eighteenth century it was ground off better quality glassware. Early-nineteenth-century blown molded glassware also bears the pontil mark, but again it was removed gradually. As its demise was slow it is not possible to date glassware accurately by its presence.

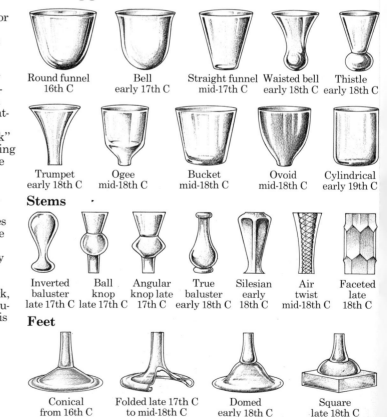

Drinking glass bowls

Round funnel 16th C	Bell early 17th C	Straight funnel mid-17th C	Waisted bell early 18th C	Thistle early 18th C
Trumpet early 18th C	Ogee mid-18th C	Bucket mid-18th C	Ovoid mid-18th C	Cylindrical early 19th C

Stems

Inverted baluster late 17th C	Ball knop late 17th C	Angular knop late 17th C	True baluster early 18th C	Silesian early 18th C	Air twist mid-18th C	Faceted late 18th C

Feet

Conical from 16th C	Folded late 17th C to mid-18th C	Domed early 18th C	Square late 18th C

Types of decoration

Many people think of glass as a plain, colorless material, but this is far from the truth. Over the centuries glassmakers have invented numerous decorative finishes for the material.

Engraved glass

Engraving—a mat white motif on polished glass—is produced by scratching with a diamond bit or by grinding a line with a revolving abrasive wheel. Diamond engraving was used as early as the sixteenth century, but wheel engraving became increasingly popular from the eighteenth century onward.

A rarer form of engraving known as "stipple" produces a delicate light and shade effect by varying the density of minute chips made with the diamond or steel tool.

Painted and enameled glass

Designs painted directly on to glass are often worn, but retouching is usually a fairly simple job (see p. 44). With back-painted glass, however, the paint is protected and therefore does not wear so easily. This type of painting appears perfectly flat from the front. Glassware was often decorated with gilding, especially on rims. This, too, can be retouched.

Enameled glass is the most durable finish because after painting the enamel is fired in a kiln until it fuses, becoming an integral part of the glass.

Enameled-glass biscuit barrel

Cut glass

Glassware can be faceted by cutting it with an abrasive wheel. This technique enhances the reflective and refractive qualities of the material. On early cut drinking glasses the work was restricted to stems—the only part thick enough to cut without risk of shattering the piece. But, with increasing skill, all manner of glassware was cut.

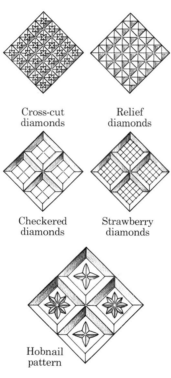

Cross-cut diamonds

Relief diamonds

Checkered diamonds

Strawberry diamonds

Hobnail pattern

Molded glass

To make blown molded glassware, a bubble of molten glass on the end of a tube is placed inside a metal mold. The glassmaker blows down the tube to force the soft glass out against the shaped inner surface of the mold. Press molding, developed in the 1920s, uses a plunger to squeeze the molten glass into the mold.

The pattern on blown molded glass is evident on the inside as well as the outside, whereas the inside of a press molded piece is smooth. You can tell a molded piece from cut glass by examining the edge of the pattern. Cut patterns have crisp, sharp edges, molded patterns are rounder.

Cased or cameo glass

This effect is made by imposing colored glass on a base layer of clear glass. Each layer may then be cut through or etched to reveal the color below. The best pieces have a thick layer of colored glass, but cheaper types were merely dipped in the more expensive colored variety.

Amber cased-glass goblet

Millefiori

To create this effect tiny rods of colored glass were grouped together, then cut across to reveal the pattern. Millefiori was developed in Venice, but it was made famous by French glassmakers. Genuine Millefiori is now very expensive. Countless fakes have been made, so take care when buying such articles.

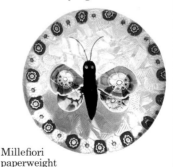

Millefiori paperweight

Acid-etched glass

Etched glass was originally made by coating a glass with wax, then scratching through with a pointed tool. Acid was applied which ate into the areas unprotected by wax, leaving the motif permanently on the surface.

Cleaning and repairing glass

Glassware, like china, can usually be cleaned effectively, but it is not so easy to repair successfully. Because of the nature of the material, most repairs will be obvious to the naked eye.

Never put antique glass in a dishwasher; instead wash it by hand. Lay a foam mat in the bottom of a plastic bowl filled with warm water and liquid detergent, and wash one piece at a time. Add a few drops of ammonia if the glass is very dirty or greasy.

Dry glassware carefully, as damp conditions can cause staining. Let the piece drain on a teatowel, then polish it with a lint-free cloth. Dry the inside of vessels with a hairdryer. Store glass in a dry, ventilated place.

Restoring a chipped edge

Careless handling can easily lead to minor damage such as a small chip on the rim of a drinking glass. If you want to use the glass, you will need to grind away the top of the rim to remove the chip. With a display piece, you must decide whether the chipped edge spoils its appearance enough to merit grinding down the rim.

1 Glue fine wet-and-dry abrasive paper to a flat surface. Dip the rim in water and rub it over the abrasive.

2 Grind over the sharp edges with wet-and-dry paper wrapped around a pencil or dowel. Polish out the finely-scratched edge with a miniature buffing wheel.

Removing stains

Alcohol will often leave dark stains on glassware. White, cloudy stains are a result of over-moist storage conditions. Decanters are the most common casualties, especially if they have been stored with their stoppers in place. Staining may be worse if hard water has left deposits of calcium carbonate.

Unfortunately, you cannot remove all stains completely, but an acid treatment is often effective.

Warning: Never add water to acid, only acid to water. Strong acids may etch old glass, so try an organic acid like white vinegar or citric acid first, soaking the stain for several days before washing the piece thoroughly in warm water. If the stain is still there, use a solution of mineral spirits (see p. 22).

Removing scratches

The surface of well-used glassware may be dulled in patches by a mass of fine scratches.

Some collectors consider shallow scratches as "fair wear and tear"—just what you would expect on old glass. No restorers polish out scratches on the base of jugs or decanters, like the example above. If a "show" part of the piece has scratches try polishing them out with a miniature buffing wheel in a flexible drive attached to your power drill. Dress the buffing mop with a very fine abrasive such as jewelers' rouge. Take care not to overheat the glassware—if the glass feels hot, stop and wait for it to cool down.

Gluing broken glass

To repair broken glass, modify the techniques used for mending china (see pp. 24–5). Be particularly careful when mending glassware because the broken edges are extremely sharp.

You can use epoxy adhesives effectively on glass, but the color of the glue will draw attention to the joint. To make the repair less obvious, use a water-clear anaerobic adhesive. This sets by the action of the ultra-violet rays in natural daylight—in bright sunlight it takes 10 seconds, and on a dull day about two minutes. The best place to work is therefore at a table in front of a shaded window in artificial light. Then when you have glued the piece, you simply draw back the curtains to expose the glass to daylight.

Mending procedure If you want to join two pieces of glass, first clean the edges carefully with acetone and attach adhesive tape to the body of the item (see p. 25). Put specks of anaerobic adhesive along the edge of the broken pieces, smoothing it out to a thin, even layer with a scalpel. Then bring the joint together, applying just enough pressure to squeeze out any excess adhesive. Tension tape across the joint on each side of the glass. Run a knife blade across the joint to check alignment, and adjust any error.

Having glued a joint, you may find that the two parts slide as you attempt to bring them together. This is because the edges of broken glass are perfectly smooth. Roughening them with fine paper can help, but this is not easy on thin glass, and you must avoid rounding the edges as this only makes sliding worse. The best solution is probably to use a minimum of glue in the first place to try to reduce the tendency to slide.

Now wipe off excess adhesive with acetone and examine the joint against the light. A perfectly-filled joint will be barely visible, but if air is present it will show up as a silver line. Run a line of adhesive along each side of an air-filled joint and blow on it to encourage it to flow into the joint. Wipe off any excess with acetone.

Finally, expose the joint to daylight for a short period, then leave it overnight to continue hardening. Clean up the joint line with a sharp knife. Avoid using abrasives—they could scratch the glass.

Filling chips, holes and cracks

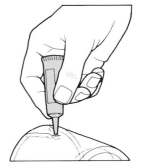

You cannot camouflage fillings in glassware with a layer of paint, and it is therefore impractical to fill any large chips or holes. However, you can improve the appearance of smaller faults by filling them with a drop of anaerobic adhesive. Back up holes with clear adhesive tape, then add adhesive and leave to harden in daylight. It will take at least 24 hours to set. When the glue has set hard, pare it flush with the surface of the glass. To do this, lay a knife blade flat on the glass, facing away from you, and run it down the joint to cut off excess glue. Finally, polish the repair with chrome polish.

You can disguise a clean crack in glass using the technique for dispeling air from a new joint.

Gluing a wine glass stem

Gluing a broken wine glass stem is the least noticeable glass repair. The gluing procedure is the same as for a simple break (see above). You must set up the wine glass so that the two halves are held together while the glue sets. Stand the glass on its rim and support the base with lumps of modeling clay. Alternatively, stretch adhesive tape across the base and down to the bowl, making sure that tension is even on all sides. Once you have supported the piece, look at it from all sides to make sure that the base is level. And if possible, wrap the glued stem with clear adhesive tape to prevent pieces sliding.

Tools and materials

The care and repair of glassware is similar to that of ceramics—you use mostly the same tools and materials (see pp. 20–1). Any special equipment is recommended in the appropriate section of the text.

It would be a sensible precaution to have a first aid kit at hand because it is very easy to cut yourself when working with broken glass.

Restoring colored glass

Colored glassware is attractive and well worth collecting. Successful repairs will be within the scope of most people. Broken sections in stained glass panels can be removed and replaced, worn painting or gilding can be retouched, and you will find that glued breaks on opaque glass are less obvious than clear glass repairs.

Mending colored glass

Some opaque colored glass filters out ultra-violet rays. If your piece is of this type you cannot use an anaerobic glue because it will not set. As an alternative, use a cyanoacrylate glue (see p. 25) or tint an epoxy adhesive (see p. 25) to match the glass. Always warm the two tubes of epoxy glue on a radiator before mixing them together to make sure that the glue is liquid.

Restoring gilding

The simplest way to restore worn gilding on glassware is to use the good-quality gold paints known as "liquid gold leaf". These are available in a range of colors from craft or art stores. The best application method is the one used for china (see p. 38).

Gilded cruet bottle

Painting glass

The technique for painting glass is very similar to that for china (see pp. 36–7). You need not worry about brush strokes showing as these paints flow, rather like a wood stain.

Glass paint is transparent, so if you need to match opaque colors use acrylic paints instead (see p. 36).

1 First you must color match your paint to the original. Mix colors on a tile or in a foil tray. When you think you have the right shade, put a speck of paint on the piece, next to a patch of original color. Wipe this off with thinner on a scrap of silk.

2 Once you are satisfied with your color match, begin to paint in the edge, using a fine artist's brush. If you go over the edge wipe off paint with thinner.

3 Finally, take a brush of paint and touch in the middle section, letting it flow out naturally. Leave the piece to dry in a horizontal position.

Restoring stained glass

Unrestored glass panel

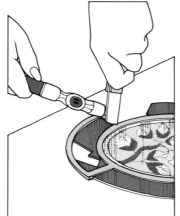

Many older homes have attractive stained glass panels in their front doors and windows. If you want to collect this type of stained glass, you can often acquire panels saved from demolished buildings in antique shops and retailers specializing in architectural features.

To wash stained glass make a solution of warm water and a few drops of ammonia, and apply it with a soft brush. Rinse and dry the glass thoroughly. If the window is large, work on a small section at a time so that you can wash off the ammonia quickly.

1 Stained glass is held in a fine framework of lead "cames". To remove a piece of broken glass cut diagonally into the corners of the lead with a knife, tapping the blade gently with a hammer if necessary. If the panel is free-standing, lay it on a flat board so that you do not distort the entire frame.

2 Use a flat-bladed knife to pry back the came. Then remove the old glass and putty.

3 Make a thin cardboard template as a guide to cutting the shape. If you are uncertain about cutting the glass, take the template to a glass store.

4 Press putty into the cames and insert the new glass. Fold the cames back into position and rub them down with a rounded burnishing tool such as a screwdriver handle. Finish the corners with abrasive paper, then solder them (see p. 227).

Restored glass To bring out the best in your work, burnish the cames with black lead paste and clean up the glass with the warm water and ammonia solution. Such panels are best displayed with a light behind them.

Restoring glass lusters

Glass luster vase

Chandeliers are perhaps the best known example of an item made up from hanging lusters. However, luster vases, candlesticks and lamps were also made. You can wash any grimy lusters along with the rest of the piece (see p. 42), but you should either remove the metal parts first, or dry them very carefully afterwards. When dry, polish lusters with acetone or denatured alcohol so that they sparkle brilliantly.

Making a replacement lustre

You can sometimes replace missing lusters with a close match obtained from an antique shop. Obviously finding a match is not easy, but it will have the advantage of being real glass. Otherwise, lusters can be made from a clear casting resin. This will not look so realistic, but it will fill the gap in the row. Casting resin with its hardener is available from craft shops and also by mail order.

Plaster of Paris is a suitable molding material for resin. But with clear resin you will get the best results if you use a finer casting plaster (from craft shops). To cast a luster you will need to make a two-piece mold (see p. 30). Coat the luster with cooking oil, half embed it in modeling clay and build a wall of clay around it. Cut the point off a plastic golf tee and lay it next to the luster. This will form a tapered hole in the mold into which you can pour the resin. Fill any gap between tee and luster with modeling clay. You should also fill the hole in the luster. Now pour the plaster in and leave it to set.

When the plaster has set, remove all the modeling clay so that you can clean the mold and luster. Turn the mold over, cut key-ways into it (see p. 31), and spread petroleum jelly on the surface. To make the second half of the mold, turn the mold over, replace the luster and tee and build a wall of clay around them. Pour in a layer of plaster and leave it to set. Remove the clay and then clean the mold as before.

For a smooth surface to your casting, seal the inside of the plaster mold with liquid wax, petroleum jelly or polyvinyl acetate glue. Strap the two halves of the mold together, sealing the joint with a little modeling clay. Mix and pour the resin according to the manufacturers' instructions, vibrating the mold to release air bubbles.

When the resin has set, open the mold and cut off the tapered peg with a junior hacksaw, shaping the end of the new luster with a fine file. Then use a regular drill bit to drill a hole in it to take the metal links.

If necessary, clean up the surface of the luster with a piece of fine wet-and-dry or silicon carbide paper glued to a flat board. Finally, polish the resin to a high gloss using a cutting compound (this is available from craft shops).

Casting a new luster Align a plastic golf tee so that it makes a hole in the mold for you to pour the resin in. See left for how to make a mold.

Renewing the links

The lusters should be able to spin freely so that they catch the light. Examine the metal rings and hooks on which they are suspended. Close up any open rings with a pair of pliers, and make wire replacements for any badly repaired metal parts.

Try to match the color and thickness of the existing wire as closely as possible. Jewelers can supply you with fine silver wire. You can also try various fuse wires, or use a sharp knife to strip down electrical cable to obtain copper wire.

The fine, tapered jaws of round-nosed pliers will enable you to twist the wire into the correct diameter to make a ring. Crop excess ends with side-cutting pliers. You should open the rings sideways rather than pull them directly apart, as this may destroy the neat circle.

STONEWORK

Collecting stonework

Very few people collect early stone statuary —it is simply too expensive. Whereas, in the past, great collectors could purchase classical sculpture, today the bulk of this is in national collections, and most people cannot afford the astronomical prices fetched by the very few pieces of Roman or Greek sculpture that come onto the market. However, eighteenth- and nineteenth-century garden sculpture is more readily available. Statues, urns, plant-holders, benches and sun dials are all very popular with contemporary collectors. So, too, are such pieces as the busts and carved plaques designed for indoor display.

Marble

When limestone is under tre- mendous pressure and heat it is transformed into marble. In its pure form marble is white, but due to the presence of impuri- ties it is often streaked or veined as well as colored. Because it is relatively easy to carve and capable of taking a high polish, it has been used for sculpture since the time of the ancient Greeks and Romans. In the nineteenth and early-twentieth centuries it was frequently used to make small decorative ob- jects for domestic use, as well as for larger, interior pieces such as fireplaces, floor and wall tiles, and tops for washstands and tables.

Carved marble figure Marble sculp- ture has been made since ancient times. This figure of Mercury dates from the eight- eenth century.

Limestone

The most common stone for architectural carvings in North- west Europe because it is easy to carve and mold, limestone is grayish-white to light brown in color, with a rough, pitted surface.

Large eighteenth-century bust of a cavalier carved in limestone

Granite

Usually gray, red or whitish in color, granite is an extremely hard igneous rock, and is there- fore not bound by any cement- ing material. Granite can be polished to a high gloss. It was used in the eighteenth century for fireplaces and some table tops, and in the nineteenth century it was widely used for monuments, urns and, to a lesser extent, garden ornaments.

Sandstone

A sedimentary or stratified rock, sandstone is composed of grains of quartz plus other materials, cemented into a solid mass. It is a warm honey color but has a fragile surface and weathers badly, eroding and flaking easily.

Onyx

Very similar to marble in appearance, onyx is a carbonate of lime deposited by water. It is available in variegated forms of green (most common of all), white, red, and golden yellow. Onyx is usually used for carved ornaments, the bases of lamps and Art Deco figurines, and table tops.

Scagliola

This imitation marble was invented in the early seventeenth century. It is made from plaster mixed with a glue in which splinters of marble, granite and other materials are embedded. Highly effective when polished, it was often used as a substitute for marble on table tops.

Soapstone

This stone has a smooth, slightly greasy feel and can be red, yellow, white, green, bluish-gray or brown in color. A magnesium silicate (a variety of talc), it is so soft that it can be cut with a knife. It is most often found in the form of oriental carvings.

Plaster

Although plaster casts are not true stonework, they can sometimes be mistaken for stone. However, plaster is very soft and easily damaged. Any chips will reveal its chalky white core. Painted plasterwork should be preserved, rather than repainted. You may have to employ an expert restorer to do this for you.

Alabaster

True alabaster, as used by the ancient Egyptians and in the Middle East and China, is a lime carbonate, but a softer lime sulphate is also described as alabaster; and you are more likely to find pieces made from this sort. It resembles marble, being smooth and translucent and capable of taking a high polish, but it is far less durable, scratching easily. It is found in a range of colors—white, yellow, pink and light brown—and it is often veined. Alabaster has been used for centuries in Europe for tomb effigies and church figurines. Since the eighteenth century it has been used to make clock cases, vases, lampstands and ash trays, and, in rare cases, chimney pieces.

Artificial stone

The first artificial or composition stone was developed in 1760 by Eleanor Coade, the largest manufacturer of figurines and ornaments in England. From 1840, several other cheap artificial materials became available. Artificial stone is made from stone fragments bound together with cement.

Composition stone vase This late nineteenth century piece is in a classical Grecian style.

Buying tips

The biggest problem faced by potential buyers of sculpture is how to tell whether the piece is genuine antique stonework or a cast reproduction.

- Examine any chipped areas— they might reveal a plaster or cement core.
- Look at the underside of the base—if it is open it may reveal a hollow casting. And it may be unfinished, giving away the fact that the rest is painted or bronzed to imitate a superior finish.
- Flush lines—raised lines tracing the joint between the parts of a mold—are never found on carved work.
- Although castings made from an original, weathered antique will have convincing cracks or chips, they are unlikely to be discolored by a long accumulation of dirt, as such damage on a genuine piece would be.
- Look at the veining carefully —if the piece is a reproduction the veins may be painted on.

Caring for stonework

Stonework left outside for any length of time inevitably suffers from the action of impurities in the air. The combined results of soot, acids and sulphur streak and discolor stone so much that washing alone may not be enough to clean it. Even in rural areas, algae and lichen will leave their mark on outdoor sculpture. Do not clean stonework too enthusiastically—it develops a patina which mellows the color of freshly cut stone, a characteristic worth preserving. Also soft stones form a crust which helps to preserve the soft interior.

Tools

You will need paint, bristle and brass wire brushes to clean stone, and a buffing mop and power drill (see p. 57) to polish waxed stone. If you want to repair heavy pieces buy a masonry drill to make holes for reinforcing pins.

Materials

Ammonia Makes a solution with water to clean most stones.
Mineral spirits Use this to clean alabaster and soapstone, and to make a poultice to draw out oil and wax stains.
Blotting paper Forms the basis of poultices used to draw stains out.
Distilled water Soak blotting paper in this to make a poultice for general stains.
Bleach Removes stains from plain white marble.
Paint stripper Removes grease from white marble.
Wax polish White furniture or commercial marble polish will protect stone from dirt and stains.
Stone sealer Protects porous stones from staining.
Beeswax White beeswax or candle wax will consolidate a flaking surface.
Adhesives See p. 52.
Adhesive tape Holds glued pieces together while they set.
Brass or stainless steel rod Makes pins to reinforce joints in heavy items.
Fillers See p. 52.

Cleaning stonework

Before you attempt to wash stonework, find out what the stone is. Some respond better than others; some should not be washed at all.

Limestone and sandstone
Rather than scrub soft stones like these vigorously, you should let the action of running water soften any deposits before you attempt to remove them. Set the stonework up outside, preferably near a drain. Rig up a hose to play at reasonable pressure on the stone and leave it for about five or six hours, periodically turning the object or moving the hose to direct the spray evenly. Wearing rubber gloves and protective glasses, add half a cup of ammonia to a bucket of warm water and scrub the deposits with a stiff bristle brush. Thoroughly rinse the stone with the hose, then leave it outside to dry out.

Washing soft stone After softening deposits with running water, scrub them gently with a stiff bristle brush.

Basalt and granite
These hard non-porous stones do not absorb dirt like soft stones, and will normally respond immediately to scrubbing with hot, soapy water plus a small amount of ammonia. Use a stiff bristle brush or, if necessary, a brass wire brush.

Marble
Marble should be cleaned regularly as it is so porous that dust can penetrate it, especially if dirty water is left in hollows. Before you wash marble, dust it with a soft paintbrush to remove loose dirt and grit. Use a soft cloth to apply hot, soapy water and a little ammonia. Wash fixed items from the bottom upward to avoid streaking. Rinse thoroughly with clean water and dry with a soft cloth.

Washing marble First dust the stone, then wipe with a soft cloth dipped in hot, soapy water, working from the bottom up.

Onyx
Like marble, onyx is absorbent, so you must dust it before washing in warm, soapy water.

Plaster
Cast plaster should not be washed in water. To clean such pieces dust them with a soft brush. Do not use a cloth as this can rub dirt into the surface. Wipe greasy marks with clear denatured alcohol on a rag.

Removing stains

It does not take very long to stain an absorbent stone, so wipe off spills as soon as possible. There are several methods of removing staining from stonework, depending on its severity. However, do not use acids on soft stones like marble, alabaster or soapstone.

Coping with general stains

A damp paper poultice is a good way of removing stains. To make a poultice soak white newsprint or blotting paper in warm distilled water until it forms a pulp. Mash it up with a stick if necessary. Do not use printed newspaper because the print will add to the problem.

Spread the wet pulp in a $\frac{1}{2}$–$\frac{3}{4}$ in (1–2 cm) thick layer over the stain or over the whole object if it is small enough. First of all the stone will absorb the water, then, as the pulp dries out, the effect is reversed and, along with the water, the stain is drawn back into the poultice. When this has happened, remove the poultice, wash the area with clean distilled water, and mop it dry with a soft cloth.

Applying a poultice Spread pulp over the stain, pressing it down. When the stain appears on the pulp, remove it and rinse the stone with distilled water.

Removing oil and wax

You can also use a paper poultice to remove oil and wax stains, but let the pulp dry once you have made it, and then soak it with mineral spirits before applying it to the stone.

Removing algae and mildew

You can usually remove these from stonework by washing with a mild solution of ammonia. If this fails to work, apply a poultice as described for general staining.

Using bleach

It is not advisable to use bleach on colored or veined stonework. However, it works particularly well on white marble. Wear protective gloves whenever you use bleach. At first, try a mild bleach such as Chloramine T in a 2 percent solution in distilled water. Rinse the stone thoroughly with clean water after bleaching. For more stubborn stains, apply a solution of 1 part hydrogen peroxide (100 volume) to 3 parts of water, plus one or two drops of ammonia.

Using paint stripper

This will remove greasy deposits from white marble. Follow the manufacturer's instructions, and brush the stripper onto the marble, stippling it into any crevices and hollows. You can leave the stripper on the stone for up to an hour, then wash the piece several times with clean water.

Cleaning alabaster and soapstone

Proceed cautiously when you try to remove a stain from alabaster or soapstone. Use a cloth soaked in mineral spirits wrapped around your fingertip and rub the surface vigorously. Alternatively, mix up a paste of ground chalk with clear denatured alcohol. Rub the stain with a cotton ball, working with a circular motion, then wipe it clean with mineral spirits.

Protecting stonework

Once the surface of the stone is clean, it is advisable to protect it from dirt and further staining. A good quality white furniture polish is quite safe to use on any stone if you want to put a sheen on it. If you can obtain a commercial marble wax polish this will provide a tougher surface. Seal porous stones against oil and dirt by brushing on a branded stone sealer. Very soft stone will require a second application of sealer before it is protected. A good sealer will also bring out the color of the stone.

Extracting soluble salts

Salts that have been absorbed by porous stones like sandstone or limestone emerge as white crystals on the surface. They can be brushed off easily, but it is likely that they will reappear and eventually break up the surface. To draw out the salts use a poultice of blotting paper and distilled water. Coat the entire object with a $\frac{1}{2}$ in (1 cm) thick layer of pulp, wrap it in plastic and leave it for about three weeks. If necessary, apply a fresh poultice.

Binding a flaking surface

If the surface of the stone is powdery, you should apply a material which will bind it together. Museum conservators impregnate or "consolidate" the stone with white beeswax or candle wax. This method inevitably darkens or dulls white marble, and it is not advisable to use it on alabaster or soapstone.

The stone must be heated gradually. Place it 3–4 ft (about 1 m) away from an electric heater and turn it periodically so that it is heated evenly. Meanwhile, mix the wax with mineral spirits until it has a buttery consistency, then paint it onto the stone. When all the solvent has evaporated, heat the stone gently to drive the wax into it, repeating the process until no more wax can be absorbed. Wipe off any excess, then buff with a soft cloth or a lambswool mop on a drill.

Repairing stonework

You can repair even quite heavy stonework with confidence using a suitable modern adhesive. You will need to strap the broken parts together firmly with adhesive tape, string or wire while the glue sets.

Gluing stonework

Always make a trial assembly to ensure that the meeting surfaces join accurately and to work out the best method of clamping the broken piece while the glue sets. On smaller items, stretch adhesive tape across the joint to hold it together. For larger pieces try using a string or wire tourniquet to bind the two halves.

Brush loose dirt or grit from the broken surfaces, then clean them thoroughly with mineral spirits or acetone to remove any trace of grease. Most stone is sufficiently coarse to provide a good key for the glue, but you can roughen the edge of a smooth break with coarse abrasive paper.

Apply glue sparingly and evenly to one half of the joint. Bring both pieces together, squeezing and rocking them gently until they are perfectly matched. Clamp up the joint so that excess glue squeezes out, then wipe it off the surface immediately with the appropriate solvent. If possible, prop the object up so that gravity helps to hold the joint together until the glue has set.

Reinforcing a joint

To reinforce a joint in a heavy stone item use brass or stainless steel pins. Do not use ordinary steel as it can cause rust staining. Mark the holes for the pins on one edge with a spot of paint, then bring the two halves together. This will transfer the spots to the other half accurately.

Drill holes in both sides using a masonry drill slightly larger than the pin you want to use. Check that both halves mate well, adjusting the shape of the holes with the masonry drill if necessary. Cut the pins from suitable metal rod and file notches in them to provide a coarse key for the glue. Glue the pins into one half of the piece, then glue the other half and bind up the joint tightly with tape. Leave the glue to set, then remove the tape.

Adhesives

Epoxy resin glues These glues are the most useful adhesives for bonding stonework. They are sold in two parts—the glue itself and a hardener. When the two equal parts are mixed, the setting process begins. Standard epoxy glues from a hardware store will set in about six hours. There are also quick-setting varieties which take 5 to 10 minutes. These glues are only suitable for a small piece where you can apply the glue and then clamp it immediately. Otherwise you should use the standard variety.

Epoxy glues are very thick, so before mixing the two parts, warm the tubes on a radiator to thin them. This will make it easier to get a good joint. Try to match the color of the glue to the stone you are mending by adding tiny amounts of titanium dioxide or other coloring pigments (see p. 20).

Wipe excess glue from the surface of the stone with denatured alcohol. For very porous or white stones, make sure that you use clear alcohol, as the blue dye in commercial denatured alcohol may leave a stain.

Polyvinyl acetate glues You can use white woodworking polyvinyl acetate glues to join alabaster and soapstone. Apply the glue sparingly to both halves of the joint with a brush and then tape up the joint tightly. Wipe away excess glue with acetone and leave to set.

Fillers

Epoxy fillers are ideal for most stonework. They will resist weathering as long as they are self-coloring. However, overpainting will only stand up to indoor display use. Ready-made epoxy fillers are available commercially, but you can also make your own by mixing epoxy glue with kaolin powder to make it into a putty. Use colored pigments to match the filler to the stone. For an alternative, hard-wearing filler mix polyvinyl acetate glue with kaolin or ground chalk.

Plaster of Paris and cellulose general fillers are suitable for indoor stonework, but they are soft and therefore totally unsuitable for anything left outside. Before using them you must dampen the joint with water so that the moisture in the filler is not absorbed into the stone as this will weaken the filler.

None of these fillers is suitable for filling alabaster or soapstone—to repair these blend colored waxes.

The procedures for using fillers are the same as those for pottery (see p. 27). Once the filler has set and you have smoothed it off, fake any veining with acrylic or oil paints, using methods similar to those described for touching in wood grain (see p. 110).

METALWARE

Collecting metalware

All kinds of decorative and utilitarian objects are made in metal, and metals themselves differ widely in their nature and value—from the expensive silver of engraved salvers to the cheap cast iron of firedogs. You can usually recognize metals by their color and weight. However, some alloys can be difficult to identify at first glance.

Silver

There is a considerable difference in value between a piece made from silver that is more than 90 per cent pure and one made from silver that has been mixed with a quantity of a base metal. Yet it is impossible to distinguish them by eye until the silver content is practically halved. To get round this problem Britain and some other countries have passed laws which oblige silversmiths to have their wares assayed and marked according to the percentage of silver they contain (see p. 233). These marks were applied in addition to the maker's "touch" marks.

There were no regulations binding on American silversmiths as there were in Britain. However, they did apply touch marks.

Testing the purity of silver

If your piece does not have any silver marks, there is a simple test that a pharmacist might be willing to carry out for you. This involves cleaning a small, inconspicuous patch and making a scratch deep enough to expose any metal. When a drop of nitric acid is applied to a scratch it reacts in one of three different ways. If it turns green and effervesces your piece is base metal; if the acid turns a dark gray the silver content is less than 92.5 per cent; and if it turns a light gray you have a sterling silver item. The acid should be washed off the piece with running water immediately after the test.

Gold

See Jewelry on p. 76.

Copper

Polished copper is reddish brown in color, but will tarnish to a dull brown. It is most often found in the form of domestic ware—kettles, jugs and saucepans. These are often coated with tin on the inside to prevent copper poisoning. Many reproduction items are available.

Bronze

Bronze is an alloy of copper and tin that ages to a deep brown. It is an ideal casting metal, and is therefore most often found in the form of statuettes. It was also used for early weaponry. There are two casting methods —*cire perdue* is superior to sandcasting. Reproductions are usually made in spelter. A close examination should tell you if the piece is made from this lighter, poorer quality metal.

Nineteenth-century French bronze

Brass

Brass is a common, yellow-colored alloy of copper and zinc. It is easy to recognize unless it is heavily tarnished, when it can be a brown or greeny black color. It was used to make a wide range of items.

Pinchbeck

This brass alloy has a much higher copper content than brass. Developed by an eighteenth-century clockmaker, Christopher Pinchbeck, it was used to make jewelry and other small items. Although originally known as "poor man's gold", it is now highly collectable.

Sheffield plate

Sheffield plate was made for about 100 years from the mid-eighteenth century until the invention of electro-plating. The process involved fusing a small amount of silver onto a copper backing. In the 1770s Sheffield plate was made with silver on both sides, and such pieces can be difficult to distinguish from solid silver. A silver strip was used to cover bare edges. Examine the joints for the tell-tale thin gray line of tin solder.

Although not as valuable as solid silver, Sheffield plate is very collectable. It does not bear hallmarks or date stamps, but will usually have a maker's touch mark.

Electro-plating

In 1840 a process was invented to deposit a thin layer of silver onto a base metal. It is called electro-plating. The amount of silver used is very much less than for Sheffield plate, and is applied after the object has been manufactured. Not all electro-plate will be marked, but it often bears initials (see p. 234).

Nickel

Nickel takes a shine that resembles silver. It was used to plate items before chromium-plating became popular.

Nickel silver

This alloy of nickel, copper and zinc—also known as German silver—was often used as a base for electro-plated ware.

Tin

Tin is silvery in appearance and is most often encountered as a non-toxic lining to jelly molds, graters or cooking utensils. It may also be used to coat steel which would otherwise rust.

Lead

Tarnished lead is dull gray, but it looks silvery when cut. Lead antiques are not common, but the best-known types are toy soldiers—both the heavy solid-cast types and the lighter hollow castings.

Steel

Steel is an extremely tough alloy of iron and carbon that is capable of maintaining a sharp edge. For this reason it has been used for centuries to make tools and weapons. Steel swords were often damascened (see p. 56).

Britannia metal

This alloy was invented in the late eighteenth century and is made from tin, antimony and copper. It resembles pewter, but is stronger and more silvery in color. It became a cheap substitute for pewter. It was used as a base for a great deal of electro-plated domestic ware.

Chromium

Chromium is a plating on base metal. When clean, it has a bright, white finish. Chromium is extremely hard and is found as a protective finish on twentieth-century "Art Deco" ornaments, cocktail shakers, and furniture fittings.

Pewter

Pewter is basically an alloy of tin, but at various times its composition has changed, with different amounts of lead, copper, antimony and bismuth being added. It normally has a grayish patina with a soft sheen. It has been used for centuries to make tableware. Pewter ware usually has a maker's touch mark (see p. 234).

Eighteenth-century pewter flagon

Iron

You should be able to distinguish wrought iron from cast iron. Wrought iron is hammered into a two-dimensional pattern—often scrolls and twists—and the pieces are welded together to form a grid. Cast iron items are made in a mold and are normally in one piece or, at most, several large pieces bolted together. They are fully three-dimensional. Cast iron is brittle, and when broken the inside is gray, and has a coarse texture.

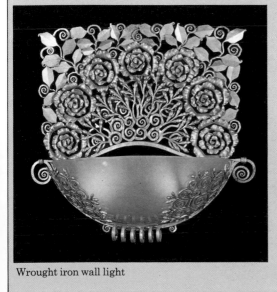

Wrought iron wall light

Cast iron gas fire

Applied decoration

Apart from purely utilitarian objects, most metalware is decorated in some form. Here we explain how some popular methods of decoration are produced.

Engraving

This line work is cut into metal with pointed tools known as gravers. Under a magnifying glass, the lines appear as sharp, triangular furrows.

Detail of engraved silver-gilt wine coaster

Etching

This is produced by scratching through a protective coating of wax. When acid is applied, it bites into the exposed metal. The wax is then removed and the surrounding metal is polished. Etched lines are not as sharp as engraving.

Damascening

This technique involves inlaying metals into engraving. The inlay is hammered to spread and lock it in place.

Niello

This technique emphasizes engraving or etching by filling it with a black powder made from silver, lead, copper and sulphur. When heated, the powder fuses into the metal, darkening the line work. The surrounding polished metal contrasts strongly with the dark decoration.

Niello-decorated silver snuff box

Repoussé

This is the term for raised decoration which has been punched out from the back of the metal.

Embossing

Strictly speaking, the term embossing means the same as repoussé, but it is often used to describe any form of relief work.

Chasing

If raised decoration is worked from the front with punches and chisels it is known as chasing. This technique is often found in conjunction with repoussé.

Piercing

A method of producing patterns by cutting right through the metal with saws or punches.

Painting and printing

You can usually identify hand-painted metalware by the relative freedom, or, in some cases, crudity of the designs. This may be due to a "folk" influence, like the colorful domestic tinware known as barge or toleware, or because it was applied by factory workers as part of a production line. Japanning is a form of paintwork applied to tinware, then baked on to produce a durable, heat-resistant finish.

Advances in printing made it possible to produce elaborately decorated, cheap tinware for pressed toys and containers. The tin plate is printed first, then pressed and stamped into shape. As a result, you will often see examples where the printing is not completely registered with the pressing. Printing looks quite flat and even in color, and is often very detailed.

Painted toleware molasses jug

Damage checks

★A simple repair
★★Some experience needed
★★★A difficult repair—not for beginners

★★Shallow **dents** can be pushed out, but avoid creased metal—it cannot be restored to its original shape.
★★**Holes** in sheet metal are not easy to repair unless you can reinforce them from behind (see p. 63). You can fill holes in castings successfully, but disguising the repair takes practice.

★★★**Deep pressings**, particularly in brass, sometimes exhibit parallel cracks. These are caused by corrosion, and are very difficult to repair.
★Minor **scratches** can be polished out of most metals. But do not buy scratched bronzes or pewter unless you are prepared to accept them as they are. Scratches cannot be removed without destroying patina.
★**Tin boxes and toys** are often held together by folded joints. If any have sprung open you can solder or glue them.

Buying tips

● If you buy a cast iron fireplace, you should ask if it has been stored outside for any length of time. Cast iron is porous and can absorb water, so it should be thoroughly dried out before finishing.
● Worn plated items can be stripped and replated by a professional, but this can be expensive so make sure that the asking price reflects this fact.
● Small items that have been accidentally crushed can sometimes be bought for a scrap price. With patience, you may be able to restore them. Make sure that nothing is missing.

Tools and materials

A garage is a good choice for siting metalwork tools and a work bench. If you use the bench for auto maintenance, clean off oil and filings before repairing antiques. Cover the bench with hardboard. When this cover becomes worn or stained replace it. Store your tools behind the bench—either in a tool rest or hung from pegboard. Unless the bench is in front of a window, install a strip light above it, and use an adjustable lamp to light your work.

Tools

Antique metalware incorporates such a wide variety of metals and methods of manufacture that it is difficult to recommend a tool kit to cover all contingencies. You will need a comprehensive kit of general metalworking tools including hacksaws, punches, scribers, pliers, snips and engineers' hammers. In addition, you will probably need several of the specific tools listed here.

Polishing brush A soft hair brush is useful for polishing decorative metalware.

Chamois leather Use this soft leather to buff polished metal.

Power buff and grinder To burnish metals to a high gloss buy a cloth buffing pad for a bench-mounted drill or grinder. A 6 ins pad is a useful size.

Nail brush This brush is stiff enough to scrub away any dirt and grease without scratching.

Air brush This very fine spray gun (see p. 35) is useful for applying lacquer.

Stake Use a purpose-made former to push dented metal back into shape. Hardwood is ideal, but a softwood stake will do.

Soft-faced hammer A plastic or rubber-faced hammer will shape metal without leaving hammer marks in the surface.

Rubber mallet As above, but generally for working over larger areas.

Soldering iron Choose a large electric soldering iron with a tapered head.

Propane torch This produces an intensely hot flame which will quickly heat metal for hard soldering. Cheap blow lamps will also do the job, but a torch that is finely adjustable will enable you to produce better results.

Engineer's vise A strong bench vise will withstand the strains of hammering and bending of metal. Large versions are bolted through the bench itself. Lightweight vises clamp to the edge.

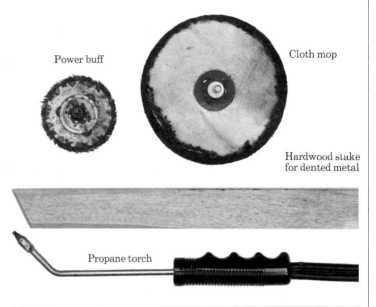

Power buff

Cloth mop

Hardwood stake for dented metal

Propane torch

Materials

Rust remover Use this to treat corroded steel and iron.

Paint stripper Removes old lacquer or paint from brass, copper or cast-iron items.

Paraffin Use this to dissolve rust on metal and to make up abrasive pastes.

Calcium carbonate Removes corrosion from some metals by electro-chemical action.

Ground chalk This fine abrasive powder removes fine scratches.

Jewelers' rouge As above.

Emery paper and cloth This hard black sandpaper takes out deep scratches from metal. Emery is too coarse for soft metals like silver or copper.

Ammonia Use a mild solution to clean lead.

Denatured alcohol This will clean grease from any surface, and remove excess epoxy glue.

Buffing soap A mixture of fine abrasive and wax for use with a power buff.

Metal polishes Liquids, pastes and wadding are available.

Lacquer A clear lacquer based on acrylic resin prevents polished metal from tarnishing.

Epoxy resin glue This adhesive produces extremely strong bonds between metal.

Cyanoacrylate glue This glue sets hard in seconds, and is useful to join small components.

Solders and fluxes Solders are low melting-point metals used to make a joint. Fluxes remove oxides which would otherwise hinder a strong bond.

Steel wool Use very fine steel wool to clean corrosion from hard metals and to clean up a joint prior to soldering or gluing it.

Metallic pastes and powders These will blend in a filling with surrounding metal.

Cleaning metalware

When cleaning metalware, always support it on a pad of soft cloth—if you lay soft metal directly on a table you could damage it. You should take extra care when cleaning objects composed of mixed materials because metal cleaners may damage the other substance, and washing or dipping may dissolve the glue fixing it to the metal. For example, bone or ivory-handled cutlery should not be left to soak in hot water.

Caring for silver

Silver is an attractive metal which actually improves in appearance with long-term cleaning and handling, developing a subtle patina with a slight bluish tinge. However, exposure to the air tarnishes it quickly, forming a brown, or sometimes even purple, coating of silver sulphide. And the presence of salt or sulphur in the air accelerates tarnishing.

Washing silver
You should wash silverware every time you use it. Also wash it before polishing it to make sure that you have removed all the dust, because even minute grains of grit can scratch the metal. Make sure you remove mild acids such as fruit juice, vinegar or salad dressing as well as traces of egg or salt from tableware as soon as possible to prevent tarnishing. Wash silver items one at a time in hot, soapy water, using a soft cloth to swab the metal. Rinse in hot, clean water and dry thoroughly to prevent stains. A thorough buffing with a soft cloth may be all that is necessary to give silver a deep shine, but if the metal is tarnished you will have to use a commercial polish.

Polishing silver
The traditional habit of wearing white cotton gloves to polish silver is not an affectation; it prevents you from scratching the metal with your fingernails and stops the acid in your skin tarnishing clean silver.

There are various commercial products available to polish silverware—you can choose from impregnated cloths, creams, foam paste and liquid polishes. Perhaps the best solution is to use a long-term silver polish—these produce a chemical barrier which preserves the shine longer than standard polishes. Apply polish to the metal with a clean, soft cloth, using a fresh area of it every time a piece gets dirty. When you have removed all the tarnish, burnish the silver with another soft cloth. Clean decorated silver with a soft nailbrush and use a soft hair brush to polish it. Wash the silver a second time to remove all traces of polish. Then burnish the piece with a dry cloth or chamois.

You can clean plated silver in exactly the same way as solid. However, any polish removes a small amount of the silver plate every time, until eventually it wears away completely. Take particular care on raised edges—these wear very quickly. You may prefer to clean plated items in a dip (called silver blue) which eliminates the sulphide, leaving the silver intact (see right).

Storing silver
To preserve the polish on domestic silver wrap it in dry, acid-free tissue paper. You can buy specially impregnated cloth or paper from a jeweler. Put the wrapped silver into polyethylene bags to seal out the air. If you intend to store the silver in an enclosed area such as a drawer or cupboard, add silica gel crystals in muslin bags to the packing material. These will absorb any moisture and also keep the silver dry.

Using a chemical dip

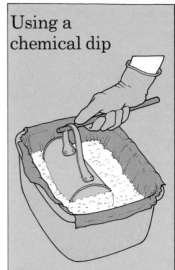

Chemical action will clean copper, brass and silver without removing metal. Do not try to clean different metals in the same silver blue dip. And never dip inlaid or enamelled pieces.

Lay aluminum foil in the bottom of a plastic bowl or bucket, and place the metalware on it. Wearing protective gloves, dissolve half a cup of sodium carbonate (washing soda) in two pints of very hot water and pour it over the metalware. The solution will bubble violently as the corrosion is transferred chemically from the object to the aluminum. After a minute or two, use wooden tongs or a stick to lift the object out. It may still appear tarnished, but if you rinse it under hot water and dry it on a soft cloth you may reveal clean metal. If traces of tarnish remain, wash them off with the solution used for corroded brass (see opposite). If necessary, dip the metal again.

Once you have rinsed a silver piece, dry and burnish it immediately to avoid water stains. Do not touch silver with rubber gloves—they may leave black marks. You can dip silver-plated items, but if any base metal is showing, leave the piece in the solution for only a short time.

Caring for brass

Brass is not particularly prized for patina, but it is much admired in a polished condition. Unless a piece has been lacquered, washing alone will not restore the metal; you will need to use metal polish and sometimes a softening solution. You can lacquer polished brass to protect its shine.

Removing corrosion

If a polish with a commercial liquid or impregnated wadding does not remove tarnishing, mix a level tablespoon of salt and a tablespoon of vinegar in half a pint of hot water. Using extremely fine steel wool, swab the brass with this solution. It is not necessary to rub hard as the solution will dissolve the corrosion. When the brass is tarnish-free, wash it in hot soapy water, rinse and dry it, then apply polish. To treat badly corroded brass that shows signs of verdigris, immerse it in a dip or use rust remover.

Caring for copper

Copper will corrode from a beautiful reddish-brown when clean to a dull gray-brown. If it is neglected, it will eventually produce bright green patches of verdigris. You clean and polish copper like brass; however, you should not use the harshest methods as these might affect the patina. Chemical dipping is quite safe, but unless tarnishing is very stubborn, do not use steel wool. Instead, use a coarse cloth such as burlap to apply the salt and vinegar solution, and follow this with metal polish on a soft cloth.

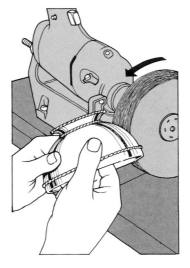

Buffing brass

Although you can polish brass by hand, it is easier to buff simple objects to a high gloss using a mop fitted to a bench grinder. Buffing is not suitable for decorated or delicate items. With the machine running, apply a stick of polishing compound to the mop. Use the compound sparingly as a thick deposit can form on the metal. Removing this deposit is hard work. Hold the brass object against and just below the center of the revolving mop. Keep the piece moving with its edges facing downward. Do not try to buff objects that are difficult to hold.

Lacquering metal

You can coat polished ornamental silver, copper and brass with a clear lacquer to preserve the finish. The most suitable lacquer for antique metals is based on an acrylic resin which will remain clear indefinitely, unlike polyurethanes which will yellow slightly.

Lacquered metalware kept indoors may remain tarnish-free for years, requiring only an occasional wash. When it eventually needs refinishing, remove traces of old lacquer with acetone, or, in the case of polyurethanes and acrylic resins, with a paint stripper. Polish the metal, then wash the piece in warm, soapy water. Use a nail-brush to remove all traces of metal polish because these show up as a white deposit when lacquered. Now rinse and dry the piece. Apply lacquer with a large, soft brush or by spraying through an airbrush (see p. 35). Spraying is preferable if the item is very fragile or intricately made. Work in a warm, dust-free atmosphere.

If you use a brush, work reasonably quickly so that you pick up wet edges before the lacquer begins to set. Try not to cover an area more than once, and make sure that the lacquer does not collect in recesses. If any brush marks show when the lacquer has barely set, warm the item on a radiator; this can encourage marks to flow out.

Caring for bronze

Bronze develops an attractive patina which you should preserve at all costs, or you will devalue the item considerably. Never use abrasives or metal polishes on bronze. Simply wash the piece in warm, soapy water, and then dry it thoroughly. If you want to display a bronze outdoors, protect it with a thin coating of wax polish.

"Bronze disease"—green, powdery spots—is a form of corrosion only found on ancient bronze artifacts and therefore it is outside the sphere of this book. If you have such a piece you should seek the advice of a conservation expert at a museum.

Caring for rusty iron and steel

Iron and steel will corrode badly in the presence of moist air, forming a layer of rust. If this is left unchecked, it will pit the metal, and eventually destroy the object. To combat rust, soak lightly corroded pieces in paraffin for several hours before rubbing off the softened rust with fine steel wool. For quicker results, especially with badly rusted items, use a commercial rust remover. You can protect decorative items from further corrosion by coating them with a little wax polish or some light machine oil.

Wrought iron

Wrought iron is most often found outside in the form of gates, railings and garden furniture. However, some decorative interior pieces were made. Use a chemical paint stripper to remove any old, flaking paint. Then treat the metal with a rust remover and inhibitor. Wrought iron looks best painted black. A special black paint is available for this purpose. But ordinary paint will be perfectly adequate for indoor pieces. You must use a lead primer before applying the top coats.

Metal fireplaces

Specialist companies often sandblast fireplaces to a silver gray, sometimes buffing them, then lacquering them.

Restoring chromium

You will often come across twentieth-century collectables which are plated with this metal. Although by some criteria these are not strictly antiques, they are sought after by many collectors and dealers. Art Deco figurines are particularly prized.

To wash grease and dirt from a chromium surface use a soft brush and soapy water. If there is any slight discoloration, remove it by adding a few drops of ammonia to the water. Do not use abrasives as they will damage the thin plating. Rinse and dry the metal, then use a cream chrome polish to restore its brilliance.

Chromium does not rust, but if the plating has worn thin, the metal underneath (usually copper, iron or steel) may be corroded. To restore such a piece you will have to ask a professional to treat and replate the object.

Cast iron

The casting process allows a degree of decoration that is impossible with wrought iron. Craftsmen took full advantage of this to make ornate door furniture and stops, cooking stoves and ranges, and to furnish the fireplace. Fenders, trivets, fire dogs, grates, firebacks and surrounds, and sometimes even mantlepieces complete with mirrors were made in cast iron.

Treat rust with remover, but if a piece has been left outside for some time, make sure that it has thoroughly dried out before finishing it. Many cast iron items are covered in layers of paint, and stripping cast iron fittings often reveals detail that was completely obscured. Either prime and paint cast iron or lacquer it to prevent corrosion.

Caring for pewter

Pewter develops a gray patina over the years. Many collectors find this attractive, but some polish the metal to a silvery finish with metal polish. Although it may have started out with a bright finish, you risk spoiling the value of a pewter piece by polishing it.

You can remove any slight dull oxide staining by applying a mild abrasive powder such as ground chalk or rottenstone. Use an oily rag, or make it into a paste with kerosene. To remove heavy corrosion immerse the piece in kerosene for a couple of days. Wipe powders or kerosene from the piece with denatured alcohol, wash in warm, soapy water, rinse and dry.

Do not store pewter near oak as this wood contains an acid which will attack the metal.

Caring for lead objects

Lead is most commonly found as lead mounts on furniture, small figures and toys, and garden or architectural fittings. Do not retouch painted lead items, such as toy soldiers, without consulting an expert first.

Lead oxidizes to a pale gray color. This oxidization is perfectly stable and requires no treatment. Remove any light staining with rottenstone on an oily rag, then clean the piece with denatured alcohol. Advanced corrosion will look like a white powder. Treat it in a bath of a very mild vinegar and water solution, followed by another mild solution of calcium carbonate and water to neutralize the acid. Then wash in several changes of clean water.

Caring for gold and ormolu

Few antique collectors can afford to buy gold except in the form of jewelry, and therefore the procedure for cleaning gold is given in that section (see p. 79).

Cleaning ormolu

Ormolu—gilded brass or bronze decorative mounts fitted to furniture, clocks, china and glass—is a form of gold. The gold coating is extremely thin, and will normally have worn through on the raised edges of antiques. It is best to accept such wear as inevitable, rather than attempt to retouch it with inferior materials.

To clean ormolu, remove it, taking careful note of its position and preserving the fixing pins or screws. Put on protective gloves and wash the ormolu in a mild solution of ammonia, brushing dirt from the decoration. Rinse immediately with clean water and dry with a cloth, burnishing gently. If you cannot remove ormolu, mask surrounding areas and clean with a Q-tip moistened in the ammonia solution. Rinse with fresh cotton dipped in clean water. Never use a metal polish on the gilding.

Opaline glass container with ormolu finial

Restoring metalware

With metalware, as with other antiques, you should only attempt repairs that are within your present level of competence, and never work on a piece that is very valuable. There are many simple jobs that you can tackle and a lot of cheap metalware is available that you can practise on with confidence.

You should consider whether the damage is worth restoring before you embark on a repair. Many minor blemishes on antique metalware are acceptable, and a clumsy repair often looks worse than the original damage.

Eliminating scratches

To remove scratches from metalware use a fine abrasive to grind the metal down below the level of the damage. Although metal polish is slightly abrasive, if you are unhappy with the result after polishing, mix up a paste of ground chalk with denatured alcohol, kerosene or mineral spirits. Using a circular motion, apply it on a cloth wrapped around your fingertip. Wash the piece and polish again.

You can clean up badly scratched brass and copper with successively finer grades of emery paper, using oil as a lubricant. Finish with ground chalk and a metal polish.

Caution: You should never use coarse abrasives on soft metals like silver and pewter. And even mild abrasion will damage bronze patina.

Filling holes

You can fill painted cast iron with a commercial epoxy filler. For self-colored metals, make a filler by mixing epoxy glue and metallic powders (available from art stores). Thicken this mixture by adding a little kaolin and powdered pigments to vary the color. Leave the filler to set overnight, before rubbing it down with fine abrasive paper.

If further camouflage is necessary, try applying the metallic paste sold in art stores as a colorant for picture frames. Rub it on with your fingertip or thin it with mineral spirits and paint it on with a brush.

Back a hole in thin metal with modeling clay (see p. 34). When the filler has set, remove the clay and reinforce the inside of the piece with thin fiberglass cloth (obtainable from an auto accessory store).

Knocking out dents

"Smithing," or the shaping of metal, is a skilled craft. You should therefore take valuable items that are badly dented to a professional. This is particularly important if the metal is creased, as inexpert treatment can produce a split. However, you can press out small dents in soft metals easily.

Hammering the metal can create faults that did not exist before. To correct these, follow the initial shaping by "planishing"—tapping the area with a wide-faced hammer to remove minor ripples. Use a plastic-faced hammer or at least a new, smooth engineer's hammer with the edges rounded off. Hold the piece firmly against the stake, making light taps with the hammer.

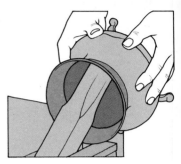

Removing dents in copper and brass Shape the end of a hardwood "stake" to match the curves of the piece. Clamp the stake in a vise, and hold the piece over it, feeling for exactly the right place to put pressure on the dent. Steadying the piece with both hands, press against the shaped end of the stake. Adjust the position to ease the dent out.

Pushing out dents in pewter and lead Pewter and lead are so soft that you can manipulate them with your fingers alone. Use your thumbs to push a dent back, then lay the piece on a thick layer of newspaper so that you can rub the area with the ball of your thumb to remove traces of damage.

Restoring a dented base If your piece has a dented flat bottom, first place it on a hard surface. If the base has a rim, make up a stake to fit inside it to support the bottom of the vessel itself. Position another stake on the inside and tap the end with a hammer.

Restoring a crushed item

Various small, personal items such as snuff boxes, match cases and thimbles were made in soft precious metals. These were always very thin, and therefore easily damaged. You can often come across such an item on sale cheaply.

To restore it, shape a piece of hardwood to resemble the blade of a paper knife, but carefully round the end and edges. Smooth the tool with abrasive papers and give it a light coating of wax. Next, work it into position (see below). Then slide the blade to and fro, gradually burnishing the item roughly into shape. When you can ascertain the true shape of the piece, make up another hardwood former that fits snugly into the item. Wax this former and coax the metalware over it by rocking and twisting the piece or tapping it on your palm. Once the former is in place, you can use your fingers to shape the piece and also to smooth out any creases.

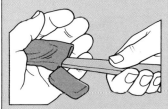

Inserting the first former Gentle levering and twisting will gradually work the point of the tool inside the crushed metal item.

Removing creases Hold the item, with the former in place, and tap it gently with a lightweight hammer.

Repairing broken metal

The method you select to repair broken metalware will depend on your experience, the nature of the break and the property of the metal. If you are inexperienced, and the joint is not going to be put under any strain, glue is probably the best choice. However, if the joint is going to be under pressure, and you have mastered the technique, you should use lead solder (see p. 64).

Using glues

Modern glues have made it possible to repair broken metalware which would previously have been abandoned as unmendable. Adhesives are particularly suitable in cases where you cannot use heat—such as when joining low melting point metals like pewter or lead. Extreme heat will also damage the patina of metalware and inlays or fittings in materials like wood or ivory. And because glues are safe and easy to use, they are a good choice for a beginner.

However, if the joint is going to be put under strain, you should use lead solder instead. The same applies if the joint has only a small surface area. You cannot glue thin sheet metal edge to edge for instance, unless you back up a joint with an additional metal strip.

Cyanoacrylate glues are suitable for small repairs, but a two-part epoxy adhesive will produce a stronger joint.

Repairing a broken fireplace

Cast-iron fireplaces are normally attached to the wall by two lugs just below the mantle shelf. Once you have loosened these, you can lever the surround away from the wall. In some cases, the fireplace has a second pair of lugs that are covered by the skirting board. If you miss these, the metal can crack right across one side piece.

A broken fireplace that has split across one side is a good candidate for repairing with glue because the fireplace will not be under a lot of strain once it is on the wall. Also it would be difficult to heat up, although you could have it welded by a garage.

Scrub the joint and the back of the fireplace with warm, soapy water. Use denatured alcohol or acetone to degrease the joint. Then stand the fireplace on its head so that you can position the smaller piece of metal on it. Mix up the adhesive, and apply it sparingly along one edge. Position the broken piece in place, rocking it gently to seat it properly, and squeeze out excess glue. Tape the broken piece tightly in place with adhesive tape. Wipe away excess glue with denatured alcohol. Leave the glue to harden overnight. Once it has set, lay fiberglass cloth (obtainable from an auto accessory store) across the back of the joint to reinforce it.

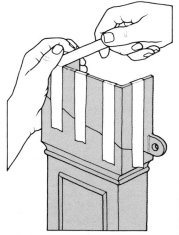

Gluing broken metal Once you have cleaned and glued the joint (see above), keep the two halves firmly in contact with adhesive tape. Leave in place overnight until the glue has set.

Repairing metals with soft solder

Particular metals melt at different temperatures, and the moment at which they liquefy is called the melting point. Solder is a metal which has a lower melting point than most metals. Consequently, it will flow into a heated joint in another metal of a higher melting point. Once the solder has cooled, it acts as a bond in the joint.

Soft solder is an alloy of lead and tin. It has such a low melting point that you can apply heat locally with a soldering iron, thus reducing the likelihood of damaging any surrounding materials like wood or ivory unless they are in direct proximity to the joint.

As long as the metal is clean, a soldered joint will be stronger than one made with adhesive. Solder is therefore preferable if the joint is going to be put under load or stress.

Before you solder metal you must clean up the joint, and then clean off the oxidization that forms immediately on the surface by using a solvent flux. Some active fluxes will corrode metals unless you can wash them from the joint after cooling. Passive fluxes will not harm the metal, so it is safer to use these whenever possible.

In order to soft solder a joint its surface area must be reasonably large—for example, a folded joint—and the two edges must be in close contact. And the metal you are repairing must be a good conductor of heat. The easiest metals to solder are tin, copper, brass and lead. You must be careful not to melt lead. Pewter is even more vulnerable, and requires a special low temperature solder, so unless you are very experienced, take the piece to a professional.

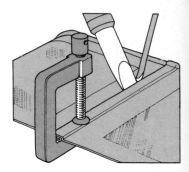

Mending a joint in tinware
Soft solder is an ideal choice to mend the folded joints found in antique metal toys and containers. Clamp the joint, then run solder and iron along it (see p. 227). However, if heating would damage the paintwork, use an adhesive instead. Before soldering, clean the inside of the joint with fine steel wool on a screwdriver tip.

Repairing metals with hard solder

Hard solders are made from different metals with a range of melting points, all of which are considerably higher than soft solders. A joint made with hard solder is much stronger. However, the much higher temperature involved will ruin any patina on the metal. And you will have to remove any combustible material such as wooden fittings or ivory inlay.

Use a blow torch to heat the solder. Although you should try to localize the heat as much as possible, the whole piece will get hot.

Items constructed from several different elements were made using a range of solders, starting with that with the highest melting point for the first joint, and gradually reducing it for each subsequent joint. If you attempt to repair one joint in a piece with several, there is therefore a danger that other components will not remain intact when you heat the piece. Therefore, it is always wise to seek professional advice, especially with a valuable silver piece.

Soldering a hollow brass candlestick

Cast hollow candlesticks often break in half, usually across a narrow section of the column, due to local thinning of the metal. Because they were made in one piece, you will not have to worry about them falling apart once heated. And it is acceptable to buff brass.

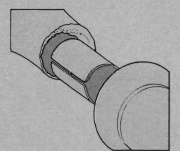

1 Join the two broken halves with a shim or spacer of brass sheet rolled up so that it fits tightly inside the candlestick. This shim will enlarge the surface of the joint, and stop it sliding sideways and going out of line.

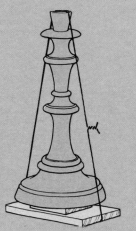

2 If the shim is a tight fit, no clamping will be necessary. Just weight the candlestick or plug each end with wood and wire the two halves together.

3 Once you have soldered the joint (see p. 227), the next step is to clean it up with fine files and emery cloth wrapped around shaped sticks. When you have cleaned and buffed the piece, the thin gray joint line should be almost invisible.

FIREARMS

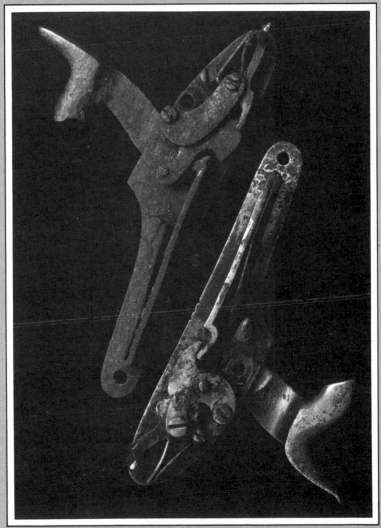

Collecting firearms

Most antique firearms on sale are flintlock or early percussion weapons. Their construction is relatively simple, and an amateur will find them fairly easy to restore. Later guns are more sophisticated and more difficult to repair, and many require a firearms certificate.

Weapons made before the advent of flintlocks are extremely valuable, so if you are lucky enough to own one take it to an expert restorer. Of course, many flintlock and percussion weapons are valuable, but you can still find some at a reasonable price.

Buying tips

● Any gun that is in surprisingly good condition may be a working replica, rather than a genuine antique. You should ask to have the weapon authenticated by an expert, especially if the asking price is high.
● Look for proof and maker's marks (see p. 234) when buying a gun. Make sure you do not remove such marks accidentally when restoring a badly corroded gun—they may help you to date it and they can affect the value of the piece.

● Never test a gun by cocking it without the vendor's permission —this action may break a weak main spring.
● If possible, you should ask to see the lock mechanism to check its condition. This is especially important if the gun is expensive.
● Dents and scratches are to be expected on the wooden stock of genuine antique guns—this type of damage will not affect the value of the piece unless it is very severe.

Legal requirements

If, like most collectors, you do not fire your genuine antique guns, you will not need a firearms certificate. For legal purposes an antique gun is defined as one that is over one hundred years old, and not designed to use a metallic cartridge.

If you do decide to use your gun, you should make it safe by getting a gunsmith to reproof the barrel. This is not advisable, however, as the barrel may split under test and thus ruin a valuable piece. In any case, a modern stamp mark will be added which is undesirable to some collectors.

Most enthusiasts prefer to fire working replicas. These are, of course, modern guns, and you may need a firearms certificate to own one. Ask your neighborhood Police Department what the legal requirements are in your State.

Damage checks

*A simple repair
**Some experience needed
***Skilled work—not for beginners

Examine any gun you intend buying carefully and systematically, and look out for the following points.

The stock
**Splits are most likely to occur at the weakest points— either where the stock is thinnest (at the wrist) or where there is short grain (at the forend).
**The mortise that houses the lock is sometimes split at the bottom by a broken main spring.
**An old split that has been taped or bound together is relatively simple to repair. If it has been nailed, however, you should look out for metallic stains and be prepared for further damage as you attempt to remove the nails.
*Woodworm is usually easy to treat unless it is extensive (see p. 129).

The lock
*A corroded outside is easy to clean. And a well-fitted lock may still be well preserved on the inside.
*Check the screw and top jaw which holds the flint. They may be missing or have been replaced by incompatible parts. Restoration is possible.
**If the lock mechanism or its mortise show any sign of having been tampered with to make the lock fit, the entire lock may be an unsuitable replacement.

The barrel
*Corrosion is simple to deal with if not too severe. However, if the barrel shows signs of blueing or browning consult a professional.
*Missing or damaged sights can be replaced or repaired.

Stock furniture
*Is the ramrod broken? Remove it to check. It is possible to mend or replace it.
*Is any stock furniture missing or out of style? It may be possible to replace parts.

Dating a weapon

The various test and makers' marks found on a gun will give you a clue to its age, if not an actual date of manufacture (see p. 234). But there are several other features of the design and mechanism found on a gun which can tell you its earliest possible date—for example, an English gun with a Birmingham proof mark cannot be earlier than 1813. However, use these features only as a rough guide, as many were incorporated in guns over very long periods. Furthermore, at any one point in time, features that were out-of-date in industrialized countries were still in use in less technologically advanced ones.

Conversions carried out in the past can also introduce further complications. A flintlock, for instance, may have been converted to percussion at a time when a flintlock would have been considered merely old-fashioned. Certain types of conversion are easy to spot—for example, a percussion nipple fitted to a flintlock pan. Although it would be foolish to convert any antique weapon now, such contemporary conversions are valid examples of a period of transition, and could be included in any collection.

Rifling

The term "rifling" is used to describe spiral grooves inside the barrel which impart a spin to a ball or bullet to stabilize it in flight, thus improving its accuracy and range. You may be able to detect rifling simply by looking down the muzzle. And it can be inferred with the presence of effective sights as these would be pointless if rifling was not present.

Any type of gun can turn out to be rifled, as this feature was first used in the late fifteenth century. However, it was rare until the advent of percussion guns in the nineteenth century.

Double barrel

Shotguns or fowling pieces with double barrels became practical around 1810, when improved breach design made it possible to reduce the length of the barrel, and hence the weight.

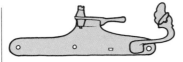

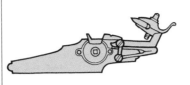

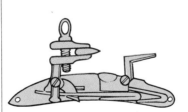

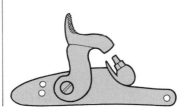

Matchlock

This design was introduced in the mid-fifteenth century. A glowing "match" attached to a pivoted arm is brought down onto the priming powder by operating a trigger. Matchlocks were cheap to produce, and were therefore still in use in the seventeenth century.

Wheel lock

The earliest wheel locks were made at the beginning of the sixteenth century. When the trigger is pulled, a spring-operated wheel is turned against a piece of iron pyrites, sending sparks to the priming pan. Any genuine wheel lock is valuable, as they were always expensive.

Snaphaunche

In most countries this form of flintlock was made until the mid-sixteenth century. However, they were still being made in Morocco in 1885. Unlike the true flintlock, the flint and priming pan cover (see p. 71) operate separately.

Miquelet

Another early version of the flintlock, the miquelet is not known to have been made before 1600. It has a combined steel and pan cover (see p. 71), but is distinguished from the true flintlock by its large external main spring.

Flintlock

The true flintlock was developed by Marin le Bourgeoys between 1610 and 1615. It incorporates the best of both previous locks, with a combined steel and pan cover (frizzen) and an internal spring (see p. 71). It was the natural successor to the matchlock for military purposes. The design was in continuous use with little change until about 1830.

Percussion lock

In the early nineteenth century gunsmiths were experimenting with systems that produced ignition of the charge by using an element which would detonate when struck. The system which became widespread by the 1830s was the "percussion" lock.

Tools and materials

You will need relatively few tools to restore early firearms, although some of them are specialized types. Firearms are essentially a combination of metals and wood, and the tools you need reflect this. However, rebuilding many of the weapons developed after flintlock and early percussion firearms is so complex that you should read special books on the subject or consult an expert about tools and working methods.

Tools

Screwdrivers You will need a selection of screwdrivers to dismantle locks and stock furniture. You must match screws exactly to a screwdriver head to avoid damaging the slot.
Pin punches Use metal punches and hammer-driven drifts to knock out tapered metal pins.
Brass wire suede brush This cleans corroded steel safely.
Pliers You need combination, flat- and needle-nosed pliers.
Main spring clamp This device compresses springs while you take apart the lock.
Files A few smooth files are useful for cleaning up scored metal.
Hacksaw blade Use this to clear screw slots prior to removing screws.
Bench vise An engineer's soft-jawed vise will hold the gun steady and protect metal parts from damage.
Hammers Use a lightweight pin hammer for general work, a medium-weight engineer's hammer for driving punches and a soft-faced hammer to strike metal parts that a standard hammer would damage.
Woodworking tools A small general woodworking kit will be useful for repairing the stock (see pp. 98–102).
A checkering chaser This home-made tool cleans and crisps checkering on the wooden stock.
Cleaning tools To clean an antique barrel you will need a gunsmith's rod, brushes, mops and jagg (a toothed attachment for passing a cleaning rag down the barrel). You can obtain these from modern gunsmiths.

Gas-torch or blow-lamp Use this to heat metal to break down corrosion by expansion and contraction.
Work bench Use a firm bench with a vise mounted close to one leg. Lay out metal and wooden components on old newspaper or carpet to protect them from metal filings.
Power tools These tools have their place in gun restoration, but they should be used with caution. A power drill is particularly useful for drilling small, accurate holes. Light pressure can be applied with the power on, whereas hand drilling requires considerable pressure when working on metal. A power buff and even a wire brush can be used to clean up a steel barrel, but only if it has no decorative engraving or inlay.

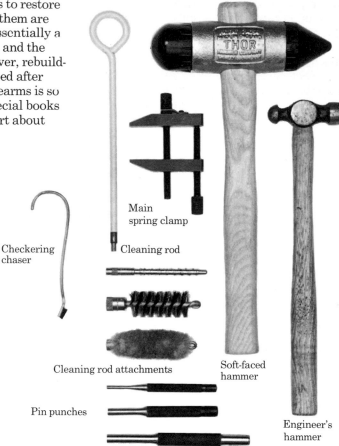

Checkering chaser

Main spring clamp

Cleaning rod

Cleaning rod attachments

Pin punches

Soft-faced hammer

Engineer's hammer

Materials
Rust remover See p. 57.
Lubricants A light machine oil is necessary for lubrication and to protect clean metal from corrosion. Use graphite-free penetrating oil to free rusted components.
Steel wool Use 00 and 000 grades to clean metal and wood.
Linseed oil This is the best finish for the stock. Boiled linseed oil dries faster.
Emery paper Use this on badly corroded steel. Make sure you do not remove any engraving, inlays or stamped marks.

Is it loaded?

When you acquire an antique firearm, it is most important that you find out whether there is still a charge in the barrel. With muzzle-loading weapons, you can determine this by comparing the apparent internal length of the barrel with the outside. To measure the inside, pass a wooden dowel down the barrel until it is in firm contact at the breech end. Mark the position of the muzzle on the dowel and withdraw it. Hold the dowel alongside the barrel, aligning one end with the muzzle, to compare the internal measurements with the external length. If the far end of the dowel aligns with the touch hole or nipple then the gun is not loaded, if it falls short, the weapon may be loaded.

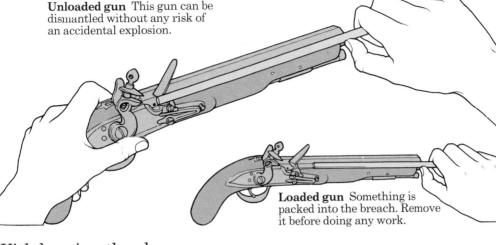

Unloaded gun This gun can be dismantled without any risk of an accidental explosion.

Loaded gun Something is packed into the breach. Remove it before doing any work.

Withdrawing the charge

Because the charge may have been in place for a long time, steel, lead and salts in the gunpowder may have produced heavy, localized corrosion. Withdrawing such a charge is like removing a cork from a bottle—carried out efficiently with the correct tool it is a simple task, but any mistakes make the job twice as difficult.

The gun may have a "worm" or screw at the end of the ramrod designed to remove the charge. If it has not, make an extractor by soldering an ordinary wood screw with the head removed into one end of a brass or steel tube. Solder a drill bit plus a shim or spacer in the other end.

Wood screw extractor

Centering device

1 Push the screw through a cardboard disk that matches the bore and pass it down the barrel, driving it into the "wad" (a paper or cloth packing on top of the ball). The disk will center the screw on the ball. Now try to pull out the wad. If the ball does not roll out, you will have to use the end with the drill bit, wrapping some tape around the brass tube in order to improve your grip.

2 Drive the drill into the lead, making a small hole in the ball. Then remove the drill, turn the tube round and drive the screw end into the hole, using the cardboard centering disk again.

3 Withdraw the ball and tip out any loose gunpowder. Insert the screw once more to make sure that no wad remains behind the ball. Finally, check that you have removed the charge by comparing the internal and external lengths of the barrel again (as described above).

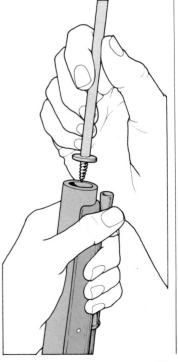

Cleaning and restoring guns

Before starting to restore a firearm, strip it down into its separate components, inspecting each part for damage or wear. Spare parts are available by mail order. The procedure given here is suitable for long guns and pistols, and the procedure for percussion cap locks is similar to that for flintlocks.

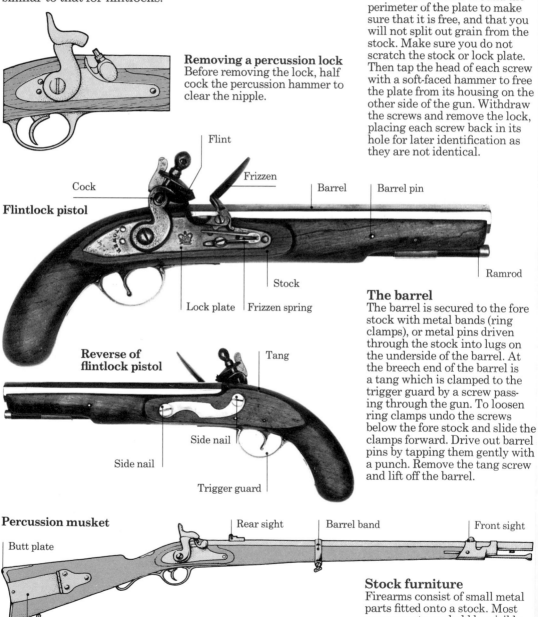

Removing a percussion lock
Before removing the lock, half cock the percussion hammer to clear the nipple.

Flint

Frizzen

Cock

Barrel

Barrel pin

Flintlock pistol

Ramrod

Stock

Lock plate

Frizzen spring

Reverse of flintlock pistol

Tang

Side nail

Side nail

Trigger guard

Percussion musket

Rear sight

Barrel band

Front sight

Butt plate

Patch box cover

The lock
The lock is held in place by screws or "side nails" which pass through the stock into the lock plate. Clean out the screw slots and turn the screws a couple of times with a well-fitting screwdriver. Run a blade around the perimeter of the plate to make sure that it is free, and that you will not split out grain from the stock. Make sure you do not scratch the stock or lock plate. Then tap the head of each screw with a soft-faced hammer to free the plate from its housing on the other side of the gun. Withdraw the screws and remove the lock, placing each screw back in its hole for later identification as they are not identical.

The barrel
The barrel is secured to the fore stock with metal bands (ring clamps), or metal pins driven through the stock into lugs on the underside of the barrel. At the breech end of the barrel is a tang which is clamped to the trigger guard by a screw passing through the gun. To loosen ring clamps undo the screws below the fore stock and slide the clamps forward. Drive out barrel pins by tapping them gently with a punch. Remove the tang screw and lift off the barrel.

Stock furniture
Firearms consist of small metal parts fitted onto a stock. Most components are held by visible screws or drive-out pins. Always tape screws or pins to their fittings to avoid confusion when you reassemble the weapon.

Cleaning up the lock

The condition of locks varies enormously. Even if the outside of a lock is badly rusted, if it fitted snugly in the stock the mechanism on the inside may still be in almost mint condition. However, if the gun has been neglected you can expect to find some corrosion to deal with. Before attempting to operate or dismantle the lock, remove the flint if it is present, then immerse the mechanism in penetrating oil.

Your first step should be to free the main spring. Begin by fully cocking the mechanism to compress this spring, keeping your fingers away from the trigger sear and the underneath of the cock or hammer. Then clamp the main spring (see above right). This is an important operation as the spring could break if you allow it to slip out of the cramp and spring apart suddenly. Let the cock or hammer down slowly into the fired position, then remove any retaining screws before lifting the main spring out of the lock.

Next remove the central fixing screw, and ease the cock or hammer off its square shaft. Before you attempt to remove the sear, make sure that there is some movement in its pivot screw. If there is not, treat it with penetrating oil. Compress the sear spring using a pair of flat-nosed pliers. Now remove the pivot screw and release the sear spring.

No other internal component is under load, so to dismantle them simply remove the screws, taking careful note of their position. Finally, remove the frizzen by depressing its spring with pliers or by levering against the underneath of the flash pan with a screwdriver. If the gun is a quality piece, wrap tape around the jaws or tip of the pliers or screwdriver to protect the metal. Remove the screws to disengage the frizzen then the spring.

Scrub all the parts of the lock with rust remover, taking care to preserve any maker's marks on the lock plate. Lightly oil the parts before assembling them in the reverse order.

Dismantling a flintlock You must clamp the main spring to remove it from the lock, preferably with a special tool from a gunsmith. As an alternative, you can use a toolmaker's cramp or mole grips.

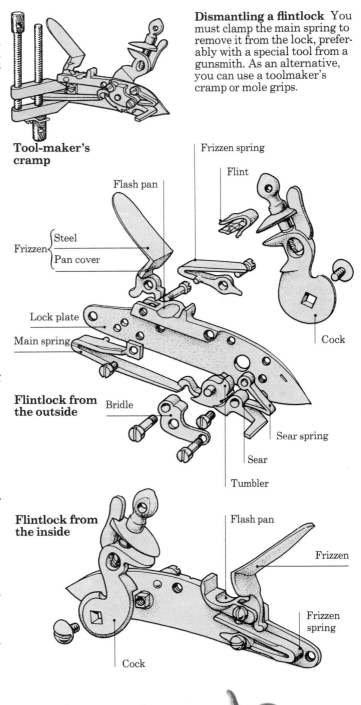

Tool-maker's cramp

Flintlock from the outside

Flash pan

Frizzen { Steel / Pan cover

Lock plate

Main spring

Bridle

Frizzen spring

Flint

Cock

Sear spring

Sear

Tumbler

Flintlock from the inside

Flash pan

Frizzen

Frizzen spring

Cock

Dismantling a percussion lock The procedure for taking apart a percussion lock and a flintlock is identical, except that a percussion lock has a hammer rather than a cock and it has no frizzen.

Restoring the barrel

Before you begin work on the barrel, remove any adjustable sights and extract the percussion nipple. Also remove the threaded breech plug that blocks one end of the barrel. To do this, up end the barrel in a can of penetrating oil and run a little oil down it to penetrate the thread from the inside. Then grip the breech plug in a vise and try to free the thread by twisting the barrel. To improve your grip wear rubber gloves. If the plug proves difficult to free, use a strap wrench on the barrel or heat it to expand it and break down corrosion.

If the inside of the barrel is rusty, use a phosphor bronze brush (available from a gunsmith) to clean it. Fit the brush to a cleaning rod, dip it in rust remover and pass it up and down the barrel. Rinse it with hot water and repeat as necessary. Clean out the touch hole with a sharpened stick or brass or aluminum wire.

Treat the outside with rust remover, rubbing it into the metal with a nailbrush or a brass-wire suede brush. Rinse and dry the barrel using a jagg to pass a cloth down the inside. Then clean up the outside with fine steel wool and progressively finer emery paper. Take care to preserve any decorative "flats" and maker's marks on the barrel. Wash and dry the barrel once more, then rub an oily rag over the outside and pass a lightly oiled mop down the bore.

Oil the threads of the breech plug and then replace it. The plug must go all the way home or the barrel will no longer align with its fixings in the stock.

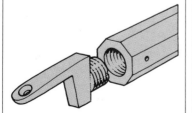

Fitting the breech plug Make sure that the threads are clear of debris first. Take care when you start to screw in the plug as corrosion may make it cross-thread.

Restoring stock furniture

Stock furniture is made from brass, steel or precious metals. It is often best to remove the furniture prior to cleaning it. For the procedures for cleaning and restoring metal stock furniture see pp. 58–61. As well as having metal fittings, the stock itself can be inlaid with ornate decorative metal. You should be very careful when restoring a gun that has engraving or inlay on the stock as these decorations can be very delicate.

Inlaid stock
The stock of this late-seventeenth-century pistol is decorated with pierced brass and steel inlay, and the lock has relief chiseling.

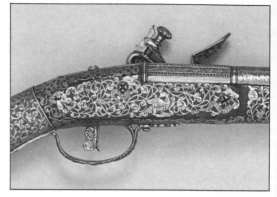

Stock with decorative mount This seventeenth-century gun has a silver mount.

Replacing a broken nipple

If the percussion nipple has broken as a result of excessive corrosion from the inside, you should replace it with a reproduction part or commission a metalworker to make one. Soak the nipple in penetrating oil, then try to move it with a wrench. Heat the barrel if necessary, concentrating on the metal opposite the nipple. If the flats on the nipple are rounded over try taking it out with a bolt extractor. When you drive this in to the central hole it will bite into the metal, providing enough turning force to extract the nipple.

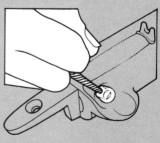

Using a bolt extractor Open up the hole in the nipple with a drill, leaving sufficient metal for the tool to grip. Turn the extractor anti-clockwise.

Renovating the stock

The wooden gun stock will show all the signs or wear and tear that you find on any woodwork —dents, splits, holes, and wood-worm attack, for example. Treatment is the same as for furniture (see pp. 105 and 129). If possible, remove any stock furniture before you begin work on the wood. Protect decoration you cannot remove with masking tape.

Scratches and abrasions are more acceptable on firearms than on fine furniture. However, this acceptability depends on the extent of the damage, and whether it occurs on those parts of the gun where you would expect heavy wear. You can plug holes with matching wood (see p. 224). If you are offered cheap badly damaged guns, never turn them down, as you can use them to provide wood and spare parts.

Once the stock is prepared, you should apply linseed oil (see p. 111). Rub the oil on with a brush, then wipe it over with a soft cloth.

Cleaning checkering

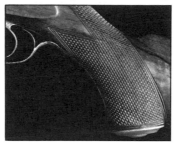

Checkering—cross-hatched "V" grooves—is found on pistol grips, the wrist or small of the stock, and the fore end of long guns. Its function is to improve the grip. Constant handling wears off the high points and fills the grooves with dirt and grease. Use an old toothbrush to scrub out dirt and grease with a mixture of four parts mineral spirits to one of linseed oil.

If you have stripped the stock down to bare wood, you can sharpen checkering with a chaser—a tool made from a short length of triangular file. Choose a broken file with relatively coarse teeth, and grind the nose at an angle to form a point similar to that of a graver. Solder a length of flat steel wire to the top of the chaser and bend the other end to fit into the heel of your hand.

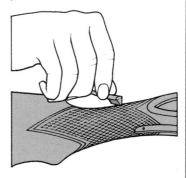

Cleaning procedure Use short strokes of the chaser to clean the checkering. Start in relatively clear grooves in order to establish the line.

Displaying guns

After you have handled a weapon, mild acid in your sweat can etch fingerprints on metal parts. Always wipe guns over with an oily rag before putting them aside. Apply a little linseed oil to the stock if it appears dry, and lightly oil the lock mechanism from time to time.

To display long guns and also protect them from dust, you should store them in a glass-fronted display cabinet.

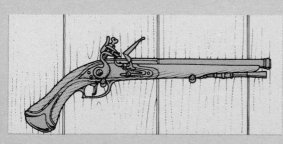

Wall hanging Oiled guns will stain wallpaper, but you can display them on wooden paneling, supported on two short lengths of dowel angled upward.

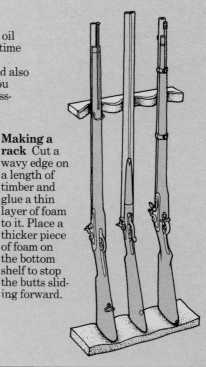

Making a rack Cut a wavy edge on a length of timber and glue a thin layer of foam to it. Place a thicker piece of foam on the bottom shelf to stop the butts sliding forward.

Restoring pocket pistols

As their name implies, pocket pistols were small guns carried by ladies and gentlemen for their personal protection. A special type of mechanism known as a box-lock was generally used. This mechanism was usually fitted with a central hammer or cock. But percussion-cap pocket pistols fitted with side-mounted hammers can also be found. Most pocket pistols have a "turn-off" barrel. The gun was loaded by unscrewing the barrel from the breech block. A powder charge was loaded into the upturned breech, the ball set in a recess, and the barrel screwed down over it.

Dismantling a box-lock mechanism

For an amateur restorer, dismantling a pocket pistol for cleaning (see pp. 70–1) is not particularly difficult. A flintlock pistol is dismantled in the same way as the percussion type, except that it is the frizzen which is first removed from the former and the nipple from the latter. Removing the nipple should be straightforward. The frizzen's removal is slightly complicated by the presence of a spring. Remove this before trying to remove the frizzen pivot screw. Loosen the screw slowly to relax the spring before removing it. Then remove the pivot and frizzen.

Unscrew the two butt-fixing screws. The first is through the top-plate tang, the second underneath the butt. Withdraw the butt by pulling it straight back. Take care not to lever the butt sideways. Its sides are thin where it has been cut away to clear the mechanism and can be easily split.

The lock mechanism can now be tackled. Never try to remove the cock pivot before releasing the main spring. Access to the spring is gained by lifting the cover plate. Remove the two fixing screws at the front corners of the plate. Fully cock the mechanism to compress the main spring. Lift the cover plate out of the way and grip the spring with the toolmaker's clamp or small pliers. Do not compress it further.

Pull and release the trigger and at the same time push the cock forward to disengage it from the main spring. Unscrew and withdraw the cock pivot screw from the side. Lift out the cock and cover plate, which can

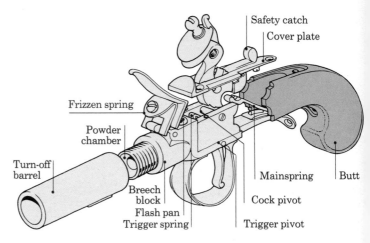

Safety catch
Cover plate
Frizzen spring
Powder chamber
Turn-off barrel
Breech block
Flash pan
Trigger spring
Mainspring
Butt
Cock pivot
Trigger pivot

now be separated. Note the gap between the jaws of the clamp. There is no need to do this with the pliers as it will reset itself. Release the clamp and disengage the relaxed spring from its locating lug.

Drive out the trigger pivot using a punch no larger than the pin's diameter. Extract the trigger. The trigger spring is located by a lug fitted into a hole at the front of the box. Pull it out with needle-nosed pliers.

Remove the trigger guard by first unscrewing the rear fixing screw, which passes through the bottom of the box. Rotate the guard to unscrew it from the base of the box.

Removing the barrel

Round barrel with lug

Octagonal barrel

Round barrel with star-shaped muzzle

The "turn-off" barrel of the pocket pistol is screwed onto the breech block. A special key is used to tighten the barrel to ensure a fit that is tight enough to withstand the charge. In most cases the key slips over the barrel. With a round barrel a projecting lug locates in a notch in the key. An octagonal barrel key may have a notch to clear a foresight. However, some round barrels use a key which fits into the muzzle of the barrel—the muzzle is grooved to form a star shape which takes a square key. Use whichever key is required to release the barrel. If the barrel is particularly tight and will not come free, give the key a sharp tap with a rubber mallet. Once free, unscrew it by hand.

JEWELRY

Collecting jewelry

Although gold, silver and precious stones tend to be valuable, many pieces made from semi-precious materials are modestly priced. Most of the problems you are likely to encounter with jewelry are associated with broken fittings, settings or clasps. For this reason, before you put on a piece of antique jewelry make sure that any clasps and catches are safe. Full insurance is important —jewelry is easily lost or stolen.

Buying tips

● Some brooches are meant to have overlong pins. Under the misapprehension that an ill-fitting replacement pin has been substituted, some people file them shorter, but in fact this devalues the piece.
● Real pearls have a rougher texture than imitation ones, which are quite smooth.
● If you have a necklace in your possession which you know to be strung on its original thread, do not restring it unless absolutely necessary. It is worth more in its original state.
● It is rare to find a piece signed by its maker, but it is worth examining any Art Nouveau style jewelry for signatures. Show signed pieces to an expert —they could be very valuable.

Damage checks

*A simple repair
**Some experience needed
***Skilled work—not for beginners

*****Missing** stones are easy to spot if fairly large, but carry a magnifier to check groups of smaller ones. You will probably have to get a jeweler to replace them for you.
Examine **pins and clasps carefully before buying. Most damage occurs to these working parts.
****Large glass beads** on necklaces can have sharp edges to their holes. These will soon wear through the thread. If you buy a piece with beads in this condition, grind down the edge of the hole with a diamond bit in a pin vise before restringing the necklace.

Precious metals

Gold
Pure gold is hardly ever used to make jewelry, because it is a very soft metal. Other metals are therefore added to make an alloy. The amount of gold in the alloy is expressed in "carats," 24 carats being pure gold. There are currently four standards for gold—9, 14, 18 and 20 carat. The number represents the proportion of gold out of 24 parts. Before 1932 both 12 and 15 carat gold were recognized, but both were superceded by 14 carat.

Gold jewelry will usually have a manufacturer's mark, as well as the test ("assay") marks applied by the country of origin (see p. 234). Some countries test and mark imported goods too.

Colored gold
The type and amount of metal mixed with pure gold affects the color of the resulting alloy. The type of metal in the mix also determines the properties of the gold. For example, if silver is added, the gold will be malleable and whitish in color, whereas adding copper will make the gold harder and give it a redder tinge.

Rolled gold
The process of rolling gold involves fusing a thin sheet of solid gold to a thicker backing sheet of a base metal. The sheet is rolled out to make it extremely thin, and then used to manufacture the item. There are no regulations governing the quality of the gold used, so it will not be hallmarked.

Gold plating
Gold plated items are made from base metals with a very thin coating (thinner than rolled gold) of gold transferred to the item by electrolysis. Such pieces are not hallmarked, but they often bear the words "gold plated."

Silver
Silver is harder and stronger than gold. Details of its composition are given in the metalware chapter (see p. 54); for marks see p. 233.

Settings

The method of securing a stone in a piece of metal jewelry is known as a setting. Settings may be open or closed. In a closed setting the stone is fixed in solid metal, whereas in an open setting the metal is cut away behind the stone to allow light to reflect through. Metallic foil is often placed under a stone in a closed setting to mimic this.

Encabochon
The stone is set in a small box of metal, the edges of which are bent over in order to hold the stone in place.

Carved setting
The stone is set into a socket cut into solid metal and secured by burring over the edges of the hole.

Millegrain
Tiny grains of metal are pushed up to hold the stone at its edge. The setting is so fine that virtually no light is cut out.

Claw setting
Metal "claws" hold faceted stones firmly. The top edge of each claw is bent over to grip the stone just above the widest part (the girdle).

Gem stones

The value of gem stones is determined by their relative scarcity, individual size and beauty. Technically they are divided into "precious" and "semi-precious" by their hardness on a scale of 1 to 10. Diamond is the hardest gem; it is rated 10 on this scale. Any stone rated at 9 or 10 is also considered precious. These include emeralds and rubies. Stones like garnets and opals are rated as semi-precious.

Semi-precious materials

Amber

Amber is fossilized pine tree resin; it ranges from red to yellow in color and it can be either clear or opaque. Pieces that contain embedded insects are considered more valuable nowadays. At one time such inclusions were considered second-rate, and amber was often reconstituted (melted down, filtered and molded) to produce beads of an even color.

Reconstituted amber is genuine, and you should treat it as such. There are many synthetic copies made from plastic and glass; to the eye, some are indistinguishable from the real thing. To find out if a piece is genuine, use the test on p. 84.

Coral

The skeletal remains of tiny marine creatures form coral. It is generally dark pink, but occasionally pale pink or white. In jewelry, it is usually found as small polished beads or as branch coral—tiny, uneven sticks—threaded to form a necklace or bracelet. Coral is also set into precious metals. Plastic copies are easy to spot when molded into bracelets, but fake beads need careful scrutiny.

Tortoiseshell and horn

Cut from the shell of the sea turtle, tortoiseshell is a mottled brown and black in color. Horn, which is cheaper, ranges from a translucent milky brown to a darker, browny gray. Horn was sometimes dyed in a variety of colors.

Mother of pearl

Mother of pearl is the lining of the mollusk shell, and is composed of the same material as a pearl.

Ivory and bone

Elephant's tusks are generally used to make ivory. In some ways, ivory resembles wood—it has a definite grain of darker lines visible on its pale cream ground. It is sometimes difficult to distinguish bone from ivory. However, bone does not have such a smooth grain, and it may have small, dark flecks, all of which run in the same direction.

Jet

This highly polished black stone, made from fossilized wood, was extremely popular in Victorian times as mourning jewelry. You should watch out for glass and hard-molded rubber substitutes.

Jade

Real jade is very hard and cold to touch. It can be green, yellow, blue or white in color. Jade has been used to make jewelry and carvings since prehistoric times, especially in the Far East.

Enamel

Enamelware may be opaque or translucent, and it usually has intricate patterns or designs. Enamel is made by fusing colored glass powders to a thin sheet of metal. In some cases, the areas of color are separated by thin metal wires soldered to the base—this type is called *cloisonné*. In another sort of enamel the base metal itself is engraved, and these hollows filled with glass; this is known as *champlevé*. For a third type, enamel is fired directly onto the metal, designs added with more enamel, and a second firing given.

Cuts for stones

Cabochon

Before jewelers developed methods for cutting stones they domed and polished them.

Table cut

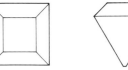

This is a simple faceted cut for softer stones.

Rose cut

This cut was developed in the sixteenth century to enhance the brilliance of stones. All the facets are triangular, and the back of the stone is flat.

Brilliant cut

This cut, developed in the seventeenth century, has 58 mathematically designed facets. It takes full advantage of the reflective and refractive qualities of the stone and consequently is used most often for diamonds.

Emerald cut

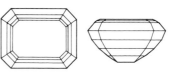

This rectangular cut is used for brittle stones, like emeralds and aquamarines, because it reduces the risk of chipping.

Tools and materials

Valuable, finely made jewelry should only be repaired by a professional. However, you can clean valuable jewelry without fear of harming it, and you can mend many less valuable pieces, turning them into highly desirable decorative objects.

For a work bench use a small table placed in good daylight. Because small pieces of jewelry can easily be lost, work on a tray with raised edges, or better still, make up a work board with raised lips on three sides and glue a half-round wooden molding across the front edge to hold beads in place.

Never clean jewelry over a sink. Instead, use a saucer of water on your work table in case you accidentally wash a stone from its setting. And keep spare parts and pieces of half-assembled jewelry in small packets or boxes. Label these clearly, because you can easily lose a spare part if you fail to identify it.

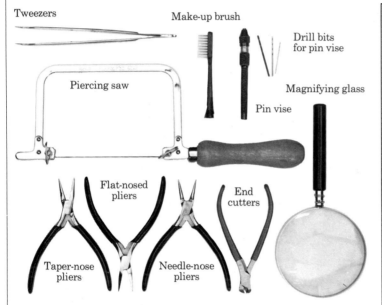

Tweezers
Make-up brush
Drill bits for pin vise
Piercing saw
Magnifying glass
Pin vise
Flat-nosed pliers
End cutters
Taper-nose pliers
Needle-nose pliers

Tools

Small pliers Choose pliers with smooth rather than serrated jaws because these would mark soft metal. You will need flat-nosed, taper-nose, needle-nose and round-nose pliers.

Clippers These are useful for cutting wire. End-cutting types are the most versatile.

Needle files Use these for delicate shaping and repair.

Piercing saw If you fit a piercing saw with a fine jeweler's blade you can use it to cut soft metals as well as to shape sheets of ivory, bone and tortoiseshell when repairing inlay.

Make-up brush A small, fairly stiff eye make-up brush is useful for scrubbing fine engraving or settings. Alternatively, use an old toothbrush.

Magnifier You must have either a jeweler's eyeglass or a magnifying glass to inspect jewelry for damage and also to carry out very delicate operations successfully.

Sharp knife You will need a knife with disposable scalpel blades.

Tweezers A pair of tapered tweezers will be useful.

Pin vise To set reinforcing pins in broken jewelry use a small finger-operated drill and very fine drill bits.

Artist's paintbrush Use this to wash branch coral pieces and to clean out crevices in carved work such as jet.

Beading needle You may need to use this very fine, long needle when restringing a necklace. Obtainable from craft or jewellery suppliers.

Materials

Jewelry dip This chemically cleans metals. You can obtain it from almost any jeweler.

Denatured alcohol and acetone Use denatured alcohol to clean most precious stones and jade; use acetone to clean enamel.

Powdered magnesia This powder is used to dry clean pearls, opals and turquoise.

Almond oil A rich oil that will clean and revive several semi-precious materials. It is stocked by most druggists.

Hydrogen peroxide (20 volume) In very rare cases you use this to bleach ivory.

Cold cure lacquer and paints Use these to restore enamel.

Colored wax crayons Mix ordinary crayons to make almost any colored filler.

Adhesives You will need epoxy resin, white, cyanoacrylate and anaerobic glues (see pp. 25 and 43).

Findings Replacement brooch pins, necklace clasps and ear clips or wires are available from specialist jeweler's suppliers.

Nylon or silk thread Use this to restring necklaces.

Caring for precious metals

Antique jewelry was hardly ever made from pure gold. Since gold is soft, jewelers added other metals to it in order to make an alloy hard enough for practical purposes (see p. 76).

Much antique jewelry is also made from solid and plated silver, but the purity of the metal is expressed in different ways from gold (see p. 54). Silver is harder, and therefore stronger than gold. It is often used as the base for gold-plated jewelry.

Cleaning gold and silver

Unlike other metals, gold does not tarnish. You can clean it by buffing with a soft cloth. To remove greasy accumulations in engraving or chain links, immerse the piece for a few minutes in a commercial jewelry dip (available from most jewelers). But if the piece has stones embedded in it, you should not use a dip as it may damage them.

Use a small, soft brush to remove any stubborn dirt, but take care not to damage the gold. Polish the item dry with a clean cloth. Alternatively, wash gold in warm, soapy water and use a new eye make-up brush or a very small toothbrush to remove any dirt.

Gold plating is very easily rubbed off, so always dry plated items gently. Silver will tarnish with exposure to the air, but you can remove this either by immersing the item in a jewelry dip or by giving it a gentle polish (see p. 58).

Cleaning precious metal A gentle brushing with a small, soft brush will usually remove dirt from crevices. You may need to immerse the piece in warm, soapy water if the dirt is very stubborn.

Storing jewelry

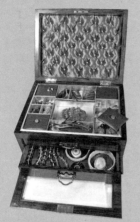

Some stones are extremely hard and can easily scratch softer metals or stones if you keep pieces loose in your jewel box. Other stones are extremely brittle and may chip. You should therefore store pieces separately in compartments or small boxes, or wrap each one individually in acid-free tissue or cotton. You should hang chains from hooks or lay them out rolled individually in tissue paper to stop them tangling.

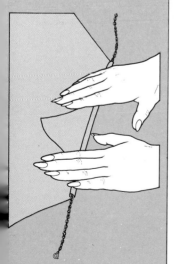

Wrapping up chains A good way to store chains so that they do not tangle is to roll each one in a separate sheet of acid-free tissue paper.

Coins and medals

You should only clean coins and medals with a soft cloth or pad of cotton. Never use polish or abrasives. Keep them in special cabinets or plastic wallets, and retain any presentation cases, to protect them from tarnishing. Try to handle them by their edges only. If a coin has been made up into an item of jewelry, then its value as a coin is already diminished and you can safely clean it using the appropriate method for the metal.

British
1st World War medal in silver

Repairing jewelry

You should inspect your jewelry from time to time, particularly recently purchased items, for signs of damage or weak points which might suddenly give way. Close up any open links, and if they are made of soft gold ask a jeweler to solder them. Replace any temporary links made from wire or thread. Make sure that all clasps are in working order and that brooch or tie pins close securely. Consider attaching a safety chain to brooches and bracelets. You can buy clasps, links and chain from a jeweler's supplier.

Repairing clasps

Make sure that clasps are working properly. They may appear to be closing, but under an unexpected load they can part suddenly. There is little you can do to repair a barrel screw clasp. If the thread is worn, it is only a matter of time before you lose it altogether, so replace it as soon as possible.

Bolt ring

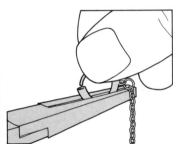

V spring
or box snap

Barrel clasp

Bolt ring See that the bolt on a bolt ring goes all the way inside the ring and does not just come to rest on the rim. If the bolt is slightly bent push it back. But if the spring is weak, replace the ring.

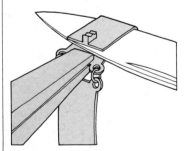

V spring You may find a V spring which, because it has been crushed, no longer locks in the catch. Pry the spring open with a knife blade until it locks securely. Sometimes the spring will break along the fold line as you try to open it. If the catch itself is valuable, get a jeweler to solder the spring for you; otherwise buy a replacement.

Mending earrings

Sometimes you may have to re-shape the wire hooks for pierced ears with round-nosed pliers. It is important to check ear clips to make sure that they are tight enough. Depending on the design, adjust the spring until it operates positively.

Hooked ear wire

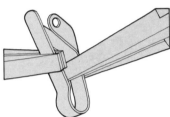

Ear clips

Adjusting ear clips Gently open out the bottom of the fitting with flat-nose pliers.

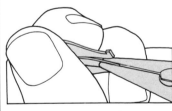

Mending bent clips The center prong may be crushed. Use needle-nose pliers to adjust it.

Screw fitting
cup and pin

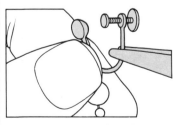

Adjusting screw clips Use needle-nose pliers to bend the stirrup on screw-threaded earrings until the clamp screws tightly against the ear lobe. If the screw is tight, lightly oil it. Also examine it to see if it is bent.

Replacing links

If you cannot buy a link of the right size, make a replacement from hard gold or silver wire.

1 Wrap the wire tightly around a nail to form the required number of links. An oval nail will act as a "pattern" for oval links.

2 Slip the wire off the nail, then use clippers or a jeweler's saw to cut out the individual links.

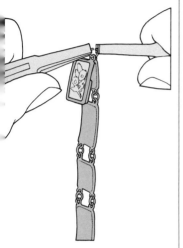

3 Use two pairs of pliers to open an individual link sideways, then hook it in place and close it up. Adjust the shape of the link until the ends are pressed firmly and securely together.

Fitting a safety chain

A safety chain is a wise precaution against losing a valued piece of jewelry. If the clasp breaks on a bracelet or brooch the chain will prevent it slipping unnoticed to the floor. You can buy ready-made chains with a link at each end for fitting to an eye on each half of the clasp. A safety chain for a brooch has a small safety pin on one end that attaches to your clothing.

Repairing brooch pins

The pin, hook and hinge that form the fastening at the back of a brooch must be in the correct relationship to one another before the spring action of the pin itself will work.

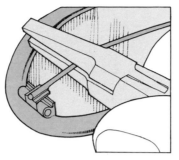

Kinked pin Do not try to bend a kinked pin back to shape—this often strains the hinge. Squeeze it with smooth, flat-nosed pliers, working up and down the length while turning the pin around.

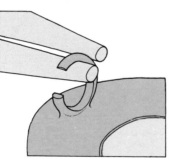

Crushed hook Gently reshape a crushed hook with needle-nose pliers. Once again, use a pinching action to bend the metal to avoid breaking the hook. A jeweler can solder a broken hook for you.

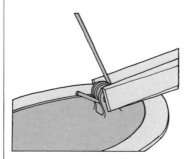

Flattened hinge Pressed metal hinges are sometimes flattened. Lift up the flanges on each side of the pin and adjust them with

pliers until the dimples engage with the loop in the end of the brooch pin.

Adjusting the stop
The hinge end of a brooch pin should operate on a stop which puts enough tension on the pin to hold the point in the hook.

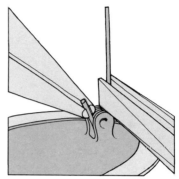

Opening the looped end You may need to open out the looped end of the pin if it has been squashed. Using needle-nose pliers open it out until it bears against the base of the hinge.

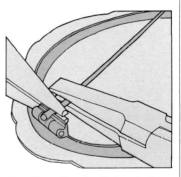

Bending the pin If the pin has been flattened you may find that you need to increase the intentional bend in the pin just in front of the hinge. Pinch the pin gently with flat-nosed pliers.

Precious and semi-precious stones

Before working on jewelry with inset stones, inspect each piece closely with a strong magnifier to make sure that none of the stones is loose. Never attempt to reset valuable stones —take them to a jeweler. You can, however, glue semi-precious opaque stones with epoxy adhesive or cyanoacrylate glue.

Before you embark on cleaning, look to see whether the back of the stone is open or enclosed. If the piece is mechanically set, with an open back, wash it to remove dirt and grease. Immerse in a jewelry dip for two minutes, loosening grime with a make-up brush. Pat the stones dry with a soft cloth. If the back of the stone is enclosed, you should not soak the setting—instead use a Q-tip ball moistened in dip. Remove stubborn grease with a brush dipped in denatured alcohol, then wipe over with a Q-tip moistened in water before drying carefully. Use the same method for strung necklaces.

Cameos and intaglios

Shell
cameo brooch

Moonstone
intaglio ring

Carved from semi-precious stone, cameos and intaglios are designed to exploit the layers of color in the depth of the material. Cameos are also made from shell. Both types are set into metal frames to make rings, brooches and lockets. Cameos carry an image, normally a portrait head, which stands out in relief. Intaglios are made by cutting the design into the stone. To clean them, dip a Q-tip in warm, soapy water and wash the stone with it. Scrub out stubborn dirt from carving with a make-up brush. Rinse with a Q-tip dipped in clean water, then dry.

Stringing a necklace

A broken necklace obviously needs to be restrung, but you should also consider renewing the thread of an unbroken string if it looks worn. Buy nylon or silk thread. It must be at least as thick as half the diameter of the hole in the bead. Knot good-quality beads individually so that if the thread breaks you only lose one.

Before you start, sort out beads in stringing order. They may get larger toward the center, and vary in pattern and color.

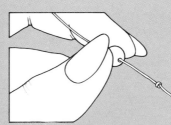

1 Tie a knot 3 ins (7·5 cm) before the end of the thread. Feed the first bead up to it.

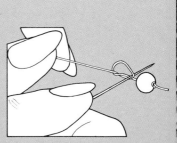

2 Tie the next knot, using a needle to pass it up to the bead. Use your thumbnail to tighten the knot against the bead. Continue along the necklace in the same way.

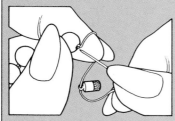

3 Once you have made the final knot, pass the thread through the clasp ring and back through the last bead. If necessary, use a needle or stiffen the end with balsa cement.

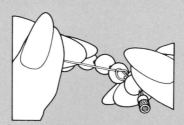

4 Pull the thread out behind the first bead and knot it around the thread at that point.

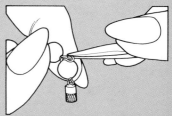

5 Cut the thread, leaving about ¼ in (6 mm) at the end. Coat this with balsa cement and lose it inside the second bead. Attach the second half of the clasp in the same way at the other end.

Semi-precious materials

Semi-precious materials have been admired for their beautiful color and texture over the centuries, and they have been used to make jewelry of all kinds. Also, because they were found in larger quantities than precious stones, they have been used to make decorative objects.

Caring for ivory and bone

Ivory reacts to moisture and heat, both swelling and shrinking. Unequal movement will lead to splits or cracks. For this reason, never display ivory in direct sunlight or next to a radiator. Also, sunlight will bleach ivory.

Although bone is not normally as valuable as ivory, you should treat bone objects with respect because heat and moisture can distort and damage them too. Clean and repair bone exactly as you do ivory.

Store ivory and bone wrapped in dry, colorless, acid-free tissue paper, in a place where there is some air circulation so that there is no risk of mold developing.

Cleaning procedure

Before you clean ivory, always brush off dust from the surface with a soft paintbrush to prevent it getting washed into tiny cracks. Because it is absorbent, never immerse ivory in a liquid for cleaning. If it is in good condition you can safely wash it with a ball of cotton dipped in warm, soapy water, then squeezed almost dry. Rinse with a cotton ball dipped in clean water and then dry it with a soft cloth.

A better method, particularly if the piece is cracked or crazed, is to use almond oil. This removes surface dirt and revives the natural shine of the material. Wipe dirt from the surface, then use a cotton ball to rub oil in. Finally, polish with an absorbent cloth.

Ivory yellows naturally with age, a process which is accelerated if it is kept in the dark for long periods. Never bleach ivory without expert advice—

patina is valued in old ivory. Also some ivories are artificially colored to highlight carving or engraving, and the bleach would ruin this. But if a piece of ivory has absorbed some liquid has stained it badly, you will have to use bleach to restore it. Mix a paste of ground chalk and 20 volume hydrogen peroxide, spread it evenly over the whole piece with a palette knife, and leave for about one hour. Brush off the paste, then wash the residue off the surface with a cotton wad dipped in water. Finally, dry and oil the ivory.

Making repairs

You can use both epoxy resin and polyvinyl acetate glues. Tape the joint together or weight it until the glue has set. Glue pegs cut from scrap ivory or small matchsticks into holes to reinforce joints.

Fill holes and chips with epoxy putty tinted to match surrounding ivory (see p. 27). Some restorers use this to fill cracks too, but as ivory can absorb moisture, there is no guarantee that the crack will not close up again. If it has been filled with a hard material like epoxy, the piece could split even further. A safer procedure, therefore, is to fill in any cracks with toning colored wax (see p. 78).

Caring for jet

To clean jet, brush off loose dust with a soft brush, then wash with a Q-tip or make-up brush dipped in warm, soapy water. Rinse with clean water on a cotton ball and dry with a soft cloth. To remove stubborn greasy marks rub with the inside of a bread crust. Brush any crumbs from inside crevices or mounts with an artist's paintbrush.

You can make almost invisible joints in broken jet by mixing black pigment with epoxy adhesive. For small breaks use cyanoacrylate glue. If an epoxy paste filling is not glossy enough, touch it in with black cold cure lacquer, or fill small holes with black wax.

Caring for jade

Wash jade with warm, soapy water, using a toothbrush or make-up brush to remove dirt and grease from the carving. Make sure that you do not soak a glued setting. Dry on a soft cloth, and polish to restore sheen. Wipe with a little denatured alcohol to remove fingerprints and add brilliance.

It is best to glue heavy jade objects with epoxy resin, although this may show up on clearer types of stone. You can glue lightweight jade ornaments with cyanoacrylate adhesive. Epoxy resin fillings will simulate the color of opaque jade. For small chips in clearer jade use drops of anaerobic adhesive (p. 43).

Cleaning opals, turquoise and pearls

Moisture damages these stones, so never wash them, just "dry clean" with powdered magnesia. Place the piece in a screw-top jar of powder, shake gently for a few minutes, then leave overnight. Remove powder with a soft cloth or brush.

Caring for amber

Amber ranges from red to yellow in color, and it can be either clear or opaque. Real amber is lightweight and does not "tinkle" like glass when rattled together. It is also warm to the touch. To find out if an amber piece is real, rub it on wool fabric. If it is genuine, it will generate static electricity which will pick up tiny scraps of tissue or fluff. It will also give off a faint smell of pine trees.

Never use alcohol or any chemical solvents to clean amber —they will affect it, leaving the surface mat. For this reason, too, take care with perfume and hair sprays as these can damage amber jewelry. Soaking in water will also cloud the surface, so if you want to wash an amber piece, use a Q-tip dipped in warm, soapy water and wipe the piece dry immediately afterwards. A bread crust or almond oil will clean amber safely. And often just a gentle buffing with a chamois or cloth will restore its brilliance.

Making repairs
Clear cyanoacrylate glue is preferable to epoxy resin adhesive. With epoxy resin, the joint line may be visible in translucent amber. And, because you will need to use denatured alcohol or acetone to clean excess epoxy from the surface, you risk damaging the amber.

Caring for mother-of-pearl

Mother-of-pearl is often cut and carved into jewelry and buttons, or inlaid into decorative objects. Never use strong solvents on it or soak it in water. It responds well to rubbing with the fingers, as the natural oil in your skin will remove all but the most stubborn grime. If necessary, wipe it with a rag dampened in milk, and dry with a soft cloth.

You can repair chipped mother-of-pearl with cyanoacrylate glue. Glue loose inlays back in place with a thin layer of epoxy resin adhesive. Strap the inlay in place with tape and weight it down until the glue has set.

Caring for coral

You cannot soak coral in any liquid, but you can wash it with warm, soapy water applied with a Q-tip. Clean large pieces by rubbing them carefully with breadcrumbs.

Branch coral necklaces are very difficult to clean because they are made up of small, irregular pieces. You should not soak the thread because it is likely to rot. Just wash a few pieces of coral at a time with an artist's paintbrush dipped in warm, soapy water. Dry them immediately using another dry artist's brush to absorb the moisture.

Making repairs
You can repair most coral jewelry with cyanoacrylate glue. When you are joining very small pieces you may find that fine tweezers and a modeling clay support are helpful. Glue large pieces with tinted epoxy resin adhesive.

Caring for enamel

Opaque or translucent enamel is usually mounted as a panel in a metal surround. It was made into jewelry, boxes and other small decorative items. It can be extremely valuable, particularly when it is delicately painted. Therefore, you should never undertake restoration without consulting an expert.

Cleaning procedure
Examine enamelware closely with a magnifier for signs of previous restoration. If you detect any, take the piece to an expert for renovation as you could clean off the repair. You should be particularly careful if the enamel appears to be flaking. If in doubt, take the piece to a jeweler.

The safest way to clean enamel that is in good condition is to wipe it gently with acetone on a soft cloth. You should test a small, unobtrusive area of the piece first. Take care not to wash the dirt into any cracks or crazing.

Caring for tortoiseshell and horn

Both these materials were used to make domestic and personal objects such as combs, shoe horns, jewelry, buttons and buckles. They were also used as inlay for boxes, furniture and dressing table sets.

To wash horn or tortoiseshell wipe them with wads of cotton dipped in warm, soapy water. Use almond oil to clean and revive them.

Making repairs
You can glue both horn and tortoiseshell with an epoxy adhesive. When relaying a piece of inlay, apply the glue thinly and evenly and weight or strap it down tightly until the glue sets. You can fill small areas of lost inlay with molten wax, mixing the colors to merge with the surrounding tints.

Making repairs
If an object is carelessly handled or dropped, pieces of enamel can chip off. Do not try to push back dents in the metal mount as this could result in even more enamel flaking off. Instead, use epoxy paste to fill the dents flush.

Restore opaque enamel like china (see pp. 27 & 35–8). Do not attempt to repair translucent enamel until you are very experienced at restoration. It is difficult to match the color and finish, and very hard to disguise the joint. If the repair is well done, however, you should only see a hairline crack. The base metal reflects light back through the material. To achieve the same effect, either scrape the base metal with a knife point, glue a tiny piece of varnished silver foil behind the repair, or paint the base with pearlized nail polish. When the surface is dry, match the color with inks, then gradually fill the enamel flush with clear varnish or cold cure lacquer.

CLOCKS

Collecting clocks

Old clocks are attractive as well as useful possessions which, by virtue of their design, variation of materials, and quality of craftsmanship, have a wide appeal to collectors.

If the appearance of clocks is more important to you than whether they work or not, consider buying one with a faulty movement just for its case. You could then try to find a contemporary movement. Do not reject a clock with a damaged case. You can buy replacement wooden moldings and brass fittings from clock suppliers.

Buying tips

● If you are contemplating buying a clock as an investment go to a reputable dealer, who will be able to guarantee its working condition and authenticity. Buying from auctions can be risky. Only spend your money when you have gained a sound knowledge of the subject.

● If you already have some experience of clocks, you should try auctions. Look out for clocks or movements beyond repair as they can be a source of spare parts. Missing parts should not put you off making a purchase as components are available from suppliers.

Damage checks

  ★ A simple repair
  ★★ Some experience needed
★★★ Skilled work—not for
    beginners

★★ General damage to the case will be obvious. Look to see if parts are missing by a change of color or tell-tale fixing holes.
★★ A clock movement is difficult to inspect when it is in its case, unless it has glass panels. A valuable test is to try winding it. Here a selection of keys is useful. If tension is felt, then the spring is likely to be in working order.
★★★ If the clock **does not run** try turning the train carefully by hand. If the key turns with no resistance and a rattling is heard, the spring is probably broken. This can be replaced, but the chances are that the gear train is also damaged. In such a case you should not buy the clock.

Dating clocks

Dating and valuing clocks can be difficult as many styles have been reproduced, and genuine early movements have been modified in later years to improve their timekeeping. Also, old movements are sometimes married with cases that are not contemporary with them. The design and development of clock movements and cases is a complex subject and you should refer to books on clocks, particularly if buying for investment.

The key points to look for are: the size, shape, construction and finish of the dial; the style of the hands; the type of case and the materials used; the quality of the movement; the presence of engraving and its quality; the type of escapement (see p. 87); the method of powering the movement. Names and dates will make things easier, but not all marks are genuine.

French clock This ormolu and white marble French-movement clock, c. 1900, has an additional key hole for winding the striking train.

American clock This turn-of-the-century clock (below) was inexpensive but is nowadays regarded as very collectable.

English clock This oak-cased clock has three winding holes —for the going train, the striking train, and the chime.

How a clock works

A clock which only tells the time is properly referred to as a timepiece. The movement consists of a gear train, which is a series of meshing toothed wheels and pinions (small toothed wheels) pivoted between brass plates. On early examples an open frame was used.

Power is applied at one end and regulated at the other. This arrangement of wheels is known as the "going train." Strictly speaking, a "clock" should have a bell to sound the hour. A separate set of gear wheels known as the "striking train" is used to operate the bell.

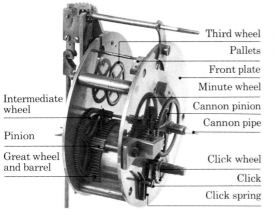

Third wheel
Pallets
Front plate
Minute wheel
Intermediate wheel
Cannon pinion
Cannon pipe
Pinion
Great wheel and barrel
Click wheel
Click
Click spring

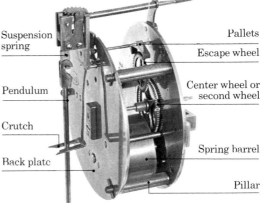

Suspension spring
Pallets
Escape wheel
Pendulum
Center wheel or second wheel
Crutch
Back plate
Spring barrel
Pillar

Powering the train

The power is applied to the largest and slowest-turning wheel of the train, known as the "great wheel." In long-case and some wall clocks the power is provided by a falling weight. The weight may be suspended by a rope or chain through pulley wheels in a 30-hour clock, or by a gut line around a barrel in an eight-day clock.

The introduction of the coiled spring as an alternative power source allowed clocks to be portable, but was unable to provide a constant rate of power.

Regulating the power

To overcome the problem of the coiled spring, English clocks used a "fusee," a conical spindle attached to the great wheel. It was so shaped to compensate for the decline in power as the spring ran down. A line of gut or fine chain is wound in a spiral groove around the fusee and attached at one end to the spring barrel. When the spring is fully wound—by winding the fusee arbor—its full power acts on the small end of the spindle. As it runs down, the line acts progressively on the larger end of the spindle.

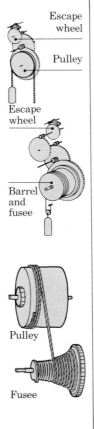

Escape wheel
Pulley
Escape wheel
Barrel and fusee

Pulley

Fusee

The going barrel

French clocks were also spring-driven, but the spring barrel and great wheel were made in one piece, known as the "going barrel." It worked by restricting the spring inside the barrel so that the more efficient middle of the spring was used.

Going barrel

The escapement

The going train is controlled by an escapement, which is a device governed by a pendulum or balance wheel in order to regulate the release of the power. The escapement acts on the last wheel, which is the weakest in the train and is known as the "escape wheel." It is, or would be if it were free to run, also the fastest. However, the wheel is interrupted by the escapement. The interrupter is usually a center-pivoted steel arm with shaped ends or pins known as "pallets." An arm known as the "crutch" is fixed to the pallet arbor and locates with the pendulum. The balance wheel, which uses a hair spring to make it oscillate, is linked to the escape wheel by the lever arm, which carries the pallets. Each pallet engages with a

Pendulum escapement

Barrel wheel

tooth of the escape wheel as the arm is rocked by the pendulum or balance wheel. The pallets and teeth of the escape wheel are so shaped that as the pallet moves away from the locked tooth it is given a little push or "impulse" in order to keep the pendulum or balance wheel in motion. The escape wheel rotates the distance of half a tooth before it is arrested by the descending pallet at the other end. It is this rocking motion of the escape wheel's pallets that gives the clock its characteristic "tick-tock" sound.

The motion work

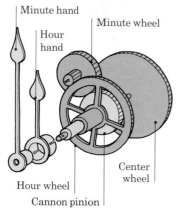

Minute hand

Minute wheel

Hour hand

Hour wheel

Center wheel

Cannon pinion

The hands are carried on a separate train of wheels and pinions mounted between the dial and the front plate and known as the "motion work." The "cannon pinion" carries the minute hand and forms a friction fit with the arbor of the center wheel, which drives the motion wheels. It revolves once every hour.

The hour hand is attached to the hour wheel, which rotates about the pipe of the cannon wheel, thus allowing the hands to revolve concentrically. A third gear wheel and pinion known as a "minute wheel" connects the two. The hour hand is geared to revolve once in twelve hours. The friction device on the motion work, which may be a flat or coiled spring or a tapered fit, allows the hands to be turned to time without turning the main gear train.

Tools and materials

The clock repairs covered here require only a few special tools and these are listed below. Some materials for cleaning movements can be bought from hardware stores, while others are available only from clock material suppliers.

Tools

Workbench A bench that you can sit down at, with a worktop that is about chest high, is most suitable for this sort of close work.
Fluorescent light A table-top fluorescent lamp fitted with an adjustable arm will give good, cool light.
Vise A small engineer's vise is generally adequate.
Hand vise This is used to hold small parts and to unwind springs.
Pliers Flat and needle-nosed pliers are most useful.
Eye glass This is used for close inspection of fine work. Choose a magnification to suit your needs.
Screwdrivers A set of watch-maker's screwdrivers from $\frac{1}{32} - \frac{1}{8}$ in (1–3 mm) is generally suitable.
Tweezers Fine-pointed tweezers are needed to hold small parts.
Paint brushes A selection of small decorator's and artist's bristle brushes are useful for washing parts with safety and cleaning solution.
Brass wire brush This is used to clean steel wheel arbors.
Hand brush You will need both a medium and soft clock-maker's bristle brush for cleaning and polishing the clock's movement.
Jars and dishes A flat dish and jars are used to hold cleaning fluid.

Materials

Safety solution This is used to wash off oil and dirt from the movement.
Ammonia Mix with water and liquid soap to make cleaning fluid. The fumes are unpleasant, so use in a well-ventilated room.
Clean rag Use only lint-free rag for cleaning.
Chalk block This is used with a brush to polish brass.
Pegwood Use pegwood sticks to clean out bearings and fine details. Pegwood is available from clock material suppliers.
Fine steel wool This is used to clean steel parts.
Fine abrasive paper Use this to rub down steel clock hands for refinishing.
Metal polish A proprietary polish is used for cleaning brass.
Silvering powder A preparation used for silvering brass dials.
Lacquer Use this to finish

the polished metal to prevent tarnishing.
Blue lacquer A colored lacquer for finishing clock hands.
Enamel paint This is used for touching-in dial numerals.
Artist's oil paint To paint in missing decoration on a dial use this type of paint.
Black wax This is used to fill engraved numerals.
Monofilament Use mono-filament to restring eight-day clock weights.
Braided rope This is used to restring 30-hour clock weights.
Tapered pins These are used to secure various parts of a clock movement. They are available in packs.
Clock oil For lubricating pivots and bearing surfaces use this fine oil.
Labels Use tie-on labels to identify parts of a dismantled clock.

Maintaining and repairing clocks

The maintenance and repair of clocks must be carried out with great care. You will probably know your own practical limitations, but if you are unsure of the history of your clock it is best to have it valued. If you are worried about any aspect of repair work, take the clock to a clock specialist.

Preparing for restoration work

Thorough cleaning of the movement is essential if the clock is to keep good time. Lay sheets of absorbent paper over your table and cover this with plain paper. You will need screwtop jars, small glass or china bowls, and a flat tray. Have at hand a supply of clean, lint-free rag, a selection of cleaning brushes, and a chamois. Wear rubber gloves to protect your hands and keep oil from your skin off metal parts. After cleaning (see following pages) check the parts for wear. Inspect pivots, pinions, wheel teeth, and bearing holes. Pivots can be bent through mishandling or grooved through wear, holes can wear oval and need bushing to true them, and broken wheel teeth require remaking or replacement.

Restoring the case

Repair, clean, and polish wooden clock cases as you would furniture (see pp. 104–111). Chipped veneer can be patch-repaired (see p. 107). Replace missing inlay by taking a rubbing of the shape and cutting a new piece to fit (see p. 107). Brass or ormolu metal mounts that have tarnished are best removed for cleaning. Extract the brass nails by careful leverage or remove the screws. (For cleaning see pp. 58–61.)

What makes a clock stop?

The problems listed in the chart below are all characterized by the clock stopping. Some repairs, marked with one box, you can do yourself. Others, marked with two boxes, need professional attention.

Cause	Remedy
Unwound mainspring	☐ Wind the spring
An accumulation of dirt and dried oil in the movement	☐ Strip and clean
A broken mainspring	☐ Replace the spring
Bent gearwheels	☐☐ Have new wheels made
Stripped gearwheel teeth	☐☐ Have a new wheel made
Worn pivots or bearings	☐☐ Have bearings bushed
Pendulum escapement out of "beat"	☐ Bend the crutch
Damaged hairspring in balance wheel escapement	☐☐ Have a new escapement fitted
Hands bent and catching	☐ Remove and straighten

Winding clocks

Get into the habit of winding a spring-driven movement regularly. Wind an eight-day clock every week, for example. In this way the same part of the spring is used, which gives a more constant rate of power and therefore better timekeeping.

Use only a key that is the correct size on the key arbor. Steady the clock with one hand and wind the spring by a set number of turns. Usually, six to eight complete turns will fully wind the spring. On some clocks "stop work" limits the number of turns to four or five.

A French barrel movement, which is clamped into the case by a back plate, has a tendency to rotate slightly in the case as the key is turned. This will upset the beat of the pendulum and must be avoided. Steady the movement by holding the bezel, or outer rim, of the clock face. If movement occurs tighten up the clamping screws at the back.

Regular winding of a weight-driven long-case clock is not so critical for timekeeping as the weights give constant power to the movement.

Putting a pendulum clock in beat

A pendulum clock must be "in beat" to run continuously and to keep time. The tick-tock sound of the clock should beat evenly. The pallets should be even in relation to the escape wheel when the pendulum is vertical. Bend or move the crutch arm slightly one way or the other to put it in beat. When bending a crutch hold it steady near the top to prevent straining the pallets. Cardboard packing can be used under one side or the other of the clock to determine which way it is out, but this should not become a permanent feature.

Regulating a pendulum

A pendulum clock is made to run faster or slower depending on the pendulum's length. Shortening it makes the clock run faster, lengthening it slower. Adjust length with the nut at the bottom. On some French clocks a key at the top of the dial is used for fine adjustment.

Dismantling a clock

Start by removing the pendulum. (With a weight-driven clock, you must first remove the weights.) Next take off the hands. Pull out the tapered retaining pin. Pull the hands off carefully. If you have to lever them off protect the dial with thin wood or plastic. Be particularly careful if the dial is an enamelled one.

Unscrew the fixings holding the movement in the case and lift it out. On long-case and early bracket clocks screws or bolts were used to secure it to a seat board. With some long-case clocks the movement simply stood on the seat board. Later, bracket-clock movements were held with metal brackets fixed to the back plate and the sides of the case. Remove the dial if it is attached to the movement (see p. 92).

Releasing a wound spring

Before you can start stripping the movement on a spring-driven clock the power must be let down. The spring tension can be released by running the train. This is done by removing the escapement pallets to let the spring run free. This is not advisable, however, with finely made old movements as the dirt in the bearings can cause unnecessary wear.

The correct way is to hold the spring arbor firmly with a large key or hand vise and let the spring down slowly by releasing the click wheel. Take great care as a runaway spring can strip teeth or buckle wheels in the gear train. Turn the key slightly as though to wind the spring and disengage the click from the click wheel.

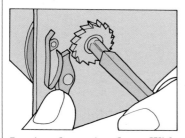

Letting the spring down With the click clear, let the spring down slowly. Re-engage the

click while you reposition your grip on the key or hand vise. Work in this way, releasing one or two teeth at a time.

Releasing a spring with stop work

A spring barrel in some movements may be fitted with "stop work." This is designed to stop the spring unwinding fully and being fully wound. Let this type down as described above until the stop is reached. The remaining turns on the spring are released once the barrel is removed from the movement.

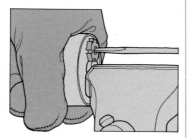

Using a bench vise Grip the winding square in the end of the vise. Unscrew the stop work retaining screw and remove the star wheel. Let the barrel slip slowly in your hand to release the remaining spring tension.

Removing the wheels

Study the works carefully and make notes and sketches indicating the positions of the parts. A little time spent at this stage should ensure that you will remember where things go when reassembling the clock. Unscrew the pallet cock from the back plate and lift out the pallets and crutch or remove the balance escapement. Remove the motion wheels and their cocks from the front plate.

Now, with the movement on its back, you can remove the pins or nuts securing the front plate to the pillars. Lift off the plate and extract the wheels. One way to keep things in order is to insert the arbor of each wheel in its relative position in the lid of a cardboard box. This should also ensure that the wheels are kept the right way up. Keep the other parts in the box. Assembly follows the same method in reverse (see p. 94).

Removing oil and dirt

Use safety solution to wash oil and dirt from the movement without changing the color of the brass. Half fill a jar with it and pour a little into a bowl. Soak a few parts at a time in the jar, adding others as you work. Very small items can be strung together by using a length of fuse wire.

Remove each piece and wash away the oil and dirt in the bowl, using a soft bristle brush. Use a stiffer bristle brush on wheels and textured parts.

Clean out holes and awkward corners or engraving with sharpened pegwood (see p. 88). After using the pegwood you may need to rinse again in clean safety solution. Dry the parts thoroughly with lint-free cloth. A hairdryer may be useful for awkwardly shaped parts.

Commercial non-ammoniated cleaning fluids are available which will loosen dirt and remove tarnish. These are worth buying for better-quality clocks.

You can make you own cleaner for removing tarnish and old lacquer with household ammonia and liquid soap. Dilute one part of ammonia with four parts of hot water, then add two or three squirts of liquid detergent and stir. A weaker solution can be used if the tarnish is light. Make sufficient cleaner to fully cover the parts to be cleaned. Never leave the brass partly covered as a dark tide mark can result. This stain is difficult to remove and requires a longer soaking, followed by laborious treatment with metal polish.

Soak the parts in the cleaner as required. The cleaner loosens the dirt and tarnish, much of which will float off if agitated. Lift each part in turn from the jar, immerse it in a bowl of the cleaner, and brush away dirt.

Finally, rinse off all traces of the solution with safety solution or clean water and a brush. Clean out holes and grooves with sharpened pegwood. Dry each part with the cloth and put aside. The brass should now be tarnish-free but relatively dull and ready for polishing.

Cleaning steel parts

Wash blued steel parts in safety solution. Wash and brush bright steel parts with a brass wire brush. Slight rust marks can be rubbed out with very fine 0000 steel wool. Revolve steel wheel arbors in a small pad of steel wool held between forefinger and thumb. Take care not to damage the pivot pins. Use a commercial rust remover for heavy rust, following the manufacturer's instructions. Wash off well with water and finish with the wire brush or steel wool.

Cleaning springs

This can be a tricky job, so take the simplest option first. Remove the cover from the main spring barrel by gently levering it out of its groove with a screwdriver or, preferably, by tapping the back end of the arbor on the worktable. Inspect the spring and if it appears to be free of thick, congealed oil simply apply about ten drops of clock oil and refit the cover. If rust is present the spring should be replaced. If the spring is gummed up it must be cleaned. Both procedures require the spring to be removed.

Carefully grip the barrel in shaped wooden blocks in a vise. Unhook the inner end of the spring from the arbor with pliers, then lift out the arbor. With a slight twisting action, as if to wind it, slowly pull the spring up and out. As more of the spring comes out you will find it easier to dispense with the pliers and use your hands. Wear leather gloves for protection while doing this. Unhook the outer end of the spring from the barrel wall. *Never* stress the spring by stretching it.

Clean the spring with a rag soaked in safety solution. Draw the loosely coiled spring through the rag held between needle-nosed pliers. Dry it with clean rag in the same way. Clean the barrel and arbor before replacing the spring. Attach the outer end of the spring to its hook in the barrel. With gloved hands, feed the spiral spring into the barrel turn by turn. Fit the arbor, check that it is the right way up, and engage the spring on its hook. Apply

fresh clock oil to the spring and fit the cover. With small barrels you might be able to snap in the cover by hand pressure. For larger or tight barrels make shaped wooden blocks to clear the rim and each end of the arbor, and refit the cover in a vise. Oil the arbor bearings.

Balance hairsprings are very delicate and are best left attached to the balance wheel and platform or cock. Loose dust can be lifted carefully with a fine sable artist's brush. Do not oil these springs. Should old oil and dirt be present try using a commercial cleaner, following the instructions.

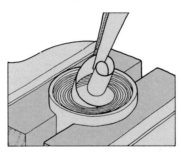

Removing the spring When doing this you should wear leather gloves to protect the hands.

Cleaning hands

Wash clock hands in safety solution and dry with a cloth. Marked or rusted hands should be rubbed with very fine abrasive paper, buffed to a polish, and reblued. A blue steel lacquer is available that can be applied by brush to retouch a blued hand or can be used to refinish the polished steel.

To blue hands using the traditional method, place them on a brass plate or bed of dry sand in a flat can and heat evenly on a stove. Watch for the color of the bright steel to change to blue. Quickly remove them from the heat using tweezers and immerse in clean motor oil. Wash off the oil with safety solution and dry. Alternatively, use a bluing salt from clock material suppliers. Heat the crystals until liquid and immerse the polished hands. Heat until the hands are blue in color, remove and quench with cold water.

Polishing plates, wheels, and other components

The traditional way to polish brass clock parts is to use a clock brush and a chalk block. Charge the brush with chalk powder by drawing it across the block and then work it over the metal. The rubbing action and the fine abrasive properties of the chalk impart a high shine.

Pegwood, available from specialist suppliers, is used in lengths, with one end sharpened to a round point, to clean out the holes and pinion leaves. Polish the edges of larger holes or piercings with a strip of cloth or chamois leather. Grip one end in a bench vise, pass the free end through the aperture, and with the cloth or leather pulled taut briskly rub the part along it.

A commercial metal polish can be used if preferred. Be sure that all traces are removed from the holes and engravings, otherwise the polish will show as white deposits when dry.

An early long-case clock will not require a high finish as many of its hand-finished parts are textured in their making and are not intended to be highly polished. French movements, particularly in carriage clocks, which were designed to show their movements through glass panels, will have been highly polished, however.

Handle the clean parts with tissue paper while working or, better still, wear cotton gloves. For small parts use tweezers. Finger marks, especially when on plates, look unsightly and the oil from your skin will quickly tarnish the metal. Replace the wheels in their respective holes in your box lid and store all the other pieces, wrapped in tissue, in the box.

Cleaning and repairing dials

Early dials were nearly square in shape. Three separate elements made up the dial: a brass face plate, a chapter ring, which carries the numbers, and decorative brass corner pieces known as spandrels. Generally, the center of the back plate, which was surrounded by the chapter ring, was textured by some form of tooling to give a mat finish. The corners to which the spandrels were applied were smooth and polished. Some dials had their centers engraved. Roman numerals were commonly used for the hours and Arabic for the minutes. A silver finish was usually applied to the chapter ring and engraved numerals were filled with black wax.

The arched dial became popular in the early eighteenth century and was used to display additional small dials or decoration. By the middle of the century round and painted dials were made. The painted dials had plain white backgrounds or were decorated with flowers or pictorial scenes. Plain white enameled dials with black numerals were used on French clocks from the early eighteenth century and later on English clocks.

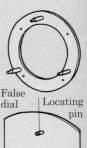

Enamel clock dial This dial is from an original French movement.

Mass-produced clock dial This reproduction dial is suitable for a mass-produced clock.

Break-arch dial A reproduction break-arch dial with moonphase for a longcase clock, made of brass.

Dismantling and cleaning dials

Generally, dials are fixed to the front plate of the clock's movement by dial "feet." Tapered pins are used to secure them. The feet may be screw-fixed to the back of the dial or permanently riveted in place (see right). Steady the movement on the bench and use nose pliers to pull the tapered pins from the dial feet. Sometimes a pin may be bent because a mis-aligned hole has strained it. To remove a tight pin use a twisting action, carefully pulling at the same time.

Brass dials with an applied chapter ring and spandrels are best cleaned with the clock cleaning solution and polished. Do not use the cleaner or metal polishes on silvered parts. For dials that are part silvered, all silvered, painted, or enameled, wash only with mild soap and lukewarm water. Then rinse thoroughly, and dry the dial with a clean, soft cloth.

Riveted dial foot

False dial With brittle enameled dials a false dial (see top right) is used to carry the dial feet. The dial itself is prevented from rotating by small pins (see bottom right), either projecting from the false dial or soldered to the back of the dial before it is enameled.

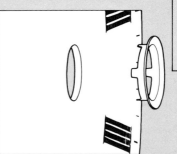

False dial | Locating pin

Cleaning keyholes On enameled dials, keyholes are usually lined with a brass rim. When cleaning, take care not to damage the thin metal.

Repairing dials

Before attempting repairs on the dial consider the value of the clock. In some cases it is better to accept damage caused by wear and tear than to have the dial repaired or restored. If you have a valuable piece in need of work seek the services of a professional dial restorer. More recent mass-produced clocks are unlikely to be valuable and their dials can be repaired at home.

Silvered dials

The silver coating used on clock faces is very thin, and over-zealous cleaning can expose the brass underneath. If this is the case, you can re-silver the brass with silver chloride powder. Degrease the surface with safety solution and wash with soap and water. Wear rubber gloves.

1 Apply the powder with a dampened soft cloth or cotton pad. Dip the cloth or pad in the powder and work over the surface with a circular motion until it is even in color. Rinse in clean water. A fixing powder is applied in the same way. Alternatively, use a clear lacquer (see p. 88). Retouch numerals with enamel paint.

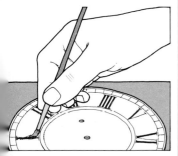

2 For a dial which has lost all its wax you could try applying

your own with black heelball. Warm the metal with a hair-dryer and melt some wax in a dish. Paint it into the grooves and when set wipe off excess with denatured alcohol.

Painted dials

To meet the demands of mass-production dial painting became a specialized trade. Through repetition the dial painters were capable of producing dials quickly and skilfully. Layers of primer were used to smooth out any unevenness in the surface and the numerals and decoration were applied over the background color. You will need artistic ability for this.

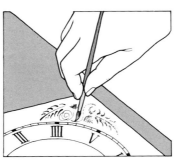

Painting in numerals These can be touched in with a fine sable brush and enamel paint available from art stores. If the color has been rubbed away look across the surface in good light. Traces of the markings should be seen and these can be used as a guide for painting. Use artist's oils to touch in pictorial scenes.

Enameled dials

This type of dial is brittle and needs careful handling, particularly when removing the hands. The classic and highly legible white enameled dial was produced by fusing the enamel to a copper plate. In some cases the numerals may be painted on the surface or applied to the polished surface before final firing.

Repairs to enameled dials are difficult. Nothing can be done to restore a cracked dial fully. A replacement is often required—but if it carries an important name this is unwise. If you can find an identical dial on a clock

that is otherwise beyond repair you will be fortunate. One solution is to apply a printed facsimile dial in the style of the original. These are available from clock material suppliers. This does nothing to enhance the clock's value, however.

A chipped edge can be repaired with an epoxy adhesive and kaolin powder, touched-in with paint (see pp. 84 and 88).

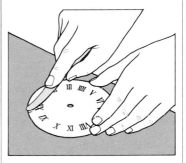

Repairing a chipped edge Mix the epoxy adhesive, kaolin powder, and titanium dioxide to a paste that approximates to the color of the enamel. Apply it with a knife blade and when set rub down with fine abrasive paper and polish with an abrasive cream. Match with paint. Numerals that have been affected by the repair can be painted in carefully with a fine sable brush and black enamel.

Replacing missing hands

Suppliers of clock parts usually stock hands in a range of styles and sizes. Consult illustrated books to decide the style best suited to your clock. Make a drawing of the design and try to match it from the supplier's range. You may have to compromise. The size of the hands is important since the minute hand should reach the minute ring and the hour hand should fall on the base of the numerals. If you cannot take the dial to the supplier make a paper pattern for reference.

Assembling a clock

Once the clock has been cleaned, repaired and restored, assemble the movement in the reverse order to dismantling. Fit the corner pillars to the back plate and then insert the wheels and barrels into their respective holes.

Carefully locate the front plate over the pillars and pivots and secure with new tapered pins. Fit the motion wheels, click work, cocks, pallets, and crutch. Apply a touch of clock oil to the pivots only.

Setting up a fusee

Old gut line is liable to break, causing serious damage to the wheels. Replace it with mono-filament or braided monofilament while the movement is dismantled. Wire is also used or, with better movements, a fine chain. Remove the great wheel from the back of the fusee. Pass one end of the monofilament through the single hole in the fusee and tie a knot in it. Re-assemble the fusee.

1 Attach the unknotted end of the monofilament to the barrel through the three holes. Set the fusee and barrel between the plates as described. Loosely fit the barrel click work on the out-side of the front plate. Slowly wind the monofilament onto the barrel, keeping it even. Hold it taut.

2 Tension the spring by wind-ing the barrel arbor by half a turn. Locate the click and tighten its screw. The main spring is now "set up." Fit the pallets and crutch assembly. Wind the spring using the fusee arbor. Guide the monofilament onto the fusee spiral as it is wound.

3 A fusee chain is made with hooks at each end. The round hook locates in the fusee hole, while the "barbed" hook fits into the barrel.

Setting up the weights

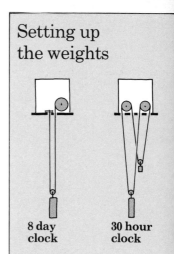

| 8 day clock | 30 hour clock |

With an eight-day clock, knot one end of the weight mono-filament into the barrel. Fit the assembled movement into its case. Pass the free end through the weight pulley and tie it to the seat board. A toggle which bridges the hole is sometimes used. Fit the weight and wind the barrel with the key. Check that the monofilament winds evenly onto the outside of the barrel. The length of the monofilament should not be so great as to overrun the end of the barrel.

Thirty-hour clocks with a striking train have a con-tinuous loop of rope or chain to carry the weights. Pass a length of monofilament over the movement pulleys and weight pulleys as shown. The monofilament should pull in a clockwise direction. Close the end link of the chain to form the loop or splice the rope (see left). Attach the weight and counterweight to their respec-tive pulleys. Pull down on the counterweight to wind both the going and striking trains.

Splicing a rope

Soft braided rope is used for suspending clock weights and is made up of twelve strands around a central strand. It can be difficult to splice, but with patience the amateur should achieve reasonable results.

Cut the rope to the required length and pass it through the pulleys. Bind the rope with a small elastic band about 2 ins (5 cm) from each end. Unwind the strands back to the band and separate evenly. Lay the strands end to end.

1 Apply a fabric adhesive to the strands and glue them to-gether. Overlap them about $\frac{3}{8}$ in (9 mm) and roll the joint between your fingers. Work carefully to ensure that each pair is glued in turn. When the glue is set, tie the center strand with a small reef knot to pull the two banded ends together.

2 Using a darning needle, pull one of the glued loops along and then out through the braided rope, working a little at a time and following the weave. Work the next loop back the other way. Pull all the loops, alternating their direction in this way. Stagger the exit off the loops along the rope and cut the loops off flush.

FURNITURE

Buying furniture

Apart from the major museums and country houses, few people buy antique furniture purely to build a collection. Most of us buy or inherit ordinary, solidly built old pieces that we use for their original purpose. There are many repair jobs you can safely carry out on this type of furniture, but if the piece is particularly old or valuable it is best to consult a professional restorer first.

If you follow the care guidelines on the opposite page, and polish pieces regularly, they are likely to last and look good for years.

Genuine or reproduction?

It is useful to know whether you are being offered a reproduction or fake or a piece of furniture that is genuinely old. A reproduction is a piece made as an honest copy of earlier furniture and sold as such. However, it may be offered as a period piece by a later owner. A fake, on the other hand, is made and sold with the intention to deceive. It is very difficult for anyone but an expert to spot a really good fake because the makers know exactly what you are looking for to determine age, and they imitate these features too. However, because reproductions were not made to fool you deliberately, they are usually quite easy to detect.

Your first clue is the general appearance of the piece. An old piece of furniture will show signs of wear and tear, whereas a reproduction might have perfectly crisp edges on corners, moldings, legs and stretcher rails. Next, look at the finish closely. A reproduction will be very even in color, but an old piece will have mellowed, perhaps faded slightly in parts, and the polish will sometimes have worn off the high points of carving and from areas of hard use like the arms of chairs. Chipped or blistered veneers are also a good sign of authenticity, as these are not reproduced by a modern manufacturer. If it has been well cared for, the wood of a genuine piece will have a deep, attractive sheen, known as patina, that is virtually impossible to fake.

Ultimately, the ability to detect a genuine antique is a question of gaining experience and knowledge, and developing an eye for whether a piece looks "right".

Conversions and marriages

Because certain large old pieces are not in great demand, some dealers buy them cheaply and convert them into items which have a greater value. The "converted" piece will have the patina and wear of age, so how do you find out whether or not it has been doctored? Look for new strips of veneer in tell-tale places— for example, along the back of a desk, where a dressing table's mirror would have been sited. Recut wood is another sign— look for newly stained edges.

A similar practice is known as a "marriage". This involves putting together bits from separate items to make a new piece. Check that the wood of top and bottom sections matches. Any inlay or carving should be carried through on both parts. And both halves should be in proportion.

An example of a "marriage"

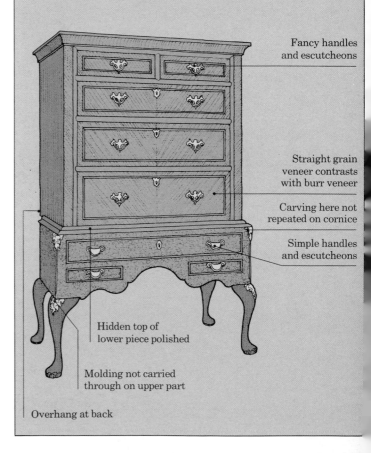

Fancy handles and escutcheons

Straight grain veneer contrasts with burr veneer

Carving here not repeated on cornice

Simple handles and escutcheons

Hidden top of lower piece polished

Molding not carried through on upper part

Overhang at back

Caring for antique furniture

Strong light and heat can damage wooden furniture, so consider carefully where you position your antiques. Do not stand a piece of furniture in direct sunlight for long periods at a time. If you must place an item in such a position, move it occasionally so that it does not discolor. Do not put it directly in front of a radiator either, as this can dry out the wood causing shrinkage problems. Central heating creates an over-dry atmosphere which can damage antiques. To counteract this, you should attach humidifiers to all your radiators.

Treat soft finishes like French polish with respect as they are easy to damage—use heat-resistant mats for hot mugs and plates, and coasters under glasses. You should wipe up any spills immediately.

Inspect furniture for woodworm from time to time. Look especially at unfinished surfaces—the backs and undersides of pieces.

Identifying wood

A vast range of woods have been used for furniture making, and you would have to be an expert to identify most of them. Here we have covered some of the very popular woods which have been in continuous use for centuries.

Oak This wood has a beige to pale gray background with a darker-brown flecked grain pattern. It is very hard, with open pores.

Pine This wood is yellowy cream in color, with a pale beige, sometimes very wild, grain. Veneers adhere well to it, and so it became the most frequently used wood for cabinet grounds after oak. Although pine is often finished in a clear polish today, it was never considered as a show wood in the past, and was usually either painted or veneered.

Walnut This wood has a creamy brown background with a highly figured dark brown to black grain. Its main use was as a veneer for chests and cupboards, but it was also used in solid form to make chairs and table frames.

Elm Because elm has a high resistance to splitting, it was often used for carved solid chair seats. It is very pale beige in color.

Maple This light-colored wood has a close, heavily figured grain. The "bird's-eye" and "curly" types have been used for centuries for decorative veneering.

Mahogany From the beginning of the eighteenth century right through the nineteenth, mahogany was a popular wood for all kinds of furniture. The earliest and best types of mahogany came from Cuba, then Honduras. The color ranges from a reddish to a dark brown. Not as figured as walnut, it is a dense wood with an even grain. This makes it ideal for furniture, particularly when carved.

Satinwood This is a light, yellowish wood which can be very figured. It was used a great deal for veneered cabinet work from the end of the eighteenth century until the early twentieth century. By this time, however, cheaper woods were often stained or finished with tinted polish to imitate it.

Some wood types

Oak   Pollard oak   Elm   Maple

Scotch pine   Oregon pine   Mahogany   Satinwood

American walnut   English walnut   Ebony   Padouk

Tools and materials

You will need a fair-sized workshop if you are going to restore furniture properly. Apart from housing your workbench and tools, you will have to store materials and still leave plenty of room for the item itself. A garage or a well-lit basement room are possible sites. Make sure that you have an adequate supply of daylight and good artificial light for working in the evening. If your lighting is poor, you will miss small blemishes which will mar a finished job once it is taken into a properly lit interior.

You should install an adequate number of electrical socket outlets, preferably along the back of your workbench. You will have many flammable materials on hand—especially polishes, lacquers and wood shavings—so it is wise to keep a fire extinguisher in your workshop. And store your materials out of reach of children, or in a lockable cupboard.

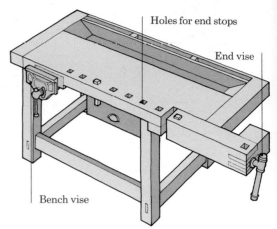

Holes for end stops

End vise

Bench vise

Woodworker's bench There is no substitute for a good hardwood carpenter's bench. In addition to a special woodworker's vise, it should have an end vise.

Tools

The nature of furniture restoration is so varied that there are many tools you will find useful, if not essential. Though you may have some woodworking tools already, you will probably want to supplement them with a few more specialized items.

Rule You will need a folding or retractable steel tape calibrated with imperial and metric measurements to allow you to check one system against the other instantly.

Try square Use this to mark or check right-angles. Choose one that has a blade not less than 9 ins (23 cm) long. A combination square is a good buy as it will also mark 45° angles and includes a spirit level.

Marking gauge This scribes a line parallel to an edge or face, working with the grain. You set the stock to the required distance from the marking pin and hold it firmly against the edge of the work while pushing the tool forward. The pin scribes the line as it goes.

Cutting gauge This is similar to the marking gauge, but has a sharp flat blade to mark the line across the grain.

Mortise gauge This is another marking gauge, but with twin pins which you adjust to mark

both sides of a mortise or tenon simultaneously.

Compass Use this drawing instrument to mark a pencil line to a set radius. To protect the work from the point, tape a piece of cardboard to the surface.

Calipers This measuring tool has two legs which you can set finely by a screwed nut. Use it to measure internal and external diameters of turned parts.

Needle template Use this to copy the profile of a molded or shaped part. It has a row of straight needles which slide in a carrier to mimic any shape against which they are pressed.

Marking knife A woodworking marking knife has a short, thick stiff blade and is ground on one side. Hold the flat side against the guide and score a line where a cut is to be made. Some craftsmen use a well-sharpened penknife instead.

Punches You will need a center punch which has a blunt point for marking the center of holes before drilling. You will also need a nail set, with a flat tip for driving nail heads below the surface of the wood.

Rip saw This is the largest size of handsaw, and has coarse, chisel-shaped teeth. It is used for cutting with the grain only

when cutting planks to size.

Cross-cut saw This is slightly smaller than the rip saw, and has finer teeth which are sharpened at an angle for severing wood fibers. It is designed primarily to cut across the grain of the wood, but can also cut with the grain.

Panel saw This small handsaw is a useful general-purpose tool for cutting sheet materials and for cross-cutting.

Tenon saw This general-purpose bench saw has a heavy brass or steel capping along the back edge to keep the blade rigid.

Dovetail saw Similar to the tenon saw, this has very small teeth for cutting fine joints.

Coping saw This saw has a narrow blade tensioned across an open frame for cutting tight curves in timber.

Fret saw This saw has fine teeth for cutting curves in thin sheet material. Its deep frame allows you to cut a long way from the edge of the board.

Compass saw This has a narrow, tapered blade for cutting holes in areas that are too far away from an edge for a coping saw to reach. You must drill a starter hole so that you can insert the blade tip.

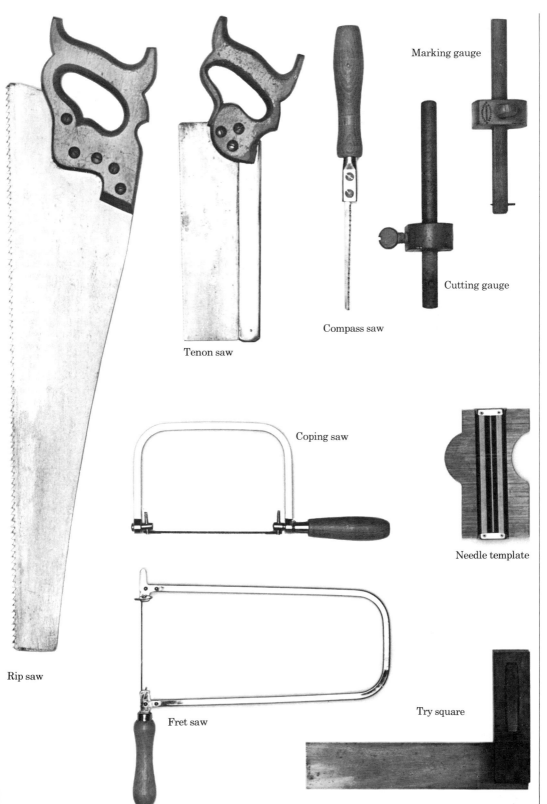

Tenon saw

Compass saw

Marking gauge

Cutting gauge

Coping saw

Needle template

Fret saw

Try square

Rip saw

Bench hook This is a sort of cutting board. It hooks onto the edge of the bench, allowing you to hold a piece of wood against the end block or stop while you are sawing it.

Miter box The angled slots in the sides of a miter box guide a saw blade when cutting miters or right-angle joints.

Bench planes These will accurately square and smooth wood. There are different sizes of bench plane: a try plane with a very long sole for planing mating edges, a smoothing plane with a much shorter sole, and a general-purpose jack plane which falls between the two. If you cannot afford all three, start with a jack plane.

Block plane Use this small plane in one hand for trimming end grain and detailed work.

Combination plane This is not an essential tool, but it is extremely useful to restorers because it is so versatile. It has adjustable fences and guides, plus a variety of blades, which will cut grooves, rebates and beading. There is an even more sophisticated version, known as a multi-plane, which will cut a wide variety of moldings too.

Spokeshaves Use these to smooth curved surfaces. You will need one for convex shapes and a rounded sole version for concave curves.

Cabinet scrapers These are simply pieces of sheet steel with a burr raised along one edge. This acts like a miniature plane, scraping tiny shavings from the wood to clean and smooth it. Shaped scrapers will work curves.

Files and rasps Woodworking files have teeth much like those used to shape metal, but they are much coarser. Rasps have long triangular teeth for rough shaping wood. Flat, half-round and round types are available.

Chisels You will need a range of chisels, not only in different sizes, but also a selection with specially shaped blades to carry out specific tasks. Firmer chisels with a rectangular sectioned blade are a strong, general-purpose tool. Beveled-edge chisels are lightweight paring tools especially designed for working an undercut like a dovetail joint. Mortise chisels have strong, square blades to lever out the

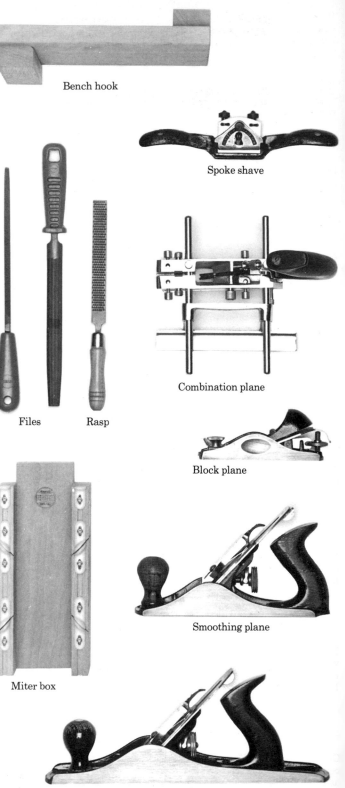

Bench hook

Spoke shave

Files   Rasp

Combination plane

Block plane

Miter box

Smoothing plane

Jack plane

Beveled
-edge
chisel

Beveled
-edge
chisel

Lathe
gouge

Lathe
gouge

Phillips-
head
screwdriver

Straight tip
screwdriver

Cabinet
screwdriver

Ball-peen
pin
hammer

Medium
weight
cabinet
hammer

Cross-
peen pin
hammer

waste wood when cutting a mortise. You will also find one or two gouges useful. They are beveled on the inside or outside for cutting concave or convex shapes.

Lathe chisels and gouges
These wood-turning tools are specially made for working with a lathe, when force is applied across the blade. Gouges are made in widths from $\frac{3}{8}$ in (9 mm) to 1 in (25 mm). They are ground on the convex side to form a square or round cutting edge. The gouge is used for rough turning and sizing. The round type is for making coves or working hollows.

Chisels are $\frac{1}{2}$–1 in wide (12–25 mm) and are ground on both sides to form a knife edge. They can have a square edge or be set at an angle when they are known as skew chisels. Use a chisel to finish the surface and cut fine detail. Scraping chisels are made in widths from $\frac{1}{2}$–1 in (12–25 mm), and are ground on one side. The cutting edge can be square, round or V-shaped. They are easy tools to use for turning, but the work will need sanding afterwards.

A parting tool is a narrow chisel, usually $\frac{3}{16}$ in (4 mm) wide and ground on both edges. You use it to cut a groove into the work to separate end waste.

Screwdrivers It is important that the tool fits the screw exactly in order to be efficient. You will need at least one large cabinet and one Phillips-head screwdriver. Add smaller ones to your kit as you need them.

Hammers A mediumweight claw hammer will be useful, especially as you can draw nails with it. Choose a lightweight cross-peen pin hammer for small nails and panel pins.

Mallets You will need a wooden carpenter's mallet for driving chisels and for tapping components together. Although you can use a softwood block to protect the work from a hammer, a soft-faced mallet is better.

Pincers and pliers Use carpenter's pincers for extracting nails and tacks. You will also need general-purpose engineer's pliers to crop wire and manipulate small sections of metal. Use pliers with pointed and rounded jaws for small items.

Clamps C clamps are very useful tools, and it is worth having several in different sizes. A couple of medium-sized sash clamps are necessary for regluing frames and clamping boards together. Large sash clamps are expensive, and it is better to rent them.

Trimming knife You will need a trimming knife with razor-sharp disposable blades. A scalpel with a variety of fine, shaped blades is also useful.

Wheel brace Buy a hand-operated drill for small drill bits.

Brace Use this for drilling large diameter holes. You can fit it with a variety of bits, including a screwdriver head for extracting stubborn screws.

Bradawl The chisel-like tip of a bradawl cuts across wood fibers to make a starter hole for very small screws.

Bench vise This proper woodworking vise is fitted permanently to a carpenter's bench. It has wide, smooth jaws and often has a quick-release mechanism that enables you to adjust the gap between the jaws quickly. Otherwise, you can use a smaller vise which clamps to the edge of a table or bench.

Workmate bench This portable bench is virtually a large vise. It is extremely useful as you can adjust it to grip a variety of objects.

Power tools A range of power tools can be expensive, but they are well worth the investment in terms of time saving and accuracy. A power drill is essential, particularly as it is capable of accepting a large range of attachments which will convert it to other uses. For example, a drill stand enables you to drill more accurately than is possible by hand. A circular saw is not essential, but it can save you a lot of work when you have to cut up a large amount of wood. A jig saw is more useful for cutting curves and large holes.

A power sander can reduce the effort of sanding large panels. Do not rely on it to provide a finished surface, however. It leaves tiny swirl-like scratches which you will have to sand out by hand before applying a clear finish. A lathe attachment is perfectly adequate for turning small items.

Brace

Jig saw

C clamps

Power sander

Sash clamp

Power drill

Circular power saw

Materials

Mineral spirits Use this to thin finishes and to clean furniture.

Linseed oil Mix this oil with mineral spirits to make a furniture cleaner. It is traditionally used for oiling wood. However, it takes a long time to dry, and there are better finishing oils available today (see p. 111).

Steel wool Use very fine grade steel wool to mat down gloss finishes. You can also use it with denatured alcohol to clean off old wax polish.

Liquid abrasives Burnishing cream, auto paint cleaner and metal polish are all abrasive enough to remove stains from a polished surface and revive a dull one.

Two-part bleach A strong commercial bleach which may even take the color out of wood.

Denatured alcohol This will remove some ink stains and can be used to strip shellac from furniture. It is also employed during French polishing to lift out linseed oil.

Wax crayons Melt these down and use them to fill tiny holes.

Filling compound A commercial product for filling medium and large holes in wood.

Plastic Wood This filler sets hard enough to rebuild chipped or broken edges.

Woodworm fluid A chemical insecticide which kills the larva of the furniture beetle and prevents reinfestation.

Candle wax Use this to lubricate sticking drawers and doors.

Chemical stripper There are several products which will dissolve old paints and varnishes (see p. 108).

Grain filler This is made from china clay or chalk plus coloring pigments bound together by a mixture of mineral spirits and linseed oil. It fills up the pores in open-grained wood.

Stains For a description of wood stains see pp. 109–10.

Wood finishes For a list of finishes see pp. 110–11.

Abrasives Abrasive papers are available in coarse, medium and fine grades (these refer to the relative size of the grit). Each grade is available as closed coat—with the grains packed tightly together for fast sanding—or open coat—with the grains widely spread to avoid clogging when sanding resinous woods.

Glasspaper is a relatively soft, yellow paper, suitable for first sanding only. It is often erroneously referred to as sandpaper, which no longer exists. Garnet paper is a better quality, reddish colored abrasive which you should use for finer sanding.

Silicon carbide paper can be pale gray in appearance and is dusted with dry lubricant of zinc oxide. Use a very fine grade of this paper for rubbing down in between coats of French polish. It is also found in black—known as "wet-and-dry" paper. This type is primarily used by restorers with water to rub down paintwork.

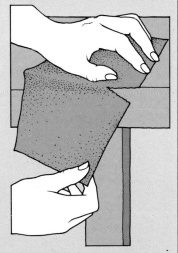

Dividing a sheet of abrasive
Fold the paper along the required line, then tear it over the edge of a bench.

Glues

Animal glue This is the kind of glue you will most often find in old joints. It is still available today in the form of cakes or beads which you have to melt in a heated glue pot. There are better glues today for joining wood, but animal glue is still used for veneering.

Polyvinyl acetate This modern water-thinned adhesive is ideal for gluing wood. It is white in color, and so is known as white glue.

Glue film Specially developed for gluing veneers, this is a sheet of glue that you lay between the veneer and the groundwork, and activate by heat (see p. 221).

Epoxy resin This is not used a great deal in furniture restoration, but you may need it for gluing back small pieces of inlay.

French polishes

All French polish is made from shellac—a substance exuded by insects—dissolved in alcohol. There are several different types for different purposes.

Button shellac This is the standard polish for antique furniture.

Cream polish This is bleached standard polish for pale wood.

Natural liquid wax Even more suitable for light woods, this is made by allowing the wax to settle out of cream polish.

Orange shellac This is a warmer colored shellac, used for finishing mahogany and similar woods.

Cleaning furniture

Over the years, a layer of dust and old wax builds up on wood, until a dull film gradually obscures its color and grain. Eventually, you will need to use a "reviver" to clean off this film and bring out the full beauty of the wood again.

If your piece of furniture is stained, the type of treatment it requires will depend on whether the damage is just in the depth of the polish or has reached the wood itself.

Cleaning wood

Wash grime from furniture with a "reviver"—a mixture of 4 parts of mineral spirits to 1 part of linseed oil—on a cloth. This will not affect any finish other than wax polish, which it lifts off along with accumulated dirt. It will not lift veneer, or raise the grain of the wood. From time to time refold the cloth so that its surface is clean. If your furniture is really dirty, use the reviver on a ball of 000 grade steel wool. Do not apply too much pressure, and work in the direction of the grain so that you do not scratch the finish beneath. Then wipe the wood with a clean cloth dampened in mineral spirits. After cleaning, you should apply a fresh coat of wax or French polish.

Cleaning painted furniture

To remove greasy deposits from painted or lacquered pieces wash them with a rag dipped in warm, soapy water. Do not flood the surface, as water can penetrate the joints and make them swell. You should wash larger items a little at a time, working upward from the bottom to avoid streaking. Finally, rinse the piece carefully with a rag dipped in clean water and then rub the surface dry with a clean, soft cloth.

Removing white patches

White blemishes are a result of the surface of soft finishes like French polish breaking up. There are a number of causes for this. Water can leave a blemish—a wet glass left on a table overnight will etch a ring into the polish. Alcohol or nail varnish remover will also dissolve the finish, and heat will melt it. Fortunately, these marks are often no deeper than the top layer of polish. To eradicate them, apply a liquid metal polish or auto paint cleaner on a soft damp cloth, rubbing down the finish to below the level of the stain. Examine the piece from different angles to make sure that no traces of the blemish remain before repolishing.

Coping with dark rings or patches

If water finds its way below the finish it often leaves a dark stain. Cutting back the finish with metal polish may be successful, but usually you will have to strip the finish locally or even bleach the wood (see p. 108).

Removing ink stains

First, try rubbing the stain with metal polish in case the ink has not penetrated the finish. If this does not work, you will find that denatured alcohol will remove some artists' inks. Damp a cloth with it, wrap it around your finger and rub the area of the stain. Use as little denatured alcohol as possible because it dissolves French polish.

If neither of these methods work, you will have to strip the polish locally with denatured alcohol or chemical stripper (see p. 108), then apply bleach to the stain with a small paintbrush (see p. 108). Touch in the resulting pale patch with wood stain and then repolish it.

Removing candle wax

If candle wax falls on a piece of furniture, wait until it solidifies, then pick it off with your fingernail or a plastic spatula. Use reviver to wash any remaining wax from the surface, then apply some fresh wax polish.

Repairing surface damage

You can expect to find dents, scratches and other minor damage on regularly used furniture. These are important clues to age and authenticity. In fact, makers of reproduction furniture often age their pieces by "distressing" them—burning the surface with soldering irons or hitting it with stones, knives and chains. When you are restoring an antique, you must decide whether to repair this type of damage or ignore it. If in doubt, leave it alone. However, if the piece is disfigured in any way, the remedies are relatively simple.

Raising dents

To raise a dent in solid wood, lay a damp cloth on it and then apply a heated soldering iron directly over the damage. The steam generated will swell the wood locally, pushing the crushed fibers back to their original level. Unfortunately, this treatment ruins the finish, so once the wood has dried sand the spot smooth and re-polish.

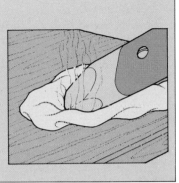

Dealing with burns

If the finish is scorched you can improve it by rubbing it with metal polish. But if the wood is charred you must scrape it off with a sharp, rounded blade. Fill the resulting hole with a stopper, or, if it is shallow, level it with polish.

Disguising scratches

You can polish out fine scratches with a metal polish or disguise them by rubbing them with shoe polish or commercial scratch remover. Fill deep scratches with wax polish or lacquer. Modern lacquers are thick enough to use directly from the tin. But with French polish, you must pour a little into a shallow dish and leave it to evaporate until it stiffens slightly.

Lightly rub the scratch flush with fine sandpaper. Use a pointed artist's paintbrush to put a layer of polish along the scratch, leaving it raised. The polish will sink as it hardens, but keep building it up until it sets raised. Scrape it flush with a knife, then buff it to a shine with metal polish.

Filling holes and cracks

Filling a hole poses no problems as it will not change in size. However, a crack could be the result of the wood shrinking in an over-dry atmosphere, and it may close up if conditions alter and the wood swells slightly. If you have had the piece for a number of years and it has shown no tendency to move, you could safely fill a crack or open joint. But if the item is recently acquired, place it in its intended position for a while before mending it. This will give it time to adjust to the new conditions. If possible, glue a crack or split rather than fill it.

The materials you use for filling will depend on the extent of the damage. To disguise the repair, match the color carefully.

Using wax

Wax is an ideal medium for filling small woodworm-type holes. Using a small soldering iron, mix wax crayons in a tin lid to get the right color. When the wax has cooled, press scrapings into the holes with a knife or chisel blade, then burnish it with the back of a piece of abrasive paper. Finally, seal the wax with polish.

Using fillers

To fill large holes use a commercial filler. These are sold by hardware stores in a range of wood-simulating colors. For an exact match, you may have to add a little wood stain. Undercut the edge of a shallow hole to provide a better key, then press the stopper in using a flexible blade such as a palette knife. With a crack, fill across it then press the blade along its length. Leave the filler standing slightly raised so that you can finish it off with very fine abrasive paper when it has set.

Using Plastic Wood

Plastic Wood is a commercial filler which sets hard. It is useful for repairing damage on an unsupported edge. Press it into place with a knife blade, shaping it roughly to match the contour. When set, sand it flush with the original surface.

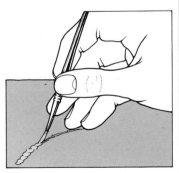

Filling deep scratches Take a brushload of your chosen polish and "paint" it into the scratch, making sure that it stands higher than the old level.

Veneers and inlays

Veneers are thin sheets of real wood glued to a thicker backing, usually a solid softwood or cheap hardwood. Veneering was introduced in about 1600, not only to cope with the rising cost of hardwoods, but also to take best advantage of some of the beautiful grain patterns of these woods. Veneers were originally sawn by hand and were therefore relatively thick, but since the nineteenth century they have been machine-cut. This produces a much thinner sheet.

Colored woods (marquetry) and other thin sheet materials like brass, tortoiseshell and ivory (inlays) are often set into a veneered surface to make decorative patterns.

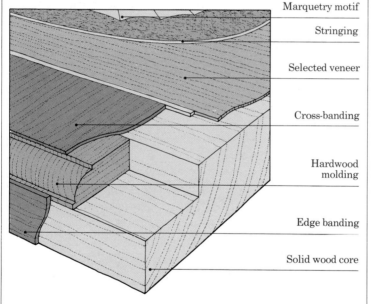

Marquetry motif

Stringing

Selected veneer

Cross-banding

Hardwood molding

Edge banding

Solid wood core

Where to obtain veneers

You can re-use old veneer if you are prepared to strip it from badly damaged, unrestorable pieces. Strip off the polish, then lay wet cloths over the veneer. Either leave them overnight, or apply a hot domestic iron on top to generate steam and lift them quickly. Scrape and wash off the old glue while it is still soft, then lay the veneer between chipboard to keep it flat until it has dried. Put sheets of newspaper between the veneer and the boards to make sure that traces of glue do not stick them together.

Otherwise, you can buy veneers from specialist suppliers. In order to match the veneer, take a drawer or table top with you if possible, or send a piece of loose veneer to a mail order supplier. You can buy ready-made stringing, banding, patterns and even complete pictorial motifs in a range of woods to replace missing components.

Restoring dented veneers

You can raise dents by using the solid-wood method described on p. 105. But because the steam will soften the glue holding the veneer to its ground, you must clamp or weight the veneer as soon as you have eliminated the dent. Put a block of softwood over the area and fix it in place with a C or sash clamp. To apply pressure in the middle of a table top place two strips of stout timber across the table, one on top and one beneath, with a clamp at each end. Leave in place until the glue has set.

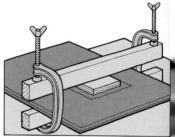

Clamping dented veneer
Once you have steamed out the dent, place a block of softwood on the area and clamp it up. This will prevent the veneer lifting.

Restoring blistered veneers

Patches of veneer can become detached if there is movement within the solid wood ground, and if these swell they will form a raised "blister." It is sometimes possible to soften the original glue and press back the blister. First, steam the area with a wet cloth and heated iron until you can lay the blister flat. Then clamp it as described for raising a dent.

If this is unsuccessful, cut a slit along the blister and work glue under it with a knife blade. Press the blister down with a wallpaper seam roller or a veneer hammer, and wipe off excess glue with a damp cloth. Stick a strip of paper tape along the slit to prevent it opening up, cover this with a piece of newsprint under a softwood block, and clamp it.

Laying loose veneers

If a veneer is lifting up at one edge or corner, glue it back as soon as possible before it breaks. Dust and grease will have contaminated the old glue, so scrape it from the veneer and ground. Brush fresh glue under the veneer and clamp it flat.

If a whole piece of veneer has become detached, clean off the old glue, apply fresh glue and replace it. Clamp it in place until the glue has set. If the original veneer is missing or badly damaged, you will have to substitute a modern veneer (see opposite).

Patching damaged veneers

You can cut out damaged sections and replace them with a new patch. This must be thicker than the original, so that you can sand it flush. If necessary, glue two pieces together.

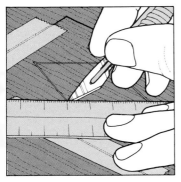

1 Tape an oversized piece over the damage, aligning the grain closely. Using a scalpel, cut a diamond or boat shape through all layers.

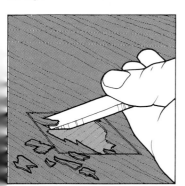

2 Lay the patch aside, chisel out the damaged veneer within the cut area and scrape out the old glue.

3 Iron a piece of glue film (see p. 221) onto the back of the new patch, and lay it in place. Protecting it with a piece of brown paper, press it flat with a domestic iron set to its lowest temperature.

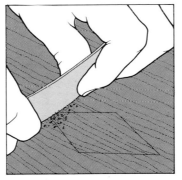

4 Rub a block of softwood gently over the patch until the glue has cooled, then scrape or sand the new veneer flush.

Replacing inlays and marquetry

Once inlay or marquetry begins to lift, it is easily broken off and lost. This will make your repair job more difficult, so replace the loose piece as soon as possible.

Clean brass, ivory or tortoiseshell inlay and glue it back with epoxy resin glue. Tape or cramp the inlay until the glue sets. Glue veneer pieces with polyvinyl or animal glue, or, if the piece is large, glue film (p. 221).

If a whole central or corner marquetry motif is missing, you may be able to buy a close match. However, if only a small piece is missing, take a rubbing of the area by laying a piece of paper over it and shade in the shape with a soft pencil. Tape the rubbing onto the replacement veneer, prick it through with a needle to reproduce the shape, and cut it out with a knife.

Motifs often include veneers that have been shaded by scorching them in hot sand, as shown below.

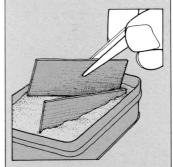

Shading veneers Heat a container of silver sand on a stove, and dip pieces of veneer into it for varying lengths of time until you get the exact amount of shading. Use tweezers to avoid burning your fingers. Cut your replacement patch slightly larger than necessary, so that, once it is scorched, you can lay a tracing of the shape over it to ensure that shading falls in the right place.

Preparing wood for refinishing

Before you attempt to refinish a piece of furniture it must be perfectly sound and clean. Never fall into the trap of believing that polish will hide minor blemishes—on the contrary, it will emphasize them. Begin by stripping off the old finish —either locally or over the entire piece, depending on its condition. Next, if the wood is stained or discolored it might be necessary to bleach it. Finally, before you apply the finish you should sand the surface so that it is perfectly flat. Then apply the stain of your choice. If you want to French polish the piece you will have to fill the grain at this stage.

Stripping the finish

In some cases you will have to strip all of the old finish from a piece of furniture in order to restore it. However, it is preferable, if possible, to restrict the repair to a small area. This way, you will not only save yourself work, but also retain almost all the antique finish.

Stripping local areas
There are several methods you can employ to strip a small area of finish—a scraper, denatured alcohol or a commercial chemical stripper. Scraping has advantages if surrounding areas might be badly affected by a liquid stripper. A cabinet scraper will remove a blemish, but if you take more than the tiniest fraction from the surface of the wood you will destroy its patina, and will therefore need to stain the patch lightly to restore its color. On veneered furniture make sure you do not scrape through to the groundwork.

Scrape more or less in the direction of the grain, changing the angle slightly from time to time. This stops you scraping a hollow in the wood. Sand the area lightly to feather the polished edges of the patch before refinishing.

Denatured alcohol is good for stripping small areas of polish. Apply with a coarse cloth or very fine steel wool. The edges of the patch will feather naturally as you work at the center. Denatured alcohol can easily spill over onto adjacent areas, so use it sparingly.

Chemical stripper will also strip a patch of finish. The best method is to dip a small ball of 000 steel wool into it, and rub the polish off in the direction of the grain. Neutralize the area with fresh steel wool dipped in mineral spirits or water.

Stripping a whole piece
To strip a whole piece of furniture use a chemical stripper. The most versatile strippers are in a liquid or light jelly-like form which you paint on and then scrape off along with the softened paint. You can use this type on molded as well as flat sections, and you do not have to wrap the furniture in plastic.

Warning: All strippers can be dangerous unless you follow manufacturer's instructions carefully. Wear protective gloves, old clothes and eye protectors. Work outside if you can, but if you have to work indoors lay newspaper on the floor and keep the windows open.

Paint on a coat of stripper, wait until the surface bubbles, then stipple on a second coat. Test a small area to make sure that the stripper has done its job, then remove as much of it as you can with a paint scraper. Use fine steel wool to remove the residue and clean out molded areas. If patches of finish remain, dip the wool in fresh stripper and rub off.

Next, wash the wood with mineral spirits on a ball of steel wool, rubbing in the direction of the grain. When the spirit has evaporated, you should sand the wood lightly with a fine abrasive to prepare it for polishing.

If the piece is covered with layers of paint it is best to use a hot air stripper. This tool blows air heated to 300°C, lifting paint in seconds. As long as you do not concentrate the stream of air in one place for too long, there is no danger of scorching the wood.

Industrial stripping

There are several commercial processes for stripping finishes from wood and metal. Most of them involve dipping the item into a tank of hot lye, then hosing it off with water. This can be very damaging to furniture, leading to weakened joints, peeled veneers, splits in solid panels and raised grain. However, there are other methods which do not immerse pieces in lye for long periods. These cold chemical strippers do not harm joints or split the wood, but the grain is raised slightly and will require light sanding. Always ask the company's advice before going ahead, and never submit a valuable item to any industrial process.

Bleaching

Once wood has been stripped it may be necessary to bleach it, either to remove stains or to lighten discolored wood. Wear protective gloves and avoid splashing other parts of the furniture or your clothes.

To remove serious stains or discoloration use a commercial two-part bleach. Apply the first solution with an old bristle or nylon brush and leave it for about 20 minutes, then apply the second solution. After about

4 hours, wipe the surface with a damp cloth, then neutralize with a solution of 1 teaspoon of white vinegar in a pint of water.

Sanding

Before you apply a stain or a finish you will need to sand the wood to provide a smooth surface. This stage is essential before the application of a water-based stain. After this, sanding will reduce the depth of color. If you have bleached the wood the final washing stage will have raised the grain, otherwise you should wipe a damp rag over the wood before you sand.

Use a medium-grade garnet or glasspaper wrapped around a cork or softwood block. Sand the wood in the direction of the grain only. Switch to a fine grade paper for the final sanding. For shaped surfaces, use a small piece of abrasive paper and your fingertips.

Filling the grain

You will hardly be aware of the pores in the wood until you apply a gloss finish, then, as the polish sinks into them, they will become very obvious. If you plan to French polish a good quality hardwood you should therefore fill the grain first. The best method is to apply successive coats of polish, rubbing down between each one.

However, the process is slow and many restorers prefer to use a commercial grain filler. These are usually oil-based, and available in different wood colors, but you will probably have to adapt the color with a little stain. Mix up a slightly darker color as the filler lightens when it dries. Thin the filler with mineral spirits, then wipe it across the surface with a piece of burlap, using a circular motion. Wipe off excess with clean burlap, using light strokes in the direction of the grain. Leave to harden, then lightly sand with a fine abrasive.

Staining wood

If you have stripped and sanded an entire piece of furniture you may feel that it looks too new, and you may want to put the color back into the wood by staining it. If you have to cope with a light patch left by bleaching or coloring a new piece of wood, staining it to match the surrounding wood is a difficult task which needs practice.

Whether you stain before or after grain filling is a matter of choice. If you stain first you can achieve a better color match with the filler, but you could remove color when you sand it. To avoid this, seal the stain with a coat of clear finish then you can sand lightly without harming it.

Applying stain

In order to absorb the stain evenly the wood must be clean and grease-free. Wipe any dust from the surface with a cloth lightly dampened with mineral spirits or water (depending on which type of stain you are using). Use a soft cloth, brush or paint pad to apply plenty of stain in the direction of the grain. Work steadily in order to pick up wet edges and avoid a streaked appearance. Never go over an area twice once it has begun to dry out, because this will make the color patchy. Once dry, wipe the surface with a cloth to remove powdery deposits.

Types of stain

Stains are available as powdered pigments for mixing yourself, but you will find it easier to use a ready-made stain from a hardware store. You can mix compatible stains to alter their color.

Water-based stains

These are easy for an amateur to use. They flow nicely, and if you apply too dark a color you can lighten the tone by wiping the stain off the surface with a damp cloth while it is still wet. This quality allows you to shade when you are matching a patched area to surrounding grain patterns.

Any finish can be applied over a water-based stain. However, it will raise the grain unless you wet and sand the wood first. And these stains can encourage veneers to blister, so it is better to use the oil-based types to stain any veneered pieces.

Oil-based stains

Not truly oil-based at all, these stains are a solution of naphtha and mineral spirits. (They are not spirit-based stains, which are made with denatured alcohol and can only be obtained from a specialist supplier.) With oil-based stains you will have to mix your own colors. Some polyurethanes react badly with oil-based stains, so test the combination on scrap lumber first. You can also use them to color French polish. Always add stain to the polish, as it separates if you mix the other way around.

Blending wood stains

Before you attempt to color a patch of new veneer or filler, try blending stains and paints on scraps of different woods first in order to familiarize yourself with the techniques.

To match veneer to surrounding wood build up the background color gradually by applying several coats of light stain. As you approach the right color you should begin to copy the grain pattern with streaks of darker color while the background is still wet. The most important part of the task is to blend the stain into the surrounding area by blotting it with a damp cloth or brush. You should avoid a hard edge at all costs. Simulate fine grain patterns using artist's oil paints (see below).

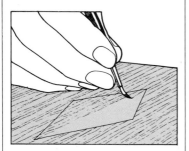

Simulating grain With a fine sable brush break up the edge of a patch by continuing the existing grain with lines of paint, blending the colors with turpentine. Leave to dry, then polish.

Disguising filler Paint in the lightest background color first, extending the area onto the wood itself. While the paint is still wet, fake the grain pattern. Brush paint out well so that it does not show as a raised texture when viewed from some angles.

Wood finishes

Applying the surface finish to a piece of furniture is a particularly rewarding part of restoration. It may well bring out the beauty of the wood for the first time. The type of finish you should use will depend on the style of the piece, the wood from which it is made, and the use to which it will be put.

Modern varnishes

Today you can buy extremely durable finishes which will resist alcohol, water and even direct heat. There is, however, a great resistance to modern varnishes by professional restorers, dealers and of course, many collectors. To a large extent such views are perfectly valid. If you can replace a finish with the appropriate traditional type you should do so. However, if you are restoring chairs and tables for hard use, there is no point in finishing them with a delicate polish, so coat them with a modern varnish.

Applying polyurethanes

You can buy ready-colored polyurethane finishes, but the clear sort is the most widely used for furniture. Mat, semi-mat or gloss finish are available. The mat finish has a very slight texture, although it looks perfectly smooth. Two-pack polyurethanes which you mix before use give off fumes which can cause discomfort. Furthermore, their shelf life is relatively short, and the quality of bonding between coats is suspect. One-shot polyurethanes which you use straight from the can are more suitable.

Apply polyurethane varnish as you would a coat of paint. Use a good quality brush, and avoid going over an area twice once the varnish has begun to set. You will need to paint at least two coats onto bare wood.

If you decide to treat an old piece with polyurethane either use a mat varnish and liven it with a coat of wax polish, or apply a gloss varnish then dip fine steel wool in wax polish and apply it to the surface in the direction of the grain.

Applying cold cure lacquer

This product is a modern two-part lacquer which is extremely hard. Unlike a polyurethane, it does not darken with age.

Mix the two parts together, then paint the lacquer onto the wood. All the brush marks will flow, leaving a flat film of lacquer. Leave it to harden for two hours, rub out any imperfections in the first coat with silicon carbide paper, then apply a second coat. Leave this coat to dry overnight. Once it has set, you can either polish it to a high gloss with a burnishing agent or give it a satin finish by rubbing it down with steel wool and then applying wax.

Reviving an existing finish

If the finish on an old piece of furniture is dull but otherwise in good condition, you may be able to revive it. This is always preferable to the more drastic step of stripping and refinishing. You can use any mild abrasive such as liquid metal polish, auto paint cleaner or one of the many commercial furniture burnishing creams. These will remove surface grime and restore an attractive polished look without damaging the patina of the wood.

Traditional finishes

Many dealers and collectors prefer these authentic finishes. Although they are not as durable as modern varnishes, it is important to use them for old or valuable pieces.

Applying an oil finish

You can use an oil finish on any wood, but it looks particularly good on teak or open-grained types like oak. And stripped pine looks very mellow when it is oiled. It is a durable, easy-to-maintain finish. When the surface begins to look dry and lifeless, one wipe over with oil will revive it.

It is best to use a commercial teak oil. Traditional linseed oil looks just as good, but it takes so long to dry that it becomes sticky and collects dust. Teak oil contains ingredients that make it dry within a few hours. Wipe a generous coating of oil onto the wood with a soft cloth, rubbing it into the grain, then wiping any excess off. You may need to apply two or three coats.

Applying wax polish

Unless you intend to restore a great deal of furniture it is doubtful whether there are many real advantages in making your own wax polish. Also, the ingredients can be difficult to obtain, whereas specially formulated furniture waxes are widely available. Although not as durable as a really hard wax, they are quite serviceable.

These waxes should not be confused with the commercial furniture polishes which have a high silicon content. The silicon can cause a problem for future restorers if you apply it directly to bare wood. Any silicon left in the pores of the wood will disturb subsequent finishes.

In fact, there are good reasons why you should not apply any wax directly to wood. Although it is a beautiful finish, wax has a tendency to collect dust which can be carried into the wood. The safest approach is to seal the wood with shellac or varnish, then apply the polish.

French polishing

French polish was a very popular finish in the nineteenth century. Indeed, many earlier pieces were "renovated" using French polish to replace their old varnish or oil finish. Its appeal is due to its appearance, not to its function. It is very soft and easily damaged by water, alcohol and heat. French polish is therefore best reserved for furniture which will be used very carefully.

Making a rubbing pad

Most restorers use a "rubbing pad"—an absorbent pad of linen and cotton—to apply French polish. To make one take a handkerchief-size square of lint-free linen.

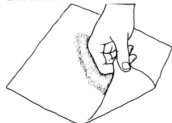

1 Place a handful of cotton in the center of the linen and fold one corner over it.

2 Fold in the loose fabric at the sides, and twist it into a tail behind the pad.

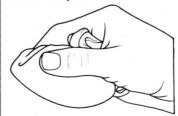

3 Fold the tail up into the palm of your hand, squeezing the pad until it is egg-shaped. You should store your rubbing pad in an airtight screw-top jar.

Applying French polish

Small specks of dust will ruin this finish, so work in a clean, draught-free, day-lit area. Avoid damp as the shellac goes cloudy. For a description of types of shellac see p. 103.

Pour shellac into the cotton before you wrap your rubbing pad. Press the bottom against clean scrap wood to squeeze out the excess as well as to distribute it evenly. Then dab linseed oil onto the bottom with your fingertip to prevent the rubbing pad sticking.

It is most important to distribute the shellac evenly, making sure that there are no bare patches, and never allow the rubbing pad to stop on the surface. Sweep the rubbing pad onto the surface using overlapping circular strokes. When you have covered an area once, go over it again with figure-eight movements. Finally, finish with straight strokes across the grain, sweeping on and off the surface at each end. As the rubbing pad begins to dry increase the pressure slightly. If it starts to stick, apply a little more oil to the bottom.

Leave your first coat to harden for about 20 minutes, then apply a second coat. Once you have put four or five coats on, leave it to harden overnight. Next day rub it down lightly with self-lubricating silicon carbide paper. Wipe dust from the surface with a cloth dampened in denatured alcohol. Then continue building up coats.

When you have built up a good body of polish you must lift out the linseed oil. To do this, add denatured alcohol to the rubbing pad, and apply straight strokes to the polished wood. When the rubbing pad starts to dry add more spirit. Leave it to evaporate for a few minutes, then "spirit off" again. Use a clean, soft cloth for the final polish, then leave the piece in a dust-free atmosphere for a few days to harden.

Buying chairs

Chairs were rare until the early seventeenth century—most people sat on stools, benches or chests. The earliest form of chair was developed from the chest by extending one frame to form a back support. A variety of designs followed, most of which fall into one of three categories: frame, stick or bentwood.

Ladderback chair

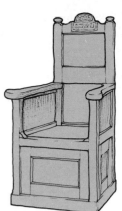

Joint chair

Types of chair

It would take a whole book to cover all the different designs and types of chair. Here, we have shown some of the most common ones as an aid to identification. Upholstery is dealt with on pp. 134–5.

Ladderback chair A rustic type of chair with a rush seat and curved horizontal slats forming a back rest.

X-frame chair Contemporary with the joint chair, the X-frame design was originally a folding chair. The seat cushion was supported on webbing.

Balloon back This was a popular style for bedroom and dining chairs from about 1820 through the nineteenth century. The cresting rail is jointed into the back legs to form a continuous, sweeping curve.

Stick or Windsor chair A traditional country chair with a solid wooden seat and turned legs, stretcher rails and back spindles.

Joint chair This early design of chair has a frame and panel construction which was based on the design of chests. In later chairs the panels were dispensed with to form the more familiar open frame.

Bentwood chair This mass-produced chair became popular from the middle of the nineteenth century. The legs, back supports and stretcher rails are made from continuous lengths of steamed, bent beech.

Side chair These lightweight chairs are often painted or gilded, and have canework seats. Many are carved to look like bamboo.

Corner chair In this ingenious style the back rest is supported on three legs instead of the usual two. The user sits across the diagonal of the seat.

X-frame chair

Bentwood chair

Balloon back chair

Side chair

Windsor chair

Corner chair

112

Damage checks

*A simple repair
**Some experience needed
***Skilled work—not for
  beginners

The **joints between the cresting rail and legs of a balloon back are often damaged as a result of people lifting the chair by the rail alone.

Bentwood chair

*Check that the **bolts** in the back legs are firm. Have they been replaced by ones that are too small? The original nuts are square and are locked in place by a folded tab on the washer.

*The original **pressed plywood seat** may have been replaced with modern ply or hardboard.

*Check that the **front legs** are glued firmly into the seat rail, and that the reinforcing screws on the inside are present.

*Examine the various **screwed joints** to make sure that no screws are missing or replaced with unsuitable ones.

Frame chair

****Joints** are sometimes crudely repaired with nails. These can be difficult to remove without damaging surrounding wood.

Stick chair

Lean on the **seat with both hands and apply a circular motion to it to make sure that there is no movement in the leg frame.
If a **solid seat warps, the chair will rock when placed on a flat surface.

Check for **splits, particularly across the short grain of curved legs and where turned detail creates a weak point.

The **rear side rail joints are most vulnerable. Tip the chair on its back legs, then apply force to the front seat. If there is any movement at the joints they may need regluing or even re-building. It is particularly important to carry out this test on upholstered chairs where you cannot see the frame.
Look to see if the **joint has been reinforced with metal brackets on the inside. This is a sure sign of damage.

Check that the **back spindles and arm supports are securely glued by holding down the seat while pressing back on the top cresting rail.

*Look for **splits** in the stretcher rail.

Dismantling and repairing chairs

Whether you intend to reglue loose joints or mend a broken component, you will probably have to dismantle at least part of the chair in order to make a good repair. In general, an old chair will have taken more punishment in its life than any other type of furniture. It will probably have been rocked on its back legs countless times, putting severe strain on the joints between the legs and seat rail. Shrinkage makes things worse, and the advent of central heating has exacerbated this problem. Once the glue in one joint fails it transfers more load onto the others, and eventually the extra stress may cause components to break.

How is the chair constructed?

Before you attempt to take a chair apart, examine it carefully to see how it was originally constructed, otherwise you will risk breaking a joint if you try to force it. Also mark each joint with masking tape to help you during re-assembly.

Bentwood chairs

Bentwood chairs are mostly bolted or screwed together, so they are easy to dismantle. The only glued part is the joints where the front legs go into the underside of the frame. You will normally find a wood screw reinforcing this joint from the inside of the frame.

Stick chairs

These chairs are simply constructed by plugging turned components into round, tapered holes. You can often remove a loose component by springing its neighbors apart. If you do have to tap a joint apart, wrap newspaper around the wood to stop any damage.

Frame chairs

Undo the side rails first, then the back and front frames. The leg to rail joints will be mortise-and-tenoned or doweled together so you must exert a straight pull on them. Use a softwood block to protect the wood, and tap the joint apart with a hammer or a mallet.

Similar joints will have been used to construct the back frame. Sometimes the back legs were jointed to the back seat rail, followed by a cresting rail plugged on top of them. Or the cresting rail may be jointed between the legs like the seat rail.

Removing joint reinforcements

Joints are sometimes reinforced to stop them being pulled apart accidentally. You *must* remove the reinforcements before you dismantle the chair.

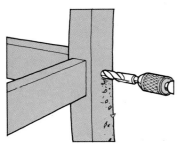

Drilling out dowels Dowels may be driven right through the legs, locking the seat rail tenons in place. Drill them out carefully so that you can replace them later.

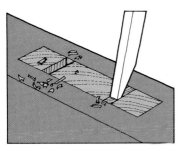

Removing tenons Tenons pass through the leg and may have wedges driven into them. These spread the tenons to dovetail them in the mortise. Chop out wedges with a chisel.

Removing wooden plugs Look out for wooden plugs which might cover a woodscrew. Chop out the plug so that you can remove the screw and replace it with a new one (see p. 224).

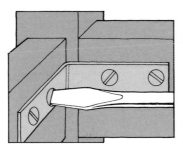

Taking off corner brackets Look under the seat to make sure that there are no brackets screwed across the corners. These must be removed before either rail will pull out of the chair leg.

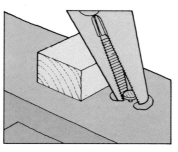

Extracting nails You will often find nails driven into a loose joint. Usually these are not original. You may have to cut away some wood from around the nail head to grip it with pincers or tapered pliers. Or cut the head off the nail and drive the shaft through with a pin punch.

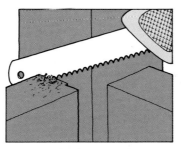

Extracting hidden wedges These are fitted to the tenon before it is inserted into a closed mortise, and are difficult to remove. You will only be able to detect them when you find a joint which starts to come apart, then jams part way. Saw off the top and bottom of the tenon and rebuild it (see p. 213).

Softening glue

There are times when you will have to soften the glue of a sound joint—to remove a broken component for instance. You should soften water-soluble glues with water or steam rather than brute force. You could wrap wet rags around a joint until water seeps into it, but this is a slow process. It is best to make a steam generator to inject steam straight into the joint. Both methods will damage surrounding polish, so be prepared for some refinishing.

To make a steam generator plug a tight-fitting cork into a kettle. Drill a hole through the cork for a piece of brass tubing. Fit a length of rubber or heat-resistant plastic tubing on the brass tube. Plug a second piece of brass tubing into the other end to make a nozzle. Half fill the kettle with water and heat it. Drill a small hole in the joint, and wearing thick gloves, plug the steaming nozzle into the hole until the joint slackens.

Restoring chairs

Chairs are subject to a lot of wear and tear,
especially on rails and joints, so it is quite
likely that you will have to tackle a few of
the repairs outlined here. When a piece you
already have is damaged, it is best to mend it
as soon as possible—you are more likely to get
an invisible repair as the two edges will not
be dirty or worn. If you buy a broken chair,
make sure you are capable of restoring it.

Repairing a dowel joint

Dowel joints (see p. 214) are
often used to join the cresting
rail to the back legs, or to hold
arms on carver chairs in place.

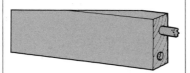

Mending a broken joint First
remove any remaining dowel.
Grip any protruding pieces with
pliers, twisting and pulling
them out. If the dowel has
broken off below the surface,
choose a drill bit that matches
the hole and drill it out. Use the
sides of the hole to center the
drill. If the dowel has broken off
flush, a large drill could wander
sideways and enlarge the hole,
so drill out the center with a
smaller drill bit, then pick out
the rest with a small gouge.

Cut lengths of dowel slightly
shorter than the combined
depths of the holes in the two
halves of the joint. Chamfer the
ends with a pencil sharpener,
and make a saw cut groove for
trapped glue to escape. Glue the
joint and clamp it until it sets.

Repairing a split mortise

Mortise and tenon joints (see p.
213) are usually found between
the seat rails and the back legs,
and between stretcher rails and
legs. Sideways pressure on this
type of joint can split the leg.

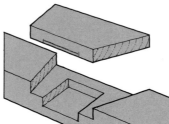

Mending a split Introduce
glue into the split with a brush
or knife blade, then clamp it. If
the side of the mortise is broken
away completely, you must first
insert a strengthening patch of
matching wood. Begin by making an angled saw cut at each
side of the mortise down to the
level of the damage. Pare out
the waste so that the bottom
surface of the housing is flush.
Cut a patch to fit the housing,
glue it and clamp it. Once set,
plane the patch flush and re-cut
the side of the mortise.

Rebuilding a damaged leg

If one end of a leg is badly
broken or worm-eaten you
should glue on a new section
using a scarf joint with an
angle of 1 in 4 (see p. 215).

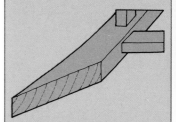

1 Cut and plane the 1 in 4
angle on the end of the leg.

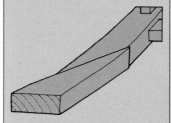

2 Cut a similar angle on an
oversize block of wood which
has a similar grain direction
to the original leg. Glue and
clamp the block to the leg.

3 Mark the shape of the original leg on the block, using
a cardboard template (the
opposite leg will provide a
pattern). Shape the block
with a saw and spokeshave.

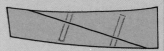

4 It is a wise precaution to
reinforce a repaired chair leg
with dowels or screws. Level
legs if necessary (opposite).

Mending broken chair rails

When a rail splits it always
follows the line of the grain.
If a serious split occurs, but
the rail is still in one piece,
glue it immediately and bind it
tightly with waxed string. If
the rail has broken in two, you
should reinforce the repair

after gluing and binding with
dowels or wood screws. Insert
a screw or dowel from each
side. Screws should be counterbored and plugged (see p. 224).
Bind the joint up again with the
waxed string, leaving this in
place until the glue has set.

Repairing a turned leg or rail

A turned component is vulnerable to breakage if under stress, especially if the short grain runs across it. You can glue broken sections of a turned leg or rail together again, but the joint will have to be reinforced by an internal dowel. There are two methods of repair—one for breaks near one end, the other for a break in the middle.

Mending a break near one end

If the break occurs near one end, glue back the broken part, holding it with a sash clamp. If necessary, bind the joint with waxed string to align it.

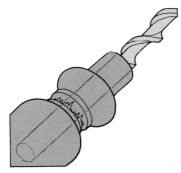

1 When the glue has set, drill down the center of the leg or rail past the level of the break line. Match your drill size to the most convenient dowel. Saw two or three grooves along the dowel to make sure that the glue can escape. You may also have to bore a tiny hole through the side of the leg or rail into the bottom of the hole to allow glue to escape.

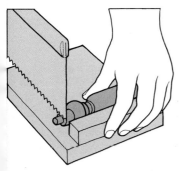

2 Apply glue to the hole and tap the dowel into it. When the glue has set, cut the end of the dowel flush with the chair leg.

Mending a break near the middle

If a leg or rail breaks near the middle you should make a dowel hole in one broken end before gluing.

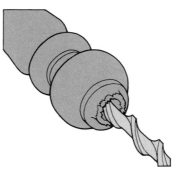

1 Drill a hole for the dowel in the center of one broken end.

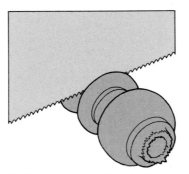

2 Choose a convenient broken section of the turned decoration and saw through the leg or rail at that point, making a registration mark for assembly later. Glue this piece to the other half of the leg, aligning the broken edges carefully.

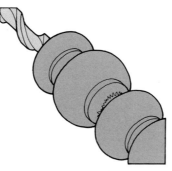

3 Using the hole to locate the drill bit, drill into the second half of the leg or rail. Prepare and glue up the dowel (see left).

Leveling chair legs

Every now and again you will come across a chair that rocks from leg to leg, even when you place it on a flat surface. To cure this, first make sure that there are no obvious faults such as a tack driven into one foot, and check that the frame is true by looking across the seat rails to see if they are parallel. Some faults—like a slightly bowed seat on a stick chair—cannot be remedied simply. It is easier to trim the legs slightly. Stand the chair on a flat board and let it come to rest in its optimum position. Ask an assistant to hold the chair still while you pack veneers under the shortest leg to make up the gap.

Trimming legs Using the veneers as a guide, mark the other three legs to the same depth. Trim them with a fine saw or a sharp chisel.

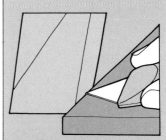

An over-length leg If one leg is too long after rebuilding, stand the chair on a board with that leg hanging over one edge. Using a knife, make a mark on the leg at the point where it aligns with the top of the board, then cut it to size.

Repairing broken tenons

A tenon is the "stud" that fits into the "slot" of the mortise in a mortise and tenon joint (see p. 213). Unfortunately, when you dismantle a chair for re-gluing, you will often find that a tenon has broken off inside the joint. If this is the case, you will have to cut out any remaining tenon to "free" the mortise and then repair the tenon (see p. 213).

A partly broken tenon

If only part of the tenon is missing, rebuild it by cutting away the broken part flush with the shoulder of the joint, then glue on a new section made from similar wood.

To make a more efficient joint you should "key" the end of the new piece into the end of the rail.

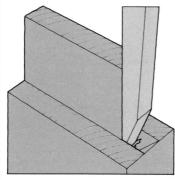

1 Undercut the shoulder using a chisel that matches the width of the tenon.

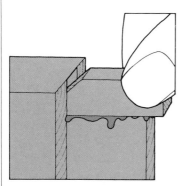

2 Cut an angle on the end of the new piece to fit the undercut, then cut it to length to match the tenon. Glue and clamp it in place.

A totally broken tenon

If the tenon is missing you will have to joint a new replacement into the end of the rail.

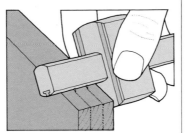

1 Square off the rail. Use a mortise gauge to mark out an angled housing for the tenon on the end and underside of the rail. Set the gauge to fit the mortise, and make sure that the housing is three times as long as the original tenon. Saw and pare out the waste with a chisel.

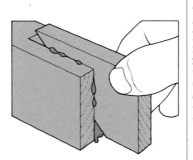

2 Cut a tenon to fit the angled housing from similar wood to that of the rail, matching the direction of the grain. Leave it slightly over-sized at the top and bottom, as this will make it easier to plane it flush when set.

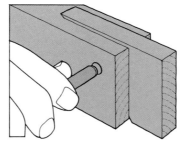

3 Glue the tenon that holds the housing closed, keeping it in place with a small C clamp. Before planing the tenon to size, glue in a dowel to lock the tenon and rail together.

Tightening loose joints

If a joint has become slack due to shrinkage, it is not advisable to rely on glue alone—you will need to find some way of strengthening it. The method you should use will depend on the construction of the original joint.

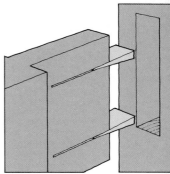

Using hidden wedges Placing these inside a closed joint is hard. If they are not exactly right, the joint will tighten before it is all the way in and you will have to remove the tenon. Gauge the hole's depth with a dowel. Cut a wedge long enough to spread the tenon just short of the bottom of the joint.

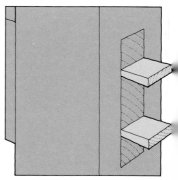

Making a through tenon Wedges will spread a through tenon in the mortise. Make two saw cuts across the tenon almost down to the shoulder. Then cut tapered hardwood wedges. Assemble the joint, apply glue to the wedges and tap them into the saw cuts. When set, saw the ends of the new wedges off and trim them flush.

Screwed joints

If a screw has stripped the thread in its hole, it is best to plug the old hole and replace the original screw.

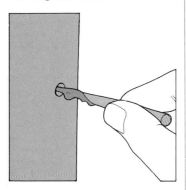

1 Trim the end of a dowel to a fine taper to make a plug for the hole. Apply glue to the dowel and tap it into the hole. When the glue has set, trim the dowel flush.

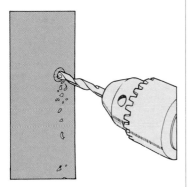

2 Drill a pilot hole for the screw (see p. 224) in the center of the plug. Then put the screw in place.

Assembling chairs

Before you can re-assemble a chair you must scrape old glue from the joints with a chisel. You can soften the glue first with hot water, but then leave the joint to dry out. The order in which you assemble the chair will depend on its construction.

Frame chairs

First, glue the front and back frames, holding them together with sash clamps. To check that each frame is accurate plane a sharp edge on the end of two battens, and hold them so that each point nestles in opposite corners of the frame. Then try the fit in the other corners. If it does not match, squeeze across the longest diagonals (use your hands or move the clamps slightly).

Once the glue has set, assemble the rest of the chair. Check that the seat frame is square, and make sure that the chair does not rock. Before you undo the clamps screw in any corner blocks.

Stick chairs

Glue and assemble the stretcher rails and plug each leg onto them, then plug this whole assembly into the underside of the seat. Tap the end of each leg to seat it in its joint, then stand on a flat surface and adjust the stance. Leave it to set.

Bentwood chairs

Bolt the seat frames to the back legs. Glue each front leg in place, twisting the joints until the reinforcing screw is located. Slip the hooped stretcher rail in place and screw it to each leg. If your chair also has hooped arm rails screw them in place too.

If any screws were originally plugged, cut new plugs from matching wood using a chisel or plug cutter. Glue plugs in place, trim them flush with a chisel, then sandpaper them. Finally, touch them up with stain and polish.

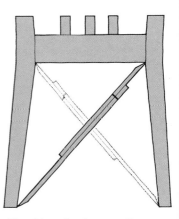

Checking the frame alignment Use two sharpened wooden battens held diagonally.

Tape each glued back spindle into the seat and then fit the top rail onto the spindles. With an armchair, you must glue the arms at the same time as the back. View the assembly from all angles to make sure it is completely even.

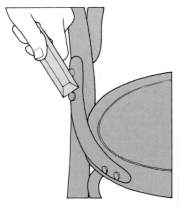

Trimming plugs After gluing in new wooden plugs use a chisel to trim them flush.

Buying tables

The structure of this type of furniture allows a great deal of freedom of design—a table can be very large or small, it can have one or many legs, and its top may be oval, square or round, with or without flaps or leaves. They range from plain, kitchen-style frame tables to fancy hardwood side tables with inlay, carving or turning. However, most tables fall into the four categories—standard, drop-leaf, draw leaf and pedestal—discussed here.

Identifying types of table

Here we have shown some of the commonest types of tables.

Pedestal table The name refers to the central column and tripod base that support the top. The top is usually circular, and frequently tips up for storage (this type is often known as a "tilt-top"). Size varies from dining tables that seat eight to small tea tables.

Side table Designed to stand against a wall, these tables have one unfinished side and are intended primarily for display. A variation, the console table, is supported at the front edge only as it is made to be attached permanently to the wall.

Gateleg table Two hinged flaps are supported on framed legs (the "gatelegs") which swing out from the central framework of the table. When not in use, the flaps hang vertically.

Tavern or frame tables This is one of the earliest kinds of dining table. It has a stout leg at each corner, and sometimes has legs half way along as well. The upper frame and stretcher rails are jointed to the legs with pegged mortise and tenons.

Draw leaf table This design has extra flaps stored under the main top.

Pembroke table This table has drop flaps at each side supported on hinged brackets.

Sofa table These small, narrow, rectangular tables stand in front of or behind a sofa. They have a drop flap at each end and two drawers.

Drum table This is a pedestal table with a deep frieze below the top that holds drawers.

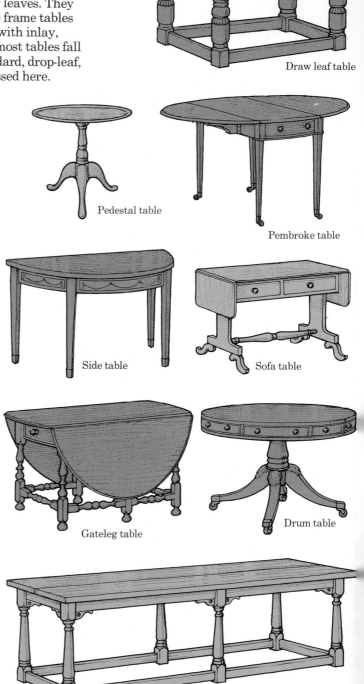

Draw leaf table

Pedestal table

Pembroke table

Side table

Sofa table

Gateleg table

Drum table

Tavern table

Damage checks

*A simple repair
**Some experience needed
***Skilled work—
    not for beginners

Standard table
Are the **joints loose or in need of repair? To check, lean on the table and push sideways.
Look for **splits or **open joints** in a solid wooden table top.
Molded edges may be broken, especially in the corners.
The **finish often suffers on table tops. If the top is badly stained be prepared to strip it before refinishing.

Draw leaf table
An infrequently used **hidden flap may be a different color to a faded top.
If a **supporting bearer is warped, use the other one as a pattern to cut a replacement.
*Are the **stops** on the underside of the bearers present? If not, glue on new ones.
*If a **flap** droops, prop it level with the top, then glue small leveling wedges between the bearers and the table frame.

Drop leaf table

Pedestal table

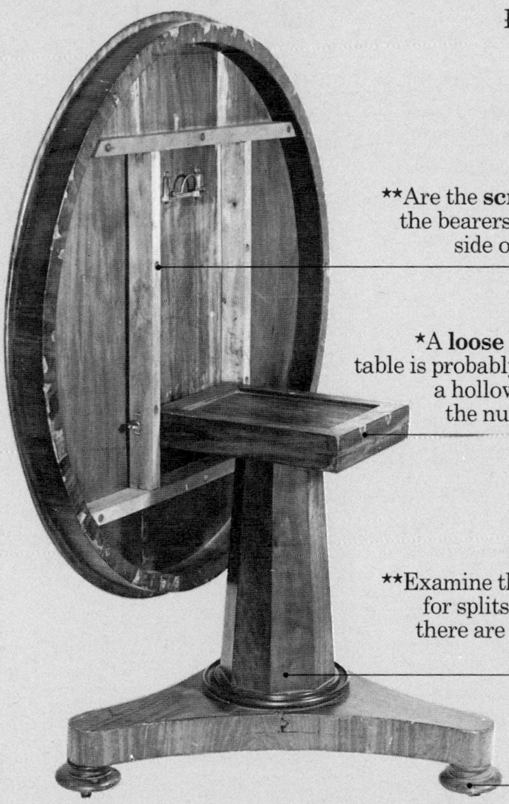

Are the **screws which hold the bearers on to the underside of a tilt-top loose?

*A **loose block** on a large table is probably bolted through a hollow column. Check the nut under the base.

Examine the **column base for splits. Make sure that there are no earlier, badly repaired breaks.

Turned feet may be broken.

The **rule joint between the flap and the fixed top could be broken. If it binds when you operate it you may have to adjust the hinges.

***The **flaps** on some tables are supported on hinged wooden brackets. Repairing these is best left to a professional.

Check for **splits here.

Are the **pivot points of a moving gate sound?

Repairing tables

When a table top is fixed rigidly to the frame, shrinkage of the wood can lead to splits along the grain, or the glued joints that hold the separate planks together can open up. When this happens you must take the top off the frame to make repairs.

Dismantling a simple table

To remove the top take out retaining screws or knock out the glued blocks with a blunt chisel. Then dismantle the frame as you would a frame chair (see p. 114).

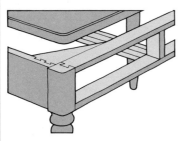

Removing a drawer rail
To allow for a drawer the top rail is turned on its side and dovetailed into the legs and adjoining rails. Tap this rail upward with a mallet and softening block before tackling other joints.

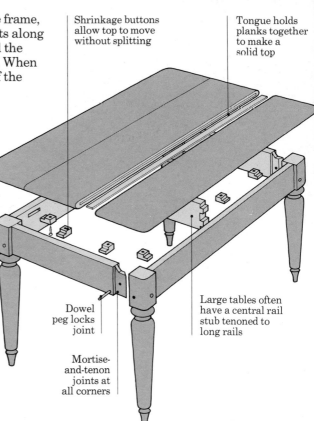

Shrinkage buttons allow top to move without splitting

Tongue holds planks together to make a solid top

Dowel peg locks joint

Mortise-and-tenon joints at all corners

Large tables often have a central rail stub tenoned to long rails

Taking joints apart

Once the glue has failed, you may find that simple butt joints, or ones held by a tongue of ply or dowels, fall apart as soon as the top is freed from the underframe. However, if a joint is difficult to dismantle, try playing steam along it to soften the glue (see p. 115).

In rare cases, joints are held by countersunk screwheads that locate in dovetailed slots in the other half of the joint. If you can see a metal screw or detect one by running a blade along the joint, you should loosen it (see right).

Loosening a joint Place a softening block at the end of one of the planks and tap it sharply with a mallet. If no movement occurs, try tapping in the other direction.

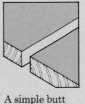

A simple butt joint is glued together

A solid or plywood tongue is stronger

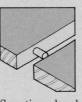

Sometimes dowels are glued into both edges

Screw heads in dovetail slots are rare

Regluing the top

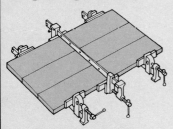

Clamping a rectangular/square top

You will need at least three sash clamps and softening blocks to glue a table top. Place one clamp at each end on the underside and the other centrally on top. This arrangement will prevent the top bowing as you apply pressure to the clamps. You must place the softening blocks between the clamp heads and the edges of the top to avoid bruising the wood. If the edges are molded shape the blocks to suit. Carry out a trial run to make sure that you have everything you need, then paint white glue along mating edges. Rub the joints together to squeeze out excess glue, then apply light pressure to the clamps.

Wipe off any glue that is forced out so that you can inspect the joints. If they are not lying flush, lay a block of wood across each joint and strike it with a hammer until the edges line up perfectly. Put extra pressure on the clamp and clean off the glue again.

Check that the top is flat by laying a straight edge across it and raise or lower the clamps to take out any slight bowing. Replace any dowels or tongues during the gluing. If the joint was held by screw slots, a slight turn on the right screw may pull the joint closed. If this does not, remove them and make a glued butt joint.

Replace the top on its frame, using the original fixings. However, if the top was screwed rigidly to the frame, or held by glued blocks, install shrinkage plates (from hardware stores) to allow the wood to move in future.

To clamp round or oval tops, you will have to make up a cradle for each side (see below) which will allow the clamps to apply force directly across the joints.

If there is a split in the top and you can easily clamp it closed, then you can just glue it. However, if the nature of the split is such that this would put too much strain on the glue, you will have to fill the crack by gluing in a piece of shaped veneer.

Clamping an oval or round top

Screw plywood to both sides of the blocks to lap over the edge of the table

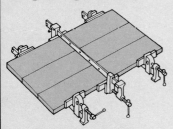

Shape softwood blocks to suit the edge of the table

Use the same arrangement of clamps for any shape of top

Rebuilding broken moldings

Many table tops have shaped, molded decorative edges. If part of a molding is split away, glue it back as soon as possible and either clamp or tape it tightly in place. If the piece is missing you must rebuild the edge with a patch of matching wood.

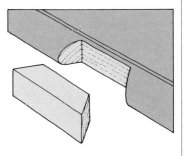

Mending damage in the center If the damage occurs in the center of the molding, let in a piece which is angled at each end. This not only makes the joint less visible, but also allows you to make trial fittings without forcing the piece into a tight housing.

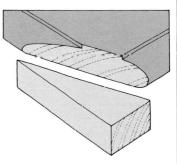

Repairing a broken corner First, plane the damaged area flat and square. Then cut and plane a block which follows the grain direction of the top. Glue both faces of the joint, and rub them together until suction holds the block in place. Tape it tightly until the glue sets. Finally, shape the patch with a plane, files and a shaped sanding block so that it matches the contours of the molding.

Repairing pedestal tables

Pedestal tables, especially the "tilt-top" ones, have their own particular defects. Because the top is only supported by the centrally placed column, considerable strain is placed on the fixing points and any pivoting mechanism. Any force applied to the table is transferred directly to the tripod base, so always inspect this carefully for signs of damage.

Coping with a loose top

A pedestal table top can be loose for a number of reasons— the bearers under the top or the block that attaches the table to the base could be loose, or the pivot points may be worn.

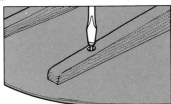

A screwed bearer

Loose bearers
The underside of your table top will have bearers or a frame known as a "cleat" screwed to it. Check this, and replace missing screws or ones that have stripped their thread (see p. 224).

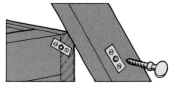

Screw bolt pivot

Worn pivot points
Examine the pivot points of your top. Large tables sometimes pivot on metal screw bolts which pass through the cleat into a threaded plate attached to the block on top of the column. Make sure that this plate is fixed securely to the block.

    If the top pivots on wooden pegs projecting from the block, these pegs, or the holes in the bearers that they sit in, may be worn. Reshape worn pegs with a file, then glue short lengths of brass tube over them to build them up to their original size. If the holes in the bearers seem worn, fit brass tube collars.

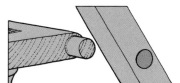

Wooden peg pivot

A loose block
In some cases, the top of the column fits into a through mortise in the block. The column top should be spread tightly in this mortise by wedges. If the block is loose, chop out the old wedges, reglue the block to the column and fit new wedges.

    Some small tables have two blocks separated by wooden columns. This structure is known as a gallery, and it allows the top to rotate as well as pivot. It is plugged onto the pedestal and held in place by a wooden wedge passing through the projecting peg. Make sure the wedge fits tightly. If the gallery has loose joints, knock it apart and reglue it (pp. 115 and 119).

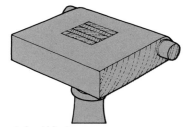

A fixed block

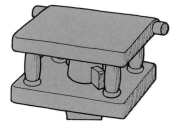

A rotating gallery

A split tripod base

Each leg of the base is dovetailed into the central column. The joint itself is very strong, but undue strain or weight can force the legs outward, splitting the column or even breaking a piece right out of it. You can glue up this kind of damage in the normal way, but clamping such an awkward shape is a problem.

Clamping a split Pull the legs toward the center and shape plywood blocks to fit over the feet, notching them to take a tourniquet.

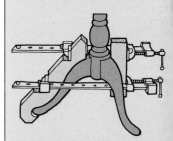

Clamping a broken leg If a leg has broken away, taking part of the column with it, make a plywood block to fit the outside of the damaged leg and hook over the toe. Notch this block so that you can use two sash clamps— one above and one below the damage. Place another block opposite the broken leg, and clamp it.

Repairing drop-flap tables

To save space, some designs of table have a sectioned top that allows you to fold part of the table surface away when not in use. The two most common varieties are the Pembroke table, where the flap is supported on hinged brackets, and the gatelegged table, which incorporates a pivoting frame that positions a leg directly under the flap.

Solid wooden tops unsupported by a frame will share common problems. You can mend a broken gate and adjust a binding flap (one that rubs against the central fixing board), but if the flap is badly bowed it can be difficult to repair, and is therefore best left to a professional restorer.

A binding rule joint

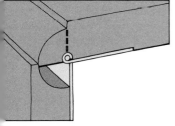

Section through a rule joint

The joint between the flap and fixed top of a drop-leaf table is known as a rule joint. It supports the flap along the drop edge while in use, and hides the hinges with the flap down. If the joint sticks, try rubbing candle wax along it.

If the wax does not help, examine the hinges. Make sure they are in good condition—a bent or worn hinge can throw the flap out of line. If you have to adjust the position of the hinge, unscrew it and plug the old screw holes. Then move the hinge leaf forward on the fixed panel until the knuckle is directly below the small step from which the quadrant of the joint springs (above).

If the flap binds at one point only, the hinges may be recessed incorrectly. If the flap binds near the horizontal, pare the timber below the hinge leaf until the leaf lies flush. If the joint binds just before the flap hangs vertically, pack thin cardboard under the leaf.

A broken gate

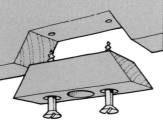

Exploded view of the repair

The pivoting frame on a gatelegged table can suffer from a variety of problems. Because the moving leg is cut to lie flush with the frame, splits can occur around these points. Glue up the split and put it in a C clamp. To repair broken legs refer to pp. 116–7.

If the hole for the pivoting dowel in the side rail happens to have split, you may find it necessary to rebuild that section. Cut out the damaged section as you would with a split mortise (see p. 116). Make a hardwood patch to fit the new housing and drill a hole in it for the pivoting dowel of the gate. Gauge its size from the one in the lower frame. Drill clearance holes on each side of the pivot holes, countersinking them to take screws. Drop the patch over the top dowel on the gate. Next, fit the lower dowel onto the bottom rail and swing the top of the gate into position, screwing the patch to the underneath of the side rail.

Fitting new castors

A castor will run badly or even jam if the small axle of the wheel is badly worn. You should be able to buy a replacement from a specialist hardware store. If you cannot get a good match, replace all the castors.

Cup castor Some gatelegged tables have castors on the movable leg.

Toe castor The splayed tripod leg on a pedestal table takes this special castor.

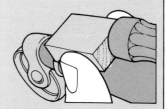

How to fit a castor Remove the fixing screws on the old castor, then tap the edges of the cup with a small block of wood and a hammer. The cup should slip off quite easily. Next, try the fit of the new castor. You may have to trim the end of the leg slightly with a file, or pack it out with very thin veneers. Once the castor fits, screw it in place. You may have to plug the old holes first.

Buying cabinets

Cabinets are, broadly speaking, storage furniture. The wide range of apparently different pieces—from a simple wardrobe to an elaborate secretary—are all basically a mixture of drawers and cupboards. Once you know how to repair these, you can repair any cabinet.

Identifying types of cabinet

There is a massive range of different pieces in this category. Here we show a few of the most common types.

Lowboy A low, shallow cabinet housing drawers and standing on four legs.

Chest of drawers A low cabinet housing a series of drawers. It stands on feet or a plinth.

Wardrobe A sizeable cupboard that provides full length hanging space for clothing. In practice, wardrobes often provide drawer and shelf space as well.

Sideboard This originally started out as a large side table with pedestal cupboards at each side for storing wine. Later examples are often vast, with several cupboards and drawers below the table surface.

Highboy A chest of drawers mounted on a lowboy. There is a variation known as a chest-on-chest—this is a double chest of drawers, one mounted on top of the other.

Dresser This form of kitchen or dining room storage cabinet comprises a table with open shelving mounted above it. Dressers often have cupboards and drawers below the table top.

Secretary A chest of drawers or cabinet that has a deep top drawer or flap with a front that falls open to form a writing surface. Usually topped by a cupboard with glazed doors.

Slant-front desk A piece of furniture, often a chest of drawers, that incorporates a slanted writing surface which falls flat to form a desk. Inside are fitted pigeon holes and drawers.

Press A large cupboard containing fixed or sliding shelves for linen storage, often mounted on a chest of drawers.

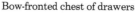

Lowboy

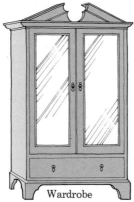

Bow-fronted chest of drawers

Wardrobe

Secretary

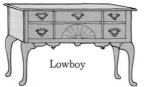

Sideboard

Highboy

Dresser

Secretary (continental style)

Slant-front desk

Damage checks

*A simple repair
**Some experience needed
***Skilled work—not for
   beginners

***Have the **trays** on a press been removed and the top section converted to hanging space? This devalues the piece and is difficult to restore.

Is the **cornice missing or damaged? It could be a replacement, as here.

Examine the **hinges for signs of wear by lifting an open door.

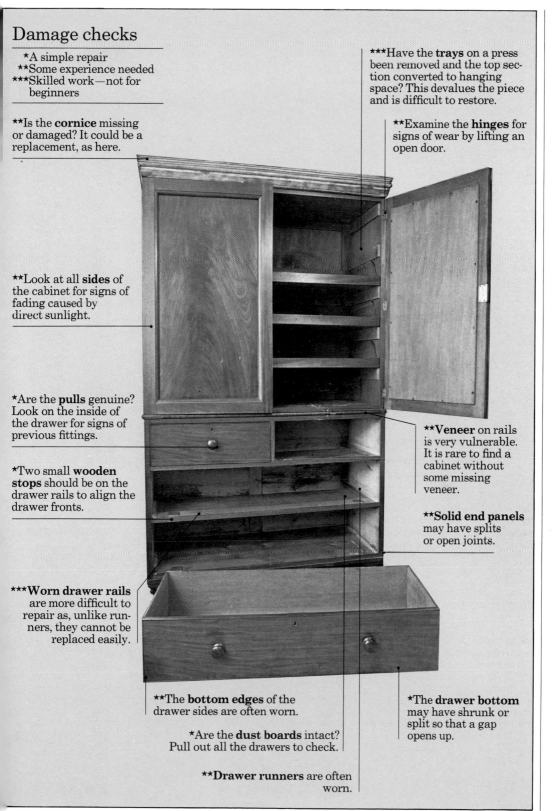

Look at all **sides of the cabinet for signs of fading caused by direct sunlight.

*Are the **pulls** genuine? Look on the inside of the drawer for signs of previous fittings.

****Veneer** on rails is very vulnerable. It is rare to find a cabinet without some missing veneer.

*Two small **wooden stops** should be on the drawer rails to align the drawer fronts.

****Solid end panels** may have splits or open joints.

*****Worn drawer rails** are more difficult to repair as, unlike runners, they cannot be replaced easily.

The **bottom edges of the drawer sides are often worn.

*The **drawer bottom** may have shrunk or split so that a gap opens up.

*Are the **dust boards** intact? Pull out all the drawers to check.

****Drawer runners** are often worn.

Restoring cabinets

Cabinets are usually very sturdily built, so it is very unlikely that you will find one that needs to be dismantled completely for regluing. In fact, a cabinet that is in such poor condition is probably not worth restoring unless it is valuable. However, most cabinets are likely to have a few of the damage problems covered in the following pages.

Repairing worn drawer runners

When you buy an old cabinet, especially one with large, heavy drawers, you will often find that the drawers run badly. If this is due to excessive wear on the runners, they must be replaced. While the back of the cabinet is off, take the opportunity to replace any damaged or missing dust panels with a sheet of plywood. This must fit the grooves in the runners and drawer rail.

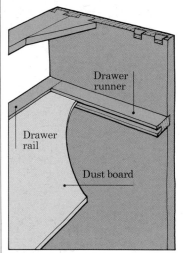

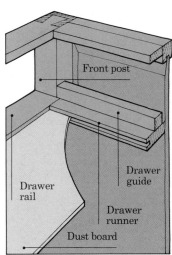

Runners in cabinets with solid end panels

In this type of cabinet the runner is located in a groove cut across the inside of the end panel. The front end of the runner is tenoned into the drawer rail which runs across the front of the cabinet. The runner is sometimes grooved to take the dust panel. When the panel is fitted it holds the runner in place. In some cases, it may be held in place at the back end by a single screw, or even glue.

To remove a rail, take off the back panel of the cabinet. This is probably screwed or pinned into rabbets all round. Slide out the dust panel and release the runner. If the runner is glued in place, tap a chisel under the back end to ease it out.

Using the old runner as a pattern, make up new ones and rebuild the cabinet in reverse order. Do not glue in the replacement runners. Instead, cut a slot in the back end of the runner for a screw. This will allow for shrinkage across the end panel.

Runners in frame and panel cabinets

Some cabinets are made from a framework of solid wood which holds thin wooden end panels. These panels are held in grooves on the inner edges of the framework. Because the inner face of the end panel is not flat, the drawer runner is set behind the side frame post (see above). It is tenoned into the drawer rail at the front and held by a single screw at the back. In addition, a strip of wood known as a drawer guide is fixed to the top of the runner to prevent the drawer from sliding sideways.

To make the drawer run smoothly, remove the runner and replace it with a new one as described on the left.

Cabinets with a central drawer runner

When a cabinet has two drawers running side by side, they are separated by a short post jointed between the two drawer rails above and below the drawers. A double runner is tenoned into the drawer rail behind this central post. A drawer guide is glued or screwed to the runner to keep the drawers apart. The runner may be jointed into or screwed through the back of the cabinet.

Once you have removed the cabinet back to replace the other runners (see left), you will be able to pull out the central drawer runner and replace it as you did the others.

Repairing worn drawer rails

The action of the drawers will sometimes wear a shallow groove across the drawer rail. The rail is seldom as badly worn as the runner. To repair it insert a patch of matching wood into a housing in the rail.

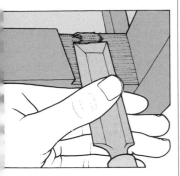

Making a housing The housing should be slightly wider at the back than the front. Cut it out by sawing across the rail to the depth of the damage, then paring out the waste with a chisel. Glue and clamp the patch in place. Leave it protruding at the front edge and top. When set, use a block plane to make the front edge flush, and a wide, sharp chisel to pare down the top.

Fitting a drawer stop

If a drawer will not come to rest in line with the front of the cabinet, the drawer stop may be missing. This is a small block of wood glued near the front of the drawer rail which catches the back of the drawer front. There is usually one each end of a long drawer, and a single centrally placed stop on a small drawer. To measure for a new stop set a marking gauge to the thickness of the drawer front, allowing for any moldings, and mark where the front edge of the drawer stop should be on the rail.

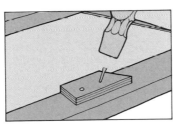

Gluing in the stop Cut a new stop from a piece of plywood or solid wood of the appropriate thickness, and glue it to the rail. Then pin or clamp the block, checking that it aligns accurately with the mark first.

Dealing with woodworm

The furniture beetle lays its eggs in cracks or crevices in wood. When the larvae hatch out they burrow into the wood, and eventually come to rest just below the surface, where they pupate. The adult beetles bite their way out, leaving tiny holes.

Many old pieces of furniture have been victims of woodworm in the past, but often they will have been treated successfully. The way to tell whether or not the woodworm is still active is to look carefully at the holes. Fresh flight holes will be clean and lighter in color than surrounding wood, whereas old ones will have darkened. Signs of fine powder in or around flight holes are another clue.

If you think that a newly-acquired piece has woodworm, treat it as soon as you can, preferably before bringing it into the house. Cut out and replace any serious damage and treat sound wood with a commercial fluid.

Squirt the fluid into the flight holes using a can with a pointed nozzle or an aerosol spray with a special applicator. As the internal tunnels are interconnected, there is no need to treat every flight hole—one every 2 ins (5 cm) will be sufficient. Brush or spray the fluid over all unfinished wood, and treat finished surfaces with an insecticidal polish.

Repairing a split panel

Any furniture which has solid panels is designed to cope with the fact that the wood will shrink across the grain. However, if the panel is held too rigidly, shrinkage will occur and the panel will eventually split. You can fill a narrow split by opening it up slightly with the point of a tenon saw, then tapping in a piece of glued veneer. To fill a wider split see right.

In some cabinets the base frame, or more often the internal drawer runners, prevent movement in the end panels. The panels in these cabinets are made from several planks of wood glued together, so instead of the wood itself splitting, the joints may open up.

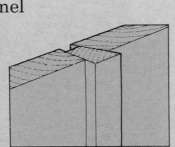

Filling a split If the gap is wide enough, choose a strip of matching timber that is slightly wider than the open joint, and plane a shallow taper along it. Scrape out the old glue from the joint with a knife blade, put glue on the strip and tap it into the gap until it jams in tightly. When set, scrape and sand the strip flush with the panel.

Drawers and doors

The drawers and doors of cabinets usually suffer most from wear and tear. Look for wear on the bottom edge of drawer sides and check that the drawer bottom has not split or shrunk. When a cupboard door will not close smoothly, either because it is rubbing on the frame or because it has to be forced shut, the hinges are often the source of the problem.

Rebuilding drawer sides

With years of use the sides of a drawer may wear down and stop running smoothly. If this has happened, you rebuild the side with matching wood.

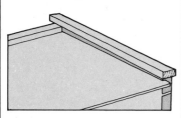

1 Turn the drawer upside down and plane a slope on the bottom edge of each side, starting just behind the drawer front. Remove wood to just below the level of the wear. Next, glue a hardwood strip to the slope, so that it is flush with the inner face of the drawer side.

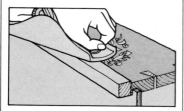

2 When the glue has set, plane the strip flush with the outer face of the drawer side.

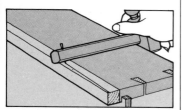

3 Set a marking gauge to the true depth of the drawer and mark a line along the new hardwood strip parallel with the top edge of the drawer side. Plane the strip down to this line. The drawer should run smoothly.

Replacing a drawer bottom

Originally, the bottom will have been made from a thin sheet of solid wood. In some cases it will have shrunk so much that there will be a gap at the front or the back. It is worth repairing this, since any contents that fall through the gap may damage the drawer rail as the drawer is closed. If the bottom is large enough, you may be able to slide it forward to close the gap.

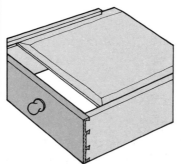

Inserting a new drawer base Cut a sheet of plywood to fit into the grooves on three sides of the drawer. If you cannot find plywood of the required thickness, buy the closest thickness and plane off a shallow angle on the underside at three edges. Slide in the new bottom and attach it with small countersunk screws.

Mending a springing door

If a door will not stay closed, examine its hinged side. If you can detect slight flexing of the hinges at the moment of closing, the door is "hinge-bound." This is usually due to a loose or badly fitted hinge.

Tighten up any loose screws that you find—one might be projecting slightly and catching on the other flap of the hinge. If you find a screw that is too big to lie flush in its countersink, remove the hinge, plug the holes, and replace it with one of the correct size.

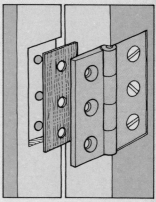

Resetting a badly fitting hinge A hinge may be mounted so that one or both of the flaps are let into the wood too deeply. Remove the hinge and cut a piece of thin veneer to shim out the housing. Put in one screw, check the door's action, then put in the remaining screws.

Adjusting a sagging door

There are several reasons why a door may drop so that it binds against the bottom of a cupboard or sticks against its twin door. First inspect the top hinge to see if it is loose. Replace any loose or missing screws. If the hinge itself is worn, replace it with a new one of similar style. If you cannot find a good match, replace both hinges, recut the housing, and plug the old screw holes. It is possible to extend the life of the original hinges by swapping them top for bottom. This will even out the wear at the knuckles. If the hinge is not at fault, the frame itself may have split at the hinge (see below).

Mending a split frame If the frame of a cupboard door splits at the hinge point it will release the screws. If this is the case, remove the door and flex the split slightly so that you can introduce some glue, then clamp it tightly. Wrap a damp tissue around a swizzle stick and use it to clean excess glue from the screw holes and housing before it sets. Finally, replace the hinge with the original screws.

Coping with a sticking door

Sometimes a door will stick even though the hinges are in good condition. Before you make any adjustments, make sure that the cabinet is standing level. If it is not, try placing a little cardboard under one front leg.

Having satisfied yourself that the cabinet is square, look to see exactly where the door is rubbing on the frame. A scuffed finish is an obvious sign, but if the contact is only slight it may only leave a shiny patch. Running a thin piece of paper between the door and frame may show where the door is catching.

If the door is made from solid wood, you can skim it with a plane until it closes satisfactorily. If it is veneered you should only plane the hinge side and the bottom edge. It is more difficult to gauge the amount of material to remove in this case, so err on the side of caution.

Mounting a new hinge

You may have to replace a damaged section of frame that incorporates a hinge housing because it is so badly split or decayed that a strong joint cannot be guaranteed. In such a case, you will need to cut a new housing and then remount the hinge. Lay the hinge in position and draw round its outline using a sharp pencil.

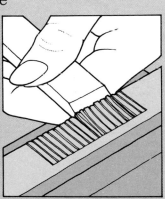

2 To cut out the housing, use a mallet and chisel. Chop across the waste wood every $\frac{1}{16}$ in (2 mm) or so, then pare it out with a chisel.

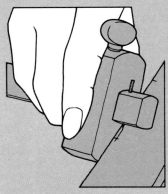

1 To locate the housing on the new wood measure from the edge of the cabinet to the edge of the hinge on the remaining housing. Mark the ends of the new housing with a knife and try square. Set a marking gauge from the edge of the hinge flap to the center of its knuckle and mark the back of the new housing. Set the gauge to half the width of the knuckle and mark the depth of the new housing.

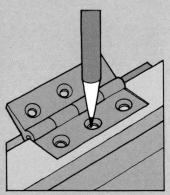

3 Check the fit of the hinge— the knuckle pin should be set halfway into the wood. Use the hinge to mark screw positions. Drill pilot holes, then screw the hinge in place.

Repairing a split panel door

Just as an antique cabinet itself may be made up of a solid frame enclosing thin sheets of wood, cabinet doors are often made using this "frame and panel" construction to reduce the risk of splitting and warping. Unfortunately, it does not always work. If the panel is restricted in its movement by pins or glue it will probably crack as it shrinks.

You can repair such damage by opening up the crack with the tip of a saw blade, then gluing in veneer, as you would for a split in a cabinet's side.

However, if the joint in the panel has opened up, it is better to glue the two halves of the panel back together. The method you should use will depend on the construction of the door. If the panel is held in a rebate in the frame by beading pinned round the inside, carefully lever out the beading with a chisel, then lift out the panel. If the panel is held in a grooved frame you may have to dismantle it to release the panel.

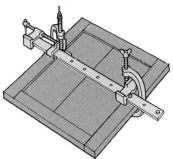

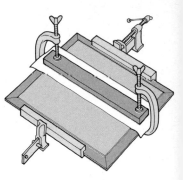

Mending a split in a grooved frame Before taking drastic action, such as steaming joints apart, which would spoil the finish, try closing up the gap by clamping a C clamp to each half of the panel. Use softwood blocks to protect the wood. Then use a sash clamp to pull the C clamps toward each other, pulling the joint together at the same time. If this fails, you will have to loosen the glued joints with steam and then tap them apart (see p. 115).

Mending a split in a rebated frame Clean up and glue the broken joint, holding the panel together with a sash clamp while the glue sets. You may have to move the clamp up or down to ensure that the panel is flat. Place softening blocks, grooved to fit over the edge of the panel, under the clamps. To stop the joint sliding apart, clamp a stout batten on each side of the panel, and insert waxed paper to stop them gluing together.

Drawer and door furniture

If you have a piece that has lost a pull or has been fitted with out-of-style pulls that you wish to replace, make sure that you choose pulls of the right period —it is just as inappropriate to replace the wooden knobs on a nineteenth-century chest with brass handles as it was for the Victorians to change the brass handles on eighteenth-century chests to wooden knobs. Unfortunately, it is almost impossible to find original sets of brass pulls, so you will have to buy reproduction ones from a specialist ironmonger. Matching reproduction metal key escutcheons are usually available —as are replacement wooden knobs.

Fixing handles

Most pulls are attached with threaded rods which pass through the wood and are secured by a nut on the inside. Metal or china knobs usually have a single screw projecting from their back face, whilst wooden knobs have their own coarse screw thread. These screw into matching holes on the drawer front.

If the thread on the back of a wooden knob is allowed to work loose it is likely to wear. To prevent this, reglue it immediately. If serious wear has occurred, make a saw cut down the center of the knob's worn thread and glue and wedge it from inside the drawer front.

Cleaning methods

Clean metal fittings with the appropriate metal cleaner. It is best to remove metal knobs, handles and key escutcheons before cleaning them. If they are difficult to remove, protect surrounding wood with masking tape to prevent dirty metal cleaner being rubbed into it. You will also need to mask plated metal when you clean the wood.

Decorative knobs

Cabinet handle with pivots

Escutcheons

Decorative washers

Swan-neck handle with pivots

Decorative backplate

Ormolu mounts

UPHOLSTERY

Buying upholstered furniture

The earliest examples of upholstery were loose cushions made to soften hard, flat solid timber seats. By the mid-nineteenth century, upholsterers had developed much more sophisticated techniques using hair stuffing and springs to "sculpt" chair coverings. These traditional methods are still used today to restore antique furniture.

Upholstery is a very skilled craft—many years of experience are required to restore some pieces. There is a great deal to learn—far more, in fact, than can be explained in this book. However, the techniques covered here are the most important ones. Once you have mastered them, you will be able to tackle more ambitious projects.

Identifying stripped frames

If you come across a frame without its upholstery you will have to decide what kind of upholstery was intended. A frame which should have a drop-in pad has rabbets or blocks on the inside of the rail to support the pad, and the polished framework has no tack holes. Overstuffed chairs have unfinished frames. To tell if they were sprung or not, look at the tack holes—if they are on the underside of the seat rail, then the chair contained springs, if they are on the top edge, then it did not. Sprung chairs have corner blocks near the rail's bottom edge, non-sprung types have bracing notched into the top edge.

Drop-in seat pad

Although no upholstery task can be described as easy, a drop-in seat pad is the simplest project for a complete beginner. Because the pad itself is removable, you can work on it at your bench unhindered by the frame.

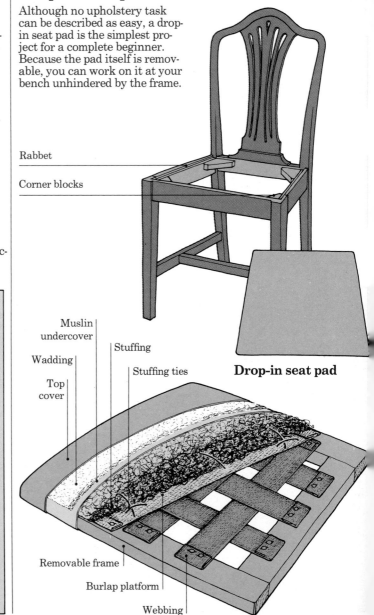

Rabbet

Corner blocks

Muslin undercover

Wadding

Top cover

Stuffing

Stuffing ties

Drop-in seat pad

Removable frame

Burlap platform

Webbing

Damage checks

*A simple repair
**Some experience needed
***Skilled work—not for beginners

***Is **the frame** in poor condition? Unless the dust panel is off, the frame will be hidden. Test it by tipping the chair onto its back legs and pressing on the front rail. If there is any movement in the back joints reject the chair. Test the front frame too.
*If the **basic cushioning** is sound (the webbing platform is intact, the springs return to form a symmetrical domed seat, and the edges of the seat are firm), you can recover it with fresh wadding and a new cover.

Sprung overstuffed seat

Once you can successfully repair a sprung overstuffed chair, you are well on the way to becoming an upholsterer. This job contains all the elements of traditional upholstery—sewing and lacing a coil spring platform, judging the amount and shape of stuffing, and sculpting it with stitches. The top cover is either tacked and trimmed to the side of the seat frame, or wrapped and tacked underneath.

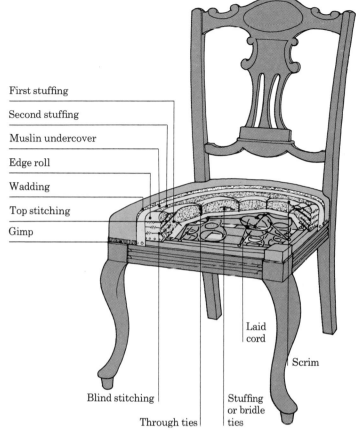

First stuffing

Second stuffing

Muslin undercover

Edge roll

Wadding

Top stitching

Gimp

Laid cord

Scrim

Blind stitching

Through ties

Stuffing or bridle ties

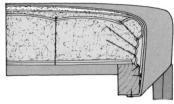

Wrapped-under cover

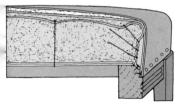

Side-fixed cover

Overstuffed seat without springs

To upholster a chair which does not have springing inside its overstuffed seat you combine the techniques used on the other two chairs shown here. The frame is webbed and the stuffing fastened on a burlap platform as for the drop-in seat pad (see p. 139). Then you make a row of stuffing ties (see p. 139) around the perimeter to build a very firm edge to the cushion. Finally, complete the rest of the upholstery as for the sprung seat (see p. 141).

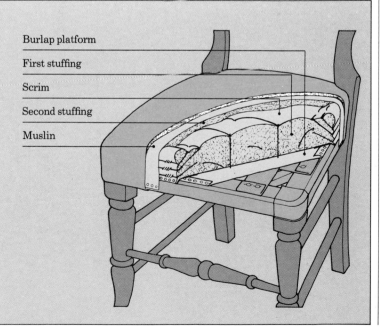

Burlap platform

First stuffing

Scrim

Second stuffing

Muslin

Tools and materials

Before you begin working, it is important
to support the chair frame at the right level
so that you can work comfortably. The best
method is to lay boards across trestles to make
a table of a convenient length and height.

Tools

Many upholsterer's tools are
specialized items. You will have
to buy some of these, but in
many cases you can make do
with more common tools from
your existing kit.

Hammer You can use an ordinary tack hammer to upholster
furniture, but a genuine upholsterer's hammer is superior. It
has a narrow head for driving
tacks in confined areas, and
often incorporates a small claw
for removing them. Some upholstery hammers are magnetized
so that you can pick up a tack
on the face of the hammer.
This frees one hand to hold
the fabric taut.

Ripping chisel This chisel
looks like a screwdriver, but the
blade is often wider, and it is
used to drive out tacks. You hit
it with a carpenter's mallet.

Using a ripping chisel Place
the tip of the blade under the
fabric against the head of the
tack, then hit the chisel with
the mallet, at the same time
levering with the chisel handle
to lift out the tack. You can use
an old screwdriver to do this
job, but you may have to grind
the tip to sharpen it.

Tack lifter The small claw at
the end of this tool is used for
prying awkward tacks from the
frame. It is especially useful on
show wood edges where a ripping chisel would be unsuitable.

Staple gun Useful for fixing
dust panels to the undersides of
chair seats. Some upholsterers
fix the fabric temporarily with
tacks, then when they are satisfied with the shape of the upholstery they staple the fabric.

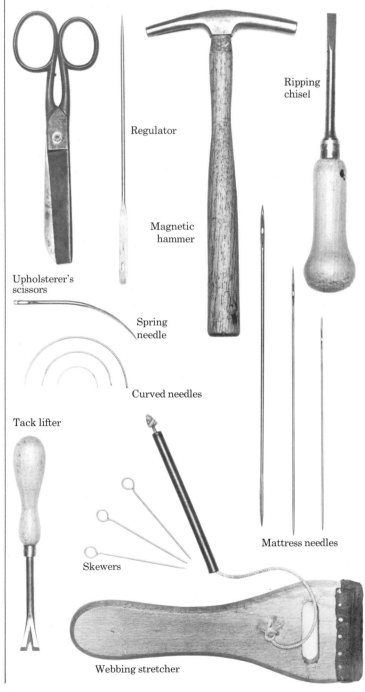

Upholsterer's
scissors

Regulator

Magnetic
hammer

Ripping
chisel

Spring
needle

Curved needles

Tack lifter

Skewers

Mattress needles

Webbing stretcher

Webbing stretcher There are professional stretchers available, or you can make one by cutting a V-shaped notch across one end of a block of wood.

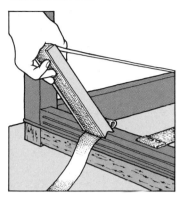

Using a webbing stretcher
When the webbing is tacked at one end, wrap the other end over the stretcher and tuck it into the notch, holding the tool against the frame. Lever down on the stretcher—this pulls the length of webbing taut across the frame.

Needles You will need several types of needle. A mattress needle (a large double-ended needle with a single eye) is used to make the special stitches which pull the stuffing into shape. A spring needle is curved, with a broad bayonet point. You use it for sewing coil springs to burlap panels. You will also need some small, curved needles to sew pleats and welting.

Regulator The pointed end of this tool is used to coax stuffing into the required position once it is covered with fabric. The paddle-shaped end can be used to shape pleats.

Scissors Choose a large pair of scissors to cut out fabric and a smaller pair for trimming.

Sharp knife A heavy craft knife with disposable blades is ideal for trimming the edge of tacked fabric.

Skewers Use these long pins to hold cover pleats in place temporarily.

Materials

Webbing Use 2 in (5 cm) cotton webbing for chair seats. This type is woven in a black and white herringbone pattern, enabling you to distinguish it from the cheaper jute webbing which is really only suitable for back rests.

Springs If you are lucky, you will be able to reuse the old springs. But if they are broken or distorted, buy replacements from an upholstery supplier. Take an old one with you to obtain a match.

Burlap This coarse, brown fabric is woven from jute. Use a heavyweight 16 oz (456 g) type for seat platforms.

Scrim A lightweight, open-weave burlap used for covering the first stuffing.

Stuffing materials For the first stuffing a vegetable fiber such as palm fiber or the finer type made from coconut husks and known as coco fiber is used. The best material is used for the second (top) stuffing, and is a mixture of animal hair.

Wadding A thin sheet of cotton faced with paper, wadding is laid over the muslin undercover to prevent the hair stuffing working through the top cover.

Muslin This thin, unbleached fabric is used to cover the second stuffing.

Cambric A cheap, black fabric stretched across the underside of chair seats in order to finish them.

Top covers It is essential to use a strong, closely woven fabric for the top cover. The better the quality however, the more you will have to pay. Antique chairs look best covered with traditional fabrics like tapestry, brocade, damask and velvet.

Trimmings These are applied to upholstery to cover exposed rows of tacks. There is a huge range of decoratively woven braids and gimps. Some chairs are finished with a row of decorative round-headed nails, usually driven through a cover strip.

Tacks Upholsterer's cut tacks have wide, flat heads for gripping fabrics. They also have very sharp points so that you can push them into wooden frames before hammering them home. You should use $\frac{5}{8}$ in (16 mm) improved tacks for fixing webbing, burlap platforms, temporary tacking and to anchor laid cord. Use smaller $\frac{3}{8}$ in (10 mm) or $\frac{1}{2}$ in (12 mm) to finish tacking covers.

Gimp pins These small colored pins are used to fix braid to the seat rail.

Buttons Forms covered with fabric are used to pull down deep upholstery. If you do not want to cover them yourself, a local upholsterer or supplier may be able to cover them.

Latex adhesive Use this white glue for fixing braid.

Twine Strong brown twine is made in several thicknesses. Use a No. 1 twine to sew springs in place and for through ties. Use thinner No. 2 twine for stitching a firm edge roll on a stuffed-over seat. Most upholsterers wax twine before use by drawing it across a block of beeswax. This helps it to hold a tight knot.

Laid cord Thick jute or hemp cord is used to lace coil springs together.

Welting cord This soft cotton cord is wrapped in top covering fabric and used to finish a seamed edge. It is available in three thicknesses—$\frac{1}{4}$ in (6 mm), $\frac{3}{16}$ in (5 mm), and $\frac{1}{8}$ in (3 mm).

Threads Use strong thread to close pleats and attach piping. Match the color of the thread to the top cover so that it does not stand out.

Restoring existing upholstery

Few of the antique upholstered chairs offered
for sale are in pristine condition. Your first
decision should therefore be whether the
chair needs merely cleaning and a few simple
repairs or whether it requires new upholstery.
If the piece needs to be re-upholstered, there
is no point in cleaning the top cover because
you cannot refit it. However, if the seat itself
is in good condition and the fabric merely
dirty, it should respond to gentle cleaning.

Caution: Do not discard genuine period
fabric if there is any way of restoring it.

You can tackle the job yourself, using a
foam shampoo. First, test the fabric to make
sure that the colors do not run (choose an
inconspicuous area). Clean the fabric by rubbing the foam into it with a sponge, working
from clean areas onto dirty ones. When dry,
vacuum or brush the surface.

Minor repairs

Small tears and missing buttons are easy to repair. You
may need to replace worn
welting (see p. 230), or close up
open seams with a ladder or
slip stitch (see p. 230).

Repairing torn fabric
Small, triangular tears can be
mended by gluing in a patch of
fabric with latex adhesive.

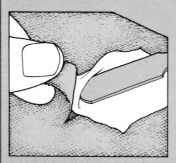

Gluing in a patch First, lift
the torn fabric so that you can
work the patch in with a regulator until it is directly under
the hole. Then carefully paint
latex onto the patch with a
small brush, and press the tear
into the glue. If necessary,
hold it closed with skewers
until the glue has set.

Replacing a button
Use a button mold which
matches the other buttons on
the chair, and cover it with
some spare material cut from
inside the frame. Remove
the back cover of the chair
and push a mattress needle
threaded with fine twine, eye
first, through the stuffing from
back to front. Leaving the
needle in place, pull the twine
free and thread on the button.
Rethread the needle, then pull
it back through the stuffing.

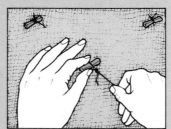

Securing with a toggle Tie
a slip knot at the back of
the fabric (see p. 230), with a
toggle (a small patch of rolled-
up fabric) placed underneath.
Shape front pleats with a regulator, then pull twine tight.
Slip stitch the cover back.

Removing stains

You can avoid many stains simply by wiping off spills immediately, then sponging the area
with a little clean water to remove any residue which might
discolor the fabric. However, if
a stain is left when the fabric
dries, lather up a little upholstery shampoo on a sponge and
rub the stained area with this
foam. Leave the fabric to dry,
then vacuum it. Unfortunately,
if the cover is dirty, cleaning
may produce a light patch; in
this case you will have to shampoo the whole piece.

Greasy spots are more difficult to remove. Try a commercial dry cleaning fluid on
a cloth, rubbing toward the center of the stain so that you do
not spread it. Then wipe the
area with a damp sponge. Another way is to make up a poultice by mixing an absorbent
powder such as fuller's earth or
talcum with some dry cleaning
fluid. Leave it on the stain until
dry, then brush off.

Larger stains can be dry
cleaned with an aerosol cleaning fluid. Spray this onto the
fabric and wait for it to evaporate. It leaves a powder which
you brush or vacuum off.

Candlewax can be picked off
the fabric with a fingernail, but
it will usually leave a stain behind. To remove this, lay some
blotting paper over the mark
and press it with a lukewarm
iron so that the wax is absorbed
into the paper. You may have to
iron it several times, using a
clean area of the paper each
time, before the stain is completely absorbed.

Chewing gum is notoriously
difficult to remove from upholstery. You must get it off before
it begins to attract dust. Put
some ice cubes in a plastic bag
and place this on the gum to
freeze it. When the gum has
hardened, chip it off.

Ripping off

Ripping off is an upholsterer's term for removing old upholstery. This is a filthy job, so put on old clothes and wear a face mask. Begin by removing the dust panel, covering fabrics and webbing, using a ripping chisel or tack lifter (for show wood) to get the tacks out. Work all round the frame, always driving in the direction of the grain to avoid splitting the rail. You will have to hold a drop-in seat pad in a bench vise.

Cut the twine holding the springs to the coverings and compress them with your hands. As long as they are not broken, and will return well, you can re-use them.

Discard all the old covering material, unless you find horsehair. This top-quality stuffing can be revived. Tease it apart to shake out all the dust, then wash it in warm, soapy water. Tease it out once more and leave it to dry.

Repairing a chair frame

Before you begin to upholster, carry out any repairs and refinishing necessary (see pp. 105–119). The rails on a chair that has been upholstered many times may be splintered and need reinforcing.

Reinforcing wood To make sure that your tacks grip, stipple woodworking glue on to the rails and then lay a piece of burlap over it. Paint more glue on top to saturate the burlap, then rub it down onto the rail with a block of wood.

A drop-in seat pad

Many dining chairs have a loose upholstered pad which drops inside the seat rails to rest on rabbets. This pad is an ideal first project, since, although simple, it incorporates techniques required for more difficult examples.

Stage 1

Begin by stretching upholstery webbing across the cleaned wooden frame of the pad. Most pads are webbed on top of the frame. But occasionally drop-in pads include small coil springs (see p. 141), in which case tack the webbing to the underside.

Clamp the frame to a bench, and work out the position of each web. If in doubt, space them about 1 in (2·5 cm) apart.

1 Leaving the webbing in a roll, fold 1 in (2·5 cm) over. Place it fold uppermost on the rail and drive in five tacks. Use the stretcher to tension the web across the frame. A tensioned web should "ring" when tapped.

2 Fix the web on the other side with two or three tacks, then cut off the roll, leaving about 1 in (2·5 cm) of webbing to fold over the tacks. Drive two more tacks through the fold.

3 Stretch the front to back webs, then weave and tack the cross webs in the same way.

Stage 2

Cover the webs with a panel of heavyweight burlap about $\frac{3}{4}$ in (18 mm) larger all round than the frame. Make a 1 in (2·5 cm) fold along one edge and tack it every inch (2·5 cm). Stretch the panel across the frame, tacking it every 2 ins (5 cm). Fold excess burlap over the tacks and drive another tack between each one.

Stage 3

To hold the stuffing to the burlap panel you must make a series of stuffing ties across it.

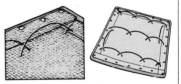

1 Thread a half-circle needle with a length of No. 1 twine, making a slip knot (see p. 230) at one corner of the panel. Sew three or four rows of loose ties.

2 Make sure that you can fit two fingers under each tie. Finish with a double hitch (p. 230).

Stage 4

Now you are ready to add the stuffing, tucking it carefully under the securing ties. You should use either coco fiber or palm fiber (see p. 137) for this stage.

1 Tuck bundles of your chosen fiber under each tie, teasing the fiber bundles out to form even rows. Start at the far edge and work forward.

2 Add extra stuffing between the rows. Then pile up the teased stuffing on top, building it up to a height of about 4 ins (10 cm) in the middle.

Stage 5

Tear a muslin undercover 2–3 ins (5–7.5 cm) larger than the frame. Stretch it across the stuffing, attaching it with a temporary tack in each rail.

1 Hold the frame vertically, with one corner on the bench, propping it between your body and arm so that your fingers can hold the fabric against the underside of the frame. Drive in three or four temporary tacks. Turn the frame onto the other corners and tack the edges in the same way. Remove the four temporary tacks. Stretching the fabric diagonally, pull each corner over the frame and tack.

2 On one edge, remove the tacks that hold the fabric. Tension it and smooth over the stuffing using the flat of your hand.

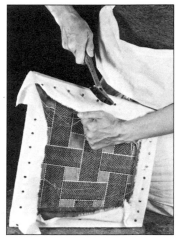

3 Hold the fabric against the frame while driving a row of evenly spaced tacks from the center to each corner. After every three or four tacks, stretch and smooth the fabric. Tack the opposite edge, then the other two sides. Finally, tension the corners one at a time, driving home a tack in each. Adjust the pad shape with a regulator if necessary. Tack neat pleats at each corner, and then trim the fabric close to the tacks.

Stage 6

Before you fit the top cover, cut a layer of wadding slightly larger than the pad and lay it squarely on top.

1 Holding the wadding down with one hand, pluck at its edges to feather it off so that it does not show as a ridge under the cover. Cut the top cover 2 ins (5 cm) larger all round than the pad, and cut a notch to mark the center of each side. Then mark the middle point on the underside of each rail with a felt-tip pen. Lay the pad on the cover, aligning the center marks as you tack it in place. Use the procedure described for fitting the muslin undercover in Stage 5.

2 Once you have fitted your top cover (above), the final task is to fit a dust panel to the underside of the pad. Stretch and fix it in a similar way to the first burlap panel (see p. 139), but turn the edges under all round. Make sure that it covers all the tacks and follows the edges of the pad.

A sprung seat

A great many antique dining chairs feature sprung overstuffed seats. Restoring one of these involves the traditional techniques of building up a thick seat pad using coil springs and horsehair or fiber stuffings. On some chairs the undercover and top cover are tacked to the side of the rail just above the show wood. Where no show wood exists, you wrap and tack both covers under the rail.

As for the drop-in seat, attaching the webbing is the first step (see p. 139). To allow for the springs, it should be tacked to the underside of the frame seat. Space the strips so that each spring can be positioned directly over an intersection of webs.

Stage 1

All dining chairs have four or five coil springs per seat. You can sew the springs in place with the chair either standing on its legs or laid on its back.

1 Arrange the springs so that their twisted ends face toward the center, forming a domed seat. If you have a central spring, face its twisted end toward the front of the seat. Use a spring needle threaded with No. 1 twine to stitch the coil springs to the webbing.

2 Starting with the central spring, pass the spring needle through the web close to the outside of the bottom coil and back down close to the inside of the coil, then make a slip knot (see p. 230). Leave the thread intact and make three half-hitches (p. 230) around the same coil at equal intervals.

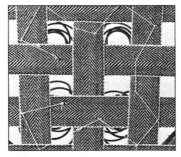

3 Do not cut the thread—carry onto the next spring, sewing it in place with four half-hitches. Link all four springs, tying off with a double hitch (p. 230).

Stage 2

To make sure that all the springs work in unison, lace their tops together with laid cord. This cord is anchored to the seat frame with $\frac{5}{8}$ in (15 mm) improved tacks. Drive two tacks halfway into the top edge of each side rail, aligning them with the position of the springs. Then cut four lengths of laid cord, each twice as long as the depth of the seat.

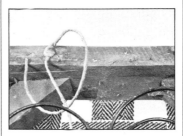

1 Knot one length of cord around one back tack, leaving 9 ins (22 cm) hanging. Drive the tack home to grip the cord.

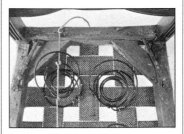

2 Compress the first spring and tie a clove hitch (see p. 230) around the second coil from the top. Then take the cord diagonally across to the top coil and tie a lock loop (see p. 230).

3 Compress the next spring, lock-loop the cord to the top coil, take it down to the second coil and knot it with a half-hitch. Tie the cord to the tack leaving a 9 in (22 cm) tail. Repeat with the other side springs.

4 Now lace the springs across the seat in the same sequence. Whenever you cross one cord over another, tie a lock loop as this helps to make a firm seat platform.

5 Take the end of each cord hanging from the tacks up to the top coil of the nearest spring and tie it on with a double hitch.

6 Throughout the lacing process you should be keeping the tension the same on all the cords. If you have done this, the springs will lean outward to form an even dome shape, providing a good foundation for the stuffing.

Stage 3

The springs must be covered with a heavyweight burlap panel to prevent the stuffing you apply subsequently falling through the seat.

1 You should cut out a heavy-weight burlap panel about 1 in (2·5 cm) larger all round than the frame of your particular chair. Temporarily tack the panel to the top edge of the seat rails. Position the burlap accurately by tensioning one side at a time. Then fold the edges of the burlap over and tack it permanently in place on all four sides.

When tensioning the burlap panel you should make sure that you do not compress the springs any further. Extra compression may make the lacing slacken so that the springing will not function.

2 To attach the burlap to the top of the springs, use the same method you employed when sewing the springs to the webbing (Stage 1). This will prevent movement between them which would wear through the burlap.

Stage 4

This stage involves stuffing the seat with coco fiber and covering this with scrim.

1 Make a row of stuffing ties (see p. 139) around the sloping side of the seat platform. Tuck handfuls of fiber under the ties, then fill the center to a height of about 4 ins (10 cm), teasing the fiber out with your fingers.

2 Cut a panel of scrim to cover the fiber. Fix it temporarily with one tack in the center of each rail, and make diagonal cuts into the two back corners to fit around the legs.

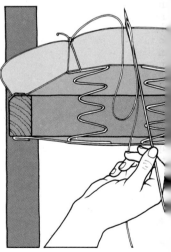

3 Make through ties between the scrim and the burlap to pull down the center of the seat. Thread a mattress needle with No. 1 twine and start with a slip knot in one corner on top, then pass the needle through the seat. As soon as the threaded end of the needle emerges underneath, move it about $\frac{3}{4}$ in (18 mm) to one side then push the threaded end back up through the seat so that it emerges near its original entry point.

4 Make another stitch about 4 ins (10 cm) to one side of the first and criss-cross the seat at 4 in (10 cm) intervals. At the last corner, tie thread (you pull it tight when the edge is tacked).

5 Remove one temporary tack and firm up that edge by stuffing a little fiber under the burlap. When you put tension on the burlap, the stuffing should form a firm, square edge if held in the crook of thumb and forefinger. Next, tuck the edge of the scrim under the stuffing with your fingertips. Pinch the scrim and pull it down, then closely tack it along the chamfered edge of the seat rail. Stuff more fiber in either side to build up the edge at the corners until it is hard.

6 Fold the edge in at the corner under the stuffing, tacking it to the rail as before. Work round each side in this manner.

7 Pleat the front corners to get rid of any excess fabric. Take up slack on the through ties and finish them off with a double hitch (see p. 230).

Stage 5

This stage involves shaping and firming up the scrim-covered edge of the seat pad using a series of special upholsterer's stitches.

Blind stitching

Blind stitches pull the stuffing against the side wall of the seat cushion. Use a regulator to pull the fiber up into the top corner of the seat to form a squarish edge. Then thread the mattress needle with No. 2 twine and make a row of blind stitches just above the tack line.

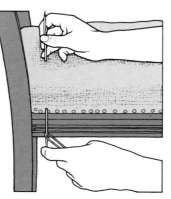

1 Start the blind stitching by pushing the needle into the scrim at an angle of 45°, about 1½ ins (4 cm) away from the back leg of the chair.

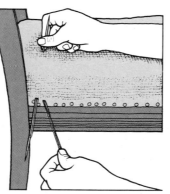

2 Pull the needle through the scrim and stuffing, but just before the eye emerges, angle it towards the chair leg and push it back so that it emerges just in front of the leg above the tack line. Pull the needle out completely, tie a slip knot in the twine and then pull the stitch tight.

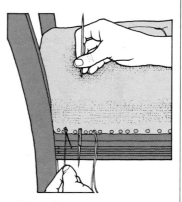

3 Move along 2 ins (5 cm) and insert the needle again at 45° and position it to emerge 1 in (2·5 cm) behind its point of entry. Just before the eye emerges, return it again to exit next to the first stitch.

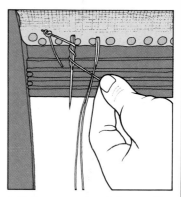

4 Before you extract the needle from the stuffing, wind the thread around it three times to bind the stitch.

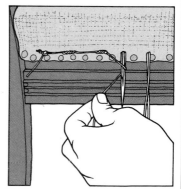

5 Pull the needle through the stuffing, tighten the stitch, make a row of stitches around the pad. Finish with a double hitch.

Top stitching

Once you have finished the blind stitching, you sculpt a square corner to the seat pad. To do this, you must sew two rows of top stitching around the pad using a mattress needle threaded with No. 2 twine.

1 Regulate the edge again, then insert the needle about 1 in (2·5 cm) away from the leg and about $\frac{3}{4}$ in (19 mm) above the row of blind stitches. Push the needle right through the seat pad at an angle of 45°.

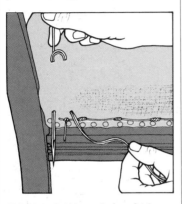

2 Move the threaded end 1 in (2·5 cm) back toward the leg and push it through the stuffing at the same angle so that it emerges next to the leg and the same $\frac{3}{4}$ in (19 mm) above the stitches. Pull the needle through and slip knot the twine. Pull the stitch tight.

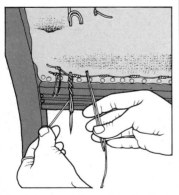

3 Make a stitch next to the first, but wind the twine around the needle three times as it emerges. After one row of stitches make another about $\frac{3}{4}$ in (19 mm) above, regulating as you go.

Stage 6

Make another series of stuffing ties across the scrim. Build up a 1 in (2·5 cm) layer of teased animal hair across the seat as described on p. 142.

1 Tear out an undercover of muslin about 4 ins (10 cm) larger all round than the seat and lay it over the second stuffing. Smooth the stuffing into an even dome as you pull down on this muslin cover.

Tack the muslin to the rail just above the show wood. Tack each side of the seat, working from the center of the rail toward the corners. Now proceed to neaten the muslin at the edges.

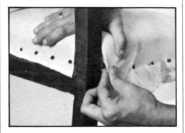

2 Make diagonal cuts into both back corners, then tuck in the excess fabric to make a neat folded edge against the leg.

3 The method for neatening the front corners varies. For a rounded corner, make two pleats, one each side. Or wrap fabric around the corner, folding excess into one front pleat.

Stage 7

Before fitting the top cover, place a layer of wadding over the pad, tearing it off all round to just above the bottom tack line (see p. 140).

Fit the top cover in exactly the same way as a muslin one (see Stage 6). After you have tacked the new cover in place, trim any excess material away with a sharp knife. Make corner pleats (see Stage 6), but cut away the excess fabric from inside the folds. Finally, if the pleats gape, close them up with slip stitching (see p. 228).

Finishing off

Two things remain to be done. First, a burlap dust panel must be fitted. This is simply stapled to the bottom of the chair (see p. 140). Second, braid must be pinned and glued over the tacks along the side and back rails.

Attaching braid Fold under one end of a length, and gimp pin it just in front of one leg. Paint latex adhesive on the inside of the braid and stick it round the frame, folding the other end under and pinning it. Run another length across the back edge of the chair.

CANE
AND RUSH

Buying caned or rushed pieces

Canework—interwoven thin strips cut from the glossy surface of the rattan stem—was introduced to Europe from India and China, and first became popular in Europe and America in the seventeenth century. Originally, it had a simple, open mesh, but gradually a closer, more decorative pattern was used.

Rush-seated chairs are known to have been made in Europe since the Middle Ages. And they have been in use in America since the arrival of the Pilgrim Fathers.

Caring for cane and rush

Canework will dry out and become brittle in a dry, centrally heated atmosphere—a humidifier will prevent this. To wash dirty cane or rush dip a cloth in warm, soapy water, wring it out and wipe over the surface. Rinse several times with clean water, as residues of soap may encourage mold. Rush is particularly vulnerable to mold, so leave the piece out in the sun to dry.

Bentwood rocking chair with cane panels

Detail of canework

Rush-seated ladder back chair

Detail of rushwork

Damage checks

*A simple repair
**Some experience needed
***Skilled work—not for beginners

Before examining the cane or rush itself, you should inspect the frame of the chair for damage (see p. 113).
*__Damage__ to cane and rushwork is immediately obvious. It is possible to cut out one broken cane and thread in a new length, but at best this is a temporary measure. You need not worry that recaning or rerushing will prove to be too difficult—in a short time you will be able to produce acceptable work.
***__Splits__ running from hole to hole along a seat rail can be difficult to close up in such a way that the frame is strong enough to support the caning.

Tools and materials

You will require very few tools and materials to work with cane and rush seating, and most of these will probably be in your basic tool kit already. If you do not want to restore the chair frames yourself (see pp. 114–9), you can employ another restorer to repair and refinish the chairs ready for reseating. You will not need a workshop for these jobs—just set the chair up so that you can work at a comfortable height in good daylight.

Tools for caning

Sharp knife Use a heavy-weight craft knife to cut out cane seats.

Clearing tool This is an improvised tool for clearing old pegs from frame holes. You can use any stiff metal rod of suitable diameter, such as a large nail with the point filed flat, or you could grind the tip from an old Phillips-head screwdriver.

Cane lever To lever up tight canes, thus enabling you to thread another cane, the best tool is a bayonet-pointed spring needle.

Long-nosed pliers Taper-nosed pliers will help you manipulate the cane.

Temporary pegs Use a short length of center cane or plastic golf tees to hold the canes while you work.

Pin hammer Use a small hammer to drive pegs into the holes.

Clippers End or side-cutting clippers are useful to cut lengths of cane and to trim the ends that hang below the seat.

Tools for rush seating

Rush lever An old, worn screwdriver or chisel will act as a lever to ease the last few cords into place and to manipulate knots.

Sharp knife Use a strong craft knife to trim off the rough ends of the rushes underneath the seat.

Strong scissors Use a large pair of scissors to trim the rushes before you begin work.

Roller An old lawnmower roller is useful to flatten the finished seat.

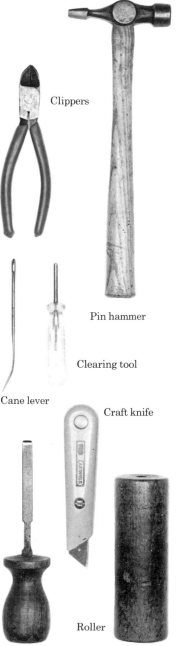

Clippers

Pin hammer

Clearing tool

Cane lever

Craft knife

Rush lever

Roller

Materials

Cane Cane used for seating is split into standard widths, numbered from 1 to 6. As you gain experience, you will be able to decide which width is best. As a guide, use the following sizes:
No 2 cane—all the front-to-back and side-to-side work.
No 3 or 4 cane—slightly wider cane for the diagonals.
No 6 cane—for beading edges.
No 2 cane—to loop over the beading cane.

Before you use cane, moisten it to make it supple. Take a bucket of warm water and immerse enough cane for one stage of the work at a time. Leave for a couple of minutes, then put it in a plastic bag to keep it moist. If the cane starts to dry out, wipe it over with a wet cloth.

Pegging Use No 14 or 16 center basket-weaving cane to peg holes, or trim wooden dowel to make tapered pegs.

Rushes Freshwater rushes are available from specialist suppliers, although supplies can be limited at certain times of the year. Rushes will be dry and brittle, and you must make them pliable. Sprinkle them with a watering can and leave for a few minutes to soften. Salt water rushes must be soaked for about 2 hours, then wrapped in a wet blanket.

Soft string Use string to tie rushes to the frame.

The six-way canework pattern

There are several patterns which can be used to weave a cane seat. The most common one is the six-way pattern. Although a finished example looks very complicated, once you grasp the simple principles of caning, it is just a matter of careful repetition.

Whenever you weave with cane, make sure that you always work with the shiny surface uppermost. If you run a piece of cane between your fingers it will feel smoother in one direction than it does in the other. Weave it in the smoother direction so that it does not catch.

Preparing the frame

Before you begin to clean and refinish the chair frame you must remove the old, worn cane chair seat. Using a sharp craft knife, cut out the main panel inside the frame. Then punch out any wooden pegs from the holes, and carefully pull out the remaining pieces of cane with pliers. Now you can clean and refinish the chair frame (see pp. 108–11). Once the frame is in good condition, you can start to recane the seat. Have all your tools and materials at hand, and dampen the cane before use (see p. 147).

Stage 1

Start by taking a long strip of dampened No 2 cane and peg it into the central hole in the back rail of the chair. If there is an even number of holes, choose one immediately next to the center of the rail, and peg the cane into it.

1 Now take the end of the strip of No 2 cane and thread it through the opposite hole on the front rail of the chair.

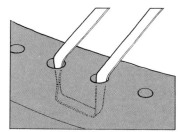

2 Pull the cane taut, at the same time making a half-twist on it so that its underside faces the next hole, and peg it in place. Take the end of the cane through the next hole, keeping the cane flat along the bottom of the seat rail. Make a half-twist so that the cane faces the back of the seat, and move the last peg into that hole.
  Thread the cane through the opposite hole on the back rail, make a half-twist toward the adjacent hole, and move the peg again to plug that hole.

3 Continue threading cane across one half of the seat, moving the peg each time. Leave the back corner hole free—this is needed for a later stage. Do not leave the cane slack or put too much tension on it, as you will find it difficult to weave later.

4 Eventually you will have to start a new length of cane. Peg the first piece into a hole, leaving at least 3 ins (7·5 cm) hanging below the rail. Plug the new cane into the next available hole in the opposite rail.

5 Lace the other half of the seat. Make sure that you leave the back corner hole free.

6 If the seat frame is tapered, you will still have a few holes left at each end of the front rail, even though the back rail is full. Fill in each side using the same method, selecting holes in the side rails which will keep the cane running parallel. But leave the front corner holes free.

Stage 2

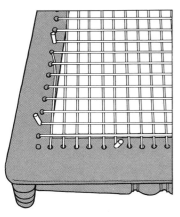

This stage involves placing a second series of canes at right angles to the Stage 1 canes. Avoiding the front corner hole, start by plugging one end of a strip of dampened No 2 cane into the next hole on the front rail of the chair.

You simply lay this series of canes on top of the first ones—there is no need to weave them over and under. As before, you must leave both the back corner holes free as they are needed for a later stage.

Stage 3

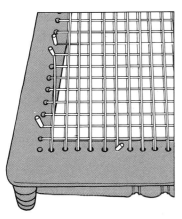

In this stage a second series of canes is positioned parallel and to the right of the Stage 1 canes. You work in exactly the same way as Stage 1. Again, do not weave the dampened cane over and under—just lay it on top of the Stage 2 canes. When threading the cane through the holes it is important to ease it to the right of the Stage 1 canes.

Stage 4

Stage 4 traces the path of Stage 2, but this time the cane is woven between those already in position. Plug one end of your length of cane into the Stage 2 starting hole. Working toward the left-hand side of the seat, pass the length through the first pair of canes, weaving over the nearest cane then under the second. Weave through a couple more pairs in the same way before you pull the working cane through. Continue in this manner across the seat, then back again, reversing the weaving pattern on the return leg by passing the cane under the first cane of each pair then over the second. Work each cane above those inserted in Stage 3.

Stage 5

The next step is to begin weaving the diagonal canes. Now you will put into use those corner holes you left free earlier. As before, you use dampened No 2 cane.

1 Weave the first diagonal cane by plugging one end into the empty back right-hand corner hole. Weave the cane toward the corner of the seat diagonally opposite, passing it under the front-to-back pairs of cane, and over the side-to-side ones. Pull the cane through after every three to four pairs.

2 When caning a tapered seat, the path of the first cane will not coincide with the actual corner hole. Instead, it will fall on a hole in the front rail, perhaps two or three away from the corner.

3 Pass the first cane down and up through the next hole on the right in the usual way, then weave it back across the diagonal, and pass it down the hole that it started from.

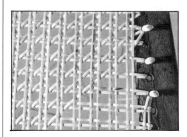

4 Pass it up through the next hole and weave it back across the chair until one half of the seat is caned. To keep the diagonals parallel on a tapered seat you will have to decide which hole to use from time to time. Occasionally you will have to use a hole in the side rails twice, in which case, make sure that two canes woven in Stage 6 go into the same hole on the opposite side rail so that the pattern can be repeated.

5 Weave the other side of the chair in the same way. When you come to the front left-hand corner hole, pass through it twice to repeat the pattern in the opposite corner.

Stage 6

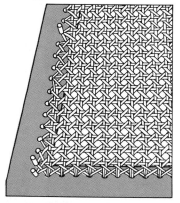

Weave a second set of diagonal canes at right-angles to the first. Start in the back left-hand corner hole and repeat the Stage 5 sequence except that you weave over the front-to-back pairs and under the side-to-side ones. When you come to those holes filled twice on the opposite side rail during Stage 5, pass through them twice.

Beading the edge

The most satisfactory finish to a cane seat is achieved by pegging alternate holes, then covering the holes with a length of wide No 6 cane held in place with narrower No 2 cane. To make a peg, push a length of center cane into the hole and use clippers to cut it off just above the surface of the seat rail. Tap in the pegs with a hammer, then drive them below the surface with a clearing tool. When you come to a temporary peg, cut it off and drive it below the surface.

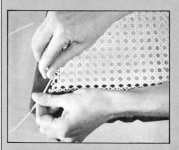

Tidying loose ends Sometimes you will find that a hole you want to skip is temporarily pegged. In such a case, pass the short end of the loose cane up through the next hole, pulling on it from above until you have driven a permanent peg home. Before beading, trim off the end.

1 Begin beading by passing the end of a No 2 cane through a back corner hole from the underside. Bend about 1½ ins (3·5 cm) over to follow one line of holes, then push the end of a No 6 beading cane into the same hole from above. Secure both canes with a peg.

2 Bend the beading cane so that it covers the end of the No 2 cane. Pass the other end of the No 2 cane up through the next free hole. Loop it over the beading cane, then thread it back down the same hole.

3 Continue to the next corner. Trim the end of the beading cane and push it into the hole. Plug the end of the next beading cane into the same hole and peg both. Cross diagonally under the corner of the seat rail with the No 2 cane, threading it up through the next open hole. Continue until all four sides are covered.

4 Trim the end of the last beading cane to fit the starting hole. Pass the end of the No 2 cane up through the same hole and drive in a permanent peg. Finally, trim off any loose ends.

Rerushing a chair

Like caning, renewing a rush seat is a reasonably simple procedure. Although there are cord substitutes for real rushes, none of them matches up to the subtle coloring and feel of the genuine article. If you want to use a substitute such as seagrass, the method is similar except that the cord is already twisted.

Twisting a cord

To get a firm, corded effect, rushes have to be twisted together while they are worked. This cording of the material is only carried out on top of the chair seat.

1 Tie 2 or 3 rushes together, then hold them in your left hand while twisting them clockwise with your right. Twisting a cord tends to compress air trapped inside the rushes. Expel it by gripping the rushes tightly between finger and thumb, then give them a sharp tug, running your fingers quickly down the length. You will hear a "pop" as the rush splits to release the trapped air.

Rushes are corded for the upper part of the seat only. They are stretched underneath without twisting.

2 When you use up a length of cord, you will have to join one length of rushes to another. The best way to do this is by knotting the working bundle to a new length of rushes underneath the seat.

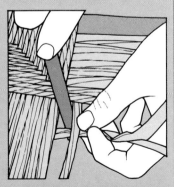

3 To keep the thickness of the twisted cord constant, you may sometimes have to add a single rush to it. You should do this at the corner of the seat, inserting the end of the new rush between the working cord and the last one worked. Then twist the new rush into the existing cord.

Stage 1

With chairs that are wider at the front than the back, your first step is to compensate for this by filling in the ends of the front rail. When the corners are filled, the gap between the two rows should be the same as the length of the back rail.

1 Tie the rushes to the left-hand seat rail with string. Twist them into a cord, then wrap this cord over the front rail close to the leg, up through the frame, over the side rail and back up through the frame. At this point in the work you will probably have to join two lengths of rushes (see left).

2 Continue across the frame to the right-hand corner, wrapping the cord over the side rail, through the frame, and over the front rail, then tie it to the inside of the side rail.

3 Continue to the next corner and repeat the wrapping procedure outlined in step 2. Work round the frame until all the corners are properly filled.

Stage 2

Start the process of weaving around the frame by tying another length of rushes to the left-hand side rail. Wrap the cord around both front corners as before but instead of tying it to the seat rail, continue right up to the back rail. Wrap the cord around both back corners in the same way, then stretch the rushes across the frame and take the cord over to the front left-hand corner again.

Stage 3

When you have woven eight or nine cords in each corner, tie the working length to the back leg and pack out corners.

1 With your fingers, pull each row of cords towards the nearest leg. Tighten up the cords and even out the diagonals.

2 Use a knife to trim off the loose ends of any rushes protruding from the bottom of the seat. Fold some off-cuts of rush in half, and tuck them into the pocket formed between the top and bottom rushes in each corner. Pack the off-cuts in tightly with the tip of a rush lever.

Stage 4

Once you have packed the corners, weave in the same way, squeezing up the corners and packing every eight or nine rows until you reach the center.

1 When you have to join rushes in a confined space, do not knot them, simply pass the working end into the center of the seat and twist both lengths together.

2 Unless the seat is square, you will fill one set of opposite rails before the other. Fill the gap by weaving cord in a figure-eight pattern between the rails.

3 At this stage the cords will have become very tightly packed, and this means that you will have to ease them apart with the tip of a rush lever in order to get the last couple of cords in. After you have completed the weaving, the last step is tying off the final cord.

4 To tie off the final cord, wrap it over the back rail and bring it to the center of the seat on the underside. Then lift up a central rush with a rush lever, hook the last cord over the tip and pull it through. Knot the cord tightly and trim off free ends. Use a ruler to bed down cords.

Rushing a chair with arms

Arm supports which plug into seat rails some distance behind the front legs require you to weave the seat in a different way. First, dismantle the arm rests and weave the rushes as far as the holes. Then for the next few rows, instead of wrapping the cords over the side seat rails, pass them through the holes. Once you have covered the inside, wrap the outer edge of the left-hand hole. Then take the cord across the seat to wrap the other hole. Finish the seat. Wet the rushes inside the holes before you insert the arm supports.

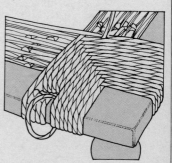

Wrapping the hole Wrap the outer edge with a rush cord. Then take this cord across to wrap the other side of the seat.

BOOKS

Collecting books

Although all of us have handled dozens if not hundreds of books, very few appreciate the ingenuity of their construction, evolved over the centuries. A well-made book should not need repair unless mistreated.

How books are constructed

Traditionally, books are made up of sections formed by folding a large printed sheet which is slit to form separate leaves. The sections are sewn together to form the book. Generally, older books have ragged edges to their leaves, whereas most modern books are trimmed square.

The pages
A book's pages—each side of a leaf—are numbered but, in addition, sections in old books were denoted by a letter or "signature". You will find these printed at the foot of the first page of each section.

The spine
The back of the spine is reinforced by open-weave fabric, or crash, glued across the back of the sections. Additional reinforcement is sometimes provided by cloth tapes or cords sewn across the spine. Headbands glued to the head of the spine were originally intended to strengthen it when the book was removed from the shelf. Now they are largely decorative.

The cover
Book covers are made by covering thick millboard or strawboard with book cloth or leather. With a leather binding, the boards were often sewn to the book with the reinforcing cord. Cloth covers, known as the case, are hinged by gluing crash, and sometimes the tapes, to the board. This joint between the book and the covers is further strengthened by wrapping the cover material round the spine and by gluing endpapers across the inside. Board and paper linings between the cloth cover and the spine allow the book to open without creasing the spine cover.

The pages

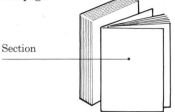

Section

The spine

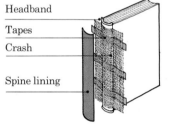

Headband
Tapes
Crash
Spine lining

The cover

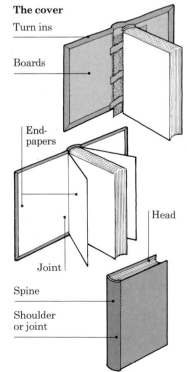

Turn ins
Boards
Endpapers
Head
Joint
Spine
Shoulder or joint

Damage checks

* A simple repair
** Some experience needed
*** Skilled work—not for beginners

*Loose leaves or plates can be glued back or "tipped in" very easily, but if several appear to be loose make sure that a whole section is not about to drop out.

***Missing pages cannot be replaced, so unless the book is rare, do not buy it.

*Missing endpapers are not difficult to replace.

* Uncut leaves—many early books have leaves with ragged edges. It is intentional on the part of the binder and the leaves should not be trimmed.

*** Stained or dirty paper can usually be renovated. However, a book which is stained extensively may have to be dismantled and resewn professionally.

* Most tears can be repaired easily as long as care is taken (see p. 157).

*** Detached section—unless you are prepared to take lessons in book binding, avoid books in which the sewing needs renewing.

*Dirty covers can be cleaned and refurbished easily.

*When the leather is dry, bindings can be revived with a dressing.

***Crumbling leather may be due to a condition known as "red rot". In such a case, seek the advice of a professional.

** Worn patches on covers can be touched in and damaged corners can be replaced.

** A broken hinge can be renewed, but if you are prepared to undertake this yourself you should ask for a generous reduction in price.

** If the spine cover is torn away, a book can be rebacked, but retain as much of the original binding as you can, including the spine cover itself. Again, a book in this condition should cost very little.

Tools and materials

Book binding and repair should not present any workshop problems for amateur restorers as these jobs require no special facilities. A firm work table covered with polyethylene sheeting and good lighting are all you need.

Tools

Knife Book binders use a cobbler's knife for trimming materials, but a craft knife with interchangeable blades is just as good.

Straight edge Use a steel rule for accurate straight cuts.

Paring knife Used for thinning leather to make short "turn-ins" and "joints". Some craftsmen use a spokeshave to skive leather (see p. 175).

Scissors Heavy-duty scissors are required for trimming.

Folder This is a smoothed plastic or bone tool used to rub down glued paper and cloth and to press joints to shape. Buy one from a book binder's supplier or make your own from plastic.

Brushes Use small artist's brushes and a $\frac{1}{2}$ in (12mm) painter's brush for applying glue.

Erasers These are used to clean dirty leaves (see p. 156).

Sponge This is used to apply paste and saddle soap. A natural sponge is best.

Needle You will need a needle to sew in a cloth hinge on leather-bound books. If possible, obtain a small-eyed book binder's needle.

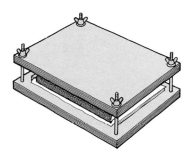

Making a book press You can make a book press from two sheets of thick plywood with a bolt and wing nut at each corner. When using a press of this type, tighten the bolts gradually, working diagonally from corner to corner to keep pressure even.

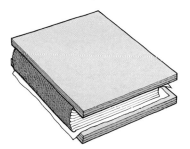

Using a book press With any press, protect the book on both sides with waxed paper and sandwich it between two sheets of plywood positioned with one edge close to the joint between the flat cover and the curved spine. This allows you to place the book in the center of the press without crushing the shoulders. Take care not to apply too much pressure to books with embossed covers.

Book press Although it may be possible to carry out some simple repairs by pressing a book under heavy weights, you will need a book press if you plan to restore books in any quantity. You can buy new presses from specialist suppliers.

Materials

Document cleaner and abrasive powder These are used for cleaning paper.

Bleach Ordinary bleach will remove stains from leaves.

Waxed paper Prevents glued leaves sticking together.

Micro-crystalline wax This is used to revive cloth covers.

Water-based inks Diluted, these are used for coloring faded cloth covers.

Saddle soap and leather dressing See p. 176.

Flour and water paste Use this mix for repairing torn paper and for cleaning old leather bindings. For gluing, mix up one part flour with two parts of water in a coffee can or a pan. Stand the can in a saucepan of water and bring to the boil, stirring continually until the mix thickens. Remove the paste from the heat and allow it to cool.

White glue Used for the structure of the book.

Tissue Use fine but strong "Japanese" tissue for repairing torn leaves.

Kraft paper A strong brown paper is used to line the spine.

Endpapers Use white bond or cartridge paper, or obtain specially printed material, such as marbled paper, from a specialist supplier.

Document repair tape This is a very thin, self-adhesive tape for repairing torn leaves. From specialist suppliers.

Crash This is an open-weave plain muslin used to strengthen spine and hinge.

Book cloth Cloths such as canvas, buckram, and linen are used dyed and starched for covering boards.

Leather Thin leather in natural and artificial colors is used for book covering.

Headbands Headbands of silk thread wrapped around a cord were originally attached to the head and sometimes the tail of the spine to reinforce it. Decorative headband ribbons are available from a book binder's supplier.

Cleaning books

As long as there is no damage to the book, you should start by cleaning the inside and then treat the cover. With a leather book, apply a paste wash first to make the book supple enough for subsequent repair work. After the repairs, apply a leather dressing.

Cleaning leaves

You can clean paper leaves and endpapers using the methods for artwork (see p. 165). The erasers, bread, and document cleaner are suitable for removing dirt and finger marks from any part of the book. Pencil notes can be erased in this way too, but not ink. Avoiding printed portions of the page, try gently abrading the surface with a very fine silicon carbide paper. Use small, circular strokes and check constantly against the light that you are not wearing through the paper.

Crayon can be lifted by coating the area with rubber-based adhesive, leaving it to dry, and then rolling the adhesive off with your fingers. Repeat this if some crayon remains. The adhesive sometimes may raise fibers from the surface of the paper, so test it before using on printed matter.

Colored endpapers can be cleaned with document cleaner, but avoid harsher methods. Coated endpapers that have a slightly powdery texture are very fragile and should not be touched.

Bleaching paper

Books are often stained with small brown spots, a condition known as foxing. Along with other stains, foxing can be bleached out, but the leaves have to be removed. If the staining is widespread the book will have to be dismantled and resewn. This is best left to a professional, who will bleach out the stains at the same time. To remove single pages, soak a piece of thin, soft string in water, lay it in the hinge of the book next to the page for removal, and close the book for about a minute. The water softens the page along a straight line so that it pulls out easily.

The other portion of the leaf left in the binding will probably be secure enough without further attention, but if necessary remove it at the same time.

Pages that are "tipped in"— that is, stuck to the adjacent page along the inner edge—can be removed by peeling back the glued joint.

Bleach individual pages as for artwork (see p. 165) but not so much that they look completely different from the rest of the book. After bleaching, put back their original stiffness by sizing the paper with a very runny flour and water paste. Apply it to both sides of a page with a small sponge, working outward from the center. Leave the page to dry on white blotting paper, then press it flat (see p. 155). Finally, tip the page back (see opposite) into position.

Treating mildew

A book damp enough to develop mold may have warped boards and cockled leaves with heavy staining. This will require professional attention. But if mildew has barely taken hold, stand the book on end with the boards open and the leaves fanned out. Leave it like this in a dry, airy environment, separating the leaves from time to time. Once the mildew has become powdery, you can then take the book outside and use a soft brush to remove deposits.

If damp conditions are affecting your books take action immediately to make sure that the problem does not worsen. Locate and treat the source of damp, examine your books for signs of deterioration, and thoroughly clean the shelves. At the same time inspect the shelves for woodworm as these pests will bore through books as well as wood (see p. 130).

Cleaning the top

Books invariably collect dust on the top. Holding the book tightly closed, blow the dust off the top. Use an artist's brush to clean dust off the headband and inner edges of the covers. If absolutely necessary, use a barely moistened ball of cotton to wipe the top clean from the spine to the foredge. Do not use water on any gilded edges, instead rub them over with a dry cotton pad.

Cleaning covers

Cloth covers are more easily cleaned than leather, but both benefit from careful attention.

Cloth covers

Wash grimy cloth covers with a damp sponge. Do not soak the surface, and keep water away from the pages. Be particularly careful if there is gold lettering or decoration on the cover as it can wash away easily. When the surface is quite dry, rub in micro-crystalline wax with circular strokes and polish with a soft cloth.

A faded spine can often be revived with a coat of wax. More extensive areas of fading are difficult to rectify. On inexpensive books you can, if you wish, recolor such areas using water-based inks applied with a cotton pad.

Scuffed or worn patches of cloth can be disguised by rubbing in colored starch scraped from new book cloth. Choose a piece which matches the book closely and dampen the surface. Scrape with a knife to form a moist paste. Dab the paste onto the worn area with your finger.

Leather bindings

Clean a dirty leather binding with saddle soap, followed by a treatment with leather dressing (see p. 176). Leave it to soak into the leather for a couple of hours, then buff it with a cloth.

Give old, dry leather books a "paste" wash to clean and consolidate the surface at the same time. Dip a damp sponge lightly in flour and water paste and rub it into the surface with circular strokes. Leave the leather to dry and then apply a dressing.

Repairing books

Book binding is a skilled craft which takes years of experience to perfect. Unless you can attend a class, you are advised to leave difficult tasks to a professional, especially with leather-bound books. Most of these are bound with different methods from those used for cloth-covered books. It requires a greater degree of skill to restore leather books properly and to avoid spoiling expensive materials. However, certain repairs are not beyond the ability of the amateur.

Dealing with a crease

Books are often found with corners folded as book marks. Such creasing can be difficult, if not impossible, to remove. Rub it down with a folder and put the book in a press. If this is unsuccessful, put several sheets of blotting paper under the leaf, damp the crease, and then cover it with more blotting paper before pressing it with a warm iron.

Replacing a leaf

You will often find that a single leaf has become loose. Glue it back with a little polyvinyl adhesive. If necessary, trim the inner edge so that the other edges of the leaf align with the other pages. Lay a piece of paper on the leaf as a mask, leaving a $\frac{1}{8}$ in (3 mm) wide strip of the inner edge projecting from the mask. Paint glue thinly across the strip from the mask outward.

Gluing the leaf Align the leaf with the book, then press the glued edge flat. Lay waxed paper into the hinge.

Torn leaves

Although a torn leaf can be glued like a damaged print (see p. 169), it should be reinforced to cope with the extra strain it will be subject to. Use document repair tape, applied on one side only. Rub it down with a folder to exclude the air and make it almost invisible. Never use ordinary adhesive tape.

Alternatively, using the flour and water mix, paste a strip of tissue paper over the damage. Tear a strip of tissue so that the frayed edge will be less noticeable. Place waxed paper beneath the leaf, then brush paste along the torn edges. Paste the tissue and use the brush to lay the strip in place. Brush the edges down carefully, place waxed paper on top, and close the book. When you remove the waxed paper, peel it with care from the leaf. Printed matter will be visible through the tissue patch.

Adding a corner

A corner torn from a leaf can be replaced using methods similar to those described on p. 170. If printed matter is missing, however, it is debatable whether the repair is of any value. Reinforce the joint with tissue paper.

Filling holes

The method for filling insect holes is described on p. 169. However, as several leaves could be involved, this could be a laborious task. Lay waxed paper under the affected leaves, and then fill the holes with pulped paper. After you have filled a hole, paste a small patch of tissue paper over it.

Covering worn covers

The corners of a book are vulnerable, and take a great deal of wear and tear. If possible, glue loose worn cloth or leather back onto the board. If the covering is worn away, wrap the damaged corner with new material. Leather patches can be dyed, while you can color new cloth with water-based inks.

If the laminated layers of the board itself are separating, work some glue into them with a brush and squeeze them back together. The following technique is for patching corners.

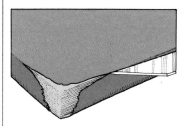

1 Slit the cloth along the outer edge of the board away from the corner in two directions to form a triangular flap. Slide the knife under it carefully as old leather is often brittle. If you wish to preserve the endpapers do the same on the inner edge.

2 Cut a triangular patch from new covering material that fits under the flap and projects about $\frac{1}{2}$ in (12 mm) or so from the edges of the board. If you are using leather, make sure that it is skived so that it is as thin as possible (see p. 175).

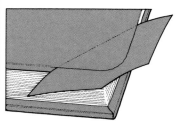

3 Paint polyvinyl glue on the patch and board. Slip the patch in place and use your fingers to rub it down, including the flap. Trim the corner from the patch about $\frac{3}{16}$ in (5 mm) from the board, or a little more with leather.

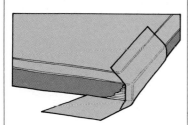

4 Fold one side over the edge of the board and rub it down on the inside.

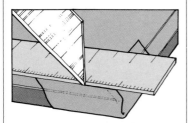

5 Rub the folded corner down with your thumbnail and fold over the other edge, pressing it down with the folder. Trim the edge to match the existing "turn-ins".

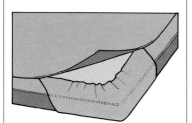

6 Thin leather will stretch more than cloth, so that excess material can be gathered under the endpaper to produce a smooth, rounded corner. It is best to coat a leather patch with a couple of coats of glue, leaving the first to soak in before applying the second, to make it supple.

7 Trim any frayed edges from the raised flaps, and carefully paint polyvinyl acetate adhesive (white glue) onto their undersides. Rub the flaps down with the folder, placing a small piece of acetate over leather to avoid bruising it.
  Wipe the area carefully with a clean, damp sponge to remove any glue that squeezes out.

Repairing a broken joint

The joint between a cover board and the book itself is covered by the endpapers. If it becomes slack or is broken, the entire case separates from the book. Damaged endpapers are a sign of a strained joint, and the repair will be better if you renew it completely. The methods described here are for cloth-covered books only. Leather bindings require a stronger and more complicated joint.

1 Carefully cut through the endpapers and crash hinge with a knife. Some books are bound with cloth tapes sewn across the spine for strength. The ends of these tapes are glued to the board cover under the endpapers; cut through these as well. As long as they are securely stitched to the spine they will continue to fulfil their function.

2 If the sections of the book need to be resewn have the job done by an expert. If the book is otherwise sound, apply flour and water paste to the spine and let it soak in for 10–15 minutes. Carefully scrape the spine with the back of a table knife to remove softened glue and crash. You can leave the old endpapers glued to the inside of the cover and place new ones over them.

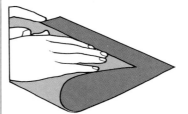

3 The grain of the new endpapers must run parallel to the spine, so test the paper by folding it under your fingertips, but do not crease it. Now try the

same test at right angles to the first. The fold offering the least resistance runs parallel to the grain.

4 Cut endpapers which are about $\frac{1}{4}$ in (6 mm) larger all around than the cover. Fold them in half and crease them firmly. Mask the endpapers as shown for regluing a single leaf.

5 Tip one set of endpapers to the first and one to the last section of the book so that a crease aligns with each shoulder. Rub them down with the folder and leave them until the glue sets.

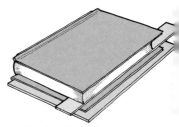

6 To trim the endpapers to size, first lay the book on a piece of scrap cardboard. Place a steel rule between the book and the endpapers so that it is aligned accurately with the edges of the leaves. Holding the book firmly with one hand, trim off the excess paper with a knife.

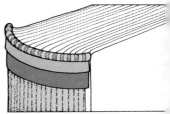

7 Glue headbands which closely resemble the original to the spine with white glue.
  Cut a piece of crash which matches the length of the spine but projects $\frac{3}{4}$ in (18 mm) from

Rebacking a cloth binding

each side. Paint white glue on-to the spine and rub the crash down with the folder.

8 Strengthen the spine further by gluing on a piece of kraft paper. It should run from shoulder to shoulder, but be slightly short top and bottom. Make the grain of the paper run parallel with the spine.

9 Wrap the case around the book and check that it fits snugly, with equal margins. Holding the book firmly, open one half of the case. Slip waste paper between the endpapers.

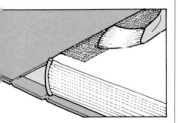

10 Paint a thin coat of white glue under the projecting crash and rub it down onto the end-paper and into the shoulder. Brushing outward from the spine, apply white glue thinly but evenly over the rest of the endpaper, then substitute the waste with waxed paper.

1 Carefully close the spine against the book, press the edge of the cover into the joint, then close it over the endpaper and rub it down with your hand. Do not open the cover again until the glue has set.

2 Do the same with the other endpaper, then put the book in a press (see p. 155). Apply firm pressure for about five minutes, then reduce it slightly, leaving the book in the press for a further hour.

If the cover spine is split along the joint line, it should be replaced with a new cloth backing. Unless the crash hinge and endpapers are perfect, it is worth replacing them at the same time. Leather bindings require a different treatment (see p. 160).

1 Separate the book and cover, then provide new crash and end-papers as described in the section opposite.

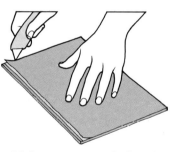

2 Make a cut across the board near the joint line about $\frac{1}{4}$ in (6 mm) from the edge. If there is any form of decoration on the cover, cut along it to disguise the joint. Cut the cover back $\frac{3}{4}$ in (18 mm) along the outer edge of the boards as you would for repairing a corner (see p. 157), and turn back the flaps.

3 Cut the new cloth spine so that it is $\frac{3}{4}$ in (18 mm) oversize top and bottom and so that it fits around the spine with enough left to tuck under both flaps. If necessary, dye the cloth to match the cover.

4 Cut a spine lining from thin cardboard, the same length as the boards and fitting from shoulder to shoulder across the book's spine. Paint white glue onto the back of the cloth and on one board under the flap.

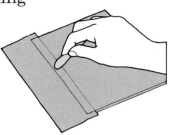

5 Slip the cloth under the flap and rub down with the folder. Turn the board over and position the book accurately on it, then put the other board on top.

6 Place the spine lining cardboard against the spine, then rub the cloth up over it. Paint white glue under the other flap and slip the edge of the cloth under it with the folder tip before rubbing them down.

7 Take the case from the book and adjust the lining if it is not centered between the boards.

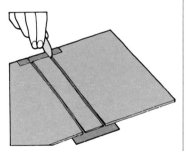

8 Turn the cloth over top and bottom, rubbing it down into the joints with the folder. Turn the case over and rub down the entire length of both joints.

9 Carefully paint white glue onto the underside of both flaps and rub them down, wiping off any excess glue with a damp sponge.

10 Put the book back in the case with waxed paper between them and leave it under a light weight for about an hour to dry off thoroughly. Attach the case to the book (see above). Use a damp sponge to wet the original cardboard lining on the old spine, then scrape it off. Trim the edges of the spine cover and glue it to the new backing with white glue.

Rebacking a leather binding

Leather-bound books can be re-backed by the amateur, but the technique needs practice.

1 Many books have decorative endpapers which are worth preserving. Tip hinged endpapers to the first and last sections and cut flaps along the inner edge of both cover boards, then peel back the glued-down endpapers. Cut similar flaps on the outside faces (see p. 159).

2 Cut strips of book binding cloth about 1 in (2.5 cm) wide and the same length as the end-papers. Tip them onto the book, face down, so that they are right up to the shoulders.

3 Sew the cloth hinges to the first section of the book with linen thread. Start at one end, pushing the needle at an angle through the shoulder of the book and passing the thread through a couple of times to secure the end.

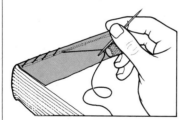

4 Now make $\frac{1}{2}$ in (12 mm) over-sewn stitches along the shoulder. At the far end do not cut the thread but take it across the spine and continue stitches along the other shoulder, tying the thread off at the other end.

5 Glue on headbands, plus a strip of crash to cover the spine which runs from shoulder to shoulder only. Make and attach a hollow (see right) to the spine.

6 Cut a new spine cover to match the original. Skive the edges carefully (see p. 175).

7 Work flour and water paste into the inner face of the spine cover, leave for five minutes then paste again. Meanwhile paint polyvinyl (white) glue onto the boards under the outer cover flaps.

8 Slip the spine cover under one flap and rub both down. Use a strip of acetate to avoid bruising the leather. Mold the leather around the spine and stick the edge under the other flap.

9 Apply white glue under each flap and rub them down. Wipe with a damp sponge. Peel cover off hollow and lay it face down.

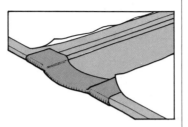

10 Turn in the top and bottom of the spine, but encourage a slight curve at each end. Insert the book, "setting" the boards by pressing joints down well. Mold shoulders by binding thread around the joints.

11 Mold the spine's top to form a "head-cap" so that it curves in slightly over the headband. Slip card under each cover board. Place the book between ply-wood boards and weight it over-night.

12 Cut the thread, and remove the waste card. Cut the corners off a cloth hinge, and coat the hinge with white glue.

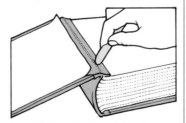

13 Holding the board firmly against the book, fold the hinge over it, rubbing it into the joint and over the board, working it under endpaper flap. Glue flap down. Repeat steps 12 and 13 with the other hinge, re-insert waste card and place book in a press.

Making a hollow

A hollow is a flattened tube with one side glued to the book's spine, and the other side to the spine cover.

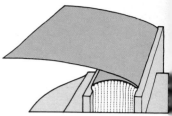

1 When a book is opened, the tube opens too, allowing the spine cover to spring back in a curve and not break. To make a new hollow, you should place the book between boards in a bench vise and glue a sheet of kraft paper to the spine with white adhesive. The grain of the paper must run with the spine (see p. 158).

2 Fold the paper over once to mark the width, then carefully peel it off the spine. Fold it over once more onto the glued side.

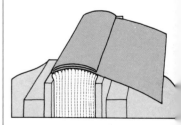

3 Lay the folded paper back on to the spine, having added more glue if needed.

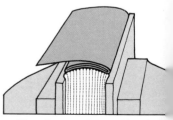

4 Glue the top of the roll and fold the rest of the sheet over again. Trim off the excess with scissors along the spine as well at the top and bottom.

PAINTINGS, PRINTS AND DRAWINGS

Collecting pictures

Many people think of the art market as an exclusive club for the very wealthy who collect priceless masterpieces. However, this type of artwork only represents the very top end of the market. As long as you are interested in pictures more for their aesthetic quality than for their investment value, you will find collectible items at modest prices.

Prints

Print collecting is a worthwhile introduction to collecting artwork, as prints are, in general, inexpensive and they embrace a wide range of types, subjects and periods.

Relief printing
This technique uses a wood block to make an image—those parts which are not to be printed are cut away, leaving the design standing out in relief. Ink is rolled onto the surface and transferred to the paper by light pressure.

Prints produced by this method are known as woodcuts or wood engravings. The woodcut is the earliest method; it produces a picture with relatively crude, thick black line work. A wood engraving is a finer process— the design is cut into the end grain of a block of hardwood with tiny chisels or "gravers." The effect of this is to produce much more delicate line work than on a woodcut.

Detail of a wood engraving

Intaglio printing
With intaglio printing, the image is incised into a metal plate. These plates were made from copper until the early nineteenth century, after which they were steel. Ink is rolled onto the plate which is then wiped clean, leaving ink in the grooves only. When the plate and paper are forced together in a press, the ink is transferred. This also leaves the mark of the plate "framing" the picture.

Line engraving A line-engraved plate is cut by hand on metal, using gravers to draw the image. Line engraving is slightly raised on the surface of the paper, as a result of the paper being forced into the ink-filled groove under pressure. This is visible with a magnifying glass.

Hand-tinted line engraving

Drypoint This technique is similar to line engraving in that the line is "drawn" directly on to the plate with a sharp point. No metal is cut away—the displaced metal is left raised on either side of the scratched line. The scratch and the raised metal both hold ink, producing a heavy, rich printed line.

Mezzotint The whole surface of the plate is textured with a spiked rocker, to produce an overall even, soft black. Then to record the design, parts are scraped and burnished.

Detail of a mezzotint

Etching The etching plate is covered with a thin layer of wax which is then scratched through with a needle. The plate is then immersed in acid, dissolving the exposed metal. The depth of the line is determined by the length of immersion. Under a magnifying glass, an etched line will not appear consistently solid, as in places the acid will have eaten into crumbling wax.

Eighteenth-century etching

Stipple engraving Areas of the plate are textured by pricking with a pointed tool. Magnified, the image can be seen to be made up of tiny dots.

Soft ground etching This type of print has a softer appearance than a standard etching; it can resemble a pencil or crayon drawing. A piece of paper is laid over a plate covered with etching ground mixed with tallow. The image is drawn onto the paper, which is then peeled off the plate, removing the ground immediately under the drawn lines.

Aquatint Fine, powdered resin is applied to the plate and fixed with heat. When this is treated with acid, a small metal point is left under each grain of resin. These points print white, while the surrounding metal prints black.

Lithography This process relies on the fact that grease repels water. The design is drawn in grease crayon on a piece of zinc, aluminum or limestone. Water is then applied, which the greasy marks resist. When ink is introduced, it in turn is resisted by the water, adhering to the marked areas only. Paper is pressed onto the inked stone to transfer the image.

Detail of a nineteenth-century lithograph

Detail of an aquatint

Paintings

Antique paintings will fall into one of the following two categories, determined by the medium used.

Watercolors Pigments bound in a water-soluble gum are known as watercolors. This medium produces delicate paintings with flat, transparent washes, and was usually used for small scale pictures on absorbent paper.

Oil paintings Oil paint was first developed during the Renaissance. Its colors can be very rich and dark, and are easily blended into one another. Oil paint can be built up in thick layers so that the texture of the paint itself contributes to the quality of the picture. Most oils are executed on stretched canvas, although they are occasionally found on wooden panels.

Nineteenth-century watercolor

Nineteenth-century oil painting

Drawings

This is a relatively inexpensive area in which to start collecting—an original antique drawing will cost less than a watercolor or oil by the same artist. The field is not just limited to pencil sketches; many other drawing media have been used.

Pencil

Look out for drawings made as preparatory sketches for paintings, since although they may not be signed, they could be the work of a named artist.

Ink

Black drawing ink is most common, but colored ink drawings can also be found, especially in sepia or brown. These are generally less permanent than black. Inks were often diluted and applied to the drawing as a wash. Quills were used to apply ink until the eighteenth century, when steel nibs appeared.

Nineteenth-century ink drawing

Chalk

Chalk is a versatile medium; it can produce a wide range of tones and textures. Drawings in black and in red chalk are the most common types. White chalk is generally used as a highlight on drawings made with other media.

Pastel

Drawings made with this medium have a soft appearance similar to those produced with chalk. The crayons used are made from pigment and fine chalk bound together with gum, and they are often very colorful. Pastels first became popular in the eighteenth century.

Early twentieth-century pastel

Charcoal

Perhaps the oldest drawing medium, charcoal is produced from partly burnt wood. Drawings are usually very dense black, and free in style. Charcoal does not last well, and therefore examples are not particularly common.

Silver point

In this case, the name describes the process—a specially coated white paper is scribed with a very fine, pointed needle made from silver. This technique produces extremely delicate, gray line drawings.

Crayon

Non-powdery colored drawings may be made with crayon. This drawing medium first came into use in the early nineteenth century.

Nineteenth-century crayon drawing

Buying tips

● Avoid pictures on very thin, delicate papers—they are difficult to restore. Torn prints and drawings on ordinary weight paper can be mended, but repairs are rarely invisible, so expect a large reduction in price.
● If you buy artwork unframed do not pay a lot for a "laid" print (one that has been glued to its backing board) as it is not always possible to soak it off for renovation.

Damage checks

*A simple repair
**Some experience needed
***Skilled work—not for beginners

Prints, watercolors and drawings

*Most **stains** on prints and on drawings other than chalks and pastels are very easy to remove. Ink and grease stains are the exception.
*Brown **rust-like marks** on a print are known as "foxing." This fungal attack is easy to bleach clean.
****Holes** in paper produced by a boring insect can be filled.
****Missing corners** can be replaced, but this is not easy.

Oil paintings

***Is the **surface flaking or blistering?** This type of restoration should not be attempted by an amateur.
*****Holes and tears** can be patched, but you will need to employ a skilled painter to retouch missing paint. An extensively torn painting will have to be relined.
***If the **tacks** holding the canvas to the stretcher are rusting, the canvas around them may be weakened and in need of relining.
****Dirty varnish** will probably have to be stripped.
A **misty appearance in the varnish is known as "blooming." It may need to be stripped off.

Tools

Craft knife and steel rule Use these to cut mounts accurately and to splice a new corner onto a print.
Domestic iron Use for pressing artwork flat.
Wide artist's brush Choose a wide, flat type to apply varnish to an oil painting.
Triangle, T square and drawing board These are essential for ruling decorative borders on picture mounts.
Ruling pen An adjustable ruling pen, available from technical drawing suppliers, is used to draw borders.

Materials

White blotting paper Use this to dry washed prints and remove grease stains.
Art gum eraser A soft eraser to clean artwork.
Document cleaner This abrasive powder will remove surface dirt from paper.
Household bleach Diluted bleach will eradicate stains from prints and drawings.
Mineral spirits and alcohol These make a solvent for removing old varnish.
Natural resin varnishes Natural varnishes are best for coating paintings.
Wallpaper paste Used to repair torn artwork.
Document tape Reinforce torn paper with this tape.
Mounting board An acid-free rag board is best.
Painting canvas Use scraps to patch holed paintings.
Rabbit glue This is ideal for patching damaged canvas, but latex glue can be used.
Spackling compound Used for filling torn canvas.
Wet-and-dry paper Extra-fine paper is used for rubbing down spackling compound.
Brass strip Use $\frac{1}{2}$ in (12 mm) wide strip to make clips to hold the stretchers in place.
Epoxy putty This putty is used to repair frames.
Dental compound Makes molds for frame repairs.
Metallic colors For retouching gilded frames.

Cleaning prints and drawings

The methods of producing artwork are so varied that you can never be absolutely sure if the cleaning techniques you want to use will be safe; therefore you should always proceed with caution. The broad guidelines given here should reduce any risk to a minimum, but if you are in any doubt as to the nature of a picture, consult a dealer or restorer. And always practise on worthless artwork before tackling anything of value.

What can I clean?

Most black and white printed matter is quite stable and can be washed and bleached safely. But colored work is more of a problem. As very little printed color was produced before the late nineteenth century, a lot of prints were hand-colored, either at the time of manufacture or, more often, at a later date. If you wash and bleach a hand-colored picture you will probably lose the color, so it is best to take this type of print to an expert for cleaning.

Thin or delicate papers are too fragile to be soaked. And "paper" that has a shiny surface should not be cleaned. It might turn out to be parchment which distorts in water, or it might be paper coated with a special material which will be damaged by soaking.

You should never attempt to clean pastel or chalk drawings. You cannot tell whether they have been protected by "fixing." If you fix them yourself before cleaning you will only seal in the dirt.

Most ink drawings will have been made with carbon ink which can be washed and bleached. To make sure that it is waterproof test a small part with a damp paintbrush before you begin the cleaning process.

Surprisingly, pencil drawings are not harmed by water or bleach. The only danger is that of erasing them, so avoid rubbing the surface while you are cleaning them.

Dry cleaning

Marks and blemishes on prints and drawings other than pencil, chalk or pastel can be removed by erasure as long as they are on the surface of the paper only.

Try the gentlest method first. Start by brushing the marks with a soft artist's brush. This will remove any powdery deposits such as surface dust or dry mold.

If the mark persists, shape a piece of soft white bread into a small ball and make short, light strokes in one direction only. Brush away any crumbs with a soft brush.

To remove stubborn marks, buy an eraser known as an art gum eraser from an art supply store. Stipple the surface with this very soft eraser to pick up loose dirt, then take out remaining marks with gentle strokes. As the surface of the eraser becomes dirty, knead it to get a clean surface.

Some marks respond well to a very fine abrasive powder called document cleaner (available from art supply stores). The powder comes in a sealed open-weave bag. Squeeze the bag over the print to sprinkle powder onto the surface, then rub it gently with the bag to remove the blemish. Document cleaner is so fine that it is possible to clean even hand-colored prints with it, but try it on a small, inconspicuous area first.

Removing a mount

To remove a print or drawing from its frame, cut away the seal of brown paper or tape from the back, keeping the knife blade as close to the frame as possible. Then pull out the retaining nails or brads with pliers and lift out the backing board. In an old frame, the backing will probably be a thin sheet of solid wood or brown strawboard. You should not reuse such materials because in damp or humid conditions their high acid content causes staining. If a previous framer has applied a mark to the backing keep it for reference, but store it separately.

If the picture itself is lying against the glass, but not stuck to it, you can lift it out for cleaning. And if the picture is hinged to a mount, the old adhesive may be brittle with age, in which case the tape will peel off easily. However, if it does not, slit the hinge carefully with a knife.

The print or drawing may have been "laid down" or glued to the backing board. In such a case, as long as the artwork can be immersed in water safely, you should soak it off. Lay the print face down in a shallow bowl or tray, and pour boiling water on the back. Leave it to soak for a while, checking periodically until the board has floated off.

Once the picture is free of its mount, lift it out of the water as shown below. If there is a thick residue of glue on the back, lay the picture face down on a sheet of glass and carefully wash the glue off with a large, soft brush.

Lifting a print out of water
To lift a wet print either slide a sheet of glass or plastic under it, or spread your fingers out so that they support the wet paper over a wide area. Never lift a wet print or drawing by its corners.

Removing stains

Most blemishes on prints and drawings can be removed easily by applying a gentle bleach. Oil and grease stains, however, need a different treatment.

Washing in bleach

Professional restorers use strong chemicals to remove stains, but inexpert use of these can seriously weaken the paper. You should only use a mild bleaching solution; this will take out all but the most serious staining. If the marks persist after such treatment, you should consult a professional restorer.

In a shallow tray, mix a solution of one part of ordinary household bleach to twelve parts of cold water (see p. 165). Slide the print under the surface of the solution, face uppermost. Keep checking on its progress, and as soon as the staining is eradicated, pour away the solution. It should not be necessary to leave the artwork in bleach for longer than 10 minutes.

To rinse out the bleach pour fresh water into the corner of the tray until it covers the print. Leave to soak for 5 minutes, pour it away and add more water. After four changes of water, carefully lift out the artwork as described left, and place it face down on clean white blotting paper to dry.

You can touch out isolated stains which occur outside the picture area by applying a little bleach solution with a small brush. Then wash it out with a brush dipped in water. Although this is a useful method for artwork which cannot be immersed in water, it often results in a pale patch in place of the original dark stain.

Fungal attack

Fungal growth can occur on any paper stored in damp conditions. If you catch the problem early, you can deal with it by merely brushing off the mold. However, some fungal growth will stain paper. The most common variety, known as "foxing," leaves orange-brown spots—but these can be bleached out.

If you suspect that a framed picture will be subject to humid conditions you can protect it by sealing the glass, print and backing into an air-tight sandwich using adhesive tape over the edge of all three elements. You must make sure that the tape on the front of the glass is hidden by the edge of the frame.

Evidence of fungal attack

Oil and grease stains

Bleaching will not remove oil and grease marks. Some restorers therefore attempt to spot out such stains with a substance such as lighter fluid. Although this can be successful, in some cases it merely spreads the grease over a wider area.

A safer method is to lay one or two sheets of blotting paper on the artwork and use a warm domestic iron to draw the grease out of the print into the blotting paper. The same method can be used to remove candle wax stains, but you must carefully pick off any solid material first. If this method is not completely successful, take the picture to an expert.

Ink stains

Some inks, such as ballpoint pen, can be bleached out as described above. But, if you cannot bleach out an ink stain, you should take the artwork to a professional restorer.

Cleaning paintings

Since it takes an expert to authenticate an artist's work, even when it is signed, it is best to get the picture valued and authenticated before you tackle any kind of restoration. Inexpensive paintings can usually be cleaned safely by an amateur. But if the picture is very valuable, take it to a professional. Water-color paints, in particular, can be fragile, and the restoration of this type of picture is best left to a professional.

Taking a painting from its frame

Any painting on paper will be framed behind glass just as drawings and prints are, and you remove it in the same way, but if it is laid on board, do not soak it off as this will damage the paint layer. Paintings on canvas are framed differently. The canvas is tacked over a simple wooden frame which can be expanded with wooden wedges to tension the canvas. This "stretcher" locates in deep rabbets in the frame. This type of painting is rarely glazed.

Many old paintings are held in the frame by nails either bent over behind the stretcher, or driven at an angle through the stretcher into the frame. Use pliers to withdraw any nails, pulling them out at the same angle to avoid splitting the frame or stretcher.

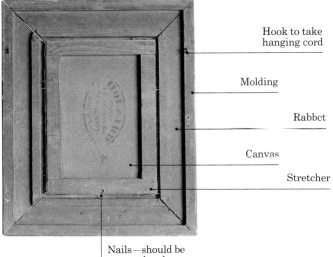

Hook to take hanging cord

Molding

Rabbet

Canvas

Stretcher

Nails—should be removed and replaced with brass clips

Preparing a canvas for cleaning

Before you can clean or repair a canvas it must be retensioned. Make sure that the painting is strong enough to take the strain, especially along the front edge of the stretcher where the tension is greatest. And examine the tacks for signs of rust, as this may have rotted the canvas. If the canvas itself seems strong enough, you can drive copper tacks between the old ones, but if the canvas looks weak you should have it relined by a professional. Relining involves gluing the old canvas to a new piece which can take the strain of tensioning. This is not a job which should be tackled by an amateur. Because a professional is able to reline a lot of paintings at once, you will find that the prices are usually quite reasonable.

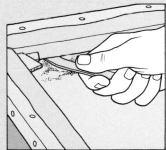

Cleaning out dust Before you tension the canvas you must clean out any dirt trapped between it and the stretcher as this will show through on the front. Use a strip of cardboard with the corners rounded off to gently rake out the debris, and then brush the stretcher and the edge of the canvas until clean.

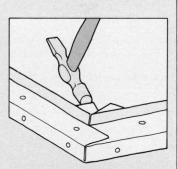

Tensioning the canvas Using a lightweight hammer, tap in the small corner wedges, working around from corner to corner to even out the tension. Any wedges which have fallen out should be replaced. Re-insert them with the end at an angle to the stretcher, not square onto it.

Cleaning and stripping varnish

Oil painting with damaged varnish

Old paintings were protected with a layer of natural resin varnish. Over the years, this varnish will have discolored and absorbed dirt, obscuring the true colors of the paint beneath. A few paintings can be restored by cleaning off surface dirt only, but in the majority of cases the only way to clean the painting effectively is to strip off the old varnish. If the varnish is cracked or flaking, you should take the painting to a professional restorer as any stripper that can penetrate to the paint layer itself will destroy the picture.

Before you begin to clean a painting, tuck folded newspaper or strips of cardboard between the stretcher and the canvas. This prevents the impression of the stretcher showing through on the front. Discard this packing once the cleaning is completed.

Removing surface dirt
Try cleaning a corner of the painting first, using a small swab of cotton dipped in clean water and wrung out until it is just moist. Make small, circular strokes, and examine the swab occasionally to see how much dirt is coming off. If this process makes no appreciable difference, you will have to strip the varnish. But if it appears to be successful, work over the whole painting with clean, moist swabs. Clean a small area at a time, drying it with fresh swabs before moving on. To

avoid damaging the painting, it is essential to keep the back of the canvas dry, and to use only light pressure.

Stripping old varnish
The solvent used to clean a painting should be of the minimum strength necessary to dissolve the varnish. Any stronger, and it increases the risk of damaging the paint layer. Make a test at the edge of the painting by wiping it over with a swab moistened in mineral spirits. Unless the painting has been protected with a wax varnish, the swab will be clean and you will have to add a little alcohol. Mix the two thoroughly, adding more alcohol until the varnish begins to dissolve. The ratio should never be more than 50 : 50, as alcohol is a powerful solvent. Once you are satisfied with the strength of the solvent, moisten your swab with it and start to clean the painting using light, circular strokes. Constantly check the surface of the swab to make sure that only varnish is being removed. If you inadvertently begin to pick up paint on your swab, lightly wash the area with mineral spirits in order to neutralize the solvent.

Sometimes an artist will apply fine work over the varnish so take particular care when cleaning areas of detail such as faces: you may need to reduce the strength of the solvent in such places.

Oil painting stripped of varnish

Revarnishing

Once you have cleaned off the old varnish you should apply a fresh coat to keep the painting clean. Traditional copal, mastic or damar varnishes are still available from good art supply stores, but they are expensive. If you prefer, you can use a modern synthetic picture varnish. It is not economical to buy varnish in bulk because it is difficult to keep in good condition once opened.

In the past, painters often applied varnish to their pictures with their fingertips. The advantages of this method of application are that it is economical, and you are unlikely to get air bubbles or debris in the varnish. Cover the open top of the bottle with your fingertips and tip it up to wet them. Spread the varnish on the painting in light, circular strokes for an evenly distributed coat. Although you need only a thin coating of varnish, you can, if necessary, apply a second coat when the first has dried.

As an alternative to your fingers you can use a wide artist's brush (reserved solely for varnishing). Paint the varnish on first in one direction, then the other, to spread it evenly and encourage the spirit to come to the surface.

Caution: Only varnish a painting in dry weather. Damp or humid conditions will make the varnish "bloom," producing a misty coating that resembles condensed breath on glass. If blooming occurs, lightly swab the surface with mineral spirits, leave it to dry, and then varnish it again.

Repairing prints and drawings

Torn or creased artwork can be repaired successfully by an amateur, but you will find it difficult to get perfect results unless you have done such work before. If you have no experience, buy a similar paper from an art supply store and practice the repair first.

Mending a single tear

Prints and drawings are usually made on relatively thick, soft paper. When this tears, the edges of the tear are "feathered," and they overlap one another just enough to enable you to make a reasonably successful repair. Use a paste designed for hanging lightweight wallpaper, but make sure that it contains a fungicide.

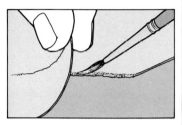

1 To glue a straight tear at the edge of a print or drawing, apply the minimum of lightweight wallpaper paste to one edge with a very fine artist's brush. Then turn the print over and paste the other edge.

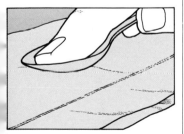

2 Mate the two edges carefully, then lay the artwork between sheets of waxed paper and press the repair with the back of a spoon. Put a heavy book on the top until the paste sets.

3 As an extra precaution you can reinforce the glued joint by sticking a piece of document repair tape along the back. This extremely thin tape (available from art supply stores) is hardly noticeable when burnished down. Do not use ordinary self-adhesive tape as this will stain the repair.

Reassembling torn artwork

Although it is possible to patch together several pieces of a print using the method described for a single tear, the repair will be very weak and you will find it difficult to mate all the edges perfectly. A better method is to glue the pieces down on a stiff backing card. This would not be recommended by museum conservators, but it is hardly likely to devalue artwork that is very badly damaged already, and as long as you use a water-soluble paste the process can always be reversed. When wet, the joints look unsightly, but there is no need for concern, as they will not be so noticeable when the glue has dried.

1 Coat the card and the back of the pieces of artwork with lightweight wallpaper paste and leave them to dry. Apply another coat of paste, and, while still wet, slide the pieces around on the backing card, aligning the damaged edges carefully. The artwork often looks unsightly at this stage as all the joints show up badly when damp.

2 When you are satisfied with the position of the pieces, lay a sheet of waxed paper over them and flatten with a rolling pin. Then cover with blotting paper and press with a warm iron.

3 Leave the pasted artwork between two sheets of weighted hardboard overnight. When dry, remove the hardboard.

Taking out creases

Creases or fold lines left on prints or drawings can be removed quite easily. Moisten the back of the crease with a cotton swab dipped in water, then, protecting the print with blotting paper, press the crease flat with an iron. Alternatively, you can "cold press" the print by sandwiching it between sheets of hardboard and leaving it under a heavy weight overnight.

Filling holes

Many old books have suffered from infestation by boring insects. If a print has been extracted from one of these at a later date it may have small holes or trails right through it. To fill these holes, make up a pulp from matching paper by cutting a thin strip of paper from the edge of the print and mashing it up in hot water with a spoon.

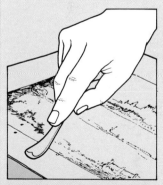

Applying the pulp Put the print on hardboard and dampen the damage site with water on a cotton swab. Press tiny amounts of pulp into the holes with the back of a spoon, then flatten the pulp with an iron. When dry, the pulp and paper fibers will have become interwoven, locking the filling in place.

Replacing a corner

There is only one answer to the problem of a print or drawing with a missing corner—you must graft on a new one. The first task is to match the paper. You may be able to salvage sufficient paper from a worthless print in the same series, or, if yours is from an incomplete book, cut a patch from one of the other pages. Of course, if the print has very wide margins, it may be possible to cut a strip from the edge of the print itself.

Grafting on a patch

When preparing the new paper you should bevel the edges of the print and the patch; this helps them to mate together.

1 Overlap the patch on the artwork and tape it on with masking tape. Cut through both pieces of paper with a sharp knife, holding the blade at an angle so that you are cutting matching beveled edges.

2 Glue the edges with wallpaper paste, then reinforce them with document repair tape, or mount the print onto backing card.

3 When the paste is dry, lightly rub the joint with flour paper. Press lightly, and rub in one direction only. Then trim edges.

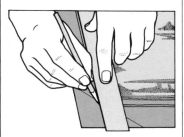

4 If necessary, touch in missing borders with a ruling pen (see p. 165) to match the new corner to the rest of the print.

Repairing paintings on canvas

Small holes and tears in the canvas can be patched quite easily, but large splits or tears should be dealt with by a professional. And missing areas of paint that have resulted from such damage should only be retouched by a skilled painter. Take paintings with blistered, cracked or flaking paint to a restorer.

Patching a hole

Hold the canvas up to the light and examine it for small holes. Any you find should be patched before they get worse.

1 Start by cutting a square of matching painting canvas large enough to cover the hole and give a generous border.

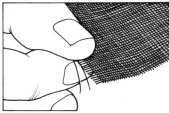

2 Fray the edges of the patch so that it will not show through on the front. Now prepare to glue the patch in place by cleaning the back of the canvas in the vicinity of the hole with mineral spirits. Try to obtain animal glue, but if you cannot, use a latex adhesive instead. Do not use spirit-based glue since it will lift the front of the painting.

3 Once the canvas is dry, coat the patch with glue and, with the painting face down on a smooth surface, smooth the patch down onto it.

4 Place a piece of polyethylene over the patch and weight it down with a book. Leave it until the glue sets.

(see p. 165)

Mending a small tear

A fresh tear can be patched in the same way as a hole. If the edges have frayed, trim off any loose ends—they can protrude from the painting's face and be difficult to cover.

1 Lay the painting face down on a smooth surface, and glue the patch in place over the torn edges. Then leave it until the glue has set.

2 Turn the painting face up and fill any gap along the tear with stopping, using a palette knife and working across the tear.

3 When dry, rub the stopping down with very fine wet-and-dry paper. Use a tiny patch of paper and do not use a lubricant. Stopping is easy to rub down, so there is little risk of harming paint.

4 Once flush, the repair is ready for retouching. Unless you are a skilled painter with a sound knowledge of traditional methods and materials, you should take it to a professional.

Framing pictures

The main distinction in framing methods is between those with glass and those without. Traditionally, oil paintings are framed without a protective covering of glass, while frames for prints, watercolors and drawings are always glazed.

Types of frame

Traditional wooden frames can be made up from a large range of moldings. Cutting these moldings to size to fit the artwork exactly is difficult unless you have a miter box to cut the joints, and miter clamps or a web clamp to glue up the frame. If you do not have these, simply find a gallery or store where you can select a molding and then have the frame made up by a framer.

If you want to make a frame yourself, you will find that clip-together aluminium kits are extremely easy to put together as they are already cut to size and mitered. However, the range of sizes is limited and the effect may not be appropriate to your picture.

As an alternative, you can make a cheap frame by sandwiching the print and its mount between a sheet of hardboard and a sheet of glass, holding them together with special clips available from art stores. This method is not recommended for long-term framing as the edges of the sandwich are open, and therefore the artwork is not protected from dust.

Aluminum frame

Traditional gilded frame

Clip frame

Plain wooden frame

Framing paper artwork

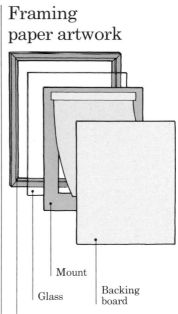

Mount

Glass

Backing board

Frame

To calculate the size of the opening in the window mount, measure the picture area of the artwork and allow a margin all round. It is impossible to give a ratio that will suit all pictures, but most will look balanced if you make the bottom margin very slightly larger than the other three. Never cover the plate mark (see p. 162).

Once you have decided on the size of the mount, take the measurements to a framer and ask him to cut the molding of your choice and a piece of thin picture glass to fit your frame (non-reflective glass is not essential). At the same time choose the color of the window mount. Use the glass as a guide to cut out the backing card and the outside of the window mount. A framer may be willing to cut you a beveled window. Otherwise, you could cut a square-edged window yourself, and draw on a decorative border.

Drawing borders
Using a ruling pen, draw a simple border of parallel lines with diluted drawing inks or metallic marker pens. Once you have inked in the border, carefully paint the area between the lines with clean water, then apply a wash of color before the water dries.

Mounting paper artwork

The picture and window mount is held in one hand, and adjusted with the other until the picture area is aligned in the window. Ask a helper to secure the picture temporarily with masking tape.

1 Using wallpaper paste, glue thin paper along the top edge of the picture to hinge it to the mount.

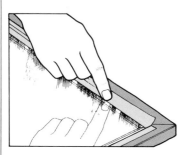

2 Seal the edge of the glass to protect the picture from dust. Use masking tape, making sure

that it is hidden by the molding rebate. Then, with the glass in the frame, lay the mount and picture in place. Remove the temporary tape.

3 Lay the backing board on top of the picture and secure it by driving small pins or nails into the edge of the molding.

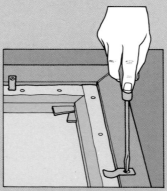

4 Either seal the edge of the backing board with masking tape, or glue a piece of brown paper across the frame back.

Framing an oil painting

Frames for oils on canvas should have a rabbet to take the stretcher. Home-made clips cut from thin brass sheet can then be used to hold the stretcher in place. The clips are screwed to the back of the frame so that they overlap the stretcher securely. To attach these clips to the frame drill holes in the top, bottom and sides of the frame and use countersunk screws.

Attaching clips Use countersunk brass screws to hold the clips to the frame.

Repairing frames

Many antique frames are decorated with carvings or elaborate gesso moldings. Gesso is particularly vulnerable to damage, and many frames are chipped or have sections of molding missing. Use epoxy putty (see p. 27) to build up missing parts or to cast a whole new section. Add the epoxy putty layer by layer with modeling tools, smoothing it into the surrounding contours with a little water. When the putty has set hard, finish with a fine abrasive paper or small files. If a large section is missing, reinforce the putty with a length of wire glued into strategically placed holes in the frame.

Touching in with paint

Gesso frames are frequently gilded. If the frame is covered with genuine gold leaf, you should get an expert to finish it for you, but you can touch in cheaper gold frames.

On top of the new putty, paint a primer coat of umber oil paint diluted with mineral spirits. Then paint on the "gilding"—either metallic powders mixed with varnish, gold paste or ready-mixed gold paint (see pp. 35 and 38), feathering out the paint at the edges. When the gilding is dry, blend it into the frame with very diluted washes of umber oil color.

Casting broken moldings

To cast missing sections of frame make a press molding from dental composition (see p. 28) on an intact section. Fill the mold with epoxy paste, and leave it to set. Next, cut away the damaged frame section up to an edge or motif which will disguise the joint. Remove the casting from its mold, trim it to fit the gap, and glue it in place with epoxy adhesive. When set, shape the casting with abrasives and files, and fill in gaps with epoxy paste.

LEATHERWORK

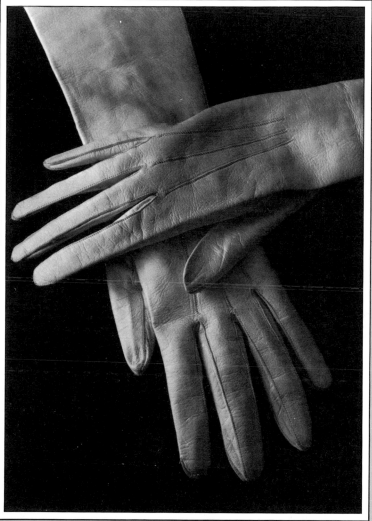

Collecting leatherwork

Today cheap man-made alternatives have elevated leather above the commonplace—it is now an expensive material. Yet it was once a basic material used by every level of society for all manner of items. The antique leather-work you will most often find in auction rooms and antique shops reflects this. Collectible pieces range from fine buttonbacked Chesterfield sofas and leather-covered boxes to more mundane hat boxes and other items of luggage.

Types of leather

The range of leathers, colors and finishes is so extensive that if you need to match leather you should take a sample to a supplier for identification and advice. This list is a basic guide.

Morocco
This very fine-quality goat skin is available in a range of colors. It is most often found in the form of book bindings and accessories.

Calf
This fine-grained leather is produced in a natural or colored finish, and takes tooling and carving well. Available in thicknesses of $\frac{1}{16}-\frac{1}{4}$ in (2–6 mm), it is often used for book binding.

Cowhide
A smooth-grained leather, cowhide is usually found in its natural russet shade, although it is sometimes colored. The largest hide can be $\frac{3}{8}$ in (10 mm) thick, and is sometimes split into several layers. Vegetable-tanned cowhides are used for tooled and carved work.

Sheep
This relatively inexpensive leather can be tooled, but not as effectively as calf or cowhide. It is available in a range of colors, and is usually about $\frac{1}{16}$ in (2 mm) thick. Sheepskin is used to produce suede.

Skiver
A type of thin leather produced from sheepskin, skiver is used for desk tops. It is made in a range of colors.

Reptile skins
Exotic patterned skins from alligators, snakes and lizards are available in a variety of colors. They are mainly used for expensive accessories, and were very popular in the 1930s.

1930s snakeskin clutch bag

Painted and embossed nineteenth-century leather panel

Leather processing

Leather is produced by removing hair from animal skin, scraping off fatty deposits, and then "dressing" it to prevent decay. Minerals, oil, and vegetable matter are used to dress leather. The term "tanning" is often used to describe all leather processing; but originally it applied to the vegetable dressing process only.

The mineral alum was used in an early processing method which produced pale-colored "tawed" leather. Water should not be used on it as the treatment can be washed out, rendering the leather liable to decay.

Oil has been used for hundreds of years to preserve leather and keep it supple. Its most common use is to protect ("proof") heavy suede leather.

Vegetable tanning uses oak and plant extracts. Vegetable-tanned leathers lend themselves to shaping and tooling.

The main process used today dates from the end of the nineteenth century. It involves immersing hides in a chromium salt solution to make them less prone to chemical and fungal attack. However, chrome-tanned leather is unsuitable for tooling and shaping.

After tanning, the leather is treated with oils, greases or soaps to keep it supple. Leather may be left natural in color, dyed in vats or lacquered. To make leather soft it is processed through rollers. Finally, the dressed side is polished with rollers and the flesh side is brushed.

Buying tips

- The best way to identify real leather is to examine both sides. The side you will normally look at is the dressed grain side (de-haired and finished), while the fibrous surface is the processed flesh side. With suede leather, the opposite is true—the "show" side is the flesh side buffed to a fine pile. If leather has been bonded to another material, so that you cannot see the reverse side, you must judge it on its feel and smell alone.

- Several leather substitutes have been produced over the years; simulated exotic reptile skins were a particular favorite. Boxes, for example, were often covered with mock snakeskin or alligator paper.

- Larger leather-covered items, such as trunks or furniture, incorporate a wooden frame. Always check the groundwork or sub-frame of such a piece as faults in the wood may be difficult or expensive to repair. A small outbreak of woodworm can be treated with a commercial fluid, but you should test it on an unobtrusive area first to make sure that it will not stain. In some cases fumigation may be a better method for dealing with this pest; you should consult a leather goods store about this treatment.

- Some neglected leathers can show signs of wear, or more seriously, decomposition. If the leather feels dry, and has cracks and abrasions caused by wear and tear, it can be treated with a dressing. However, if some of the fibers are crumbling into a red powder, decomposition known as "red rot" has set in. This non-curable chemical attack is caused by the absorption of sulphur dioxide which, combined with moisture, degrades the fibers.

Tools and materials

The range of leatherworking tools is extensive, but for the amateur restorer a basic tool kit supplemented with one or two special tools should be sufficient. Unless the piece is very big, you will not need a large work area —a kitchen table covered with newspaper or plastic should be sufficient.

Brass wire suede brush

Selection of paring knives

Tools

Straight edge Use a 3 ft (1 m) metal rule or straight edge when marking and cutting.

Knives To some extent, the type of knife you should use is determined by the work. You can use a craft knife, scalpel or even a very sharp penknife for straight cutting and small shaping work. But for general-purpose leather cutting, including skiving, you should buy a shoe knife. For working on thick leather a special round knife might be worth buying if you are going to undertake more than the occasional repair.

Scissors You will need a good-quality, heavy-duty pair of shears for leather cutting.

Hammer A general-purpose woodworking hammer will be useful to press down glued joints, or flatten stitching.

Brass wire suede brush Designed for cleaning and finishing suede.

Needles Straight harness needles for stitching leather range in size from 00 to 6—the higher the number the finer the needle. Use curved upholstery needles where seams are difficult to work with straight needles.

Skiving a patch
When you cut a patch of leather you may have to thin the edges to avoid a visible ridge.

Using a knife to skive a patch Carefully pare a taper on the flesh side of the patch.

Using a spokeshave to skive a patch Clamp the leather level with the worktop edge and then trim it with a sharp spokeshave.

Materials

Thread and wax Strong thread is available in various thicknesses and colors. Use beeswax to wax it, and thus make it easier to work.

Saddle soap This special formula cleans, softens and protects dressed leather.

Solvents Mineral spirits, surgical alcohol, acetone and lighter fluid will all lift grease stains. *Warning:* These substances are flammable—only use them in a well-ventilated room, away from naked flames.

Spirit soap Dilute this with mineral spirits to remove dirt and grease.

Fuller's earth A dry, absorbent powder that can be used to lift grease stains.

Trichloroethane 1.1.1. stabilized A non-flammable solvent (from drugstores or industrial suppliers) which removes stains.

Hide cleaner A cream dressing that cleans leather and restores its natural oils.

Leather reviver A specially formulated dressing which will revitalize dry leather. It incorporates an insecticide and fungicide.

Microcrystalline wax A fine wax polish that will enhance the color of leather, protect it and bring out a shine.

Nylon gossamer fabric Ultrafine nylon tissue used to reinforce torn or worn pieces. It is normally bonded with a flexible acrylic adhesive.

Polyvinyl acetate glue Used to bond leather or canvas patches.

Aniline dye This powdered pigment is dissolved in denatured alcohol and used to color leather.

Cleaning and finishing leather

All leather mellows with age, taking on a patina that only time and use can produce. Slight scuffs and darkening or fading in local areas are all part of this aging process and you should accept them as part of the character of the material. Dirt, however, can spoil the appearance of the leather and should be removed periodically.

Cleaning leather and suede

Whenever you use a cleaning agent you should first try it out on an inconspicuous area of the leather to test for color fastness. Then remove any dust and inspect the condition of the surface. Lightly wipe sound leather with a slightly damp sponge or cloth to pick up fine dust. Do not wet the leather.

To remove ingrained dirt you should start by trying saddle soap (see left). However, if the leather is heavily soiled or if it has a textured surface, you may find that a spirit soap cleaner is more effective. Dilute the liquid concentrate with mineral spirits —the recommended proportion is 1 or 2 parts soap to 20 parts spirit. Apply the solution with a piece of rough toweling, lightly scrubbing it over the surface for a few minutes; this will quickly emulsify dirt and grease. You can then rinse off the dirt and soap with a clean cloth and fresh mineral spirits.

To remove surface dust and lift the pile on suede, brush it with a brass wire brush. Small items (not larger than a handbag) can be cleaned with a commercial aerosol suede cleaner. This produces a thick foam which you work in with a small brush and then leave to dry. Finish by brushing the piece with a brass wire suede brush in order to restore the pile. You should take larger items to a specialist leather cleaner.

Removing stubborn dirt Saddle soap, commonly used to clean thick leathers, will remove ingrained dirt from many types of leather. Rub a damp sponge over the soap to produce a lather. Then work the lathered sponge over the leather in a circular motion. Wipe the piece with a clean, damp sponge and leave it to dry. Finally, rub it over with a soft cloth to buff up a shine.

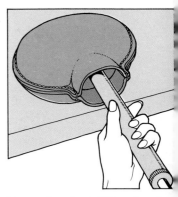

Removing dust If the piece is hollow, as in the case of a bottle, you can use a bicycle pump to blow dust away where a soft brush cannot reach.

Removing stains

Leather is a porous material and therefore it is likely to absorb oils and other substances. Often this is merely a part of the aging process and, unless extensive, should not be regarded as undesirable. The nature or shape of any dramatic marks will determine whether or not they are unsightly enough to remove. If the color of the mark is in strong contrast to its surroundings, or its shape makes it an obvious blemish —for example, a ring mark— you should treat it as a stain.

Oil or grease marks can usually be lifted with a solvent such as alcohol, mineral spirits or lighter fluid. For other stains, try spirit soap or Trichloroethane 1.1.1., dabbed on with a clean cotton pad. An application of fuller's earth may encourage a persistent stain to lift.

Coloring leather

All leathers have a color, whether it is natural or applied during manufacture. Over the years this color may fade or darken. Where the color is merely in the dressed surface, scuff marks may expose the underlying fibers. In such cases, a tinted wax polish or a shoe coloring lacquer (from shoe shops) should make the marks less noticeable. You could also try using waterproof felt-tip pens to touch in small marks.

However, worn patches and some scratches will need a stronger color with a deeper penetration. In this case, use an aniline dye powder dissolved in denatured alcohol. Since the dye is very strong, you will only need a small quantity. Start by mixing up a weak solution of dye and alcohol, adding more powder if necessary, and testing the color periodically on an inconspicuous part of the work.

Apply the stain evenly, using a cloth pad or a wide, soft brush for worn patches and a fine brush to touch in scratches. Work quickly and do not overbrush.

Before you completely recolor an antique leather article, bear in mind that after such treatment it will no longer have the look of old leather. If you think that recoloring would benefit the piece, you could use a commercial leather-renovation kit; this includes a cleaner, the colored lacquer to match your sample and a hide cleaner. Vintage auto restorers, who seem to have different criteria from those of renovators in other fields, use this treatment to bring auto upholstery up to *concours d'élégance* standards.

Reviving dry leather

Dry, neglected leather will appear dull and lifeless. It will also show signs of cracking and fraying, and feel stiff to the touch. A hide cleaning cream (available from shoe repairers) will clean light dirt from the surface, nourish the fibers, restore suppleness and freshen color.

A commercial leather reviver which also contains an insecticide and fungicide that provides protection for several years is used by professional restorers. You should repair any splits or tears before using any reviver, as it may affect adhesives. The treatment is applied with a cloth and then sinks into the surface, leaving no stickiness behind.

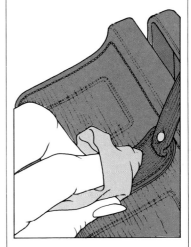

Buffing with hide cleaner
Apply hide cleaner sparingly, using a cotton pad or soft cloth, and rub it well in. Leave the piece for 24 hours, then lightly buff it with a soft cloth. If the leather is really dry, you should repeat the treatment.

Polishing leather

Leather that has been cleaned with saddle soap or treated with hide cleaner can be buffed to a shine with a soft cloth. However, for extra protection and enhanced color, it is a good idea to use a microcrystalline wax polish. This will provide a barrier against marks and spillage stains. Apply the wax sparingly, using a soft cloth for smooth leathers and a brush for textured surfaces. Buff the surface with a cloth or brush before the wax dries completely.

Repairing leatherwork

Leather is a tough covering material which will give long service, provided it is treated properly. Unfortunately, in some examples lack of care eventually results in physical damage. Splits and tears may look alarming, but they can be repaired. However, badly worn or decomposed leather should be stripped off and replaced.

Stitching is the traditional method for join-ing leather parts together, and often a dilapi-dated appearance may be caused by little more than rotted threads. You can therefore repair a gaping seam by restitching it with matching thread through the existing needle holes (see p. 230). However, holes caused by splits or tears should not be sewn, but patched from behind. If the split occurs along stitch holes patch it before restitching.

Mending a tear

Leather that has become dry and brittle is weakened and therefore liable to tear. This is especially true of upholstery leather as it is usually subject to strain as well. Remove the dam-aged panel—extract the nails or unpick the stitching—to expose the flesh side. For thick leathers, cut a canvas or skived leather patch larger than the tear and use polyvinyl or acrylic adhes-ive to glue it to the flesh side. Use nylon gossamer fabric to repair fine leathers. Weight the patch to ensure a good bond.

After patching, touch in ex-posed fibers on the dressed side with a suitable coloring—use a tinted polish or waterproof marker pen on stiff leathers. For soft leathers, try an acrylic paint or adhesive tinted with a water-soluble dye, as these will be more flexible when dry.

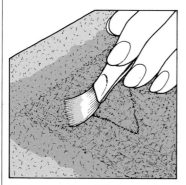

Gluing a nylon fabric patch
Brush acrylic adhesive onto the leather, apply the patch to the flesh side, then coat this with more adhesive. For light-weight leather thin the adhesive slightly with water.

Replacing a desk top

Leather is frequently used as a surface for antique desks and secretaries. The leather top is usually inset in a cross-banded veneer border, and should lie flush with the veneer, which protects its edge.

When dealing with this type of desk, try, where possible, to retain the original top. If it has started to lift around the edge, but is otherwise intact, apply polyvinyl glue to the exposed underside and press it back.

If the leather is beyond re-pair or has been replaced with an imitation material, strip it off and fit a new hide, skiver or morocco top. Some suppliers provide ready-cut tops.

1 Start by peeling off the old leather, then use a chisel to scrape away the glue and old fibers left behind. You may be able to soften the glue with warm water. When the ex-posed wood is clean and dry, sand it with medium-grit ab-rasive paper on a softwood block. Take great care when working near veneer.

2 A plain leather top is cut oversize, then trimmed to fit once in place. With a ready-tooled top, you mark and trim

two adjacent edges first. Put masking tape around the re-cess, then brush glue over the recess and the leather.

3 Lay the leather in position, with the cut edges against the veneer border. Use a roller or the flat of your hand to press the leather down, work-ing from the center outward. Make sure you do not over-stretch the leather by pressing too hard. Some shrinkage may take place, so do not trim the waste yet.

4 When the leather is nearly dry, press it into the recess with a stick or your thumb-nail. Trim away waste with a scalpel—holding it vertically and following the border or using a metal straight edge as a guide. Peel off the pro-tective tape. When the glue is dry, polish the entire top.

MUSICAL
INSTRUMENTS

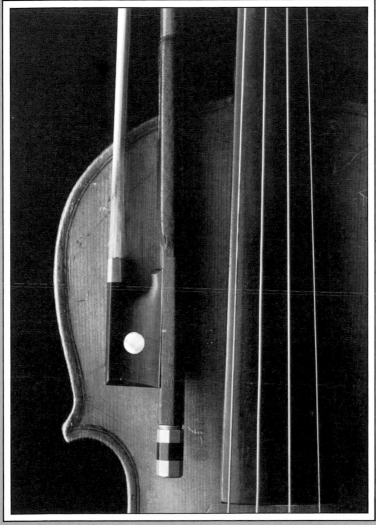

Buying musical instruments

The types and styles of musical instruments are so diverse that several books would need to be written to cover them all in detail. The three types referred to here have been chosen as representative popular instruments. When buying any musical instrument, your first impression is often a good guide to its condition —if it has no obvious missing parts and is clean and well finished it is worth further inspection. And, of course, if you are able to, playing the instrument is always a good test of condition and quality.

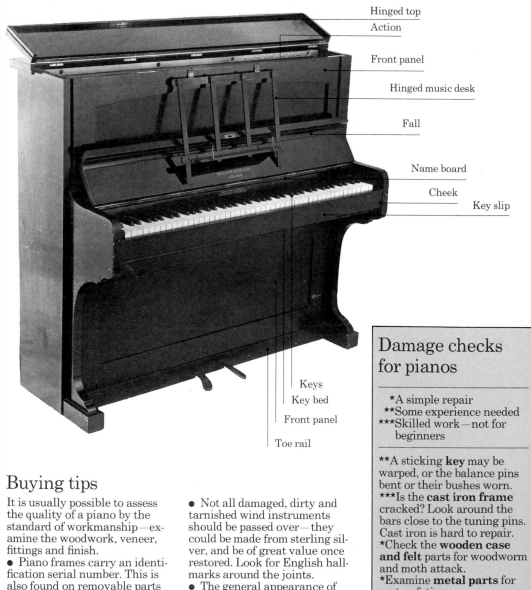

Hinged top

Action

Front panel

Hinged music desk

Fall

Name board

Cheek

Key slip

Keys

Key bed

Front panel

Toe rail

Damage checks for pianos

★A simple repair
★★Some experience needed
★★★Skilled work—not for beginners

★★A sticking **key** may be warped, or the balance pins bent or their bushes worn.
★★★Is the **cast iron frame** cracked? Look around the bars close to the tuning pins. Cast iron is hard to repair.
★Check the **wooden case and felt** parts for woodworm and moth attack.
★Examine **metal parts** for rust or fatigue.

Buying tips

It is usually possible to assess the quality of a piano by the standard of workmanship—examine the woodwork, veneer, fittings and finish.
● Piano frames carry an identification serial number. This is also found on removable parts of the case such as the rear of the front panels and the fall hollow. Mismatched numbers indicate that the case has been modified at some time. This would lower its value.

● Not all damaged, dirty and tarnished wind instruments should be passed over—they could be made from sterling silver, and be of great value once restored. Look for English hallmarks around the joints.
● The general appearance of any instrument and its case is often a good guide to its condition. If it is badly worn and the case is battered, the instrument is probably in need of restoration.

Damage check for flutes

*A simple repair
**Some experience needed
***Skilled work—not for beginners

Are the **key pads in good order? Look under the cup to check. Worn pads or keys out of regulation can cause air leaks. Worn pads can be replaced, and maladjusted keys can be corrected by the adjustment screw.
*Do the **keys** feel floppy when pressed? If so, check the springs and replace missing ones. If not, the point screws which retain the axles of the key mechanism may be loose—these can be replaced.
***Touch corks or felts** may be missing. To check this, operate each key and listen for a tapping noise rather like a typewriter.
***Any **bends** in the body or mechanism axles should be left to an expert.

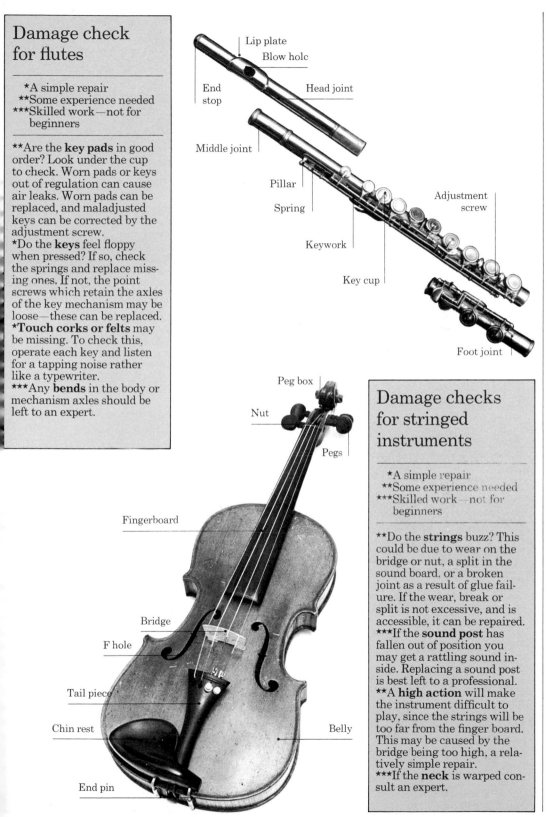

Lip plate
Blow hole
End stop
Head joint
Middle joint
Pillar
Spring
Adjustment screw
Keywork
Key cup
Foot joint

Peg box
Nut
Pegs
Fingerboard
Bridge
F hole
Tail piece
Chin rest
End pin
Belly

Damage checks for stringed instruments

*A simple repair
**Some experience needed
***Skilled work—not for beginners

Do the **strings buzz? This could be due to wear on the bridge or nut, a split in the sound board, or a broken joint as a result of glue failure. If the wear, break or split is not excessive, and is accessible, it can be repaired.
***If the **sound post** has fallen out of position you may get a rattling sound inside. Replacing a sound post is best left to a professional.
A **high action will make the instrument difficult to play, since the strings will be too far from the finger board. This may be caused by the bridge being too high, a relatively simple repair.
***If the **neck** is warped consult an expert.

Tools and materials

Many of the small tasks involved in the restoration of musical instruments can be carried out successfully on a kitchen table with a few simple hand tools. But if you are planning to tackle anything slightly more ambitious, then a similar workspace, lighting and tools to those used for furniture repair would be useful (see p. 98).

Because pianos are very heavy and difficult to move, you may find it easier to take the removable panels to the workshop for refinishing and work on the rest in situ.

Materials

Many materials used for furniture finishing are useful for restoring wooden instruments (see pp. 110–11). To prepare wood for finishing you will need mineral spirits and denatured alcohol, non-lye stripper, abrasive paper and fine steel wool (see p. 103).

Oil or spirit varnish Used to finish violins and some guitars.

Clear cold cure lacquer This two-part lacquer can be used to finish guitars.

Piano key coverings Synthetic ivory covers are usually only available in sets. If you plan to cover one key only, look for a suitable substitute in a model store.

Adhesives Animal glue was used to construct stringed instruments and should be used for repairs.

Latex fabric adhesive is used to glue back loose felt on pianos. Avoid any glue which would soak into the material and set hard.

Clock oil Used to lightly oil wind instruments.

Grease A sparing application of fine grease or petroleum jelly is used to lubricate a tight joint tenon on wind instruments.

Piano wire Stainless steel wire is used for mechanism springs on wind instruments.

Pads Skin-covered pads of felt are made to specific sizes for flute keys.

Synthetic adhesive A special adhesive is made for attaching pads to flutes. It is available from instrument suppliers.

Shellac Traditionally used to fasten pads to flutes.

Tools for repairing wind instruments

Small screwdrivers Use watchmaker's screwdrivers for the fine screws in the mechanism of instruments such as flutes.

Pliers Fine-nose pliers are ideal for gripping piano wire.

Side-cutters Use these to cut piano wire to length.

Needle files For squaring the ends of spring wire.

Cleaning rod These rods are usually supplied with the instrument. They have a slot in one end through which you pass a lint-free cloth, then push the rod and cloth into the barrel.

Tools for repairing stringed instruments

Stringed instruments are constructed chiefly of wood, and therefore a general woodworking tool kit (see pp. 98–102) is essential. In addition, the following tools will be useful.

Side or wire-cutters Used to cut strings and fret wire.

Needle files These fine files are used for shaping string notches in the bridge or nut.

Cross-peen hammer The cross-peen end is used like a veneer hammer (see p. 221).

Reach inside a guitar with it to push out misaligned splits.

Mirror A small adjustable mirror is useful for inspecting the interior of an instrument.

Flashlight A compact flashlight will illuminate the inside of the instrument and make inspection easier.

C clamps Essential when gluing a split in the body of the instrument.

Palette knife Use this to remove old glue from failed joints.

Tools for repairing pianos

The comprehensive overhaul and tuning of a piano are beyond the scope of this book. However, a good general tool kit for the repair of furniture will suffice for the repairs covered here. In addition, a brass-wire suede brush and a vacuum cleaner are useful for cleaning out dust.

Storing instruments

All wooden instruments should be kept away from extremes of temperature and humidity. Do not leave stringed instruments close to a fire or radiator or in direct sunlight, and avoid storing them too close to outside walls or windows where damp or condensation may well be present.

Pianos should be kept in a room with a moderate humidity level—over-dry central heating can cause as many problems as damp (see p. 97). A humidifier will help to maintain the correct humidity. To prevent accidental damage or blows, always place frail, awkward-shaped instruments like violins back in their case after playing.

Restoring wind instruments

Although the repairs shown here have been related to old flutes, they are equally relevant to clarinets and oboes, and the cleaning methods described can be applied to any sort of wind instruments.

It was not until the mid-nineteenth century that the all-metal flute took shape, but most of the old flutes you will come across are likely to be of this type. Earlier flutes were made of close-grained hardwoods.

Assembling a flute

First, check that the mating parts are free from dirt. Then begin assembly by fitting the head joint into the head end of the middle joint. Taking care not to grip the keys, push the head joint into place with a slight twisting action. Align the center of the blow hole with an imaginary line through the middle of the two sets of four keys. A reference line or mark is usually provided at the joint rim for this purpose. Fit the foot joint in the same way, with its key pivot bar in line with the imaginary line through the middle joint.

An overtight joint can be lubricated with a very light coating of a proprietary grease from a specialist supplier. If you cannot obtain this use petroleum jelly.

Care and maintenance

The most effective way of keeping a flute in good order is through regular and careful use. After playing, always wipe the bore with a lint-free cloth on a cleaning rod. Separate the parts, then push and pull the cloth along the length of the bore. Do not remove the end stop from the head. Wipe over the outside of the instrument with a cloth, then put it in its case.

The bore of a wooden flute can be wiped and oiled using bore oil on a pull-through cleaning cloth made from chamois leather with a weighted cord attached. Drop the weight through the bore and pull the lightly oiled leather through with the cord.

Replacing a pad

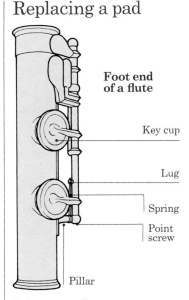

Foot end of a flute

Key cup

Lug

Spring

Point screw

Pillar

It is not usually necessary to replace all the pads on a flute at once. So, just remove the section of the mechanism attached to the key with the worn pad. To do this, unhook the piano wires from their lugs, then remove the point screws in the pillars to release the rod axle about which the offending key pivots. Now you can slide the keys off the rod, noting their order first.

Most old flutes have the flat cup style of key and key pads introduced in the mid-nineteenth century. The pads are made of a felt material covered with fine kid leather. Take other types of pad to a specialist for repairs.

Replacement pads can be bought from a good instrument supplier. Measure the diameter of the key cup, or take the key with you to make sure that you get the right size. The pads will either be glued to the cup or held by a small screw. Traditionally, shellac or sealing wax was used as a "glue". However, today a modern synthetic glue is used.

To remove the worn pad take out the screw holding it in its cup or melt the "glue" by heating the back of the cup over a flame. Wipe out the cup while the "glue" is still soft.

To fit a new screw-held pad you merely drop it into the cup and replace the retaining screw. Thin cardboard disks can be placed under the pad to adjust its height if necessary. To fix the glued type, apply synthetic glue to the bottom of the cup and press in place. Remount the key on the mechanism and hold it closed with an elastic band to bed down the pad while it sets.

Regulate the assembled mechanism with the adjustment screws. Test for air leaks and adjust if necessary.

Replacing a key spring

A key spring can sometimes weaken or fall out, and although, in an emergency, you can use an elastic band to tension the key, you should buy replacement piano wire from a supplier. If the original spring has been lost, you can calculate its length by measuring from its fixing point in the mechanism pillar to the grooved lug on the keywork. Cut the new wire to length with side-cutters, then file the ends square with a fine file.

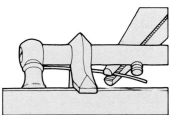

Replacing a spring Using fine-nose pliers, insert one wire end into its hole in the pillar, and put the other into the lug groove.

Restoring stringed instruments

Broken or missing movable parts on stringed instruments such as pegs and bridges, can be replaced quite easily, and slight wear can be dealt with using simple home-made equipment. However, if the damage is more severe, you should consult a professional restorer.

Replacing a tuning peg

The string tensioning pegs of a violin, viola or cello are held by friction in tapered holes in the peg box. Once the tapered holes or the pegs, or both, are worn you will not be able to tune the instrument properly.

Discard worn pegs and buy replacement ones. These are available in ebony, rosewood or boxwood, or as cheaper stained wood types. Although they come in a range of sizes to suit the size of the instrument, a new peg may still have to be cut down to fit in the hole. A replacement peg that is slightly larger than the existing pegs will not seat down level with the others. To correct this, you must trim the new peg's tapered shank (see below) so that it fits.

If a peg hole has worn, you will have to rework it (see right). A larger size of peg will then be needed to fit the re-made peg hole.

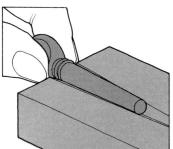

Trimming a peg Glue fine abrasive paper to plywood to make a sanding board wide enough to cover the length of the shank. Steady the peg in a V-notch cut in a softwood batten. Sand the taper with even pressure while rotating the peg. Try the peg in the hole, twisting it and noting where it rubs. Sand these areas down until the peg sits well. Cut to length and round it over to finish just above the outside face of the peg box.

Re-shaping worn peg holes

Head of a violin The tuning pegs fit in peg holes cut through the head of the instrument.

The tapered peg holes, located on each side of the peg box, can become worn or mis-shapen. When this happens, the peg will slip. An over-sized hole would need to be re-worked by a professional restorer. But if the wear is slight, you can re-shape the hole yourself, and then fit a larger peg. Use a spare peg which has a taper that corresponds to that of the original peg to make a simple hole shaper. Cut and glue a strip of fine abrasive paper to fit round the peg, then twist the peg in the holes to re-shape them. Remove as little wood as possible.

Replacing a bridge on a violin

A broken bridge, or one that is worn where the strings have cut in, must be replaced. Various makes and qualities of bridge are available, and they are all sold as either "fitted" or "unfitted". A fitted bridge has the feet shaped to fit the contour of the violin's belly. With an unfitted bridge, you must shape the feet and top edge yourself. A "De Jacques" bridge is self-adjusting—it has special articulated feet which take up the correct angle as vibration from the bowed strings causes them to settle into position.

Shaping and instaling an "unfitted" bridge

The height of the bridge controls the action—the distance between strings and fingerboard. If it is too high, the instrument will be difficult to play. Equally, the curve of the bridge is important; it must not be too flat or too round or it will affect the bowing. Before you make adjustments, remove the strings, unhook the tailpiece and mask f holes. Then support the violin on a bag of polystyrene beads.

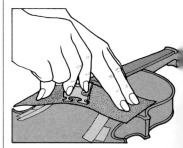

1 Take a strip of medium-grit garnet paper and curve it over the belly of the violin, with its edge in line with the center of the f holes. Rub the feet of the bridge across the abrasive, keeping the bridge upright and parallel with the edge of the paper. Work steadily so that you keep the shaping even on both sides. Remove the abrasive and try the bridge for fit. Both feet should be in full contact with the belly and the bridge upright. Make any fine adjustments if necessary.

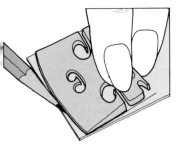

2 Next, you must make a cardboard template while the top curve is untouched. Using the new bridge as a guide, mark the top curve on cardboard and cut it out. Keep this as a record for a later stage. Now make four shallow nicks in the top edge of the bridge with a small, triangular file. Space them $\frac{7}{16}$ in (11 mm) apart, working from the center.

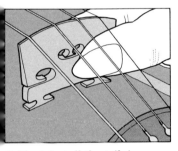

3 Next, install the tailpiece and strings, protecting the polished belly with a cloth. Lightly tension the strings. Install the bridge by passing it under the strings and pulling it up to the vertical. The stamped maker's name on the bridge should face the fingerboard.

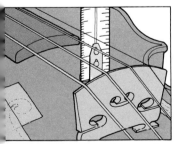

4 Now adjust the strings so that they are in their correct relationship with the fingerboard. Measure the distance between both the E and G strings and the fingerboard at the bridge end. The recommended distance

for a 4/4 violin is $\frac{1}{8}$ in (3 mm) under the E string and $\frac{3}{16}$ in (5 mm) under the G string. The bridge is likely to be higher than you want, so to adjust the string height you must deepen the notches. Slacken and disengage the E string and, if necessary, increase the notch depth with a knife-edge needle file. Keep the file upright and work down the notch until the required height is reached. Repeat for the G string, but use a round needle file.

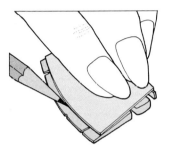

5 Remove the bridge from under the strings. Take your template and lay it over the stamped side of the bridge with the curve touching the bottom of both notches (E and G). You will notice that the curve is over to one side. Mark the curve on the bridge. Extend the notches for the D and A strings down to this line with a needle file.

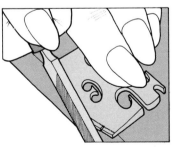

6 Using a chisel or file, pare away the bridge down to the curve, leaving a shallow notch to hold the strings. You will need to thin down the top edge and the corners that face the fingerboard as they will now be too thick. Pare or file the top edge to about $\frac{1}{16}$ in (2 mm) thick to give a parallel ridge. Finally, remove the masking tape, install the bridge as before and tune the violin.

Regluing a joint

Animal glues are traditionally used in the making of stringed instruments, and joints assembled in this way are, unfortunately, liable to glue failure. To test for this, tap around the joints listening for any change in the sound; an unglued area will not resonate.

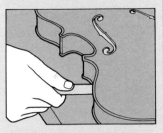

1 Before any joint is repaired, you should remove the old glue. Use a thin table or stiff palette knife dipped into hot water, and work it back and forth between the jointing faces. The heat and moisture should soften the glue so you can wipe it off the knife with a damp cloth.

2 Continue with this procedure until the knife picks up very little glue. Take care not to soak the wood with water as it will swell and weaken existing joints.

3 Allow the joint to dry, then work liquid animal glue into it with a suitable knife. Wipe off any excess glue with a damp cloth.

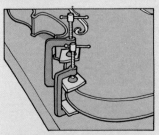

4 Apply small clamps over the joint, using a cork or fiberboard softening block to protect the wood. Leave the clamps in place for 24 hours until the glue has set.

Mending a split

Most acoustic stringed instruments have very thin soundboards, and although they are braced on the underside, a sharp blow can cause a split.

First, wipe the split with a cloth dampened in mineral spirits. If the two sides are not level, stroke the cloth in the direction least likely to catch in the grain. Then glue the split (as shown below). Finally, wipe excess glue away, cover the split with polyethylene sheet, and place a pre-shaped block of wood under it. Place one batten across the split and another across the bottom of the instrument, with a strip of fabric under it to protect the finish. Clamp the battens with C clamps.

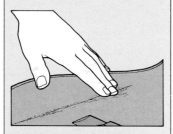

Gluing a split Use polyvinyl adhesive—it is relatively slow-setting, dries almost clear, and bonds wood very well. Work the glue into the split with your fingers, flexing the wood along the split to encourage the glue to penetrate. A cross-peen hammer worked through the sound hole will help you to manipulate the wood while gluing. Wipe away immediately the surface glue and any that runs through to the inside.

Finishing stringed instruments

You do not have to be an expert to refinish an old stringed instrument. Of course, you should not attempt any work at all on an important, valuable piece, but with old, mass-produced instruments that have no historical significance, no harm can be done by stripping the old finish and revarnishing the piece. If you are in any doubt about the value of the instrument, you should check with a specialist dealer first.

Types of finish

Stringed instruments usually have either an oil or spirit varnish finish. In addition, layers of wax polish may have been applied to maintain a shine. To determine which type has been used, test the finish. Apply mineral spirits with a clean cloth to a small patch that will not show. Wax and oil varnish will be dissolved and mark the cloth. If this does not affect the varnish, repeat the treatment with denatured alcohol. This will dissolve spirit varnish.

Violin accessory suppliers sell pigmented oil and spirit varnishes for the viol family. These are made in a range of traditional warm hues as well as a clear varnish.

A shabby old instrument may only need an application of cleaner and reviver to bring its finish back to life. Commercial cleaners and revivers are available, or you can make your own with four parts of mineral spirits to one of linseed oil. Take off the strings and all removable components before cleaning. Apply reviver on a cloth, working over the surface a little at a time. Take care around sound holes. Dry the surface with a clean cloth as the work progresses.

A sound finish can be made to shine with a burnishing cream. But if the polish has nearly worn through, you will have to apply a coat or two of varnish.

If the finish is badly crazed or damaged, you will have to strip it off and refinish the instrument. However, this should be a last resort. Use a non-lye liquid stripper, and cover any areas you do not want to strip with masking tape.

Stripping the finish Apply stripper according to the manufacturer's instructions, then scrape off the softened polish with a scraper. Wash over the surface with mineral spirits, and prepare it for polishing by lightly sanding with very fine abrasive paper, working with the grain. Apply the new polish.

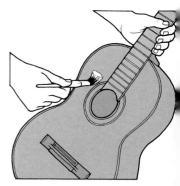

Applying varnish Brushing varnish on can be awkward because of the instrument's shape. Hold the instrument by the neck and apply varnish to the body. Hang it from a wire looped through the head to dry. Finish the neck and head separately.

Cleaning and maintaining a piano

All pianos—whether antique or not—need periodic cleaning, both inside and out. Although this may involve dismantling the case, it is not a difficult job. In addition, simple repairs such as re-covering damaged keys are within the scope of most amateurs.

How a piano is constructed

At the back of an upright piano is the substantial frame that carries the sound board and the iron frame over which the strings are tensioned. The sides of the case are attached to the back frame. And "cheeks" cantilevered from the sides carry the key bed. Toe blocks project forward at the base of the sides to steady the piano.

The rest of the piano's case, including the action and keys, is designed to be removed. It is not usually necessary to remove the top of the case for cleaning, but the top and bottom front panels, and the action and keys should be lifted out so that you can clean and inspect the inside of the piano, as shown right.

Coping with dust

Dust will accumulate inside a piano, particularly if the cotton dust panel that covers the back has worn out. Remove the front panels and brush down the components with a soft hair brush. Suck out dust with a vacuum cleaner. Replace the front panels, and install a new dust panel if necessary. Pry off the wooden strips and tacks that hold the fabric, and unscrew the bars used for moving the piano. Stretch the new cotton fabric over the back and tack or staple it in place. Replace the cover strips and refit the bars.

Taking apart a piano for cleaning

To clean a piano thoroughly, you should begin by removing the wooden panels that are above and below the keyboard. These are located in position with wooden turn buttons and dowel pegs. Next, you should remove the action and name board if you want to lift out any keys.

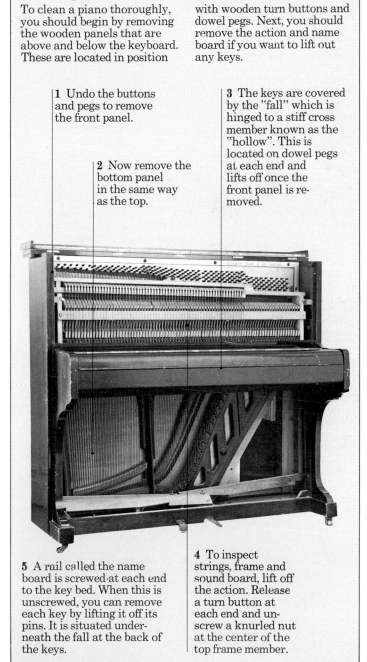

1 Undo the buttons and pegs to remove the front panel.

2 Now remove the bottom panel in the same way as the top.

3 The keys are covered by the "fall" which is hinged to a stiff cross member known as the "hollow". This is located on dowel pegs at each end and lifts off once the front panel is removed.

4 To inspect strings, frame and sound board, lift off the action. Release a turn button at each end and unscrew a knurled nut at the center of the top frame member.

5 A rail called the name board is screwed at each end to the key bed. When this is unscrewed, you can remove each key by lifting it off its pins. It is situated underneath the fall at the back of the keys.

Restoring the piano case

Traditionally, a piano case is highly polished. And, since its introduction, French polish has been used on the vast majority of decorative veneered pianos (see p. 111). Pianos with a high-gloss or ebonized finish can be restored using French polish colored with black pigment.

The first step is to repair and prepare the case, using techniques similar to those employed for furniture (see pp. 105–9). Then you must decide whether to use traditional French polish (see p. 111) or a special French polishing kit designed for the amateur. This is sold in two parts—one is the polish, and the other a burnishing liquid. You can also buy a pre-measured amount of black powder to dissolve in the polish.

Start by removing the front panels, fall and hollow, name board and keys, the action and any removable fittings. Cover the interior of the case with paper or a polyethylene sheet. It is unlikely that the underside of the fall and the nameboard will need repolishing, but mask off this original finish should any other area of these components need work.

Restoring the surface

Provided the old polished surface is sound, wax-free and sanded smooth, you can go on to apply the new polish over it. If the surface is badly crazed, however, it would be better to strip it and build up a new finish (see p. 108).

Remove all traces of wax polish with mineral spirits and fine steel wool. Work on a small area at a time and wipe dry afterward. Rub down with a fine abrasive paper, taking care at the edges as it is easy to rub through the original finish.

Repair deep scratches in the original polish by painting a thickened polish into the groove. Overfill and allow to set hard, then scrape down and sand smooth. If any deep scratches have penetrated into the wood you will have to fill them with a brand-name filler. Repair any damaged veneer (see p. 106)—if necessary you can use a non-matching type.

Applying French polish

If the original polish is well-worn or the surface has been stripped, apply two or more coats of the new polish with a brush first. Allow these coats to set for 24 hours, then rub down with fine silicon carbide paper.

You apply French polish using a special rubbing pad (see p. 111). With a kit polish, the polishing cloth (used to cover the rubbing pad) is soaked in denatured alcohol and then wrung out—this makes application easier. Build up the finish with the pad, working over the surface about 12 times. Keep another cloth in a container of spirits and exchange them as they dry out. Rub the surface down with very fine abrasive paper between coats.

A good build-up of polish should result in a gloss finish, but some smears from the rubbing pad may be detectable. Use the burnishing liquid sold as part of the kit to bring up a high gloss (see below). You should cover an area not more than 12 in (30 cm) square at a time, then repeat the process. Remove the clogged, dirty top surface of the pad after each application. Finally, dry the surface with a soft polishing cloth. This will bring out a very high gloss.

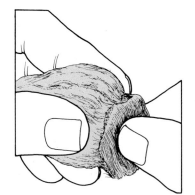

Burnishing the polish Pour the liquid onto a pad of cotton and, using straight strokes, vigorously rub it over the polish about 25 times. Pull off the clogged, dirty top surface of the pad after each application of polish.

Repairing a piano key

Piano keys are individually mounted on a frame within the key bed. They are held by a balance pin near the center of the key bed and an oval pin at the front of each key. To remove a key, take off the top front panel, the hollow and fall, and the name board (this is screwed in place at each end). Now you can either lift and slide out a key from under the action, or release and lift out the piano action to remove all the keys.

Dealing with a warped key
Lift out the offending key and check the amount of distortion against a straight edge. Dampen the wood of the key, clamp it between two straight pieces of wood, and leave it to dry. If the bend is still there, dampen and clamp the key to a piece of wood with a convex edge that opposes the direction of the warp.

Re-covering a white key
When replacing old piano key coverings, try where possible, to match the original ivory or celluloid. If you cannot, use a plastic sheet material instead. Thickness is important as all the keys must be the same height. If the new covering is thicker, pare down the top of the key or sand down the underside of the covering on a flat sheet of abrasive.

Remove the old covering by working a warmed thin knife along the joint. Use a very fine-toothed saw to cut out a new covering slightly larger in size than the key. Rough up the underside of the new cover, apply a sparing coat of white or water-soluble glue, and clamp it to the key. When the glue has set, file the cover to size and round over edges to match existing keys using a fine abrasive.

TEXTILES

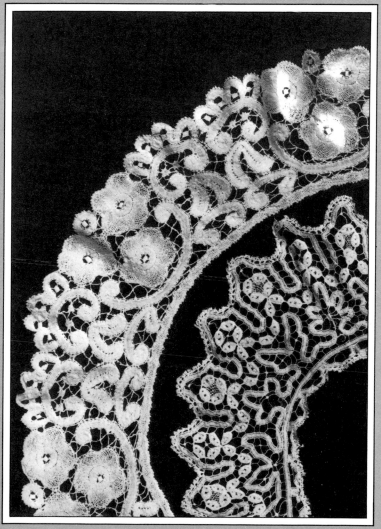

Collecting textiles

A wide range of collectibles is embraced by the description antique textiles—from "folksy" patchwork quilts to Art Deco beaded dresses. Fabrics are prone to staining, wear, and fading, so correct storage, handling, and cleaning are very important.

What is a textile?

The most common fabric construction is the weave. Woven fabric comprises two sets of threads—the warp and the weft—crossed over and under each other. This pattern is achieved on a loom. However, some textiles are either felted, knitted, crocheted or knotted rather than woven.

Woven fabrics are made in a wide range of finishes, usually decorative. For example, velvet has a cut pile and can be of cotton, silk, or wool, whereas chintz is a printed and glazed cotton. Satin has a glossy appearance and is usually made from silk, while a brocade fabric incorporates metallic threads in the weave. Crepe is a lightweight cloth, often of silk or wool, which has a wrinkled surface. And chiffon is a very light, semi-transparent fabric, usually made from silk.

Detail of a brocaded cut-velvet Art Deco jacket

Detail of a hand-painted chiffon shawl

Detail of a Victorian satin bodice

How to identify fibers

Identifying fiber types is often of importance in cleaning and treatment. Test a fiber by burning a small snippet.
Cotton (vegetable fiber) burns with a yellow flame, smells of burning paper, gives gray ash.
Linen (vegetable fiber) has a yellow flame, smells of burning grass, yields gray ash.
Wool (animal fiber) seldom produces a flame, smells of burning hair, leaves crushable beads.
Silk (animal fiber) shrivels, smells slightly fishy, and leaves a soft blob.

Types of fiber

Most antique textiles, from the lightest muslin to the heaviest velvet, are made from one of the four following natural fibers.

Cotton

Cottons were plain or hand-painted until the early eighteenth century, when block printing was introduced. Throughout the seventeenth century cotton was an expensive, luxury fabric, but by the end of the eighteenth century the Industrial Revolution had made it the cheapest textile available. Cotton is a vegetable fiber made from the cotton plant, and is used for costume, undergarments, and bed-covers.

Wool

This warm animal fiber is obtained from the coat of the sheep. It is often used for costume, upholstery, and as a thread for embroidery (for example, in needlepoint).

Silk

A delicate, luxury fabric made from the cocoon of the silkworm, silk is available in a range of weaves, including satin, velvet, and crepe. It has a tendency to wear quickly, particularly along folds. This condition is known as "ripeness." Silk is often used for costume, curtains and hangings.

Linen

This is a very strong and hard-wearing fabric made from the flax plant. It is found as tablecloths and undergarments.

Storing textiles

The storage place should be dark and, ideally, have a temperature of 55°F (13°C) and a relative humidity of 55 per cent. Do not fold textiles as fibers can weaken along the sharp creases and break. Instead, roll or pad them. For large pieces, first cover a cardboard tube with acid-free tissue paper. Roll the textile loosely round the tube, with the right side out, store the tubes flat and cover them with a dust sheet fixed in place with cloth tape. Roll small pieces individually and store them in cardboard boxes.

Store costume flat, with the sleeves and folds padded with acid-free tissue. Place more tissue between the fabric and the buttons to prevent discoloration from oxidizing metal. Do not leave brooches pinned on stored clothes.

Remove starch from tablecloths before storing. Do not use polyethylene sheeting or bags—they encourage mold. To protect items from dust, use cotton bags. Do not store dirty fabrics. Use moth balls or crystals, following the maker's instructions.

Dealing with moths and mold

Use moths balls or crystals in your closets or drawers, but make sure that they do not come into contact with the fabric. Keep the insides of closets and drawers clean and dust-free. If you do not, you will encourage pests. Check regularly for signs of moths' eggs, "frass," or holes eaten in fabrics.

Animal fibers are more likely to be attacked than vegetable fibers. If a piece falls victim, brush off all moth "frass," then vacuum (see p. 195) thoroughly to remove any eggs.

A musty, damp smell indicates the presence of mold. Discourage this by keeping your storage place damp-free and airing the textiles from time to time. A moldy piece should be dried in a warm room with air circulating. Once it is dry, brush off any mold.

Hanging costume

If you wish to hang garments, make sure that they are strong enough to take the strain. Never hang frail or beaded dresses. If you think that a dress is strong enough to hang up it is wise to sew tapes into the waistband to help support the weight. And always use generously padded hangers.

Attaching tape to a waistband

On garments with a petersham-type waistband, loops of cotton tape sewn into the petersham will take the strain off the skirt fabric when you hang the dress. Buy $\frac{1}{2}$ in (12 mm) wide cotton tape and cut off four 4 in (10 cm) long strips.

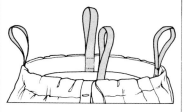

1 Sew in one strip in the shape of a loop at the middle of the front of the dress, one at the middle of the back, and one at each side.

2 Slip the central loops over the hanger center, and fit the side ones into its notches. If the hanger has no notches, use pins.

Buying tips

- To identify hand embroidery examine it on the reverse side. You will find that hand work is less regular than machine work, and often less thread is carried over behind.
- Make sure the piece is all original—you can get marriages and conversions (see p. 96) in costume.
- It is not possible to wash safely valuable and pre-nineteenth century pieces, silk items, hand-painted pieces, and old flags or banners. You should take into account the cost of specialist cleaning when you buy such textiles.

Damage checks

*A simple repair
**Some experience needed
***Skilled work—not for beginners

***Check the **seams and stress areas** on costume; for example, the underarms, collars, and cuffs—for indications of wear. Small tears can be conserved, but if the fabric is deteriorating, so that merely handling it increases the area of damage, the piece is probably past repair. Worn collars and cuffs cannot be repaired.
Is there evidence of **moths or mold? A musty smell or a few whitish powdery blotches are bad signs.
***Examine any **crease marks** carefully to make sure that the fibers are not damaged or broken.
Look for **missing areas on embroidery. Certain dyes encourage threads to rot (for example, brown on wool and black on silk).
Look for **dirt and stains. Do not pay a lot for a badly stained piece as you may not be able to remove the marks.
*Check for **missing trimmings, buttons and beads**.
Look out for **loose threads on embroidery. They may not be easy to repair.

Decorative treatments

There are many different ways that fabric and thread have been worked over the centuries to produce decorative effects. Here, we have selected some of the most common treatments.

Embroidery

This is an ancient skill, dating back to the Middle Ages, when many embroidered vestments and hangings were made for the Church. Many styles, stitches, and techniques exist, some of which are covered here. A specialist book will give you further information.

Embroidered samplers are a very popular collector's field. These panels were made by young girls to show their mastery of the different stitches.

Whitework

A form of embroidery, this is done in white thread on a white ground, usually muslin. It was used for baby clothes and undergarments.

Cutwork

This type of white embroidery is said to have been the forerunner of lace. It consists of embroidery, usually whitework, in which large parts of the background fabric between the stitches are cut away.

Broderie anglaise

This is a kind of whitework with a simple pattern of repeating open eyelets. Sometimes solid satin stitch spots or lines are added. The edges are usually scalloped.

Broderie anglaise edging on a linen shift

Lace

The earliest lace—made in the sixteenth, seventeenth, and eighteenth centuries—is in linen or, occasionally, silk. This type of lace is sought after by collectors and is quite valuable. Hand-made nineteenth-century lace, in cotton or silk thread, is less expensive.

There are three methods of making lace. The finest is hand-made needlepoint, which grew out of embroidery techniques. A single thread was used. Hand-made bobbin lace involves

Detail of hand-made lace

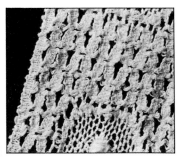

Detail of machine-made lace

twisting and plaiting up to 200 bobbins around each other and around a pattern of pins in the lace-making pillow. Machine-made lace was first introduced in the 1840s.

Needlepoint feels crisper and firmer than bobbin lace. Both hand-made types will show irregularities when examined under a glass. Machine-made lace looks very even.

Brussels, Flanders, Alençon, Chantilly, Valenciennes, Genoa, Milan, Venice, Honiton, Nottingham, Limerick, and Malta are some of the most famous lace-making centers. The appearance and design differs from region to region. If you think you have a piece that is hand-made, consult a specialist to date it and to identify its place of origin.

Drawn thread work

Threads of the ground fabric are pulled out and those left are decorated with overstitching. The overstitches serve to reinforce the weakened fabric, as well as to decorate it. This technique is often used on tablecloths and clothing.

Smocking

Simple embroidery stitches are used to gather material into regular pleats. The combination of the pleats and stitches forms an intricate "honeycomb" design.

Crochet

In the nineteenth century, panels and edgings resembling lace were often worked by crocheting techniques for trimming tablecloths, bedcovers, and underclothes.

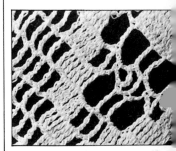

Detail of crochet "lace"

Beadwork

In this type of work beads can either be woven or threaded together in order to make a fabric, or sewn onto or knitted into the body of another fabric. Beadwork is commonly found on handbags, fire-screens, and Art Deco dresses.

Beadwork butterfly worked on net

Couching

Gold or silver thread is laid along the surface of the fabric, either singly or in double rows, and stitched in place with a more flexible, cheaper thread. This type of work is frequently found on antique oriental costume and hangings.

Detail of nineteenth-century oriental skirt with gold couching

Needlepoint or canvaswork

This is a development of embroidery in which the canvas ground is covered with yarn. It was used for upholstery and hangings. Needlepoint is worked with a needle, but it is often confused with tapestry, which is worked on a loom.

Quilting

To make cheap cotton warm, padding was sandwiched between two layers and held in place with decorative stitching.

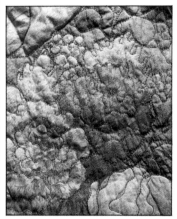

Detail of quilted chintz bag

Patchwork

This work was originally purely utilitarian—in poorer communities in Europe and America the best pieces of old clothes were cut into shapes and sewn together to make a new fabric. Arrangements of the pieces became very elaborate.

Detail of antique quilt

Tools and materials

Work in good natural light or daylight-balanced artificial light, and do not let direct sunlight fall on your work. A deep sink or bath-tub in which you can wash textiles flat is required, although you could use photographic trays on top of your worktable.

Tools

Non-rusting pins Pin washed textiles with these brass pins.
Entomological pins These very fine pins can be inserted between the threads of fabrics without causing damage. Lace pins are an acceptable substitute.
Magnifying glass Use this to help you with delicate work.
Sharp scissors For cutting threads the small embroidery type is best. To cut off backing use dressmaker's shears.
Vacuum cleaner Remove loose dust with this, screening the nozzle with nylon monofilament mesh.
Needles You should have a wide selection of curved, embroidery, and beading needles.
Press A ready-made or improvized press (two sheets of hardboard and a heavy weight) should be used to "iron" washed fabrics.
Domestic iron Use on the coolest setting for strong fabrics.
Soft hair brush This is for applying and brushing off hot potato starch, used as a cleaner.

The embroidery frame
This allows you to stretch taut the backing material and work.

An improvized press
Smooth out the fabric and place it on top of a sheet of hardboard, shiny side up. Cover with another piece of hardboard and put a heavy weight on top.

Materials

Detergent A mild type used for handwashing woollens will clean stronger fabrics.
Potato starch This is used to dry clean embroidery and lace. It is available from quality variety stores and druggists.
Acid-free tissue Use this to pad and wrap textiles.
Mothballs These prevent attack by moth.
Ammonia In solution, ammonia removes stains.
Rust-stain remover A commercial product available from druggists that removes rust and iron mold stains.
Bicarbonate of soda Used to remove some types of stain.
Denatured alcohol Used to remove grass and ink stains.
Crewel wool Use this to renew needlepoint.

Removing stains

Age-old stains are often best left—they will not move without using strong chemicals, and these will harm antique textiles. Stains of a younger vintage can sometimes be removed. Do not treat valuable or fragile pieces.
Caution: Test for color fastness first.

Use only weak solutions —several applications of cleaner are better than one strong one. Put a pad of white blotting paper, rag, or tissue under the stain before treating it. Work inward from the outer edges of the stain. Always rinse thoroughly.

This list gives common stains and their remedies.
Alcohol Use water and detergent, worked in with fingertips.
Blood Soak in cold salt water. Then rinse thoroughly.
Candlewax Put white blotting paper on both sides of the fabric. Press with an iron, then rub with mineral spirits.
Coffee and tea Soak for 10 minutes in 1 oz (30 g) borax to 1 pint (0.5 l) warm water, then rinse.
Fats and oils For thick stains, see Wax. For thin stains, dab with mineral spirits.
Grass Dab with mineral spirits.
Ink, ballpoint Dab with denatured alcohol.
Ink, marker Dab with denatured alcohol.
Ink, fountain-pen Dab with warm water, apply a paste of salt and lemon juice, leave 10 minutes, rinse.
Iron mold First try lemon juice and salt, then a rust-stain remover.
Mildew First soak in lemon juice, then rinse in distilled water.
Perspiration Dab with a solution of one part white vinegar to 15 parts warm water.

Cleaning textiles

You should never wash fabrics until you have tested them for color fastness. Always wash by hand—never in a machine, and use a special mild detergent, not a commercial soap powder. Never wash silk, tapestries, flags, or banners, and only wash frail or torn items if you can lay them out on nylon net as a support.

Washing

First test your piece for color fastness (see right). Wash antique textiles by hand in lukewarm water. Soft water or distilled water is preferable to hard water, particularly for fragile pieces. *Never* put antiques in the washing machine. Do not use commercial soap powders, but instead use the detergent marketed for handwashing woollens.

1 If the piece is fragile, lay it out on a supporting piece of nylon monofilament screening or net, and do not squeeze or rub it. Instead, merely dab it with a clean sponge. Change the soapy water as many times as necessary. When clean, rinse the piece thoroughly. You must dry antique textiles flat.

2 Place the piece on a table or board covered with polyethylene or white toweling, pinning it out with brass lace pins. Dab with white toweling or blotting paper to remove excess moisture. Leave to dry naturally.

3 A hairdryer held about 12 ins (30 cm) above the fabric will speed up drying. *Never* put antiques in a tumble dryer.

Dry cleaning

The basic rule here is *never* take antique textiles to a commercial dry cleaner. They use very strong chemicals, so that, however strong the fabric and however exclusive the establishment, the result might well be disastrous. Nor should you use dry cleaning fluids or spot cleaners yourself. You can "dry clean" antiques with substances such as potato starch, or you can take them to a hand cleaner who specializes in renovating antique textiles.

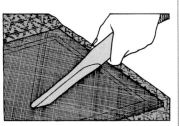

Removing loose dirt Use a vacuum cleaner for this, covering the fabric with a piece of nylon monofilament screening to protect it. Keep the nozzle about an inch above the fabric. Regular vacuuming will keep much of the dirt at bay.

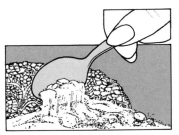

Using potato starch Stains and spots can be removed from delicate embroidery and lace with potato starch from a hardware or variety store. Heat the starch in a saucepan until it is hand-hot. Cover the piece with a $\frac{1}{2}$ in (12 mm) layer, pressing it down well. Leave for 10 minutes, then brush off.

Ironing textiles

Set the iron to a very low heat (at least one stop below that indicated by the manufacturer for the fabric). Protect the textile with a damp cloth. Fragile material should not be ironed; instead, press it in a press or between two pieces of wood and a heavy weight. You should never iron stained or dirty items as you may "seal in" the blemish or dirt, making it impossible to remove later.

How to test for color fastness

This test should always be carried out before any cleaning or stain removal is attempted. Find an unobtrusive area—on the back of the textile if possible—and dab it with a soap and warm water solution on cotton. Leave for a few minutes, then press a piece of white blotting paper on the test spot. If the paper is clean, that color is fast.

You must test every color on your piece—including the trimmings—before you can assume that it is safe to wash.

If a trimming is not fast but the rest of the article is, you should remove it carefully, wash the piece, and "dry clean" the trimming separately. Then carefully sew them back together.

Using and displaying textiles

Textiles will fade and weaken in direct sunlight, so always hang them away from window light. Samplers, pieces of embroidery, and even lace can be framed and then protected from dust with glass. Weak fabrics should be strengthened by stitching them to a nylon-net backing. Quilts can be hung on the wall from a roller or bar on tape attached to the back.

If you do not want to display a piece, or if it is too fragile, follow the storage instructions on p. 191.

Wearing a costume

Antique costume is best preserved if it is not worn, as wearing antique clothes may lead to perspiration damage, and will certainly put strain on the fibers. But never wearing an antique dress is usually out of the question for most people, especially if it is a family item such as a wedding dress or christening robe. If articles are in good condition, they can be worn occasionally if the following guidelines are observed. Avoid staining the item with modern chemical deodorants as these can rot the fabric. If possible, sew dress shields into the garment and wear only talcum powder. Wash out any perspiration stains as soon as possible. Make sure that there are no loose threads on the hems of long dresses as these can catch and lead to tears. Never try to squeeze into a garment that is too small for you.

If you do not want to risk wearing a costume yourself, but you are keen to see it displayed in three-dimensions, as it was intended to be, you can dress a tailor's dummy in it. You will need plenty of space if you want to set up such a display.

Framing small textiles

Textiles cannot be attached directly to a backing board; they must be mounted on a fabric-covered board. Measure the piece, add 1 in (2.5 cm) all round, and use these measurements to cut out a thick cardboard or hardboard backing. Smooth the edges and corners with sandpaper.

3 Center the textile on the board, pin it with brass pins, adjusting it carefully, then sew it in place with an appropriate thread and stitch.

1 Cover the mounting board with a suitable natural fabric, for example linen or cotton, keeping the grain as straight as possible.

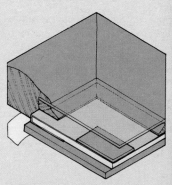

4 Either take the mounted textile to a framer or frame it yourself (see pp. 171–2). The glass must not rest on the textile—a wooden filet or an acid-free picture mount should be inserted between the glass and the board.

Clean the glass over a framed textile with a damp cloth—a dry one will create static, which could affect the fibers under the glass, weakening them.

2 Glue the edges of the fabric mount to the back of the board with white adhesive, weight it, and leave to set overnight.

Hanging a large textile

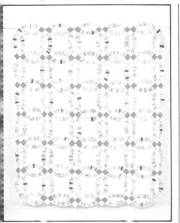

A cloth sleeve (see p. 203) can be attached to the lining and a rod threaded through it. This method is good for heavy textiles, as it distributes the weight evenly. Another method is to use strip contact fastener and a wooden batten. A third method involves sewing tabs along the back of the lining at intervals of no more than 6 ins (15 cm) and slotting the rod through these. If the lining is in the form of a visible mount, the tabs should be of the same color or, if not, they should match the textile. The disadvantage of this method is that it can cause uneven tension on a heavy textile, so it is best to restrict its use to light hangings.

The tab method
Tabs that match the lining or textile, and take a pole or rod, can be used as a way of hanging a light textile.

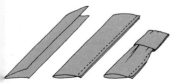

1 Make the tabs from the same material as the mount. Cut 5 in (12 cm) wide strips on the straight grain of the fabric. Fold them in half and machine-seam. Then turn them right side out.

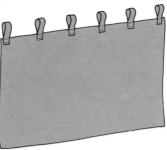

2 Machine stitch the cloth tabs to the back of the mount at intervals of no more than 6 ins (15 cm) apart.

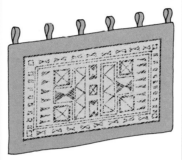

3 The textile is now ready to hang up. See right for two commonly used methods of attachment.

Strip contact fastener method
This method involves using a strip contact fastener, which distributes the weight evenly over the length of the textile.

Attaching strip contact fastener
Sew or glue the softer strip to tape that is wider than the strip, and then sew this combination to the lining along the whole length of the top edge of the hanging. Then glue or nail the rough strip to a wooden batten. You can then hang up the batten (see below).

Hanging methods
There are several ways of hanging your textile once you have prepared it. Two popular methods are shown here.

Using a curtain pole A decorative wooden or brass pole can be fastened to the wall with the brackets provided in the normal way. A textile mounted by the tab or sleeve method can be hung from it.

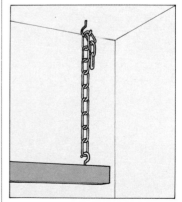

Using a chain and batten Attach a cup hook in the top of the batten and screw another hook into a ceiling joist. Then suspend a length of chain between the two. This method allows you to adjust the height at which the textile hangs.

Repairing textiles

Some repairs that you would expect to make to fabrics—darning holes, for example—are taboo for antique textiles. A darn will not look like the original weave, and it will put a strain on surrounding weak fibers, possibly causing more holes. To preserve damaged antiques, textile conservators "patch" holes by covering them over with matching fine-meshed net. This supports weak fabric, and the holes filled-in by the net do not spoil the look of the original when it is viewed from a distance.

Some sewing repairs are permissible, but only if they replace the original thread exactly as it was—for example, missing or worn thread can be filled in on a piece of needle-point or the threads that join slits in the weave of a tapestry can be replaced.

Buttons and trimmings

A wide range of materials is used for making buttons. It may be difficult to find replacements for missing buttons, but you may be able to find a similar period set, or reproductions, at a specialist button store. Make sure that the fabric is strong enough to take the weight of the button before you sew it on.

Damaged trimmings can sometimes be replaced if a suitable piece can be found. For example, the white tape used to gather the waist of Victorian petticoats can still be bought. Ask for the 100 percent cotton type.

Selection of late-nineteenth-century and early-twentieth-century buttons and braids

Attaching a textile to a supportive lining

An old textile will often need to be lined before you can display it safely. Pre-shrunk net, polyester, silk crepe, and linen are all used. Your choice will depend on the nature and strength of the textile. A light, draping textile will call for a polyester or silk support, while a light piece to be displayed flat will need net and a heavy hanging will need linen.

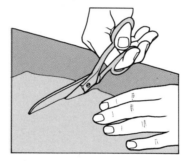

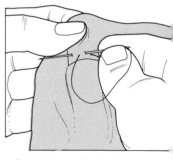

1 Cut out a patch measuring a few inches more than the area of the damage. On a small piece or a very weak item the best method is to line the entire textile. In such a case, frame up the background fabric as is done for needlepoint (see p. 200).

2 Stitch along the lines of greatest strain. Use large tacking stitches (see p. 228).

3 Do not leave knots in the textile; instead, finish the stitches with a locking backstitch (see p. 228).

Stitching up a slit in a tapestry

In some tapestries a change of color produced a slit in the weave. Originally, these slits were sewn up with silk thread. In time this weakens, however, and the slit gapes open and puts strain on the rest of the tapestry. It should be mended as soon as possible, otherwise the piece will become misshapen. Use a fine needle and strong button thread in a suitable color. Stitch between the threads, not into them.

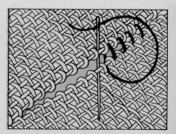

Stitching method You should use a stitch that is straight on the right side, and slanting on the back.

Mending tears in patchwork quilts

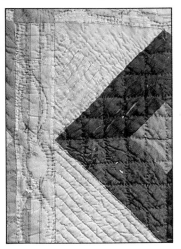

Cover tears with matching fine-meshed net tacked over the hole on the front of the quilt. Do not try to sew in a modern patch. If some of the wadding is missing in the region of the tear try to match the material you use as a replacement to the original stuffing. If matching wadding is not available, use a polyester type instead.

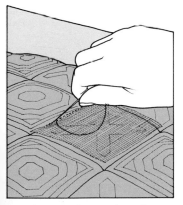

Patching with net Attach the net patch by stitching into the original stitches on the edges of the patches abutting the worn patch. Do not try to stitch through to the lining.

Mending beadwork

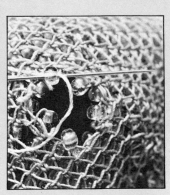

2 Thread the needle through an existing bead and then make a backstitch through it in order to hold it.

Do not attempt to resew loose beads onto beaded 1920s dresses —the chiffon ground is too frail. Just secure the remaining beads by tying off the broken thread. On strong pieces, a crocheted purse for example, you can fill in a small gap from the reverse side, using matching beads and thread.

3 Bring the needle up through the existing bead, thread on the new bead and make another backstitch to lock the new bead in place.

1 Make a temporary knot, and bring the needle up through the fabric close to the site of the missing bead.

4 Continue to thread and sew beads, "keying" them in with surrounding ones. Finish with a backstitch. Cut off knots.

Patching a broken canvas

If some of the ground on a piece of needlepoint is missing, you will need to mend it before you re-embroider the design. The method you choose will depend on the extent of the damage.

Replacing missing strands
If a few strands of canvas are missing, you must replace them before you start to re-embroider the piece. You should use a matching thread, stitching through the support when both the support and the antique textile are fixed in the embroidery frame. Make sure that the new strands match up with the horizontals and verticals of the original canvas.

Patching a hole If the hole is large, you will have to patch it with matching canvas of the same weight as the original. Reverse the textile on the support and stitch the patch in on the wrong side, matching horizontal and vertical threads. This makes the piece bulky, so avoid it if possible.

Renewing damaged areas of needlepoint

Detail of damaged needlepoint

You will need to attach the canvas to a pre-shrunk linen base and re-embroider the missing areas on the face side through both the canvas and the support. Use crewel wools, cotton, or silk, depending on the original, in suitable colors.

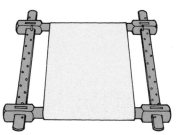

1 Take a piece of linen 2–3 ins (5–7.5 cm) larger all round than the textile and sew it to the webbing on the frame rollers. Roll the material up evenly. Insert the stretchers in the frame sides. Tension should be even all round and not too tight.

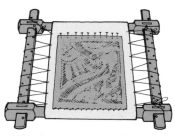

2 Pin the antique textile in place, about 3–4 ins (7.5–10 cm) below the roller, then sew its bottom edge to the support with button thread. Adjust the rest of

the textile, keeping it in place with brass pins. Now tighten the side tapes of the frame to keep the piece taut.

3 Knot the end of the thread and pull the needle through the canvas 3–4 ins (7.5–10 cm) away from the damaged area, with the knot on the right side. (After repair, cut off the knot.)

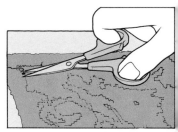

4 Next, fill in the missing area, using the same stitches as on the original. Once you have mended the damage bring the needle through 3 ins (7.5 cm) from the reworked area, and cut off the thread level with the surface. Cut off knots too. Remove the piece from the frame.

Needlepoint after restoration

RUGS

Collecting rugs

Piled rugs were originally developed by Eastern nomadic tribes who needed warm yet portable floor coverings for their tents. Rugs of this kind were unknown in the West until the fourteenth century, and it took a further four hundred years before they became common. Rugs are classified not only by their country of origin, but more specifically by the district in which they were made, or by a particular market town, village or tribal name, and, in a few cases, by the name of the master weaver. A broad classification of types is relatively simple, but even experts find it difficult to pin down certain rugs to a place of manufacture.

The design of rugs

The traditional oriental rug has a central decorated field surrounded by a border or series of borders. Patterns are often composed of motifs that form purely abstract designs. Or motifs can be stylized representations of items such as flowers, leaves or clouds.

Boteh

Gull

Palmette

Cloud

As well as motifs, there are traditional themes in rug design. A popular Persian theme is based on a formal garden with flower beds, paths, and streams or pools. Another common subject is a tree representing eternal life; this can be stylized or pictorial depending on the country of origin. Other pictorial themes worked into rugs illustrate a story or poem, or show well-known buildings or landscapes.

In some cases, the function of a carpet will dictate its design. A prayer rug, for instance, always has a niche (a representation of an arch of a mosque). This is pointed toward Mecca at prayer time. Although oriental motifs were, and still are, widely copied by Western rug weavers, their other designs reflect Western tastes and themes—for example, heraldic and floral motifs are commonplace.

Buying tips

● You will sometimes notice a color variation on hand-made rugs. This does not devalue the piece—in fact, quite the opposite. The variation occurs because the rug has been made from small batches of wool that were dyed at different times. This is usually a sign that the rug was made by a nomadic tribesman. Modern rug makers sometimes try to fake this effect.
● When you look at the back of a hand-made rug, the base of each knot is visible, and you can make out the pattern. In contrast, the pattern on the reverse of a machine-made carpet is vague. Furthermore, no hand-made rug is perfectly regular. There are always variations in the tension of warp and weft, the positioning of knots, and the shape of the side cords and fringes.

Damage checks

*A simple repair
**Some experience needed
***Skilled work—not for beginners

***Is the rug **brittle or rotted?** Check by folding the back—if it cracks audibly, do not buy it.
Look for **splits and tears by lifting the rug—they are not always obvious when it is laid out flat.
Bald patches can be difficult to repile. Examine the rug closely, as small areas are sometimes touched in with paint, and this may not be immediately obvious.

Nineteenth-century English rug with a design of lilies

Persian rug with a tree-of-life design

How a rug is made

Strong vertical "warp" threads are stretched over a loom to form the foundation of a piled carpet. They are usually made of a strong fiber such as coarse wool or goat hair. The pattern is formed by knotting short lengths of colored wool onto the warp. After every row of knots, "weft" threads are woven through the warp and beaten down with combs.

Two types of knot are used, the "Ghiordes" or "Turkish" knot and the "Senneh" or "Persian" knot. Both knots are tied around two adjacent warp threads. These traditional knots are placed directly one above the other, so the edge of any diagonal shape is made in steps.

Some rugs are made without knots; instead the pattern is formed by colored weft threads. At the edge of a colored motif the thread is passed back again rather than continued across the rug. In the simplest type, known as a "Kelim," the weft simply passes over and under alternate threads. In "Soumak" weaving, weft threads are wrapped around pairs of warp threads. As the turns slope in different directions on alternate rows, the weaving has a herringbone appearance.

Senneh or
Persian knot

Ghiordes or
Turkish knot

Identifying knots Fold the rug back along one vertical row and separate the tufts of one knot. If the two ends part to show a warp thread beneath, it is a Senneh knot. The tufts of a Ghiordes knot will not part completely, but you should see the knot base passing over both warp threads.

Using and displaying rugs

Almost any floor surface is suitable for old rugs as long as it is smooth, clean and dry. Wooden floorboards should be close-fitted, otherwise dust can penetrate the gaps and stain the rug. Make sure that a tiled floor is free of bumps or sharp edges as these will produce wear. Small rugs laid loose on a polished floor can be dangerous. Use a non-slip underlay cut about 1 in (2.5 cm) shorter all round. Many collectors loose-lay rugs over plain fitted carpets.

Caring for displayed rugs

If you must lay a rug in a position where it is in direct sunlight, turn it regularly to avoid uneven fading. Turning will also help to even out general wear. You should also be careful not to leave heavy furniture standing on one part of a rug for too long. Use furniture cups to prevent castors making a deep depression in the pile. And move your furniture around from time to time to give the pile a change to recover.

Moths lay their eggs in dark, undisturbed areas under beds and cupboards. To avoid infestation you should clean these areas thoroughly and regularly. Lift the rugs and beat them outside to dislodge any eggs, then leave them out in the sun for a few hours in order to air.

Choosing a site

A fireside rug is always vulnerable to sparks and falling coals, but you can reduce the risks by installing a screen.

Dining areas are popular spots for loose rugs, but they are not a good choice of site. Apart from the risk of staining by spilled food, the table and chairs tend to concentrate wear. Little-used rooms such as spare bedrooms are ideal sites for more valuable rugs. Antique rugs should never be used in a bathroom as they cannot be allowed to absorb any water.

Hanging rugs

Lightweight rugs make ideal wall hangings. Hang them from the top so that the stronger warp threads take the strain, and avoid positions over radiators as the heat will dry out the wool and make it brittle. Never hang rugs in direct sunlight as they cannot be turned to avoid fading.

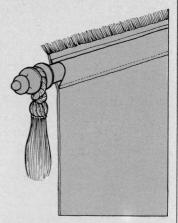

Making a "sleeve" for a hanging pole Using a curved needle, sew 2 in (5 cm) wide carpet binding to the back about $\frac{1}{2}$ in (12 mm) from the top. Allow enough slack for the rod to pass through the tape. If your rug is over 5 ft (1.5 m) wide, sew the tape on in sections, leaving access gaps for the pole so that you can fit extra brackets to support it in the middle.

Tools

Few tools are required to re-store old rugs. Most of them are common and you are likely to own them already.

Needles Use straight and curved needles with large eyes. You may need a needle threader for very thick wool.

Scissors A normal pair of scissors is used for trimming the fringes of the rug. Nail scissors with curved blades are used for trimming the pile.

Thimble Pushing a needle through a rug is hard, so use a thimble to protect your finger.

Pliers These may be needed to pull a needle through a very thick, stiff rug.

Hairdryer Speeds up the drying of cleaned areas.

Electric iron A domestic iron will help absorb grease when used with blotting paper.

Materials

Carpet shampoo Most good-quality carpet shampoos can be used on hand-made rugs as long as they are tested first. A shampoo that leaves an absorbent powder in the pile is best.

White vinegar, salt and detergent These materials are used in solution with water to remove stains.

Blotting paper Used with an iron to absorb grease from a rug.

Threads Wool or sewing silk is required to repile rugs and mend fringes. Try to match color and weight as closely as you can to the original.

To make structural repairs use strong cotton thread. It will be easier to use if you drag it across a block of beeswax first.

Squared paper and marker pens For working out a pattern before repiling a rug.

Cleaning rugs

Old rugs are just as easy to clean as new wall-to-wall carpets, but regular cleaning is more important to ensure their preservation. Dirt can damage old rugs—especially if tiny particles of grit which settle on the surface are left to be walked down into the pile where they can then begin to cut through the fibers of the material.

Beating out the dust

Dislodge dirt and dust from small rugs by hanging them on a clothesline and beating the back with an old-fashioned carpet-beater. Some people use a bamboo cane, but this can promote splits in an old rug. A beater spreads the load sufficiently to avoid this problem. When you have finished, pick up loose fluff with a hand-operated sweeper.

This process is difficult with large rugs, so use a vacuum cleaner on both sides instead. It is best not to vacuum fringes as they can get caught in the mechanism of some cleaners. Heavy, powerful upright cleaners can damage fragile rugs—only use models which have a hose with nozzle attachments. Always brush away dust from the site of the rug before you put it back.

Washing rugs

Rugs can be washed by hand at home, unless they are valuable, fragile, or made from silk. Such rugs should be treated by a professional cleaner. Avoid companies that advertise as general carpet cleaners. Although their methods are perfectly suitable for modern, machine-made carpets, they may damage old rugs. And do not use machines which generate steam or shampoo, or put old rugs in a washing machine, as prolonged soaking, particularly in hot water, can ruin the foundation of a rug.

Before you wash a rug, beat out as much dust as possible and try to remove any obvious stains. It is not worth repairing a rug before you clean it, as you will want to match threads to clean pile, but you should tack any damaged areas temporarily.

Lay small rugs pile uppermost on a table. Large ones can be laid outside as long as it is a warm day and the ground is dry. Before applying any liquid cleaner always carry out a test with it to make sure that the colors are "fast" and will not run. Dampen a white cloth with the solution and rub it lightly over a small area of the carpet. Look at the cloth to see if any

color has come off. Try all the colors, as some may be fast while others are not. If any colors appear to be running, seek the advice of an expert. Otherwise, you can proceed to clean the carpet.

Use a good-quality carpet shampoo that dries leaving an absorbent powder behind which you then vacuum or brush off the rug. Follow the manufacturer's instructions for mixing the solution, but never use very hot water. You can add a little white vinegar if you wish—this will bring out the colors. Use a white fiber brush to apply the shampoo, cleaning small areas of the rug at a time. Brush gently against, and then with, the pile. Once you have covered the entire rug, overlapping one area with the next, brush the whole area in the direction of the pile. There is no need to scrub the fringes—just rub them with a cloth dipped in the solution.

Leave the rug to dry flat in a warm atmosphere. Do not hang up a wet rug as the foundation could stretch and distort, and do not put furniture on it until it is dry. When the pile feels light and soft, vacuum or brush out the shampoo powder.

Dealing with stains

Fresh spills should be mopped up immediately so that they do not leave stains. If you know that the colors are likely to run, minimize the damage by blotting the affected area, then send it to a professional for cleaning. Otherwise, mop up the spill, then place a dry cloth pad under it and sponge the area lightly with water, making sure you do not spread the stain. When you are sure that the rug is clean, dry both sides with a hairdryer on a low setting.

Removing old stains

To remove an established stain is more difficult because you cannot always be sure what caused it. Bear in mind that a clean patch might show just as much as the original stain. Try the solutions recommended below, starting with the weakest, but always test an inconspicuous area first.

First, try washing the area with a pint of warm water mixed with two tablespoons of white vinegar. Secondly, make up a similar solution, substituting salt for vinegar. If this does not work, try one tablespoon of detergent in a pint of warm water. Finally, if the rug is still stained, use a 4 : 1 solution of warm water and carpet shampoo.

Whatever solution you use, apply it with a soft, white cloth, working toward the center of the stain, and always rinse with clean water. To dry the rug, blot it with clean cloths, then use a hairdryer on both sides.

Removing
wax or grease
First, try to pick off as much as you can with a blunt table knife. Then put several sheets of white blotting paper above and below the stain and apply a warm domestic iron to the paper.

Repairing rugs

If rugs are used on the floor they will have to put up with a great deal of punishment. Wear can be reduced with regular cleaning, but it is inevitable that you will occasionally have to repair damaged or worn areas.

Mending fringes

The fringed ends of rugs are made from the warp threads once they have been cut from the loom. Apart from their decorative qualities, their true function is to protect the pile of the rug. In normal use, fringes become rolled and folded under foot, until eventually some break off. You should replace broken fringes before further damage occurs. Begin by choosing thread which matches the existing fringe, then lay the rug face down.

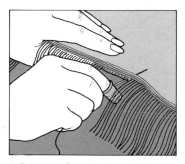

1 Insert a threaded needle into the rug, directly in line with the first broken warp thread. Allow the needle to emerge about $\frac{1}{2}$ in (12 mm) back from the edge, leaving a tail of thread which is longer than the intended fringe.

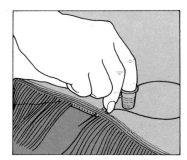

2 Pass the needle back through the same knot so that it is parallel with the first thread, emerging in line with the next warp thread.

3 Repeat this all along the damaged section, leaving long loops of thread extending from the rug. Make sure that none of these stitches is obvious on the piled face.

Tie off the last thread on the other side, then place the rug at the edge of a table so that the new fringe hangs vertically.

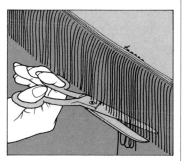

4 Use scissors to trim the loops off in line with the rest of the fringe. If the fringe is knotted, cut the loops overlength, then knot the threads to match the others before trimming the fringe to its final length.

Repairing Kelim ends

Some rugs begin and end with a short length of flat woven thread (known as Kelim work). Once the weft threads on this begin to disintegrate, you should take action as soon as possible or the knotted pile itself will be exposed to wear. Begin by removing the necessary weft threads to reach the first intact thread.

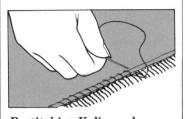

Restitching Kelim ends
Secure the edge with blanket stitching. Make each stitch no wider than four or five warp threads. Do not pull stitches too tight or the weave will distort, and check that the stitching cannot be seen on the face.

Replacing Kelim ends

If the Kelim work has disintegrated altogether, remove loose knots with a needle until you expose a secure weft thread holding a continuous row of knots. Blanket stitch the edge as before, keeping each stitch two or three knots wide.

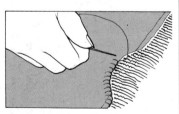

Securing the edge temporarily If the damage is very severe, and involves removing too many rows of knots, secure it by following the line of the worn area with blanket stitch. This will not look as satisfactory as a straight edge, but it will preserve the rug and prevent further deterioration until you can get an expert to reweave the missing section.

Repairing side cords

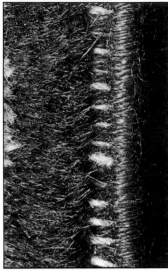

Side cords are the finished side edges on most hand-made old rugs. They are formed by binding several warp threads together with the weft threads as each row of knots is completed. This cord is often built up by an additional binding. Because the side cords are thicker than the body of the carpet, they take proportionately more wear. The binding wears first, and if this is not renewed promptly, the core itself will begin to break up.

Mending the binding
If the worn cords on a rug are detected soon enough, repairing them is a simple procedure. You simply replace the missing section with new, matching thread.

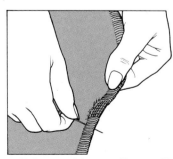

1 Take matching woollen or silk thread, knot the end, and insert the needle into the side cord on the underside of the rug a short distance away from the damaged section.

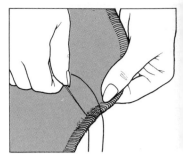

2 Using circular stitches, oversew the warp threads. The new binding should be no tighter than that of the original cord. Secure the end of the thread by passing the needle along the cord to emerge about $\frac{1}{2}$ in (12 mm) from the new binding. Then cut off the end of the thread with scissors.

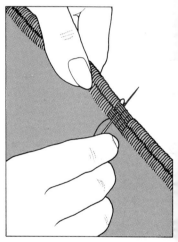

3 As an alternative to the usual style of side cord (see steps 1 and 2), some styles of rug have a double side cord. This type is formed by making figure-eight stitches. These divide the warp threads into two groups.

Mending the core
If unravelled binding is neglected, the core of warp threads will eventually break, and will have to be replaced in order to rebuild the side cord. Once you have replaced the core, the new section should be rebound as before.

Begin the repair by trimming off the broken warp threads close to the remaining binding.

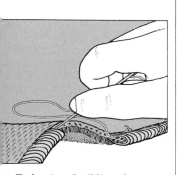

1 To begin rebuilding the core, thread a needle with carefully matched wool and insert it into a side cord a short distance from the missing section of warp thread. Bring out the point of the needle in line with the end of one of the remaining warp threads.

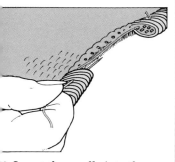

2 Insert the needle into the other intact end of the cord, picking up the opposing end of the warp thread. Bring the needle and thread out through the side of the cord, about $\frac{1}{2}$ in (12 mm) along the intact area of binding.

3 Bring the needle back to the same spot so that it emerges through the end of another warp thread, and continue joining the threads to their opposite numbers as before, until all the core threads are replaced.

4 Renew the weft threads in a similar way to the method described for attaching new fringes, closely looping the ends around the new warp core. Finally, attach new binding.

Re-piling a bald patch

Nothing spoils the appearance of a rug more than worn, bare patches on the pile. These may be the result of heavy local wear, moth infestation, or accidental burning. In the latter case, you may be able merely to trim the singed ends of the pile with scissors, but if the greater part of the knot has been destroyed, you will have to sew new knots into the foundation in order to repair the fault.

If your antique rug has large areas of bare foundation it will probably need to be re-piled by an expert. And rugs with very complicated patterns are also best left to a professional.

Once the rug has been cleaned, match the color of the knotting carefully before you begin the repair. Even a slight difference in tone may show up badly when the work is complete.

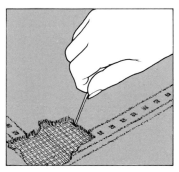

1 Using a needle, push out any remnants of damaged knots from the foundation. You should never attempt to even up the bald patch, as a ragged edge to the repaired area will be less noticeable.

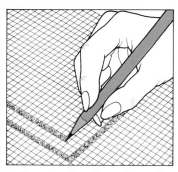

2 Examine the pile to determine the type of knot used (see p. 202). Turn the rug over and choose a similarly patterned area to count the number of knots. If the rug is very finely knotted, you may need a magnifying glass. Mark out the knots on squared paper, or touch them in with color-fast marker pens on the bare foundation itself.

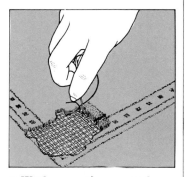

3 Work across the rug, replacing one row of knots at a time. Cut each knot slightly over-length each time so that the tufts are about $\frac{1}{2}$ in (12 mm) longer than the existing pile. Brush each finished row in the direction of the pile, and begin a new one.

4 When the area has been filled in, iron the back of the rug with a warm iron. Fluff up the new work with your fingers, and then trim the tufts to match the rest of the pile.

Mending a hole

If worn pile is left unattended, the woven foundation eventually will wear through, leaving a hole. If you notice the hole while it is still small, you will be able to tackle the work yourself. Otherwise, you will have to take the rug to a professional.

Examine the foundation threads so that you can match them (the warp and weft threads may be made of different materials). Pick loose knots from the sides of the hole with a needle, then trim the frayed edges square. Next, lay the rug face down on a flat surface, and begin to darn the hole, starting with the warp threads.

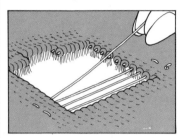

1 Insert the threaded needle about $\frac{1}{2}$ in (12 mm) from the edge of the hole, in line with the first broken warp thread. Join it to its opposite partner in the opposite side of the hole, pushing the needle into one half of the exposed knot, and bringing it out $\frac{1}{2}$ in (12 mm) from the edge. Bring the needle back through the other half of the knot, and pass it across the hole again.

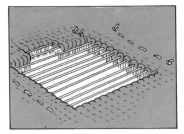

2 Continue stitching into the knots on both sides of the hole until you have replaced all the broken warp threads.

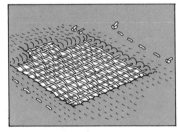

3 Replace the weft threads in the same way, but this time weave them through the new warp threads. Re-pile new foundation as described on p. 207.

Repairing a tear

A split in a rug normally occurs along either the warp or the weft threads. A tear that passes diagonally across both warp and weft threads is much more difficult to repair, because you have to make a horizontal and a vertical row of stitches.

1 With the rug face down, carefully position a cardboard tube underneath the split to raise it from the floor. Join the torn edges with a thread that matches the foundation, linking each broken thread as in darning.
Caution: Take great care when warp threads are broken—the knots on either side of the split can become detached, and you will have to replace them.

2 Start sewing just below the split, and continue sewing past the damaged section so that you secure the thread in the sound part at each end.

3 Finally, press the back of the repaired split with a warm domestic iron.

Repairing Kelim and Soumak rugs

Holes in a Kelim or Soumak are mended by first replacing warp threads, and then weaving in weft threads. Before you start, examine the pattern and choose suitable threads.

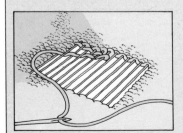

Mending a Kelim Run the thread about $\frac{1}{2}$ in (12 mm) into the sound part of the rug at the edge of the hole, then return it around the appropriate warp thread.

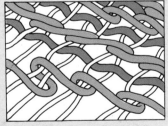

Mending a Soumak These rugs have additional weft threads wound around pairs of warp threads (see p. 203). After weaving the foundation, insert the extra threads.

BASIC
TECHNIQUES

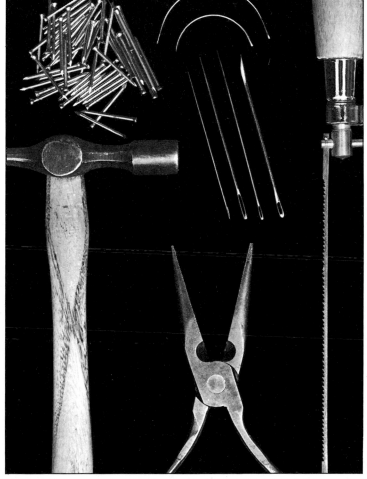

WOODWORKING TECHNIQUES

This section is intended to supplement the information on restoring woodwork. Although the majority of the techniques described here are aimed at assisting the renovation of antique furniture, they are as relevant to the repair of any woodwork.

Measuring and marking wood

Marking out replacement wood normally involves drawing round or tracing the shape from the old part. When glued in place the roughly sized new wood is reduced with a plane or chisel to the final dimensions. Making a completely new piece may simply mean drawing round an identical part. If not, you will have to measure and mark it out.

Squaring the work

When marking out a square or rectangular section of wood, first select the best side or "face". Check it with a straight edge to ensure that it is flat in all directions. If it is not, plane it flat.

Next, check the adjacent edge with a try square. Hold the stock of the square firmly against the face and look along the edge of the work with the blade resting on it. Then plane the edge true as required.

Now make a special face mark on the face side, extending it out to the prepared edge. Mark this edge, known as the "face edge", with its own symbol, to join up with the face mark. Always measure or gauge the work from one of these edges.

The face side mark

The face edge mark

Marking the length

To establish the length of the work use a rule. Mark the cutting lines across the grain of the wood with a marking knife and try square. Then indicate the waste with hatched pencil lines. Do not cut off the waste wood immediately unless necessary, as it protects the ends of the new part.

Marking simple curves

To mark small-radius curves use a standard compass. But for curves of a larger radius use a beam compass. You can make one from a length of wood with a pencil attached at one end and a pivot pin at the required distance at the other end. And for a very large curve that does not necessarily need a true radius, or for wavy curves, use a flexible strip of wood or metal as a guide. Make reference marks on your piece of work and bend the guide by hand to touch them. You will need an assistant to draw the line.

When more than one piece of wood is to be marked for cutting to complicated shapes, mark out a full-sized pattern on cardboard or paper with drawing instruments. Trace the paper pattern onto the wood using carbon-copy paper, but with the cardboard cut out the pattern and use it to draw round.

Using a beam compass

Marking compound curves

Compound-curved or double-curved shapes are those which are curved in more than one plane. Examples are a cabriole leg or the cresting rail of a balloon-back chair.

The extremes of the curve must fit into the wood to be used. Mark the shape on two adjacent faces of the block. For the cabriole leg, mark on the two outer faces. Make a cardboard template for the leg and mark round it on one face. Reverse the template and mark the adjacent face. With the rail, the shape on the front is likely to be different from the top, so mark the two sides separately.

Now cut the shape using a coping saw, then tape or panel pin the offcuts back in place as they carry the cutting lines for working the other face. If using pins, do not foul the lines.

Marking the block

Cutting out

Marking shapes for turning

If you are matching a turned piece to an existing part, use a needle gauge to copy the shape. With all the needles level, hold

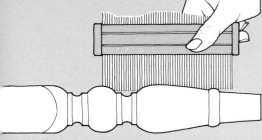

Using a needle gauge

the gauge parallel to the axis of the turned part and press it against the shape. Then transfer the shape from the gauge to cardboard to make a template. For longer turned shapes move the relatively short gauge along the shaped wood.

You may also draw out the shape full-size on cardboard, taking measurements from the existing part. Draw a straight line to represent the center line of the turning. Measure from one end all the key points of the turning, and the start and end of tapered sections. Draw lines at right angles to the center line at these key points.

Using outside calipers, measure the widths of the whole turning at these points and transfer these dimensions halved to the drawing. These measurements represent the distances from the center line to the outside edge of the template. Join up the marks. Cut out the marked template,

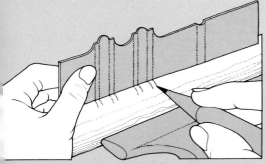

Marking the key points

which is the negative of half the whole shape to be turned. Use it to mark the key points onto the rough-turned new part, and to check the shape.

Sawing wood

Sawing accurately is a skill which has to be learned. It should not require much physical effort provided the right saw is used and is sharp. It is important that you grip the handle securely and extend your forefinger along the side. For straight-cutting a large piece of wood, one of the hand saws should be used (see p. 98). Use a back-saw for smaller bench work. Shape cutting should be done with a narrow-bladed (pad or coping) saw (see p. 98).

Supporting the work

Large jobs that require the use of a handsaw should be set up on a pair of workhorses or a Workmate bench. Rest your knee on the work to hold it steady, and get your shoulder in line with the cut. When ripsawing a long cut, you should

Making a long cut

allow the end of the work to overhang one sawhorse. Start to cut, sawing down the line about 16 ins (40 cm). Move the wood back and continue sawing between the sawhorses. Sometimes the grain causes the cut to close on the saw. In such a case, push a shallow wedge into the cut to keep it open.

When cross-cutting on a sawhorse, you can set the work up with the waste wood on your right or left. If you are right-handed and the waste is on your right you can use your knee to steady the work, while you use your left hand to reach over the saw to support the offcut.

When a larger piece is being cut off, it is better to have the waste on your left so that you can hold it with your left hand. Clamp the work to the sawhorse on your right side.

Using a bench vise

To "rip" (or cut with the grain) short lengths of wood hold them in a vise at a slight angle. Use the saw with the teeth parallel to the ground. Saw halfway through the wood and reverse the work to complete the cut.

A bench vise is used extensively to cut joints with a backsaw. Set the work up at a comfortable height. As a rule of thumb, the thinner the work the lower it should be in the vise.

You should always make the cuts vertical; this means that if you need to cut an angle you must set the wood at an angle in the vise.

"Ripping" in a vise

Using a bench hook

Use a bench hook to help you to cut small sections of wood that are difficult to hold in a vise, and for sawing the ends of a piece of wood square. Either hook the tool over the edge of the bench, or hold it in the vise while pressing the work against the stop block on the bench.

Keeping the cut square

Using a miter box

The miter box is a useful sawing jig which is used with a backsaw to help you to make accurate right-angle and miter cuts. You should hold the work

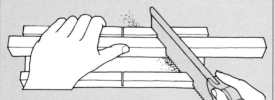

against the back stop on the bench when cutting wood in a miter box.

Cutting miters

Planing wood

When you are planing a surface true, use the longest plane you have that is compatible with the size of the work. A jack plane (see p. 100) is a good general-purpose tool for larger work, but use a block plane (see p. 100) to prepare small pieces of wood for repair work. Always position the work in a vise with the grain following the direction in which the plane will travel.

Planing end grain

It can be difficult to plane end grain as the wood splits easily on the edge farthest away from you.

There are several ways of minimizing this problem. First, always use a finely set, sharp plane. Secondly, plane toward the center from each edge. Planing a bevel down to the line on the back edge will also help, but take great care as you near the line. Small work should be held in a vise with a scrap of wood backing up the rear edge. The scrap will split, but not the work.

Planing a bevel

Shaping a simple molded edge

If you are lucky and the molding that needs repairing matches the standard cutters available with a combination plane or power router then the shaping of the edge is straightforward. If not, you will need to shape it by other means. If you cannot get hold of old wooden molding planes, you can make a shallow bead molding with a scratch stock, a simple homemade tool. Two L-shaped pieces of thick plywood are screwed together to sandwich the shaped cutter. This is made from a short length of hacksaw blade filed to the required shape. The tool is drawn along the work with its stock held firmly against the edge.

Concave moldings can be made in a similar way. Bevel the edge with a plane as much as possible and then use a scratch stock with a cutter made to the required concave shape. Finish with a sanding block shaped to fit the molding.

A scratch stock

A concave molding

Shaping curved corners

Hand-working a molding on a round corner is rather more difficult than shaping a molded edge. First, mark the radius on the corner touching both prepared edges. Saw off the waste with a coping saw (see pp. 98–9). Then plane the cut edge down to the line and form a smooth curve with a spokeshave (see p. 100). Use the spokeshave again to make beveled cuts around the corner. You will need to monitor the shape by eye as it progresses. You can use a cardboard template to check how accurate it is. Finish off the shaping with the scratch stock and abrasive paper.

Sawing off the waste

Beveling the edge

Cutting grooves and rabbets

A groove and rabbet can be cut along the grain with a plough, combination, or multi-plane (see p. 100). Set the depth gauge and side fence and then start the cut at the far end of the wood, working back along the full length.

Use the combination or multi-plane to cut across the grain. These planes are fitted with spur cutters set ahead of the blade which sever the fibers to make a clean cut.

Fine shallow grooves of the sort that might be needed for a stringing inlay could be made with a scratch stock. To work it across the grain sever the fibers first by making parallel cuts with a cutting gauge.

A groove

A rabbet

Joints

Woodworking joints are notoriously diverse, and should you be in any doubt as to what a joint is, how it is constructed, or how to repair it, then seek advice from a professional carpenter or cabinetmaker.

Mortise-and-tenon joints

The mortise-and-tenon joint is widely used for chairs and tables. A tongue, known as the tenon, is made in the rail and fits into a slot, known as the mortise, in the leg. The tenon may pass right through the leg (a through tenon), or stop short (a stopped tenon).

The tenon's size depends on the proportions of the wood and the position of the joint. Generally, the tenon is one-third the thickness of the rail. The width of the tenon can be the same as the rail, but when the rail is flush with the top of the leg the tenon is reduced in width. In order to prevent the rail twisting, a haunch is sometimes used to give a full-width tenon at the shoulder (a haunched tenon).

A mortise-and-tenon

A haunch

Cutting a stopped mortise-and-tenon

First, cut the rail to length. Mark the length of the tenon and scribe a line all round. The length is usually about two-thirds the width of the leg.

Set the points of a mortise gauge (see p. 98) to match the chisel to be used and adjust the tool to center the marks on the rail. Check from both faces that the mortise is in fact in the middle. Scribe the lines from the shoulder and over the end grain.

Set the rail in a vise at an angle and facing away from you. Saw down to the shoulder line on the waste side of the gauged lines. Turn the wood round and saw down the other side. Set the rail upright in the vise and complete the cuts level with the shoulder line. Support the rail on a bench hook (see p. 100) and saw off the waste along the shoulder line.

Mark the width of the mortise from the tenon. Scribe the thickness of the tenon with the same mortise gauge. Clamp the leg

Matching the chisel

Sawing to the shoulder

Removing the waste

firmly to the bench. Wrap tape around the chisel blade to indicate the depth of the mortise. Chop out the waste, working from the center outward. Hold the chisel upright, with the cutting bevel facing the center. Remove the wood with shallow cuts, stopping about $\frac{1}{8}$ in (3 mm) from each end. Trim away the end when the full depth is reached.

Cutting out the waste

Cutting a haunched mortise-and-tenon

Mark and cut the tenon in the same way as the stopped mortise-and-tenon. In addition, cut away no more than three-quarters of the length and no more than one-third of the width, to leave the haunch.

Mark and cut the mortise as above, but add a line for the haunch. Leave the leg over-length as the joint is made close to the end. The waste is removed when the joint is glued. Chop down to the depth of the haunch across the full width of the mortise. Then chop out the mortise.

Cutting the haunch

Cutting a through mortise-and-tenon

Mark out and cut the tenon as for the stopped tenon, but a little overlength. Mark the mortise on both faces of the leg and chop out the waste as described, taking half from one face and half from the other. Plane the exposed end of the tenon flush after gluing the joint.

Allowing for the haunch

Dowel joints

These are made with hardwood pegs that are glued into both the pieces of wood being joined together. They may be used to join wood along the edge grain or end grain to edge grain. Dowel joints are widely used in modern furniture.

A through mortise-and-tenon

Dowels are found on old chairs in which the curve of the seat rails produces short, unsuitable grain. They are also used for tenoning and for jointing the boards of table tops.

Preparing dowels

Ready-made dowels are available in a limited range of sizes. To prepare your own, buy a

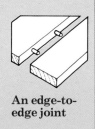

An edge-to-edge joint

An end-to-edge joint

length of ramin doweling of the right diameter. Cut the dowels to length and taper the ends slightly. With small diameters, you can use a pencil sharpener for this. Make a saw cut along the length of the dowels to allow air and glue to be expelled when the joint is clamped up.

A prepared dowel

Making edge-to-edge joints

Place the two boards in a vise with the jointing edges level. Mark lines across both with a pencil and square. Set a cutting gauge (see pp. 98–9) to half the

thickness of a board and mark across the pencil lines. Drill the holes on the center marks.

Drilling dowel holes

The diameter of the dowels should not exceed half the thickness of the boards to be joined. And the depth of the drilled holes should be slightly more than half the length of the dowel.

Making end-to-edge joints

Mark the positions for the dowels on a center line across the end grain, spacing them evenly. Drive panel pins part of the way into the marks and cut off the heads. Support the components to be joined on a flat table in

Inserting panel pins

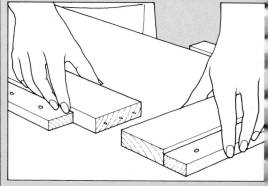

their relative positions and push them together. Remove the pins and drill the dowel holes.

Push the parts together

Halving joints

These are used for framing where strength is not critical. Half the wood is removed from each component to give a flush joint. The joint may be across the width of the wood for framework or edge-on for dividers. Both joints form a cross, so are known as cross-halvings.

Cutting a cross-halving

Use each component as a guide to marking its width on the other. Square the shoulder lines with a try square (see pp. 98–9) and knife. Set a marking gauge (see pp. 98–9) to half the thickness of the wood. Scribe a line on each edge, then extend the shoulder lines over the edges to meet the gauge lines.

Saw along the shoulder lines with a tenon saw. Keep to the waste side of the line. Make two or three additional saw cuts between the shoulder cuts to make it easier to remove the waste. Chisel out the waste, working from each edge toward the center. Carefully level cuts out.

Cutting a halved-angle

The halved-angle joint is marked on the end of the components. Scribe a single shoulder line on the face side and halfway down each edge. Mark a gauge line along each edge and across the end grain, showing the waste to be cut away. Use a tenon saw to remove it.

Bridle joints

The bridle joint is simpler to cut than a mortise-and-tenon. Sometimes it is used to join an intermediate leg to a rail.

Mark the width of the leg on the rail and scribe the shoulder lines all round. Set a marking gauge (see pp. 98–9) to not more than a quarter of the rail thickness. Mark parallel lines on each edge between the shoulder lines. Remove the waste as described for cross-halving.

Set a mortise gauge (see p. 98) to the reduced thickness of the rail. Adjust the stock to position the gauge lines as required on the leg. Mark the shoulder line of the leg to correspond with the width of the rail. Run the gauge line from the shoulder lines and

A cross-halving

A marked joint

A sawn joint

Removing the waste

A bridle joint

Cutting the rail waste

across the end of the leg.

Next, bore a hole across the bottom of the waste wood, drilling in toward the center from both sides. Using a tenon saw cut down the gauge lines. The final step is to carefully clean out the bottom corners using a chisel.

A marked and bored leg

Scarf joints

A scarf joint is used to join components end to end. The long taper provides a large glued area to strengthen the joint. Scarf joints are recommended for grafting new wood to a damaged component.

Cut a matching taper by clamping the components together. Make sure they are flush all round, with the face edges reversed, so that one faces up and one down. Plane the angle to not less than one in four.

Unclamp the components and glue the tapered faces together.

A scarf joint

Cutting the ends together

and then clamp them again between long softwood battens to prevent them slipping.

Clamping the glued joint

Mitered joints

Used to join components at an angle without showing the end grain, mitered joints often join molded sections.

Mark the length of the components on the outside face and top edge of the wood. Then cut them in a miter box (see p. 100). You hold the work against the back stop, aligning the mark with a saw slot, and place a piece of scrap wood under the pieces you are cutting. Once

A mitered joint

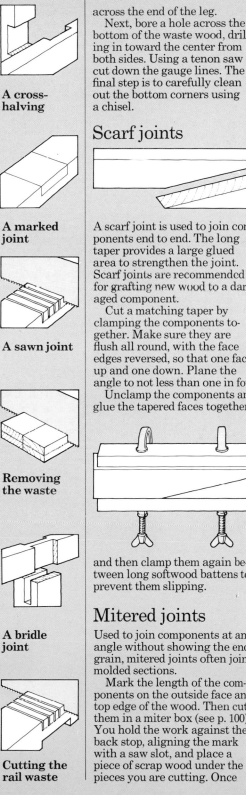

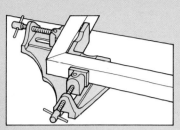

you have sawn the pieces, apply glue and use miter or tourniquet clamps to hold the joint until the glue has set.

Housing joints

Grooves across the grain of a panel that receive shelves or partitions are known as housings. A through housing shows the groove on the front edge, while a stopped housing hides it. Common housings have plain grooves to receive and support the shelf. Dovetailed housings lock the shelf, which has to be assembled from the back edge, into the side.

Cutting a through housing

Mark the width of the housing, using the shelf as a guide. Scribe the cutting lines using a knife and try square as a guide. You should also scribe a depth line on each edge with a marking gauge (see p. 99), set to about $\frac{1}{8}$ in (3mm). Then scribe the cutting lines on the edges so

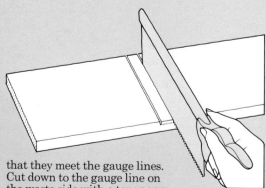

that they meet the gauge lines. Cut down to the gauge line on the waste side with a tenon saw. A straight batten cramped along the gauge line will help you to guide the saw. Pare out the waste with a chisel, working from the edge to the center. A hand router can be used to level the groove bottom.

Through, stopped, and dovetail housings

Cutting a stopped housing

Mark the groove as before, but stop the lines about $\frac{1}{2}$ in (12 mm) from the front edge. Mark the depth with the gauge on the back edge only. Drill out and clean up with a chisel approximately 2 ins (5 cm) of the groove at the stopped end. This should give enough clearance for the saw. Saw and pare away the remaining waste as before. Cut away the front corner of the shelf so that it fits round the stopped end.

Cutting a dovetail

Use the techniques described above, but mark and cut one or both sides of the groove at an angle. Score a shoulder line across the face or faces of the shelf to the depth of the groove. Mark the dovetail angle on each edge. Saw along the shoulder line and trim away the waste with a chisel to form the dovetail section.

Dovetail joints

The traditional joint for drawer making is the dovetail. It is a strong joint designed to hold boards at right angles. The interlocking shapes of the joint allow the wood used to be relatively thin without sacrificing strength. Two types of joint are usually found on drawers, the through dovetail on the back and the lapped dovetail on the front.

Cutting a through dovetail

Cut the components to length. Set a cutting gauge (see p. 99) to the thickness of the back piece. Scribe a shoulder line all round the rear ends of the drawer sides. Similarly, scribe the thickness of the sides at each end of the back.

First mark the tails, which are always on the drawer side. Square a line across the end grain $\frac{1}{4}$ in (6mm) from each end. Divide the space between them to give regular, equally spaced tails. Square the lines across the end. On average, the tails are about $\frac{3}{4}$–1 in (18–25 mm) wide.

Set an adjustable bevel or use a dovetail template and mark

Cutting out the clearance

Trimming the dovetail

A through dovetail

A lapped dovetail

Marking out the tails

Marking angles of tails

the angle of the tails. The slope is 1 in 8 for hardwoods, 1 in 6 for softwoods. Mark the waste with hatching to avoid confusion when cutting out. Set the work in a vise at an angle to present a vertical saw cut. Cut down to the shoulder line with a dovetail saw. Remove the waste between the tails with a coping saw and trim the shoulders with a beveled chisel.

Set the back piece vertically in the vise. Apply chalk to the end grain. Rest the side piece on the chalked end and hold level on a block at the other end. Scribe round the cut tails. Square the cut lines from the end down to the shoulder line. Then mark the waste again with hatching lines.

Saw down to the shoulder line. Remove most of the waste with a coping saw and finish the shoulders with a chisel. Check the fit and glue up, tapping the joint together. Use a block of wood to spread the impact of the hammer across the full width of the joint.

Cutting a lapped dovetail

Set the cutting gauge (see p. 99) to a thickness of $\frac{1}{4}$–$\frac{3}{8}$ in (6–9 mm) less than that of the drawer front. Mark a line down each end, working from the back face. With the same setting, mark a shoulder line all round the front end of the drawer side. Set the gauge to the thickness of the sides and scribe a shoulder line across the back face of the drawer front at each end. Mark and cut the tails in the sides using the method described for the through dovetail.

Mark the tail shapes on the ends of the drawer front with the ends level with the scribed lines. Square the lines down to the shoulder line.

Make saw cuts to meet the shoulder line and the line scribed on the end of the drawer front. Chop out the waste with a beveled chisel, working across and with the grain. Glue and assemble the joint as for the through dovetail joint.

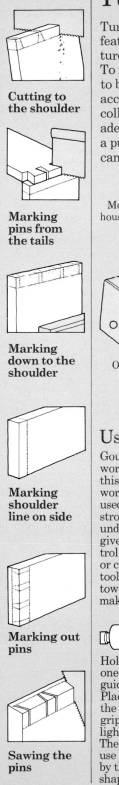

Cutting to the shoulder

Marking pins from the tails

Marking down to the shoulder

Marking shoulder line on side

Marking out pins

Sawing the pins

Turning

Turned wooden components are a common feature in furniture. In some kinds of furniture turning is the basis of the whole example. To restore such a piece you will either have to buy or hire a woodworking lathe or have access to one, for example at a school or college. A power-drill lathe attachment is adequate for medium-sized turning work, but a purpose-made machine is preferable if you can afford it.

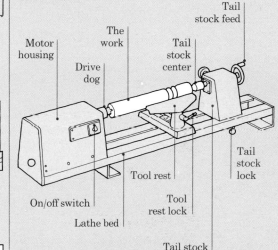

Using lathe tools

Gouges and chisels for lathe work are made specifically for this purpose and normal woodworking chisels should not be used instead. Lathe tools have strong blades ground on the underside and long handles to give the leverage needed to control the tool. In use, the gouge or chisel is supported by the tool rest and is moved carefully toward the revolving work to make the cut.

Hold the end of the handle with one hand and use the other to guide the tool along the work. Place your guiding hand over the blade for rough work but grip it from underneath for lighter work and for shaping. The size of the tool you should use with a lathe is determined by the size and the required shape of the work.

Holding the tool

Safety measures

- Work in good light and avoid casting shadows
- Avoid loose clothing
- Roll up sleeves
- Do not wear a neck tie
- Pin or tie back long hair
- Wear goggles and a mask —some wood dust is particularly unpleasant when inhaled
- Do not force the tool
- Switch off the machine when making adjustments and taking measurements
- Use a low speed for rough sizing, a higher speed for shaping and finishing
- Always use sharp tools to give a clean cut
- Reset the tool rest as the work is reduced in size, making sure that you tighten the adjusting nut securely
- Sweep the floor from time to time, as shavings can be slippery

Preparing the wood

The wooden blank from which the part is to be turned must be large enough to contain the widest part of the turning and should be about 2 ins (5 cm) overlength.

Prepare the wood so that it is square in section, then mark the diagonals on each end. Where the lines intersect mark the centers with a center punch. With a compass, draw a circle that touches all four sides at each end. Plane the corners to give an octagonal section. Tap the lathe drive dog into the center of one end of the wood with a mallet.

Set the work in the lathe with the drive dog secure in one end and the tail stock center set well into the other. Lock the tail stock onto the lathe bed. Revolve the work by hand to check that it revolves freely and is not slack between the centers. Set the tool rest so that it is level with the work and not more than $\frac{1}{8}$ in (3 mm) from the center of the wood.

Preparing the wood for turning

Turning a cylinder

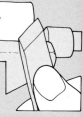

Hold a straight gouge at right angles to the work and almost on its edge. Starting from one end, push the tool along the rest to make a shallow cut. Repeat this to produce the cylinder, moving the tool rest inward and along, as the work requires. Work from both ends, turning the gouge as you do so. Constantly check the diameter with calipers. Move the tool rest along the lathe bed for longer work. As the work diminishes, reset the tool rest to maintain the $\frac{1}{8}$ in (3 mm) gap.

Using a straight gouge

Smoothing the surface
Use a skew chisel (see p. 101) for a smooth finish. Set the tool rest

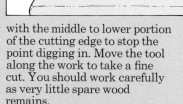

high to bring the chisel near the top of the work. Run the lathe fast. Rest the bevel of the tool on the work, with the handle below the horizontal. Raise the handle to bring the cutting edge in contact with the work. Cut

Rest tool on work

with the middle to lower portion of the cutting edge to stop the point digging in. Move the tool along the work to take a fine cut. You should work carefully as very little spare wood remains.

Lift handle to make cut

Turning shapes

Swellings, the flowing bulbous shapes found on the legs and stretcher rails of stick chairs, are formed with a gouge and finished with a chisel. Mark the swelling's highest point, and work away from it. As the work progresses, judge the shape by eye or use a template.

Forming beads

Mark the two outer limits and the center of the bead on the work. Using the skew chisel cut straight into the wood on the outer marks to the depth of the bead. For a deep cut it may be necessary to partly shape the bead and then repeat the cut.

Rest the beveled edge of the chisel on the center line. Shape half the bead with the heel of the cutting edge, rolling the chisel onto its edge as it cuts. Reverse the chisel and repeat the movement to shape the other half.

Round over the bead

Cutting coves

Score the outer limits of the cove with a skew chisel. Use a small round-nosed gouge to shape the cove, working toward the center. Hold the gouge at an angle to the work and on its edge, supported by the tool rest.

To make the cut swing the handle square to the center line, at the same time advancing and rolling the gouge onto its back. Work each half of the cove to reach the required depth.

Cutting out the center

Sanding

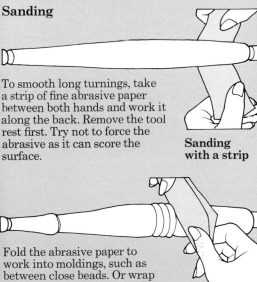

To smooth long turnings, take a strip of fine abrasive paper between both hands and work it along the back. Remove the tool rest first. Try not to force the abrasive as it can score the surface.

Sanding with a strip

Fold the abrasive paper to work into moldings, such as between close beads. Or wrap it around doweling for sanding coves. Work from the top.

Sanding the moldings

Veneering

Veneer so badly damaged that it cannot be patched should be replaced with new veneer. First strip the polish (see p. 108) and lift the old veneer by applying hot damp cloths to soften the glue. A warm iron over the cloth speeds up this process. Another way is to leave the cloths on the veneer for several days. Peel up the veneer and wipe away the surplus glue from the groundwork while it is soft. Allow the wood to dry and sand it with a medium abrasive paper wrapped around a block. Remove any remaining dry glue and key the surface by sanding diagonally across the groundwork. Dust off the surface.

Sizing with animal glue

Groundwork stripped of its veneer is not likely to need sizing. However, very soft or open-pored groundwork and also all new wood should be sized. This prevents the glue soaking in too deeply, leaving little on the surface to bond the veneer. Use animal glue, thinned to a watery consistency. Apply it with a brush and leave it to dry before you attach the veneer.

Making animal glue

This glue is commonly supplied as small beads. To make it up you need a glue pot—a tin can will do—and a larger can for the hot water in which to stand the pot. A gas or electric ring is also required. Professional glue kettles that have inner and outer containers are available. Some have built-in electric heaters. Half fill the glue pot with beads and cover with water, allowing them to stand overnight to soften. Pour water into the outer container and heat it. Stand the pot in the container and heat it, stirring occasionally until the glue has dissolved. It is ready to use when it is lump-free and thin enough to pour from the brush without forming heavy drips. Keep the glue hot all the while the work is in progress, but do not let it boil. Check the water in the outer container periodically, adding some if necessary. For small repairs it may be best to buy a can of ready-mixed animal glue.

Preparing the veneer

Select the new veneer to match the original. Cut the veneer, using a straight edge and a sharp knife, about $\frac{1}{2}$ in (12mm) larger all round than the groundwork. Make several light cuts in the case of thin, brittle veneer.

Decorative veneers are often distorted by shrinkage across the characteristically uneven grain, which makes them difficult to work. Before laying the veneer, press it between two flat sheets of blockboard or plywood, but first brush clean water onto both surfaces. The veneer can be left in the press until dry or, provided it is flat and laid promptly, it can be removed and fitted while damp.

Joining veneers

It is often necessary to join pieces together for a wide panel. This is done by first joining the pieces together with paper tape and then laying them as a single sheet, or by laying them individually and trimming the butting edges *in situ*.

Joining before laying

To make up a single sheet first trim the strips of veneer to the approximate size. Arrange the pieces side by side and face up to give the best grain configuration. Make pencil marks across the jointing edges to identify them. Lay adjacent pieces face to face, with the jointing edges together, and clamp them between two straight battens.

Trim flush the slightly protruding edges of the veneer with a finely set plane. Repeat this process on the other edges if more than two pieces are to be joined.

Trimming edges flush

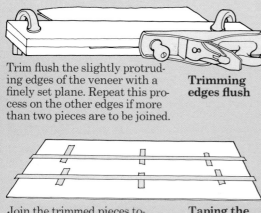

Join the trimmed pieces together with paper tape applied to the face side. Use two or three

Taping the veneers

short pieces of tape across the joint to pull it together, followed by a single strip along the full length. The veneer is now ready to lay.

Joining after laying

To join the pieces *in situ* the strips of veneer are glued to the groundwork with the edges to be joined overlapping. Make a

straight knife cut through both veneers down the center of the overlap. Peel back the cut edges while the glue is soft and remove the waste. Press back the trimmed edges to make a clean butt joint using one of the methods described in "Laying veneer

Jointing in situ

by hand." Apply paper tape to the joints to counter the shrinkage in the veneer.

Taping the joint

Laying veneer by hand

The traditional method of laying veneer by hand is to use the adhesive known as animal glue and a veneer hammer to press the veneer down. The glue is applied hot and sets as it cools. All the equipment required should be close at hand as it is necessary to work fast with this glue. Animal glue is very strong, yet its effect can be reversed by applying a combination of heat and moisture.

Before starting work check that you have: hot glue at the right consistency, a soft clean brush of the right size, a veneer hammer, an electric smoothing iron, a bowl of hot clean water, clean cloths, and some paper tape.

Try to work in a warm environment of not less than 16°C (60°F) and avoid drafts as they will rapidly set the glue. Heat the groundwork where possible with an electric iron or by standing it in front of an electric heater.

Apply an even coat of hot glue to the veneer and the groundwork. Allow it to thicken slightly, then lay the veneer in position and smooth it with the

Ironing the veneer

palm of the hand. Dampen the veneer with hot water and then press it down using the iron set to a low heat. Quickly take up

Using a veneer hammer

the hammer and with a zig-zag action press the veneer down, working from the center to the edges. Air and excess glue are squeezed out and the glue wiped away before it sets. Take care not to overstretch the veneer when working across the grain. Damp the veneer and apply the warm iron so that the glue is kept soft. Check for air bubbles by running your hand over the surface and tapping with your fingernail. A hollow sound denotes a shallow bubble which should be heated and pressed down with the hammer. Trim

Trimming the edge

the veneer with a sharp knife to within ⅛ in (3 mm) of the edge. When set, trim it flush with the edge and sand it smooth. Remove the paper tape by carefully soaking it with a wet cloth. When thoroughly dry, prepare the surface for finishing with a scraper and abrasive paper.

Caul veneering

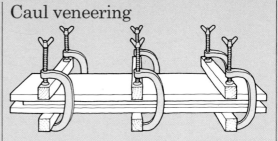

An alternative to hand laying with a veneer hammer is to press the veneer down with cauls. Cauls are made from panels of blockboard or plywood backed up by stiff wooden battens. The battens have a slight convex curve on the bottom edge which, when clamped over the boards, puts pressure on the center of the cauls first.

Animal or polyvinyl acetate glue can be used in caul veneering. The cauls should be well heated if animal glue is used. Polyvinyl is easier to use, being a slow-acting cold-setting glue.

Place waxed paper between the cauls and the work to prevent them sticking together.

Clamping the cauls

Using glue film

Glue film is a thin layer of heat-sensitive glue on peel-off backing paper. To lay a sheet of veneer, peel the glue film from the backing and lay it over the groundwork. Place the veneer on top and cover it with the backing paper. With an iron set for rayon, heat and press the veneer down, working from the center to the edges. Then press a block of wood on top.

Laying with glue film

Bandings

Decorative borders that surround the central veneered panel are known as bandings. Plain bandings have a grain running parallel with the edge of the panel, while cross-bandings have the grain at right angles to the edge.

Set a sharp cutting gauge (see pp. 98–9) to the banding width. Run the gauge around the edge of the newly veneered panel, having already trimmed back the veneer to just inside the edge. Peel off waste veneer if the glue is still soft. If not, dampen and heat the veneer to remove it.

Using a cutting gauge

Cutting the banding

Plane true one edge of the band-ing veneer using special battens (see p. 220). Plane the side grain for plain bandings, the end grain for cross-bandings. Set the cut-ting gauge a little wider than the width of the banding. Align the prepared edge of the ven-eer with the edge of a straight board. Cut through the veneer by drawing the gauge across it several times. The bands should be a little longer than the edges of the panel.

Cutting the banding

Applying the banding

Apply hot animal glue to the groundwork and to both sides of a band. Position it and press it in place with a cross-peen ham-mer. Lay remaining bandings in the same way, letting the waste at the corners overlap.

Laying the banding

Finishing mitered banding

With a straight edge and a sharp knife, miter the corners by cutting through both bands where they overlap. Make sure the straight edge is in line with the corner of the central veneer and the outer edge of the corner of the panel. Remove the waste, and press the mitered joint down with the hammer. Apply paper tape to the joints until set. Trim the edges as before.

Mitering the ends

Finishing edge banding

Edge bandings are used to cover the groundwork edges. They are cut and laid in the same way, but the ends are cut square at the corners as each strip is laid.

Replacing inlay bandings

Inlay bandings are decorative strips of veneer made up from pieces of exotic woods arranged to form patterns of contrasting color.

Inlay bandings may be let into a shallow groove in a solid top or between a central ven-eered panel and cross banding on a veneered top.

If the banding is beyond re-pair, remove and replace it with a new but traditional banding available from veneer suppliers. Use a narrow chisel to clean the recess. Apply glue to the veneer back and groove and press in place with a cross-peen hammer.

Sharpening woodworking tools

Very sharp chisels and planes are essential for good woodworking. Indeed, oddly enough, they are actually safer to use than blunt tools as little effort is required to make a cut. By contrast, forcing a dull-edged tool can lead to a serious accident if it should slip under pres-sure. Edged tools are sharpened in two stages. First, the edge is ground and honed to a fine edge. Then oilstones or hand-held slipstones are used regularly.

Oilstones and slipstones

Oilstones are rectangular blocks of natural or composite manmade stone. A combination stone with a medium grit on one side and a fine one on the other is ideal for the home workshop. Thin oil is used to lubricate it.

A boxed stone

Make a box for your stone by cutting a recess to receive it in a section of solid wood. This pro-tects the stone, while blocks of wood fitted at each end of the stone, flush with its sur-face, allow the tool to be worked along the stone's full length. Keep the stone clean and dust-free. Should the pores become clogged, wash it with kerosene.

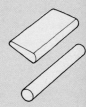

Slipstones

Slipstones are small oilstones for honing shaped cutting edges. They are used by holding the tool steady and working the stone over the cutting edge.

Using an oilstone

Chisels and plane irons come ground to an angle of 25° but need to be honed to a sharp cut-ting edge with an oilstone.

Apply a few drops of oil to the stone. Then hold the chisel or plane iron bevel side down at an angle of 30° and work it back and forth over the whole length of the stone. It takes practice to keep the blade steady and at the required angle, but a hon-ing guide is available that will hold the tool at a set angle. This guide is particularly useful for sharpening spokeshave blades, which can be awkward to hold. Keep a constant check on the beveled edge. This should show as an even line as the light

30°   25°

Grinding and honing angle

The honing guide

catches the honed section. If it appears wider at one end, and you are working without a guide, apply more pressure to the other end.

Remove the burr which builds up on the straight side by reversing the tool and holding it dead flat on the stone. Work it from side to side a few times. Repeat this light honing and reversal of the tool until the burr breaks away. Finally, strop the edge using a leather strap.

Sharpening gouges

Internally- and externally-ground gouges are honed with an oilstone and slipstone. They are ground to an angle of 25° and honed to 30°. An oilstone is used to hone outside-ground gouges.

The gouge is held at an angle of 30° to the face of the stone and worked along its length in a figure-eight movement. At the same time, the cutting edge should be rocked from side to side. The burr which builds up on the inside of the gouge is removed by working with the round edge of an oiled slipstone. You should keep the slipstone flat on the face of the gouge when doing this.

Honing a gouge

To hone an inside-ground gouge use an oiled slipstone held at the correct honing angle. The burr that builds up should be removed on an oilstone with the inside-ground gouge held flat and rocked from side to side as it is drawn across the stone.

Removing the burr on an oilstone

Grinding

A chipped blade or one that has been honed frequently will need to be reground. A power grinder is used with the tool rest set to present the blade at 25° to the wheel. Make light passes across the wheel, holding the blade square to the cutting edge. Constantly dip the tip of the blade into cold water to keep it cool. It is impossible to maintain inside-ground blades without a special grinding wheel. But you can use a slipstone to hone the full width of the beveled edge.

Sharpening a cabinet scraper

A sharp cabinet scraper should produce fine shavings. If only dust can be raised, then the scraper needs sharpening. Rub it on an oilstone or file the long edges of the plate to produce a straight, square edge. Then lay the plate flat on the bench, level with the edge. Stroke the edge with the back of a gouge, keeping it flat on the face of the plate. You will need to make about 25 strokes across the full width, pressing firmly to consolidate the edge. Repeat the procedure on the other edges.

Form the burr that produces the cutting edge by holding the plate end-on to the bench and stropping the long edge with the gouge. Work the gouge with firm strokes at an angle not more than 15° below the horizontal. The number of strokes you should make will depend on the pressure applied. You will feel the burr as a definite edge when you pass your thumb across it. Form a burr in this way on the remaining long edges as you need them.

Raising the burr

Wood screws

Screws made their appearance in furniture around 1700 and were at that time hand-made. Early screws were relatively crude, being painstakingly worked with a file. The thread was often uneven, and there was little taper and no point.

Modern machine-cut screws with tapered and pointed threads were introduced in 1851. Screws can therefore provide a useful reference for dating furniture. A machine-cut screw in an early piece would indicate that much later repair work had been carried out.

Today screws are made in a range of materials and head shapes. For the furniture restorer, however, steel or brass slotted countersunk screws are generally the only type to be found in old furniture. Screws are designated by their length, gauge, material, and head shape.

Screws

 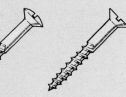

Round head Raised head Counter-sunk

Removing screws

Always use the correct size of screwdriver to remove a screw. The blade must fit the length and width of the slot. An under-sized screwdriver can slip and damage the wood and the screw slot. One that is wider than the screw head will damage the surrounding wood as it turns.

Old steel screws may be very tight due to rust. If a screw will not turn, take an old screwdriver and give it a sharp tap with a hammer. This can often shock the screw free. If this fails, try heating the screw head with an electric soldering iron. This causes the screw to expand and then to contract. Take care not to scorch the wood, however. With all tight screws, apply plenty of downward pressure on the screwdriver while turning. If a screw remains stubborn, clamp a plier wrench to the shaft of the driver to increase the turning force.

Fitting screws

When replacing a missing screw identify the type, material, and size by removing an existing one. Do not substitute steel screws for brass since some woods react with steel so that stains form around the screws.

All screws should have a pilot hole drilled into the wood to guide them and to reduce friction. Very small screws need only a pilot hole made with a bradawl. Larger screws need a pilot hole for the threaded portion and a clearance hole for the shank. Drill the pilot hole as deep as the screw is long and use a drill bit which is about two thirds the diameter of the screw's thread. For the clearance hole use a bit matching the diameter of the shank. Finish with a countersink bit if the screw is to sit flush with the wood. Some screws are set in a deep hole known as a counterbore (see below). In this case, drill the counterbore first, then the pilot and clearance holes.

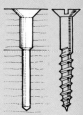

Drilling pilot and clearance holes and countersinking

Plugging a counterbore screw hole

Counterbored screw holes are sometimes used where a component such as a chair arm is screw-fixed. The screw is recessed into the wood and sometimes a plug of matching wood is fitted to cover the hole. The grain of the plug should follow that of the surrounding wood. If the plug is missing, or if it needs to be drilled out in the course of repair, a new one must be made.

Cut a new plug from the same wood, matching color and grain. Either use a plug-cutting bit in a power-drill set up in a vertical drill stand or, should the available plug cutters not match your hole, cut a plug by hand. Prepare a short length of matching wood with the grain running across its width. Make it a little larger in section than the hole. Using a chisel, pare a tapered plug and shape it as much as possible before cutting it out of the waste. Or you can turn the section on a lathe. Work carefully as the short grain will snap easily. Finally, glue in the overlength plug and trim it flush when set.

Paring a plug

Turning a plug on the lathe

METALWORKING TECHNIQUES

This section on basic metalworking techniques is intended to supplement the information given in the chapter on metalware on pp. 54–64. However, you may also find that it is a useful addition to the chapter on jewelry on pp. 76–84.

Measuring and cutting metal

Before making a cut in a piece of metal you must measure and mark out the line or shape that you want to ensure that your work is accurate. Make the cut with snips, a piercing saw or a hacksaw, depending on the type of job (see below).

Measuring metal

Use a metal rule, rather than a wooden one, for measuring sheets of metal. It is thinner and more stable than a wooden rule, so your marks will be more accurate. And it will not wear along the sides when used as a straight edge.

A flexible expanding tape is useful for measuring the circumference of round objects. Use a slide caliper to take very accurate measurements from metal parts. It can be used for internal and external dimensions.

Measuring a round section

For temporary reference marks that are not going to be cut, you can use a lead pencil, but the gray line can be difficult to see on silvery surfaces. A felt-tip pen will show up better. For lines that you are going to cut, it is best to mark the metal with a scriber. Hold it like a pencil, with the point running against the straight edge. Always keep the point sharp.

To scribe a line around cylindrical work use a strip of paper as a guide. Cut the strip with a knife and steel rule so that you produce a true edge. Wrap the strip around the cylinder, ensuring that the trued edge makes a continuous line. Tape the end down and mark out the line.

Improvized surface gauge

To mark a line on an irregular object stand the work on a flat board. Set a scriber or pencil on top of a stack of wood or cardboard off-cuts, stacked to the required height. Steadying the marker with one hand, rotate the work against it. Scribe arcs and circles with dividers. Mark the center with a punch, or cover it with tape if you do not want the metal to be marked.

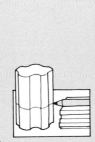

Marking with dividers

Using snips

To cut straight edges or large radii in thin sheet metal use snips. You should wear gloves to protect your hands. Start the cut well back in the jaws of the cutters, and stop short of the cutting edge tip. If you cut right through to the tip you will distort the metal. When cutting external radii, turn the work as you cut.

Using a saw

For light work like cutting inlay from thin brass sheet use a piercing saw. Start by taking a rubbing on paper. Bond the paper to the metal with a rubber adhesive, then, using the piercing saw, fretsaw around the shape. You will have to drill starter holes for the blade to cut enclosed shapes.

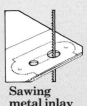

Sawing metal inlay

Cut large sections and heavy gauge metal with a hacksaw. The standard hacksaw has pins projecting from square-sectioned spigots at each end that hold the blade. Normally, the blade is fixed in the same plane as the frame of the saw, but the spigots can be set to turn the blade through 90° for deep cuts. The blades are available in several lengths, with different-size teeth. A fine blade has most teeth, and is useful for cutting thin sections. Use a medium blade for hard metals and a coarse one for large sections or soft metals.

Cutting a tube

Hold the work firmly in an engineer's vise. Protective soft jaws will stop the vise marking the surface. Set the cut line close to the jaws to prevent vibration. Use softwood blocks to hold round-sectioned work.

Filing metal

Files are used to dimension, shape and smooth metal. They can be single-cut or double-cut types. Single-cut files have parallel rows of teeth cut at an angle in one direction across the face. On double-cut files a second set of parallel teeth is cut in the opposite direction to the first set. Double-cut files are used for fast, preliminary cutting, single-cut files for precision work. Like saws, the degree of coarseness is determined by the number of teeth—fine files have more teeth than coarse files. Use the finer or "smooth" files for finishing or light work, the coarse or "rough" files for roughing and for filing soft metals. The medium files are used for general work.

Files also come in a range of shapes. Flat files are good for the general truing of flat surfaces, half-round files for flat work and internal curves, round files for smaller round holes, and the square and triangular files for other shapes and cut-outs.

Working with files

Set the work low in the vise to prevent vibration. If the metal is larger than the vise jaws, sandwich it between sections of wood.

Holding a file

Hold the file with your right thumb along the top of the handle. Grip the other end between the thumb and forefinger of your left hand. Work the file across and along the metal to true it. Keep the file level with the bench and at an angle of approximately 30° to the work, facing in the direction of the cut. Check the metal periodically with a straight edge for bumps and hollows.

Finish the edge by draw-filing to remove the cross-cut marks. To do this, hold the file at both ends and draw it along at right angles to the length of the work. Work with even pressure to avoid hollowing or rounding the edge.

Draw filing

Use a wire brush to keep file teeth clear of metal particles as these can scratch the work and make the file slip. Pick out obstinate particles with a sharp point. If you rub chalk into the file teeth before use this will help to prevent them from clogging with metal filings.

Soldering

Soldering is the technique of making an effective, waterproof, electrically conductive metallic joint between two metals. Solder is an alloy which melts when heated and sets on cooling. The proportion of the metals in the alloy determine its strength, hardness, melting point and flow properties. Soft solders are basically a mixture of tin and lead. Hard solders contain silver and brass and are sometimes called silver solder. Brazing is a form of hard soldering using brass. Soft solders melt at much lower temperatures (183°C–250°C), than hard solders do (610°C–850°C). Extremely high temperatures (850°C–1000°C) are required for brazing.

Flux

The key to a good joint is to clean the parts thoroughly and apply enough heat to make the solder flow. If the clean metal oxidizes when heated this will stop the solder from flowing and bonding to the surface. To prevent this, you should use one of the two different types of flux available.

"Active" flux is an acid which chemically cleans the surface of the metal. It is usually supplied as a liquid and you apply it with a small brush. This type of flux is corrosive, and must be washed off with water once the joint is soldered to prevent corrosion setting into the metal around the joint. However, it is easier to use than the non-corrosive "passive" fluxes, and it is effective in preventing oxidization.

The most common passive flux comes in the form of a resin paste. Passive fluxes are generally used when it is not possible to rinse the joint. Because these fluxes do not actively remove oxides, but merely protect the surface from the air, you must clean the metal thoroughly before applying them. Clean it to a bright finish using a file, emery cloth or steel wool. Once the surface has been cleaned, do not touch it with your fingers.

Soft soldering

Before you solder a piece you must heat it up with a soldering iron or blow torch. The size and type of work will determine which you should use. For light or small work such as wiring or tin-plate use a soldering iron, but for larger or thicker pieces you will need a blow torch.

Soldering irons are either heated on a stove or by an inbuilt electric element. An electric soldering iron is best as its heat is more or less constant. The iron must be able to heat the work above the melting point of the solder. The larger the iron, the more heat it can hold and impart to the work, so size is important. Soldering irons have copper bits or heads which take up heat and give it out quickly. If the bit is too small for the work the heat will be dissipated too quickly and the solder will not flow. If the solder has a crystaline look when it comes into contact with the heated work, then the iron is not hot enough.

Before you use the iron, the bit must be coated in a film of solder—"tinned". Clean the copper to a bright finish, heat it to the melting point of the solder, and dip it into flux, then solder. Clean the tinned tip occasionally in active flux.

Making a soft solder joint
Clean both halves and apply flux. Hold the joint together with clamps or weights. Put the soldering iron on the joint and allow the heat to flow into it. Hold the stick of solder against the tip of the iron and the work. The solder will melt and flow into the joint. With a long joint, draw the iron along it and the solder will follow.

Alternatively, you could tin both halves of the joint before assembly. This method is more suitable for heavier work where a blow torch is required. Clean the metal and apply the flux. Heat each half and apply the solder. It should flow over the surface, but you may have to spread it with a piece of wire. Let the solder set, apply a light coating of flux and assemble the joint. Apply heat to melt and fuse the solder.

Applying solder

Hard soldering

Hard solders are made in a range of strengths, colors and melting points. All have a higher melting point than soft solders, and require a blow torch to work them.

For the higher melting point hard solders and for brazing use borax as a flux. The relatively lower melting point solders have their own specific manufacturers' flux. These are supplied in powder form—you mix them with water to make a paste. You should clean the joint before you paint on the thin layer of flux.

Heating the work
Use a blow torch to heat up the metal. For small repair work where high temperatures are required use a small welding or brazing kit which runs off cylinders of butane gas and oxygen. The metal must be made hot before the solder will flow. To maintain the heat, build a wall of firebricks around the work. After cleaning and fluxing, set the work up, wiring the parts together if necessary. You should heat up larger pieces first with a broad flame, otherwise they may distort.

Setting up the work

Making a hard solder joint
Adjust the torch to give a "hard" flame about 4 ins (10 cm) long. The flame should have three colored elements—a small, whitish cone in the center, surrounded by a longer cone of blue flame, then an outer flame which is a more transparent blue. Use the tip of the darker blue flame to heat the work.

Heat the joint until it is red hot. Dip the solder rod in the flux and touch it on to the joint. Draw the rod along the joint, preceded by the flame. Some brazing rods are self-fluxing—a coating of flux melts before the rod, fluxing the joint when heat is applied.

For small joints place a piece of solder against the joint and then heat it. The solder will flow into the joint when the right temperature is reached.

When cool, clean the joint. Chip away hardened flux and finish with a file and abrasive.

SEWING SKILLS

This section on sewing techniques and stitches is intended to supplement the information given in the chapter on antique textiles on pp. 190–200.

You will also find that it contains useful supplementary information for the chapter on upholstery on pp. 134–44, and the chapter on leatherwork on pp. 174–8.

Basic sewing

Repairing antique textiles, upholstery and leatherwork, like any form of needlework, requires patience, care and practice, as well as a grasp of the basic stitches involved. If necessary, you should practise on fabric remnants of a similar weight and composition to the piece that you want to mend before you tackle a valuable antique.

General sewing tips

Make sure that you choose the right needle. For example, beadwork requires a fine needle specially made for beading, and needlepoint requires a tapestry needle with a round point and a large eye. When sewing an old textile—for example, repairing a seam where the original thread has rotted—it is best to put your needle into the old holes. If you cannot, insert it between the threads, not into them, as this will break them. A magnifying glass will help you to work accurately.

Use a suitable natural—not synthetic—thread. You can use cotton thread from either end of a cut length, but woollen thread will feel much rougher in one direction than the other. It should be threaded so that when you run your hand down the length away from the needle it feels smooth. And do not work with too long a thread—it will only tangle. A single thread of about 15 ins (38 cm) is probably the longest length that you can safely use.

Starting to sew

At the start of your work it is usually best to make a temporary knot on the right side of the fabric a short distance from the area you plan to mend. Once the repair is complete, you can cut off the knot, as the stitching you have worked will now hold quite firm.

Make sure that you keep your stitch tension even when you carry out repairs—if the stitches are too tight or too loose they might damage the fabric.

Starting off

Stitch glossary

This small selection of stitches reflects the sewing, upholstery and needlepoint work covered in the book. For additional information, refer to a specialist needlecraft book.

Tacking stitch
Make long, straight stitches in and out of the fabric.

Tacking stitch

Back stitch
Starting with the thread on the wrong side of the fabric, make a stitch back, then stitch forward on the wrong side so that the needle emerges a stitch's length in front of the first one.

Back stitch

Couching
With the main thread laid in place on the top surface, sew across it at intervals with a finer thread. Space stitches at regular intervals. Couching can also be applied in double lines. In this case, the over-sewn stitches are pulled tight.

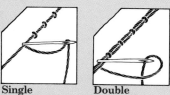
Single couching   **Double couching**

Stitch for sewing beads on fabric
Bring the needle through from the reverse side of the fabric, thread the bead, then take the needle back through the fabric to the reverse close to the beginning of the stitch.

Sewing beads

Florentine stitch

This consists of a vertical rise and drop of three threads. Begin the first stitch by working upward, then work down.

Florentine

Upright gobelin stitch

To work this simple stitch over two rows, bring the needle out and cross it over two horizontal threads, thread it through to the back, then take it over to the right across one vertical thread and under two horizontal ones, bringing it to the surface ready for the next stitch.

Upright gobelin

Horizontal tent stitch

With the needle on the top surface, take it to the right, over one canvas hole. Thread it through the fabric and move it down under two vertical threads and one horizontal one. Bring the needle out for the next stitch.

Horizontal tent stitch

Diagonal tent stitch

The stitches are made by taking the needle to the right, over one canvas hole and under two horizontal threads, working downward. Then work back up, placing the return stitches between those of the first row.

Diagonal tent stitch

Brick stitch

This straight stitch is often used to fill in backgrounds. With the thread on the surface, bring it down over two horizontal threads. Then take it through to the back across two vertical threads, leaving one canvas hole between stitches. On the second row the stitches are worked into the gaps, but one thread down.

Brick stitch

Cross stitch

Work one cross at a time before proceeding to the next. All the top stitches should slant in the same direction.

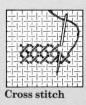

Cross stitch

Trammed stitch

This stitch is only worked between the horizontal threads on double canvas. It is generally worked with a thin thread and used as a base for more decorative stitches. Trammed stitches should be no more than $2\frac{1}{2}$ ins (7 cm) long, and the return stitches on the back of the canvas should be as short as possible to prevent snagging.

Tramming

Leviathan stitch

This star-shaped stitch is basically an ordinary cross stitch with an upright cross stitch worked over the top of it. Start by working a large cross stitch, covering four horizontal and vertical threads. Then work the upright cross, also covering four horizontals and four verticals, on top.

Stage 1   **Stage 2**

Plush or velvet stitch

Worked on double canvas, usually in a thick wool, this stitch consists of loops which are then cut to make a pile. Begin with the needle on the surface. Take it to the right over one canvas intersection, bring it out at the start again, then take it up to the same place on the right, but leaving a loop of thread at the bottom. Bring the needle out one horizontal thread down. Take the needle up and over to the left over one canvas intersection. Insert it down to the right to lock the loop in place, and bring out the needle ready to make the next stitch.

Stage 1

Stage 2

Slip stitch

The slip or ladder stitch is used to close a seam on upholstery and to hold welting in place.

Having tied a slip knot at one side of the seam, pick up the edge of the other side about $\frac{1}{16}$ in (2 mm) behind the knot. Bring the curved needle out of that side of the seam about $\frac{3}{8}$ in (10 mm) further on. Pick up the first side again about $\frac{1}{16}$ in (2 mm) from the point where the thread exits on the last stitch. Pass the thread forward again, forming a series of similar $\frac{3}{8}$ in (10mm) stitches. After every five or six stitches, pull the thread tight to close the seam.

Finish with a French knot—wind the thread a few times around the needle before pulling it through. Pull the thread tight, then pass the end under a few stitches before trimming off.

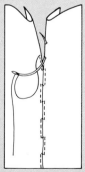

Slip stitching

Replacing welting

The cylindrical raised edge found along some seams on upholstery is known as welting. It is made by covering thick cotton cord with fabric. Welting is often the first part of the upholstery to wear, and it can be replaced as long as the rest of the fabric is in good condition.

Use skewers to hold the fabric to the stuffing. Carefully cut the threads holding the original welting in place, making sure that you do not cut the rest of the fabric. Then remove the old welting.

To make new welting, cut 1½ in (3·8 cm) wide strips of fabric "on the cross" (that is, diagonally across the weave). This will allow it to stretch over the curves. Long strips can be made by sewing several lengths together. To ensure that the grain direction is constant in the made-up strip, mark the bottom end of each piece as it is cut from the fabric, and stack them in the same order.

Join two strips by laying the

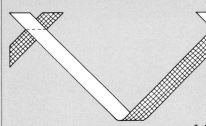

bottom end of one piece at right-angles across the top end of the other. Their patterned sides should be face-to-face. Pin, then machine-stitch the pieces together across the overlapped ends. Join as many pieces as you need end-to-end. Open the seams and iron them flat, then cut off the waste to within ½ in (12 mm) of the seam.

Buy welting cord of the same thickness as the original, and lay it down the center of the fabric strip. Fold the fabric over the cord. Fit a welting foot on your sewing machine. This allows you to sew along the edge of the cord. Place the flange of the finished welting inside the seam of the upholstery. Close the seam with slip stitching, passing the thread through the flange close to the welting.

Welting

Cutting strips

**Joining
end-to-end**

**Opening
the seam**

Upholstery knots

Several basic knots used in upholstery have been included here as a guide for anyone who is unfamiliar with them.

Half-hitch
The most basic knot of all, used for simple fixings.

Double hitch
This knot locks off the stitch shown above by tying another hitch on top. It is often used to finish off a row of stitches or knots.

Slip knot
Use this at the beginning of a row of stitches or ties. Having made the loops, pull tight the end of the thread that passes through the needle.

Clove hitch
The clove hitch is the knot used to securely tie laid cord to the springs.

Lock loop
The lock loop is a quick knot for tying springs, but only holds under tension.

Half-hitch

Double hitch

Slip knot

Clove hitch

Lock loop

Sewing leather

Thick leather is sewn together with saddle stitching. We assume that you will be repairing old leatherwork, where an existing seam has opened up.

Obtain suitable thread and two harness needles from a craft shop. Cut off a length of thread no longer than your outstretched arms, and wax it by drawing it across a block of beeswax. Thread a needle on each end, and lock them in place by pushing the needles through the thread, then pulling the threaded end right through.

Begin two or three stitches in front of the open section of seam to lock the remaining old thread in place. Pull the new thread through until it is centered. Working toward yourself, push both needles through the next hole, crossing them over always with the right-hand needle on top of the left. Continue along the seam, pulling the stitch tight as you proceed. At the end, sew back along the row for a few stitches, then cut the thread.

**Threading
a needle**

Sewing leather

Finishing off

APPENDIXES

THE SIGNIFICANCE OF MARKS AND SIGNATURES

A great many antiques bear various marks to indicate their manufacturer, quality, date of production, and so on. The study of these is a fascinating aspect of antique collecting. It is not difficult to imagine the vast range of marks that exist and, consequently, the scope of any dictionary that lists them. It would be impossible, and inappropriate, to include a comprehensive coverage here. Instead, we explain the significance of the marks you might find so that you can use detailed reference material to identify them.

Ceramics

The marking of ceramic ware has been carried on by potters for many centuries, but it was originally a spasmodic practice and not particularly widespread until the eighteenth century.

Factory marks

The idea of placing a factory mark on the base of a piece of china seems to originate from a misapprehension. In the fifteenth and sixteenth centuries Chinese pottery began to infiltrate European markets. The incomprehensible symbols on the bases of these pieces were taken to be the signature of the potter or the name of the "factory" where they were produced. In fact, they were either dating symbols relating to the reign names of emperors or good luck charms.

However, the practice of marking china with its own symbols was not adopted on any scale by potters in Europe until the early eighteenth century, when the Meissen factory of Germany first applied initials and, eventually, their now-famous crossed swords symbol. Gradually the idea spread across the continent as other respected potters chose to draw attention to their wares. Less reputable manufacturers either continued to dispense with marks, or even designed a symbol for their work which might be mistaken by an uninformed buyer for those used by the more famous makers. By the nineteenth century factory marks were commonplace.

Factory marks can be used as a method of roughly dating a piece of china. In-depth studies of the design of a particular manufacturer's marks have linked such changes with documentary evidence which proves that the factory underwent a change of ownership, the formation of a new partnership, or a move to new premises. Such occurrences can be dated fairly accurately, and much literature is available to help you. The method of application may be a further clue. Perhaps changes from an incised mark which was molded or pressed into the body of the ceramic to a printed mark will give you another clue to the date of a piece. Some manufacturers' products can be dated absolutely because they include in their marks some kind of coded system of dating based on various groupings of stars or dots, for instance.

Artists' marks

You will very often find small, cryptic marks painted on the base of china. These were applied by the painter or gilder to identify his work. A famous artist may apply her or his full signature, but in the main they are the initials or symbol of a humble factory worker, used more for the convenience of the factory owner than anything else. It is not normally possible to date china from these marks unless the artist is well-known, but some factories kept meticulous records of their workers' names and the initials or numbers they used.

When a manufacturer employed a famous designer, either on a regular basis or for a commission, they would often print the designer's signature on the work to lend it prestige. Pieces "signed" by designers like Clarice Cliff, Susie Cooper, and Keith Murray, for example, are sought after by collectors of the popular Art Deco period.

W. H. GOSS.
Impressed
1858–87

WHGOSS
Impressed
1887–1916

W.H.GOSS
Printed
1862–1927

W.H.GOSS
ENGLAND
Printed 1930–9

Clarice Cliff
Clarice Cliff
1899–1972

Susie Cooper
Susie Cooper
born 1903

Keith Murray
born 1893

Ownership marks

Early ceramics made for wealthy or important clients might bear the mark of the owner in addition to that of the maker. The only equivalent marks on less illustrious china would be the name and address of a particular retailer who perhaps held the licence to sell a manufacturer's products in one area.

Country-of-origin marks

A mark indicating the country of origin would at first sight provide no further information than that which is obvious. However, these marks deserve closer study as some are the result of legislation and thus constitute yet another method of roughly dating china. In 1891, for example, American import laws made such marks compulsory so that names like "Germany," "England," and so on, would suggest a date after 1891, while marks of the "Made in —" type were not used until the twentieth century.

Firearms

You may find makers' names or marks on any part of a gun, including the wooden stock, and they may all be different, each part being made by a specialist.

Ordnance marks

In place of a maker's name, some weapons bear an ordnance mark. This shows that the gun was assembled from separate parts, each made under government contract.

Hallmarks

Silver mounts found on weapons will usually be hallmarked, and are therefore dated, but this date does not necessarily correspond with the age of the gun itself. Their mounts would have been made in batches and sent to the gunsmith, who may have fitted them on guns years later.

Proof marks

These marks were applied to the barrel after it had been tested to ensure that it was strong enough to withstand normal use. They therefore mark the completion of its manufacture.

TOWER
1862

Tower of
London, 1862

Fredericksburg,
USA, 1776

**Birmingham
proof mark**

Liege
proof mark

Silver and gold

Items made from pure gold or silver would be too soft for practical use and the precious metal must be mixed with a base metal to make it harder. To guarantee that such an alloy contains an acceptable amount of precious metal, British silver and goldsmiths were obliged by law to have their wares assayed and struck with hallmarks.

British silver marks

The United Kingdom is the only country to have a comprehensive and consistent system of antique silver marking.

Sterling silver

British silver must contain a minimum of 92.5 per cent of the metal and 7.5 per cent of copper. Since 1543 the sterling mark has been the Lion Passant.

Other marks

British silver should bear a group of four or five marks: the maker's mark incorporating the initial of the silversmith's name, the Sterling or Britannia mark, the mark denoting the assay office, and a date letter indicating the year in which it was assayed. Between 1784 and 1890 British silver also bore the head of the monarch to show that the required duty had been paid. After 1890 the monarch's head appeared on commemorative silver only. All these marks can be identified by referring to a number of specialized dictionaries.

Britannia silver

During the period 1697–1720 a higher standard of silver was introduced. This was known as Britannia silver and contained 95.84 per cent of the metal.

American silver marks

There were no regulations binding on American silversmiths as there were in Britain. But by the eighteenth century they were applying their own marks, which followed the British custom of using the initials only, although sometimes the full surname was incorporated. The

Lion passant

Left to right:
**Manufacturer's
mark,
Sterling silver,
Assay office,
Date letter**

Britannia mark

**Monarch's
head—Queen
Victoria
1876–7**

**Jacob Hurd
18th-century
American
silversmith**

mark was usually framed by a square or rectangular box with plain or serrated edges.

Sheffield plate

It was not considered necessary to hallmark Sheffield plate, so it bears no dating mark. Makers would often mark their wares with their initials, following the custom for marking silver. However, from 1784 makers were allowed to incorporate their full name or some other emblem in their marks. From this time they registered their marks at the Sheffield Assay Office. Some manufacturers added a crown to their mark as a symbol of quality, but because such a mark might mislead the buyer into thinking the item was made from pure silver the practice was forbidden in 1896.

Henry Meredith circa 1807

Electro-plated silver

Base-metal objects which are electro-plated with a very thin coating of silver do not bear hallmarks. However, they often bear the initials EPNS—Electro-plated Nickel Silver or EPBM—Electro-plated Britannia Metal.

Gold

The hallmarks for British gold are similar in function to those for silver, indicating the manufacturer, the office at which it was tested, and the year in which it was assayed. In addition, there is a mark indicating the percentage of pure gold, which is expressed internationally in "carats."

Both rolled gold items (a similar manufacturing process to Sheffield plate) and gold-plated items are not hallmarked.

9 carat

18 carat

Pewter

Most Medieval pewter bore no maker's marks at all. The first documented use of an official mark sanctioned by the Pewterers' Company of London dates from 1474. This mark took the form of a broad arrowhead.

Touch marks

Any mark applied to pewter by the maker is known as a touch mark. From about 1550 the Company enjoined its mem-

bers to attach touchplates to their wares. These plates, about $\frac{1}{8}$ in (3 mm) thick and in various shapes, bore the touch mark of the maker known as the master mark. This identified him and showed that he had finished his apprenticeship and become a member of the Company. From the latter half of the sixteenth century this mark was applied under the pain of financial penalty.

Toward the end of the seventeenth century the ordnances of the Company grew confused. As a result, members began to apply their names and other marks in addition to the master mark, while country pewterers practiced deception by applying "London" or "Made in London" to their wares.

American touch marks

The oldest surviving American pewter dates from the early eighteenth century. There were no regulations covering its manufacture, but American pewterers copied the European tradition of marking their work with their names or symbols.

In the pre-revolutionary period the rose and crown and the lion rampant were commonly used. Then during and after the War of Independence the American eagle came into widespread use. It was normally accompanied by stars denoting the number of states in the Union. After 1825 the pewterer's name and the place of origin were applied to the piece, often in a rectangle.

Glass

The practice of applying names and symbols was not common with old glass. There was no custom until the factories that became famous started production. Some firms, the Waterford Glass Company for example, would mold the name of the factory into the base. By the middle of the nineteenth century many more companies etched, engraved, printed, or molded their names or symbols on their wares. However, this practice never became as common as it did with ceramics.

William Landsdown circa 1740 Bristol, England

Thomas Boardman 1805–1820 Hartford, USA

Rene Lalique 1860–1945 French artist in glass

Jewelry

Silver and gold jewelry is hall-marked like any other item made from either metal. There are some additional marks which you might come across.

Foreign goods

Gold ware imported to England between 1876 and 1904 bears the letter F in an oval or square, accompanied by the appropriate British Assay Office mark.

Signatures

Look out for jewelry signed by its artist/designer. A genuine signature could make the item very valuable.

Georges Fouquet 1862–1957 Goldsmith and jeweler

Furniture

It is rare to find furniture—English or European—that carries identification marks. Printed labels are sometimes pasted to the underside of drawers or on the inside of chair frames. Some manufacturers marked their wares with punches, branding irons, or stencils.

France was the exception, although until 1741 there was no standardized system of marks. However, from that date every Master of the Guild was allowed to stamp his name or, more rarely, his initials on both his furniture and his repair work. With high-class furniture a committee also gave a stamp of approval. After the trade guild was dissolved the practice of marking furniture diminished in France, only to be revived after the Paris Exhibition of 1882.

Charles Rohlfs 1853–1936 American furniture maker

Clocks

Better-quality clocks were sometimes signed by their makers. Their signatures might be printed or painted on the face or perhaps engraved on the back plate. Wood-cased clocks often have a manufacturer's label pasted inside the case.

Pictures

Most people know that drawings and paintings are usually, but not always, signed by the artist at the foot of the work. The acknowledgments on a print, however, can be confusing.

Prints

When artwork is produced by a printing process a team of specialists is involved, any or all of whom may have their names at the bottom. Their roles are described, often in full or abbreviated Latin. The chart will help you identify them.

Latin	Abbreviation	Translation
Descripsit, Delineavit	Del, Delt, Delin	Drawn by (This may refer to the original artist or the plate-maker's copyist.)
Designavit	Desig.	Designed by
Invenit	Inv.	Designed by
Pingebat	Ping.	Painted by
Pinxit	Pinx	Painted by
Aquatinta	———	Aquatint by
Aquaforti	Aqua	Etched by
Incidebat	Inc	Engraved by
Incidit	Inc	Engraved by
Sculpebat	Sc, Sculp	Engraved by
Sculpsit	Sc, Sculp	Engraved by
———	Lith, Lithog	Lithographed by
Fecit	F	Made by
Faciebat	Fac	Made by

British registration marks

Between the years 1842 and 1883 many manufacturers registered their designs with the British Patent Office. The official diamond mark was applied to the artifact, and was a symbol which incorporated the exact day of its registration. It does not prove the date of manufacture of the particular piece as the design may have been in production for years. Printed marks usually refer to the registration of applied two-dimensional patterns, and impressed marks to the design of the object itself. However, this is not always the case.

All manner of things could be registered, so each type was classified. Ceramics, for example, were Class IV. The class number was always entered in a circle above the diamond. The position of other code letters changed from time to time. From 1884, registered designs were given a code number only.

A   Class (Ceramics)
B   Day of the month
C   Parcel number
D   Month
E   Year

Ceramic design registration mark (1842–1867) 26th April 1844

Ceramic design registration mark (1868–1883) 8th August 1878

HOME SECURITY

The security of your home is important—if you have spent time and money on your antiques you will not want to have them stolen. You should install adequate locks on all doors and windows, and you may need to fit a burglar alarm. Also, it is important to make sure that you have a full, up-to-date contents insurance policy covering theft and damage.

Locks and security devices

Fitting locks on doors and windows should be your first priority. Exit doors should be fitted with strong mortise locks, in addition to any latch key locks. Also fit bolts operated with removable keys at the top and bottom of doors. Similar bolts should be fitted on French windows or patio doors. Fixed or sliding metal grilles for windows and glass doors might be worth considering, especially if your house is vulnerable because the garden is secluded.

All downstairs windows, and any upstairs ones that are accessible via drainpipes, garden walls or flat roofs, must be fitted with window locks or bolts with a removable key. Lock up your garage or other storage so that burglars cannot use your tools to break into your house. Similarly, lock up ladders.

Fit a peep-hole in your front door so that you can see callers without opening the door. And have a strong security chain on the inside of the door.

Safes and security boxes

A wall safe might be worth installing if you own a number of small, valuable antiques—a collection of antique jewelry, for example. Most safes made for domestic use are about the size of a house brick, and are installed by cementing into an interior wall. As an inexpensive alternative, you can buy a security box that is disguised as a double electric wall socket.

Most safes are fitted with extra security devices that protect them from attack by drills or blowtorch if they are discovered by a thief.

Burglar alarms

There are two types of alarm system. Passive systems are made up of various traps and observation devices, designed to operate the alarm should they be tripped by an intruder inside the home. Perimeter systems set off the alarm when someone tries to tamper with the windows and doors. The aim of this is to discourage the thief from even entering your home. With a perimeter system, it is usual to install a few passive traps in case you forget to secure the perimeter properly.

Most alarm systems operate a siren or bell, relying on neighbors or passers-by to alert the police. Some systems can be wired directly to the police station, or to a monitoring center which contacts the police on your behalf. A monitored system is obviously more efficient, but it is more costly as it involves a fee for the monitoring service.

Most alarms run off mains electricity, with batteries as a back-up in case of a power failure. However, some systems run on batteries alone. Make sure that you replace the batteries regularly.

Insurance

A straightforward house contents insurance policy will be satisfactory as long as you keep it up-to-date from year to year. If, in the event of a claim, the assessor discovers that you are under-insured, you will get only a percentage, rather than the entire value, of what has been lost. Particularly valuable pieces should be itemized on the policy, and you may need a written valuation from an expert, dealer or auctioneer. Ask your insurance company for advice. Any pieces that you take out of the house, such as jewelry, should be covered by an all-risks policy.

Keep a colored photographic record of your antiques, together with a detailed description. In the case of theft, this information can be circulated by police in an attempt to recover it. If you are unlucky enough to lose antiques in a fire, a copy of the record kept elsewhere (in a safety deposit box or at a relative's house) would be invaluable when calculating the loss. Do not leave your address with the record, in case of a break-in at the storage place.

MATERIAL SUPPLIERS

This list of materials and suppliers is intended as a brief guide to help you locate any materials used in this book that you may find unfamiliar. You will also find that some specialist suppliers of materials are listed on pages 240–1.

Material	Supplier
Abrasive paper	Hardware stores
Acetone	See solvents
Acid-free tissue	Art supply stores
Almond oil	Druggists
Ammonia	Druggists Hardware stores
Anaerobic adhesive	Hardware stores
Animal glue	Hardware stores
Art gum eraser	Art supply stores
Beeswax (white)	Specialty supply stores
Blue lacquer	Clock material suppliers
Book cloth	Bookbinding suppliers
Bore oil	Musical instrument suppliers
Braided rope	Clock material suppliers
Brass and copper polish	Hardware stores Jewelers
Buffing soap	Engineer's suppliers Hardware stores
Carpet shampoo	Hardware stores Supermarkets
Chrome polish	Auto accessory suppliers
Clear cold cure lacquer	Hardware stores
Clear lacquer	Hardware stores
Clock oil	Clock material suppliers
Crash	Bookbinding suppliers

Crewel wool	Craft and needlework stores
Cyanoacrylate adhesive	Hardware stores
Dental composition	Dental suppliers
Distilled water	Druggists Auto accessory suppliers
Document cleaner	Art supply stores
Document repair tape	Art supply stores
Endpaper	Bookbinding suppliers
Epoxy paste filler	Hardware stores
Epoxy resin glue	Hardware stores
Filler	Hardware stores
French polish	Hardware stores
Fuller's earth	Druggists Hardware stores
Glue film	Specialty supply stores
Grain filler	Hardware stores
Ground chalk	Specialty supply stores
Headbands	Bookbinding suppliers
Hide cleaner	Shoe repairers
Hydrogen peroxide	Druggists
Japanese tissue	Bookbinding suppliers
Jewelry dip	Hardware stores Jewelers
Jeweler's rouge	Clock material suppliers Jewelers
Kaolin	Druggists
Latex adhesive	Hardware stores
Latex molding material	Specialty craft suppliers
Leather	Bookbinding suppliers

Leather reviver	Specialty supply stores
Linseed oil	Hardware stores
Liquid abrasive	Hardware stores Auto accessory suppliers
Liquid epoxy adhesive	Specialty supply stores
Liquid animal glue	Hardware stores Art supply stores
Metallic paste	Art supply stores
Metallic gold paint	Art supply stores
Metallic powders	Art supply stores
Micro-crystalline wax	Specialty supply stores
Modeling clay	Art supply stores Craft stores
Monofilament	Clock material suppliers
Nylon gossamer fabric	Specialty supply stores
Oil-based stain	Hardware stores
Oil finish	Hardware stores
Oil or spirit varnish	Musical instrument suppliers
Pads, key	Musical instrument suppliers
Paint stripper	Hardware stores
Piano wire	Musical instrument suppliers
Plaster of Paris	Druggists Hardware stores
Plastic Wood	Hardware stores
Polyurethane varnish	Hardware stores
Potato starch	Druggists
Powdered magnesia	Druggists
Polyvinyl acetate glue (white)	Hardware stores
Rust remover	Hardware stores Auto accessory suppliers

Rust stain remover	Druggists (large)
Saddle soap	Shoe repairers
Shellac	Specialty supply stores
Silver polish	Hardware stores Jewelers
Silvering powder	Clock material suppliers
Silver sand	Hardware stores
Solder and flux	Hardware stores
Solvent spirits	Hardware stores Druggists
Spackling compound	Art supply stores
Spirit soap	Specialty supply stores
Stainless steel and brass rod	Engineer's suppliers
Steel wool	Hardware stores
Stone sealer	Specialty supply stores
Suede cleaner	Shoe repairers Hardware stores
Synthetic adhesive	Musical instrument suppliers
Titanium dioxide	Druggists
Trichloroethane 1.1.1. stabilized	Specialty supply stores
Two-part bleach	Hardware stores
Vinyl rubber	Specialty craft suppliers
Water-based stain	Hardware stores
Wax polish	Hardware stores
Wood dough	Hardware stores
Woodworm fluid	Hardware stores

USEFUL ADDRESSES

The following list of addresses should help you to find most of the materials mentioned in this book if they are not available from your local high street stores. This list is only a guide, as many other suppliers will stock these materials. Most of the suppliers listed on this page will provide their products by mail order.

Addresses

Craft materials

Kirchen Bros.,
Dept. MN-84,
Box C1016,
Skokie,
Illinois 60076.

Boycan's Craft and Art
  Supplies,
Dept. MC14,
P.O. Box 897,
Sharon PA 16146.

The Renovator's Supply Inc.,
2608 Northfield Road,
Millers Falls,
Mass 01349.

Tools

Garrett Wade Co.,
161 Avenue of the Americas,
New York 10013.

Black and Decker
  Manufacturing Co.,
Towson,
Maryland 21204.

Woodcraft Supply Corp.,
313 Montvale Avenue,
Woburn,
Mass 01801.

Stanley Tools Ltd.,
600 Myrtle Street,
New Britain,
Connecticut 06050.

Micro-Mark,
Box 5112, F.G. 24,
East Main Street,
Clinton,
New Jersey 08809.

Dremel,
Division of Emerson Electric
  Co.,
4915 21st Street,
Racine,
Wisconsin 53406.

Patty's Corner Inc.,
P.O. Box 565,
West Paterson,
New Jersey 07424.

Cane

T.I.E., b,
P.O. Box 1121,
San Mateo,
California 94403.

Creart,
Box 21736,
San Jose,
California 95151.

Glass

Whittemore-Durgin,
Box 2065BW,
Hanover,
Mass 02339.

Sewing supplies

The American Needlewoman
  Inc.,
P.O. Box 6472,
Dept. MC19,
Fort Worth,
Texas 76115.

Newark Dressmaker Supply,
6473 Ruch Road,
P.O. Box 2448,
Dept. A2,
Lehigh Valley,
PA 18001.

Promenade,
Box 2092,
Boulder,
Connecticut 80306.

Art materials

Badger Airbrush Co.,
9128 W. Belmont Avenue,
Franklin Park,
Illinois 60131.

Major auction houses

Sotheby Parke Bernet Inc.,
232 Clarendon Street,
Boston, Mass.
also
980 Madison Avenue,
New York.

Christie, Manson and Woods
  International Inc.,
502 Park Avenue,
New York.

Notes

GLOSSARY

A

Abrach
An obvious change of tone in the background color of a rug. It occurs because several batches of wool, colored with dyes mixed at different times, have been used.

Animal glue
A glue made from animal protein by boiling hooves and skin.

Apron
A decorative panel situated underneath the lower rail of a cabinet, table or chair.

Arbor
A spindle about which a wheel revolves, as in a clock mechanism, for example.

Arris
In woodworking, a sharp edge formed where two planes meet.

Art Deco
A fashionable style for decorative arts from 1920–1940. Derived from *Exposition des Arts Décoratifs*, an exhibition held in Paris, where the style was introduced.

Artist's mark
The initials marked on the base of painted china by the artist who carried out the color work.

Art Nouveau
A flowing, almost organic style popular in the late nineteenth century, although it did not disappear completely until the start of the First World War.

Arts and Crafts Movement
A group of nineteenth-century artists and designers, led by William Morris, who tried to restore interest in simple hand craftsmanship, in direct conflict with the Victorian taste for over-embellishment.

Assay
The official analysis of gold or silver alloy, verifying that it contains the legally required percentage of pure metal.

B

Backsight
The rearmost of two points on a gun provided for the purpose of visual alignment with the target (see Foresight).

Balance wheel
A reciprocating wheel which controls the speed of running of a clock.

Balloon back
An open, oval backrest on a chair made by curving the cresting rail to meet the back legs.

Banding
Decorative feature of furniture where strips of veneer run around the edge of panels (see Cross-banding).

Batten
Wooden strip used for strengthening or reinforcing.

Beading
A small wooden molding with a semicircular profile.

Beeswax
Made from honeycombs, this wax is sold either in its natural yellow color or in a bleached white form.

Bentwood
A furniture-making technique. Solid wooden components are bent into shape after softening with steam.

Bevel
A sloped edge.

Black powder
An explosive propellant used for firearms, composed of charcoal, saltpeter and sulphur.

Blind stitch
An upholsterer's stitch used to pull stuffing to the side of the seat in order to form a firm edge.

Blister
A small raised area of veneer where the glue holding it to the groundwork has failed.

Block printing
In textiles, printing a repeat design onto a fabric from engraved wooden or metal blocks.

Bloom
Misty appearance to the varnish of a painting. It is caused by damp conditions at the time of varnishing.

Bluing
The controlled production of an oxide film on steel to inhibit further corrosion and enhance the appearance. Bluing is achieved by heat or chemical treatment.

Bombé
A style of cabinet furniture, such as commodes, with a convex, swelling facade.

Bore
The hollow part of any tube such as a gun barrel.

Boulle
Decorative inlay composed of thin slices of brass sheet and tortoiseshell.

Bridle ties
See Stuffing ties.

Burnish
To polish with friction.

Bush
A hollow cylinder of metal in which a pivot revolves.

Button polish
A shellac polish for wood left to cool in round disks ("buttons"). Purity is ascertained by viewing a disk against the light.

C

Cabriole leg
An extended S-shaped leg design used on furniture.

Came
Lead framing for stained glass.

Carat
A unit used to measure the purity of precious metals or the weight of precious stones.

Carcass
The main structure of a piece of cabinet furniture, excluding components like doors and drawers.

Carriage clock
A portable clock with a handle. It may incorporate special components to allow for the clock not being level at all times.

Case
The outer, cloth-covered boards used to protect a book.

Cased glass
Glass composed of two layers, the outermost being colored. Usually, the outer layer is cut through in places to reveal the clear glass layer underneath (see Flashed glass).

Casein
A protein of milk, once used in the manufacture of paint.

Casting
A shape made by pouring a liquid into a mold and then allowing it to set.

Caul
A board or panel used to press veneer onto the groundwork.

Chaise longue
Strictly speaking, a full armchair with an extended seat that forms a leg rest. However, the term is often used to describe a couch with a backrest at one end only.

Chamfer
A 45° angle planed along the edge of a piece of wood to remove the arris.

Charge
The load of a gun, including powder, pads and shot.

Chesterfield
Large, overstuffed upholstered sofa. The arms and back are all of the same height.

Chiffonier
A term for a small sideboard, usually applied to pieces backed by a low mirror or an upstand with small shelves.

Chiming clock
A clock which not only strikes the numbers on the hour, but also chimes at the quarters and halves.

Cire-perdu
A "lost wax" casting process. The wax original is melted and replaced by molten metal.

Claw
A split lever on a tool for removing nails or tacks.

Clearance hole
A hole drilled in wood prior to inserting a screw to allow space for its shank.

Click
A device in a clock which acts against the teeth of a toothed wheel to allow it to move in one direction only.

Cock
(1) Pivoting arm on a firearm which holds the flint.
(2) A detachable bracket in a clock movement that supports the arbor.

Cocked bead
Raised molding around doors and drawers that protects the edge of veneers.

Color-fast
Having a stable coloring material which will not run or bleed.

Consolidating
Binding together flaking or powdery material.

Copal
A natural resin from tropical trees used to make a varnish for oil paintings.

Cornice
A deep molding which runs along the top of cabinet furniture. Often made as a detachable frame.

Corrosion
The result of the slow decay of a material, caused by gaseous or chemical action. Rust is a form of corrosion on either steel or iron.

Counterbore
A hole drilled in wood to allow a screw or bolt head to lie below the surface.

Cresting rail
The top rail of a chair back.

Crewel work
Embroidery worked in woollen thread, usually on canvas.

Cross-banding
A banding veneer in which the grain runs at right angles to the main veneered panel.

Crutch
Part of a clock escapement that transmits power to the pendulum.

D

Dammar
A spirit-soluble tree resin used to make varnish.

Distressing
Deliberate marking, denting and scratching applied to reproduction furniture to simulate an aged appearance.

Dressing
A specially formulated material for nourishing dried leather.

E

Electro-plating
The process of depositing a thin layer of a relatively valuable metal onto a base metal by means of an electric current.

Enamel, stove
Stove enamel is a special paint cured—set—by heating.

Enamel, vitreous
Glass colored by various metallic oxides applied to a metal surface.

Endpapers
Sheets of paper glued to the inside of the cover boards at the front and back of a book.

Escapement
Part of the mechanism of a clock that controls the speed at which it runs.

Escutcheon
A metal plate surrounding a keyhole. It often incorporates a pivoting cover.

F

Fake
A replica that is deliberately designed to mislead the potential buyer into thinking that it is a genuine antique.

Fall front
Flap, usually on a desk or bureau, which opens to form a horizontal writing surface.

Field
The background color of the main, central section of a rug, usually surrounded by a decorative border.

Fielded panel
In furniture making, a raised panel with beveled edges.

Figure
Grain pattern of timber.

Firedogs
Metal supports for burning logs, used in a fire hearth.

Fix
To protect fragile drawings with a chemical that prevents them from smudging.

Flashed glass
A colorless glass, dipped in a thin layer of colored glass. Similar to cased glass.

Flash groove
Grooves running away from the main cavity of a mold that allow excess molding material to escape.

Flash line
Raised seam lines on a casting mirroring the meeting point of the two halves of the mold that the casting was made in.

Flash pan
A shallow cup on a gun that is designed to hold the priming powder which ignites the main charge.

Flats
The flat surfaces of an octagonal gun barrel.

Flatware
A collective term describing forks and spoons.

Flint glass
See Lead crystal.

Fly leaf
The unpasted endpaper at the front and back of a book.

Foresight
The point near the muzzle of a gun barrel that assists in aiming the weapon (see Backsight).

Foxing
Reddish-brown spots on paper caused by fungal attack or contact with iron.

Frass
The debris left by wood-boring insects and the larvae of moths.

French polish
A shellac-based coating for wood that can be burnished to a high-gloss finish.

Frizzen
The combined steel and flash pan on a firearm.

Full binding
The complete covering of a book using one material only.

Fusee
A mechanism in a clock to compensate for the declining power of the spring as it unwinds.

G

Gallery
A wooden, cage-like structure on top of the central column of a pedestal table. It enables the table top to both pivot—tilt up —and revolve.

Gearing
In clocks, a series of meshing toothed wheels which change the speed of rotation and drive each hand at the correct rate.

Gesso
A mixture of ground chalk and glue. It is used to make a base, often carved, upon which gold paint or gold leaf is laid. Used on mirror and picture frames and furniture.

Gilding
A method of applying a layer of gold to furniture, glass and ceramics. Originally gold leaf was used, but later gold paints were also used extensively.

Glaze
A glass-like surface coating applied to ceramics to render them waterproof.

Grain
(1) The direction in which the fibers of wood lie. It is not necessarily visible.
(2) The direction in which the warp of a textile lies.

Ground
(1) The flat base material built up on a canvas in preparation for making a painting (see also Groundwork).
(2) The base material, usually linen or canvas, upon which an embroidery is worked.

Groundwork
A solid-wood or composite-board core upon which veneers are laid. Also referred to as the ground.

Gutline
A line used to support weights in a clock.

H

Hair spring
The balance spring in a clock mechanism.

Hairline crack
A virtually invisible crack, usually in china or glass.

Half-binding
A book binding where two covering materials are used—one for the spine and corners, the other for the rest of the boards.

Hallmark
A symbol struck in precious metals to designate purity, origin and date.

Hardwood
Wood cut from deciduous trees. Strictly speaking, the term does not describe the density of the timber.

Haunch
A small projection on top of a tenon when the joint comes at the top of a leg in a piece of furniture. It prevents the top part of the rail moving out of line should the wood either shrink or swell.

Head
A book-binding term for the top of a book.

Headband
A strip of cloth-covered cord situated at the top of the spine of a book. It supports the spine cover when a book is pulled from a shelf.

Headcap
The top of a leather-covered book spine which is rounded over the headband (see Headband).

Hollow
A flattened paper tube glued between a book spine and its cover. It allows a book to be opened without creasing the spine cover.

Hollow-ware
A vessel, such as a jug or bowl, designed to contain liquids.

Honing
The final act of sharpening a cutting edge.

Housing
A groove cut across the grain of wood to receive the end of another piece of wood—a cabinet shelf, for instance.

I

Impulse
The energy transferred from the clock pallet to the pendulum or balance wheel to keep them moving.

In beat
A stage that occurs when the action of an escapement in a clock is even.

J

Japanning
Imitation of Oriental lacquering, using paints and varnish.

K

Kaolin
China clay used in the manufacture of ceramics.

Kelim
A type of flat weaving used in rug making.

Kerf
Any saw-cut in timber.

Key, keying
To roughen a surface to assist the adhesion of paint or glue.

Keyways
A means by which two halves of a mold may be relocated accurately. Consists of lines or holes cut into the mold.

L

Lacquer
(1) An Oriental varnish made from a resin. It is used to coat various materials and forms a hard gloss surface.
(2) A modern clear acrylic or polyurethane coating used on wood or metal.

Ladder stitch
An upholsterer's stitch used to close a seam. Also known as slip stitch.

Lead crystal
A type of hard glass containing lead oxide, prized for its refractive qualities. Developed by George Ravenscroft c.1673. Also known as flint glass.

Leaf
A single sheet of paper within a book—comprising two pages, one each side.

Letting down
The unwinding of the mainspring of a clock prior to examination.

Lever
That part of a lever escapement which carries the pallets in a clock mechanism.

Locked out
A state that occurs when one piece of broken ceramic cannot be fitted in place because other pieces have been assembled in the wrong order.

Lock loop
An upholsterer's knot for tying springs.

Longcase clock
A clock having a case long enough to accommodate weights and pendulum (i.e., a grandfather clock).

Luster
A prismatic glass pendant, usually hanging from a vase or chandelier.

Lusterware
Ceramics covered with a metallic glaze.

M

Marquetry
Decorative veneers laid together to form abstract or pictorial motifs. Veneers made from exotic woods, and shaded or stained veneers are often used.

Marriage
An article, usually of furniture, made up of two or more antique components that originally came from separate sources.

Mask
To protect or cover an area that surrounds a surface being glued or painted.

Mate
To bring together exactly two surfaces which are to be glued.

Medallion
An elongated oblong or circular motif that is positioned in the center of a rug.

Mihrab
A niche-like motif woven into a prayer rug.

Milk paint
A casein-based primer once applied to furniture.

Miter
A 45° angled joint that is made in a frame.

Motif
A decorative element in a design. Motifs are often repeated many times in order to make an overall pattern.

Motion work
That part of a clock which transmits the power from the escapement through the gears to the hands.

Mount
(1) The backing and surround to paper artwork, usually in a frame.
(2) Silver bases or rims attached to wooden, glass or ceramic objects.

Movement
In timepieces, this term describes the complete mechanical workings of a clock.

Musket
A long firearm with a smooth-bore barrel.

Muzzle
The open end of a barrel on a firearm.

Ormolu
An alloy of zinc, copper and tin which is cast, then gilded to make decorative mounts for furniture and glassware.

Overstuffed chair
A chair with an upholstered seat which is attached to the outside of the seat frame. Also known as stuffed over.

Oxidation
The taking up of oxygen by a material to form a layer of oxide, such as rust.

P

Pallet
In a clock, the reciprocating element which transfers the amount of energy, known as impulse, from the escape wheel to the pendulum or balance wheel.

Papier-mâché
Paper pulp molded into trays, boxes and furniture. It is usually painted or lacquered.

Paring
The act of gradually shaving wood down to the required level, using a chisel.

Parquetry
Veneers laid to form geometric patterns.

Paste wash
A process of applying a thin solution of flour paste to leather book bindings in order to consolidate them.

Patina
The surface color and texture a material acquires as a result of aging.

Penetrating oil
An oil which is thin enough to seep between rusted components, such as machined screws, so that they can be dismantled.

Pigeon hole
A small compartment in a desk used for storing stationery.

Pillars
The components which hold the two plates of a clock together to form the frame.

Pilot hole
A hole drilled in wood that allows a screw to be inserted without splitting the wood.

Pinion
A toothed spindle which engages gear wheels in a clock.

Pipe
A split tube on the back of an hour hand which connects it to the clock.

Planishing
The smoothing out of dents in metal caused by the initial shaping of hollow-ware.

Plaster of Paris
Fine, white plaster used to make molds. It derives its name from the gypsum found in the quarries of Montmartre in Paris.

Plate
(1) Utensils wrought from gold, silver and other metals (not to be confused with Electro-plate).
(2) An illustration in a book, often on shiny paper.

Plating
See Electro-plating.

Plinth
The lower framework or base of a piece of cabinet furniture—often a separate component.

Pocket screwing
A method of attaching tops to tables and cabinets with deep rails. A hole is drilled at an angle to emerge from the top edge of the rail. A notch is then cut on the inside of the rail so that a screw can be inserted.

Pontil
A mark left on the base of glassware where a metal rod was attached to hold the object during its shaping and finishing.

Poultice
A paste made from absorbent powder and used for drawing stains out of ceramics and pieces of stonework.

Proof mark
A stamp applied to a gun barrel to indicate that it had been tested and was safe to use.

Quarter binding
The binding of a book where the spine and parts of the boards are covered in one material, while the rest of the board is covered in another.

Rabbet
A step-shaped recess cut along the edge of a wooden component to receive another, as when a back panel is fitted into the framework of a cabinet.

Rail
Horizontal wooden members used in furniture construction.

Red rot
A condition of old leather. It becomes dry and powdery.

Replica
A copy of an object made with similar materials and techniques to those used to make the original.

Reproduction
An object made in the style of an earlier period. Although in outward appearance it attempts to copy an original, modern methods of manufacture and materials are usually obvious under close inspection. A reproduction is not intended to deceive the buyer.

Retouch
To overpaint, usually on china, a damaged or worn area in order to disguise a repair.

Rifling
Spiral grooves on the inside of a gun barrel designed to make the projectile spin and so promote greater accuracy.

Rubbed joint
A glued joint made between two smooth surfaces. No clamps are required as suction provides enough clamping force to hold the components together until the glue has set.

Saber leg
Outward-curving leg on a chair or table.

Salver
A tray made from metal, often silver.

Sand casting
A method for casting metal using molding sand. This sand is packed around a pattern in order to form a cavity. This sand cavity is then filled with molten metal.

Score
To scratch a line with a pointed tool. Also known as Scribing.

Scribe
See Score.

Seal
To paint a porous surface with a material which makes it impervious. Also known as Sizing.

Shagreen
Skins of certain fishes made into a decorative leather. Often dyed in pastel colors, especially pale green.

Shellac
A substance derived from the lac insect and used as the prime constituent of French polish.

Short grain
Grain passing across a narrow cross-section of wood is known as short grain. It produces a weak point and the component can split along it.

Side nails
Screws which hold a lockplate to the stock of a gun.

Signature
Letter or figure applied by a printer to the foot of the first page of each section of a book. Its function is to help in the collation of the book.

Size, to
See Seal.

Skive
To shave leather on the flesh side in order to make it easier to fold, and to reduce the apparent thickness of an edge.

Slats
Thin strips of wood set vertically into a chair seat to form a back rest.

Slip stitch
See Ladder stitch.

Soft jaws
Protective covers slipped onto the jaws of a vise to stop them marking an object being held in place.

Softwood
Wood cut from coniferous trees such as deal or pine (see also Hardwood).

Soumak
A thick form of flat weaving used to manufacture Eastern rugs that makes them suitable as floor coverings.

Spindle
A round-section stick, often tapered at each end, used in the construction of Windsor chairs.

Spine
The back edge of a book.

Splat
The vertical center piece of a chair back.

Sprung
(1) Describes a piece of china which has warped after breaking, so that it is difficult to reposition.
(2) Upholstery which incorporates coil springs.

Stipple
To paint or draw with dots, often with the tip of a stiff brush.

Stock
The entire wooden component of a hand-held firearm.

Stock furniture
The small, metal components attached to the wooden stock of a gun, excluding the barrel and lock.

Stopwork
A mechanism sometimes found in a clock. Designed to improve the accuracy of the clock's time-keeping, it allows the middle turns only of a mainspring to be used.

Straight edge
Any accurate strip of metal or wood used to guide a knife or other marker when drawing a straight line. A straight edge is also used to gauge the flatness of a surface.

Stretcher
A small section rail joining either table or chair legs. Stretchers are situated below the main frame of the piece.

Striking clock
A clock which sounds the hours and perhaps half hours, but does not chime.

Stringing
(1) Thin, linear inlay on wood or metal.
(2) Glass threads wound round a mold in order to make decorative stems for drinking glasses.

Strip down
To dismantle a mechanism for cleaning or repair.

Stuffing ties
Loops of thread that hold horse-hair or fiber stuffing in position for upholstery. Also known as bridle ties.

Sub-assembly
The joining of two or three components prior to the complete assembly of an object.

T

Test strip
A piece of wood or other material used to test the effect of applying paints or dyes.

Thinner
A material, such as mineral spirits, used to reduce the consistency of another, such as paint.

Through ties
Upholsterer's stitches which pull the stuffing down in the center of a seat.

Timepiece
A clock or watch which indicates the time without striking or chiming.

Tipping in
The act of replacing a leaf in a book by applying a narrow band of glue along one edge.

Top-stitching
The act of sewing upholstery to make a firm, sharp edge to the top of the seat.

Tourniquet
A doubled length of cord wrapped around two or more components. A stick is inserted to wind up the cord, thus applying clamping force to the components.

Train
A series of toothed wheels and pinions used to reduce or increase the speed at which a clock runs.

Turn-in
The part of a book-covering material that is wrapped over the edge of the cover boards.

U

Undercut
The space under a projection, often a handle or applied decoration on an item like a vase.

V

Veneer
A thin layer of wood glued on to a thick, firm ground.

Verdigris
Green, crystaline corrosion which forms on copper. It also forms on brass, owing to its copper content.

W

Wad
A patch of leather used to ram powder and shot in a gun barrel.

Warp
In weaving, threads stretched lengthwise in the loom.

Weft
In weaving, threads taken under and over across the warp threads to form the fabric.

Worm
A spiral attachment, much like a corkscrew, found on the end of some gun ramrods. It is used to remove a charge from the barrel of a gun.

Writing slope
A box that has storage space for stationery, and opens up to form a sloped writing surface.

INDEX

ACKNOWLEDGMENTS

Author's acknowledgments: It would have been impossible to write a book about a topic as vast as that of antiques restoration without the help of many people who know more about particular subjects than we do. We are indebted to the following professionals and amateur enthusiasts who were a pleasure to work with, and who gave so generously of their time to advise us on their particular interests:

JEAN BRIDGEMAN	Pottery and porcelain
ROBIN HARRIS	Metalwork and firearms
SHIRLEY HARRIS	Jewellery
RICHARD GROOM	Clocks
DOROTHY GATES	Upholstery
TONY AND KATE HANDLEY	Cane and rush
P. F. DYKE	Musical instruments
ELIZABETH HOWARD	Books
ANTHONY CROSS	Prints and drawings
PETER SMITH	Paintings
JOHN LAWSON	Leather
JUDITH MORE	Textiles

We would also like to thank the following individuals, companies and manufacturers for their assistance: H. S. Walsh & Son Ltd, Rustins Ltd, Len Stiles Musical Instruments Ltd, J. Thibouville-Lamy & Co. Ltd, Picreator Enterprises Ltd, A. Bell & Co. Ltd, Jean O'Grady, Les and Olive Harris, Cray Pharmaceuticals.

We are also grateful to the following companies and individuals for lending us antiques for photography: Robin and Shirley Harris, Peter and Lol Matterson, Kate Handley, Judith More, Jemima Dunne, Caroline Oakes, Christopher Dorling, Alan Buckingham, Stuart Jackman, Jonathan Hilton, Roger Bristow, Debbie Rhodes, Crowthers of Syon Lodge, Park Galleries of Finchley, Warwick Leadley Gallery of Greenwich.

We would like to thank the production team at Dorling Kindersley for all their hard work and thorough professionalism.

Dorling Kindersley would like to thank: Miss Bartlett of the Royal School of Needlework, Buck and Ryan, J. Shiner & Sons Wholesalers, Falkiner Fine Paper, Hampton Court Conservation Centre, Robert Douwma Prints and Maps Ltd, Warwick Leadley Gallery, Lindy Harold of Crowthers, Françoise Sanze of Townsends, Valerie and Kate of Grapevine Porcelain Restorers, and Phelps of Twickenham for their help with materials for photography. Also thanks to Simon Adams, Debbie Rhodes and John Wainwright for additional design and editorial assistance.

All photographs by Martin Dohrn except:
Front cover: Philip Dowell
2, 6–14: Ian O'Leary
16tr: The Bridgeman Art Library
16bc: Royal Doulton Tableware Ltd
17tr, tl: The Bridgeman Art Library
17br: Victoria and Albert Museum
17bl: Philip Dowell
19b: The Bridgeman Art Library
22bl, 25tl, 26tl, 27br, 28tl, 30tc, 31bl, 34tl, 35br: Nick Harris
36–7: Tessa Musgrave
38tl, br: Nick Harris
39: Hugh Schermuly
41: The Bridgeman Art Library
42mc, tr, 43bc: Nick Harris
44bl: The Bridgeman Art Library
46: Bristol City Museum and Art Gallery
54: Victoria and Albert Museum
55t: The Bridgeman Art Library
55b: Victoria and Albert Museum
56: The Bridgeman Art Library
60: House of Steel Antiques
61, 72t: The Bridgeman Art Library
72b: Victoria and Albert Museum
79br: Spink and Son Ltd
85: Hugh Schermuly
97, 121b, 146, 161, 163tl: The Bridgeman Art Library
164tr: Mr and Mrs John Savage
174b: The Bridgeman Art Library
193br: Jane Kasmin
199tl: Hampton Court Conservation Centre
202bl, br: The Bridgeman Art Library